JUVENILE DELINQUENCY
AND URBAN AREAS

JUVENILE DELINQUENCY AND URBAN AREAS

*A Study of Rates of Delinquency in Relation to Differential
Characteristics of Local Communities
in American Cities*

By

CLIFFORD R. SHAW *and* HENRY D. McKAY

REVISED EDITION

*With a New Introduction by
James F. Short, Jr.
and New Chapters Updating Delinquency Data for
Chicago and Suburbs
by Henry D. McKay*

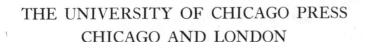
THE UNIVERSITY OF CHICAGO PRESS
CHICAGO AND LONDON

THE UNIVERSITY OF CHICAGO PRESS, CHICAGO 60637
THE UNIVERSITY OF CHICAGO PRESS, LTD., LONDON

© *1942, 1969, 1972 by The University of Chicago*
Revised edition published 1969
Second Impression 1972

Printed in the United States of America

ISBN:0-226-75125-2 (clothbound); 0-226-75127-9 (paperbound)
Library of Congress Catalog Card Number: 69-14511

CONTENTS

PART I

PART II

PART III

CONTENTS

PART IV

PART V

LIST OF ILLUSTRATIONS

MAPS

CHICAGO, ILLINOIS

PHILADELPHIA, PENNSYLVANIA

NEW MAPS

CHICAGO, ILLINOIS

SUBURBS OF CHICAGO

FIGURES

LIST OF TABLES

CHICAGO, ILLINOIS

CLEVELAND, OHIO

RICHMOND, VIRGINIA

PREFACE TO THE REVISED EDITION

The materials which are being added to *Juvenile Delinquency and Urban Areas* fall clearly within the conceptual framework set forth in the original publication. Basically these conceptions, articulated by Robert E. Park and Ernest W. Burgess about half a century ago, were grouped around the proposition that American cities, in their growth, tend to create characteristic types of areas which differ widely from one another. Furthermore, the location of the areas which are subject to most rapid change and the direction of change in these areas are assumed to be predictable.

These concepts continue to be useful. The materials presented here indicate, however, that while the differences among areas are just as great as they were during the early decades of this century, the arrangement of different types of areas within Chicago is not so orderly as it was. Events of the more recent decades suggest, in addition, that rapid turnover of population in any section of the city should be added to aging and deterioration as a possible basic element in the disruption of social life. Whatever the reason, where the social order has been seriously disrupted, the rates of delinquents are high.

Because of the increased importance of suburbs in the life of greater Chicago, rates of delinquents in suburbs have been added to the study. However, because it is not known whether the institutions involved in the maintenance of order operate in the same way in the suburbs as they do in the city, rates of delinquents in all city communities have been compared only with rates in other city communities, and suburban rates only with other suburbs. In the future, it is clear that in the study of delinquency or other urban problems an effort should be made to secure comparable data for all of the city and suburban communities.

This updated section of *Juvenile Delinquency and Urban*

Areas includes data covering a period of about 30 years. It follows that a great many persons from a variety of institutions have been involved in bringing these data together or preparing them for publication. For the most part, however, it will be possible to recognize only the contributions of the institutions which have furnished this support.

First, I should like to thank the successive directors of the Department of Public Welfare and Dr. Harold Visotsky, director of the Department of Mental Health of the State of Illinois, of which the Institute for Juvenile Research is now a unit, for the opportunity to carry out a long-range study of this type. Similarly, I should like to thank Dr. Raymond Robertson and Dr. John Halasz, successive superintendents of the Institute, and Dr. Noel Jenkin, director of research at the Institute, for their support.

The help and support of the successive judges, administrative officers and chief probation officers of the Cook County Juvenile Court are gratefully recognized. Without their support the study would not have been possible. Edward J. Nerad, now chief administrative probation officer of the Court, has been especially helpful over a period of many years. Wide use has been made of commitment data released by the Illinois Youth Commission. A breakdown of these data into appropriate units, prepared by Anthony Sorrentino, youth delinquency prevention supervisor, and Ray Raymond, youth service supervisor of the Illinois Youth Commission, has been extremely useful. In addition, I wish to thank the board of directors of the Chicago Area Project, both for its original sponsorship and its continuous support.

My debt to the late Clifford R. Shaw, with whom I worked for many years, is freely acknowledged. I deeply appreciate also the contribution of James F. Short, whose comprehensive and scholarly review of the literature of the past 25 years and discussion of the Chicago Area Project as a social movement is much more than just an introduction. It stands as a distinct contribution in its own right. Solomon Kobrin, my long-time colleague, has been a wise counselor, and Mrs. Jane Hambric has assisted ably with the art work. I am much indebted, also, to Nathan Berman, on whose shoulders has fallen the task of collecting and tabulating much of the data used in this study. Finally, I wish to express my thanks to Kota, my wife, for many years of encouragement, constructive criticism, and editorial assistance.

HENRY D. McKAY

Institute for Juvenile Research
Chicago, Illinois

PREFACE TO THE FIRST EDITION

The studies reported in this volume were started as part of the program of the Behavior Research Fund and were continued by the National Commission on Law Observance and Enforcement, under whose auspices certain parts of the material included here were published. Subsequently, the work was continued and brought to completion under the sponsorship of the Illinois Institute for Juvenile Research and the Chicago Area Project. To each of these organizations the authors are deeply indebted.

Without the financial assistance given to the Chicago Area Project by the Rockefeller Foundation, the Wieboldt Foundation, and the Chicago Community Trust, the study could not have been completed. We also wish to express our great indebtedness to the Work Projects Administration for the extensive assistance furnished.

We acknowledge with pleasure our indebtedness to Paul G. Cressey, Norman S. Hayner, Earl R. Moses, Calvin F. Schmid, Clarence W. Schroeder, and T. Earl Sullenger, who accepted the invitation to submit studies of the cities with which they are familiar. Because of space limitations, it was not possible to present all of the materials submitted originally by these men. Their co-operativeness on problems of revision and the forbearance of all with reference to delays in publication have been appreciated greatly.

It is impossible for us to thank individually all of the persons who contributed directly or indirectly to our work in other cities. However, we do wish to acknowledge the valuable assistance received from the many judges, clerks of courts, chief probation officers, police commissioners, and other officials of welfare, educational, and commercial institutions who made records available to us or who furnished maps, population statistics, and other kinds of data used in our efforts to differentiate areas from one another. In cities other than Chicago we are indebted, for very personal consideration and kindness, to Dr. W. Wallace Weaver, of Philadelphia; Dr. A. W. Stearns, of Boston; Judge Harry M. Eastman, Howard W. Green, and Dr. Charles E. Gehlke, of Cleveland; the Honorable Charles M. Hoffman and Galen F. Aschhauer, of Cincinnati, Dr. L. G. Brown, Oberlin College, for assistance in securing data in Columbus, Ohio; and Dr. Frederick M. Zorbaugh, Oberlin College, for assistance in the early stages of the study.

In Chicago we are deeply grateful to the Honorable Frank H. Bicek, presiding judge of the Juvenile Court of Cook County; Colonel Harry Hill, chief probation officer, Juvenile Court of Cook County; Lieutenant Joseph F. Healy, head of the Crime Prevention Division, Chicago Police Department; and John P. Morrison, chief clerk of the Circuit Court of Cook County, Juvenile Branch.

We wish to express our gratitude for the assistance and encouragement of Edward Haydon, Solomon Kobrin, Malcolm McCallum, and James F. McDonald, of the staff of the Department of Sociology of the Institute for Juvenile Research. We are indebted especially to Eveline E. Blumenthal, staff member, and John Clausen, formerly a staff member, for assistance in the preparation of the manuscript, and to Dr. Ruth P. Koshuk for splendid editorial assistance. The willing help of Lillian Benjamin, Lilian Davis, and Sol Z. Rosenbaum, of the Institute for Juvenile Research, also has been greatly appreciated.

Finally, we wish to express our gratitude to the Honorable Rodney H. Brandon, director, Illinois State Department of Public Welfare, Dr. Paul L. Schroeder, superintendent of the Institute for Juvenile Research, and J. C. Weigel, regional director, Office of Price Administration, and formerly administrator of the Behavior Research Fund, for their continued interest in our work; and to Dr. Ernest W. Burgess, professor of sociology, University of Chicago, and formerly director of the Behavior Research Fund, for his invaluable support and encouragement.

CLIFFORD R. SHAW
HENRY D. McKAY

May 1, 1942

INTRODUCTION TO THE REVISED EDITION

JAMES F. SHORT, JR.

In his Introduction to the first edition of this book Ernest W. Burgess referred to it as a "magnum opus in criminology," the product of twenty years of research into the ecological distribution of delinquency and the social forces and processes which account for this distribution (p. ix). Burgess summarized the major findings of the book as follows:

1. The findings of this study establish conclusively a fact of far-reaching significance, namely, that the distribution of juvenile delinquents in space and time follows the pattern of the physical structure and of the social organization of the American city [p. ix].

2. The main point . . . established by these findings is that juvenile delinquency of the type serious enough to appear in juvenile courts is concentrated in certain parts of the American city and then thins out until it almost vanishes in the better residential districts [p. x].

3. The common element (among the social factors highly correlated with juvenile delinquency) is social disorganization or the lack of organized

Henry McKay is, I believe, the only research scholar to make major contributions to this nation's two great "Crime Commission" reports: the National Commission on Law Observance and Enforcement (the "Wickersham Commission"), under whose auspices the volume *Social Factors in Juvenile Delinquency* was published in 1931; and the recent President's Commission on Law Enforcement and Administration of Justice.

It is with deep humility and gratitude, and the greatest personal pleasure, that I acknowledge the opportunity to collaborate with Mr. McKay in the preparation of this edition of *Urban Areas*. Revision of one's work surely is not the most direct or certain way to a scholar's heart. Yet, Mr. McKay has been unflagging in support of this effort, encouraging me in every way to pursue an independent course and contributing wholeheartedly to the task of updating some of the materials. Only with respect to the Chicago Area Project did he demur to my suggestion that he undertake revision. He suggested, instead, that an analysis be made of the Area Project as a social movement. My Addendum to this Introduction constitutes an all-too-brief and inadequate commentary on this point. To do more would require extensive historical and sociological analysis beyond the intended scope of this edition, and a monograph in its own right.

I am grateful, also, to Solomon Kobrin and Anthony Sorrentino, long-time associates of the Institute for Juvenile Research and the Chicago Area Project, for their helpful comments and encouragement; and finally, to the memory of Clifford Shaw, whose sociological sense continues to extend beyond the classroom—today even more than in his lifetime.

xxvi   INTRODUCTION TO REVISED EDITION

community effort to deal with these conditions. If so, the solution for juvenile delinquency and these related problems lies in community organization. Juvenile delinquency, as shown in this study, follows the pattern of the physical and social structure of the city, being concentrated in areas of physical deterioration and neighborhood disorganization. Evidently, then, the basic solution of this and other problems of urban life lies in a program of the physical rehabilitation of slum areas and the development of community organization [p. xi].

Burgess concludes his remarks with the challenge, "We must realize that the brightest hope in reformation is in changing the neighborhood and in control of the gang in which the boy moves, lives, and has his being and to which he returns after his institutional treatment. And, finally, we must reaffirm our faith in prevention, which is so much easier, cheaper, and more effective than cure and which begins with the home, the play group, the local school, the church, and the neighborhood" (p. xiii).

The book is, indeed, a magnum opus, as subsequent developments have demonstrated. In the quarter of a century since its original publication, little has happened to alter the factual picture presented, and theoretical advances and more recent programs of delinquency control are in large part extensions or modifications of those suggested here. In the remainder of this Introduction I shall discuss some of these recent developments. In so doing I will be concerned chiefly with theoretical continuity and empirical adequacy, rather than with logical or operational adequacy of the work.[1]

[1] While attempts have been made to assess one or another of these aspects of Shaw and McKay's work and are scattered in the literature, no comprehensive assessment has been published. Cf., e.g., Stuart A. Rice, "Hypotheses and Verifications in Clifford R. Shaw's Studies of Juvenile Delinquency," Analysis 40, in *Methods in Social Science: A Case Book,* edited by Stuart A. Rice (Chicago: University of Chicago Press, 1931), pp. 549–65; Christen T. Jonassen, "A Reevaluation and Critique of the Logic and Some Methods of Shaw and McKay," *American Sociological Review,* October, 1949, pp. 608–14, and in this same issue, "Rejoinder," by Clifford R. Shaw and Henry D. McKay (pp. 614–17); Howard S. Becker, "Introduction," to Clifford R. Shaw, *The Jack-Roller: A Delinquent Boy's Own Story* (Chicago: University of Chicago Press, 1966), pp. v–xviii. The most comprehensive assessment of the logical, operational, and empirical adequacy of this work is set forth in an unpublished paper by Solomon Kobrin, a longtime associate of both Shaw and McKay at the Illinois Institute for Juvenile Research. The paper, titled "The Shaw-McKay Theory," was written in 1966. I am grateful to Mr. Kobrin for making available to me a copy of this excellent paper.

The massive documentation of empirical regularities, as found in this and related work by Shaw and McKay and their associates, is rare indeed in the behavior sciences. Later research has confirmed the existence and persistence of "delinquency areas" and the association of juvenile delinquency with the physical structure of the city—including especially physical deterioration and proximity to industrial land usage—and with other human problems, e.g., adult crime, poverty, disease, suicide, and family instability.[2] In retrospect, the association of delinquency with specific social conditions seems less important than the general pattern of association and the existence of areas within cities in which a variety of social ills are concentrated. Chilton demonstrates, e.g., that delinquency rates in Baltimore, Detroit, and Indianapolis in 1940 and 1950 are associated with overcrowded housing, low income, a high proportion of unrelated individuals in household, and low education—similar to the types of relations established by Shaw and McKay. However, the association of delinquency with foreign-born populations, a persistent theme of the Shaw and McKay studies documented by both statistical and "life history" data—is absent in Baltimore and Indianapolis and slightly negative in Detroit.[3] The point here is that the social conditions with which delinquency is associated vary with historical changes and with local conditions of topography and physical structure, the nature

[2] See, e.g., Robert C. Schmitt, "Density, Delinquency and Crime in Honolulu," *Sociology and Social Research,* March–April, 1957, pp. 274–76; Robert C. Schmitt, "Intercorrelations of Social Problem Rates in Honolulu, *American Sociological Review,* October, 1956, p. 618; Bernard Lander, *Toward an Understanding of Juvenile Delinquency: A Study of 8,464 Cases of Juvenile Delinquency in Baltimore* (New York: Columbia University Press, 1954); David J. Bordua, "Juvenile Delinquency and 'Anomie': An Attempt at Replication," *Social Problems,* Winter, 1958–59, pp. 230–38; Roland J. Chilton, "Continuity in Delinquency Area Research: A Comparison of Studies for Baltimore, Detroit, and Indianapolis," *American Sociological Review,* February, 1964, pp. 71–83; Desmond S. Cartwright and Kenneth I. Howard, "Multivariate Analysis of Gang Delinquency: I. Ecologic Influences," *Multivariate Behavioral Research,* July, 1966, pp. 321–71; Robert A. Gordon, "Issues in the Ecological Study of Delinquency," *American Sociological Review,* December, 1967, pp. 927–44.

[3] Chilton suggests that, for Detroit, the negative association of delinquency and percentage of foreign born is important principally as a reflection of the proportion of white families in a given tract, rather than in its own right.

of relations between ethnic and racial groups, etc. With the re-
striction of large-scale immigration to this country, ethnic
islands have tended to disappear—with a few notable exceptions—and immigrant groups have become assimilated into the
mainstream of American life. The conflict between generations
has lost much of its ethnic flavor. Similarly, the association of
delinquency with Negro populations has been shown to vary historically and locally.

It was with respect to their methods of studying delinquency
among different ethnic, nationality, and racial groups, and their
interpretation of the data, that Shaw and McKay became involved in one of the most publicized controversies concerning
their work. Pointing to the fact that delinquency rates vary
greatly among different groups, Jonassen questioned Shaw and
McKay's conclusion "that all nationality groups evidence the
same rate of juvenile delinquency in the same urban areas and
that nationality is not vitally related to juvenile delinquency,"[4]
charging limitations of data, questionable methodology, internal
inconsistencies, and lack of logical consistency. In their tem-
perate reply to Jonassen's criticisms Shaw and McKay made
clear that they recognized many limitations of their data and
their methods, as well as differences in delinquency rates:

. . . but, as is well known, such children in America are exposed to two traditions, and in the inner areas of large cities the conventional values of
neither are transmitted very effectively.[5]

They suggested, further, that rate variations within high-delinquency areas correspond with the extent to which groups
occupy sections of these areas which are "least desirable as
measured by social and economic indexes."

Shaw and McKay drew special attention to processes which
lead to high Negro delinquency rates:

Since Negro migrants represent a group of low economic status, if not restricted in their movement they would occupy the city areas of lowest
rentals. But barriers to free movement have forced them in part into "middle-class" areas where as Mr. Jonassen has pointed out there have been in-

[4] Jonassen, *op. cit.*, p. 614.

[5] Shaw and McKay, "Rejoinder," p. 615.

creases in area rates. *The important point here is that there have been significant changes, also, in the characteristics of the community.* These changes have resulted both from low-income and from the fact that the institutions of migrating Negroes have been singularly unsuited to the problems of urban life. As a result, some of the areas which they have occupied have tended to take on the characteristics of the inner city.

The important fact about rates of delinquents for Negro boys is that they, too, vary by type of area. They are higher than the rates for white boys, but *it cannot be said that they are higher than rates for white boys in comparable areas, since it is impossible to reproduce in white communities the circumstances under which Negro children live.* Even if it were possible to parallel the low economic status and the inadequacy of institutions in the white community, it would not be possible to reproduce the effects of segregation and the barriers to upward mobility. These combine to create for the Negro child a type of social world in which the higher rates of delinquency are not unintelligible [italics mine].[6]

The controversy has continued.[7] Recent data provide evidence that, over time, Negro communities increase their ability to control delinquency. In new chapters (XIV and XVI) prepared especially for this edition, McKay presents data concerning trends of officially recorded delinquency in 74 Chicago communities (marked off by physical and social characteristics— and for historical reasons) over a thirty-five-year period, 1927–61.[8] McKay finds that four of the five communities with the most pronounced upward trends, and four of the five communities with the most pronounced *downward trends,* are Negro communities. The most significant difference between these communities appears to be the fact that the upward-trending communities have begun and completed the familiar cycle of Negro invasion, disruption of institutional life, and succession of

[6] *Ibid.,* p. 617.

[7] See, e.g., Jackson Toby, "Comment on the Jonassen-Shaw and McKay Controversy," *American Sociological Review,* February, 1950, pp. 107–8.

[8] See *Local Community Fact Book—Chicago Metropolitan Area, 1960,* ed. Evelyn M. Kitagawa and Karl E. Taeuber (Chicago Community Inventory, University of Chicago, 1963); a preliminary report of McKay's findings is found in Henry D. McKay, "A Note on Trends in Rates of Delinquency in Certain Areas in Chicago," in *Juvenile Delinquency and Youth Crime,* by the Task Force on Juvenile Delinquency, the President's Commission on Law Enforcement and Administration of Justice (Washington, D.C.: Government Printing Office, 1967), pp. 114–18.

the population to a Negro majority most *recently* in the series, while the downward-trending communities have constituted the heart of the Negro community in Chicago (the "Black Belt" south of the Loop) for more than thirty years. Thus, Lawndale on the west side, and Kenwood, Woodlawn, and (more recently) Englewood on the south side have undergone virtually complete changes in population, from middle-class white to middle- and lower-class Negro, during the late 1940's and the 1950's. Their delinquency rates have changed "from well below the mean for the city to among the highest in the city."[9] Thirty-five years ago, rates in the areas of greatest decrease were the highest in the city. They still are high, as is evidence of other social ills, such as truancy and mental illness, but they "have decreased significantly and consistently over the past thirty years."[10]

These data are consistent with earlier Shaw and McKay findings and with a more general formulation of the processes at work. The impact of rapid residential shift from an invading socially and economically disadvantaged population is such as to decrease the capacity for social control of the community. Some conventional institutions are abandoned by their traditional and stable clientele.[11] For others, as appears to have been the case of the Negro family, the invading group may never have reached a state of conventional stability.[12] Time and stability are required for the establishment of traditions and institutions. For the American Negro, time and tradition have been disruptive of stability and conventionality. But there is evidence of great change—of emerging political leadership, more stable and affluent economic institutions, more stable family patterns, perhaps even of more stable institutional forms of an "unconven-

[9] McKay, "Trends in Rates of Delinquency," p. 114.

[10] *Ibid.*, p. 115.

[11] See, e.g., Samuel C. Kincheloe, "The Behavior Sequence of a Dying Church," *Religious Education,* April, 1929, pp. 3–19.

[12] See E. Franklin Frazier, *The Negro Family in the United States* (Chicago: University of Chicago Press, 1939); also St. Clair Drake and Horace R. Cayton, *Black Metropolis: A Study of Negro Life in a Northern City* (New York: Harper & Row, 1945).

tional" nature, such as have developed among other ethnic groups.[13]

The extent to which institutional forms of the latter type can be stabilizing in a community is not clear. There is ample evidence of the socially disruptive potential of some of them.[14] Kobrin,[15] and Cloward and Ohlin,[16] however, have pointed to the *controlling* effect on delinquency of the *relations between* criminal and noncriminal elements in the community. Where these elements are integrated, through formal and informal political, economic, and even religious institutional ties, illegitimate as well as legitimate opportunity structures may be created, and control over violent and disruptive behavior enhanced. Recent data suggest that these processes are extremely complex, however, involving both ascribed and achieved statuses of youngsters and selective processes in relations between youngsters and adult. There are a number of "institutions" which have remained largely unstudied from the point of view of social control, e.g., store-front churches, neighborhood taverns, and other places of recreation (including "quarter parties" in residents' homes), common-law marriages, political clubs, social and athletic clubs, and even street-corner groups.[17]

[13] See, especially, William Foote Whyte, *Street Corner Society* (Chicago: University of Chicago Press, 1943 and 1955).

[14] See, e.g., Drake and Cayton, *op. cit.*; James F. Short, Jr., and Fred L. Strodtbeck, *Group Process and Gang Delinquency* (Chicago: University of Chicago Press, 1965); also, James F. Short, Jr., "Juvenile Delinquency: The Sociocultural Context," in Lois W. Hoffman and Martin L. Hoffman (eds.), *Review of Child Development Research,* Vol. II (New York: Russell Sage Foundation, 1966).

[15] See Solomon Kobrin, "The Conflict of Values in Delinquency Areas," *American Sociological Review,* October, 1951, pp. 653–61; also see Solomon Kobrin, Joseph Puntil, and Emil Peluso, "Criteria of Status among Street Groups," *Journal of Research in Crime and Delinquency,* January, 1967, pp. 98–118; and Ramon J. Rivera and James F. Short, Jr., "Significant Adults, Caretakers, and Structures of Opportunity: An Exploratory Study," *Journal of Research in Crime and Delinquency,* January, 1967, pp. 76–97.

[16] R. Cloward and L. Ohlin, *Delinquency and Opportunity: A Theory of Delinquent Gangs* (Glencoe, Ill.: Free Press, 1960).

[17] See my discussion in *Review of Child Development Research;* also, Chapter 5 in Short and Strodtbeck, *op. cit.*; these discussions seek primarily to understand the delinquency-*producing* characteristics of such institutions. The con-

There is further evidence, also, concerning the influence on delinquency of ethnic traditions and history. In response to the exchange between Shaw and McKay and Jonassen, Toby argued that ethnic tradition might profitably be viewed as "an intermediate structure between class position and the personality of the individual" and that differences in ethnic traditions "are presumably responsible for the variability in the placement of . . . groups in the social structure."[18] A later paper illustrated this thesis by references to differences in traditions and behavior among Jews and Italians in the United States.[19]

Jews and Italians came to the United States in large numbers at about the same time—the turn of the century—and both settled in urban areas. There was, however, a very different attitude toward intellectual accomplishment in the two cultures. Jews from Eastern Europe regarded religious study as the most important activity for an adult male. The rabbi enjoyed great prestige because he was a scholar, a teacher, a logician. He advised the community on the application of the Written and Oral Law. Life in America gave a secular emphasis to the Jewish reverence for learning. Material success is a more important motive than salvation for American youngsters, Jewish as well as Christian, and secular education is better training for business and professional careers than Talmudic exegesis. Nevertheless, intellectual achivement [sic] continued to be valued by Jews—and to have measurable effects. Second-generation Jewish students did homework diligently, got high grades, went to college in disproportionate numbers, and scored high on intelligence tests. Two thousand years of preparation lay behind them.

Immigrants from Southern Italy, on the other hand, tended to regard formal education either as a frill or as a source of dangerous ideas from which the minds of the young should be protected. They remembered Sicily, where a child who attended school regularly was a rarity. There, youngsters were needed . . . only to help on the farm. Equally important was the fact that hard-working peasants could not understand why their children should learn classical Italian (which they would not speak at home) or geography (when they would not travel in their lifetime more than a few miles from their birthplace). Sicilian parents suspected that edu-

---

verse—social control—remains largely unexplored, though Whyte and others are relevant. See Oscar Lewis, *Five Families: Mexican Case Studies in the Culture of Poverty* (New York: Basic Books, 1959).

[18] Toby, *op. cit.*, p. 108.

[19] Jackson Toby, "Hoodlum or Businessman: An American Dilemma," in *The Jews: Social Patterns of an American Group,* ed. Marshall Sklare (Glencoe, Ill.: Free Press, 1958), pp. 542–50.

cation was an attempt on the part of Roman officials to subvert the authority of the family. In the United States, many South Italian immigrants maintained the same attitudes. They resented compulsory school attendance laws and prodded their children to go to work and become economic assets as soon as possible. They encouraged neglect of schoolwork and even truancy. They did not realize that education has more importance in an urban-industrial society than in a semi-feudal one. With supportive motivation from home lacking, the second-generation Italian boys did not make the effort of Jewish contemporaries. Their teachers tried to stuff the curriculum into their heads in vain. Their lack of interest was reflected not only in low marks, retardation, truancy, and early school leaving; it even resulted in poor scores on intelligence tests. They accepted their parents' conception of the school as worthless and thereby lost their best opportunity for social ascent.[20]

Documentation of differences between Jews and Italians in criminal involvement is difficult to obtain, but available evidence suggests that Italian boys and men have had higher rates of both crime and delinquency than have Jewish boys and men.[21]

Recent research by Kobrin *et al.* finds that ethnicity and related ascribed status characteristics of the adult community are reflected in the complex hierarchy of relationships of street-corner groups.[22] Coming from a family with "clout" in the community, residential location, and being Italian (rather than Mexican or Negro) were more important in establishing the rank of groups than were prowess in such areas of group orientation and achievement as fighting, reputation, and competence in sports and organizational matters. The research of Finestone and others and the experience of the Chicago Area Project demonstrate clearly that the ethnic "flavor" of a community is important to a variety of behaviors and adjustments by the citizenry, individually and collectively.[23]

The impact of this and other research, in terms of theoretical and empirical continuity of the Shaw and McKay work, has

[20] *Ibid.*, p. 548.

[21] *Ibid.,* p. 549. See also, in the same volume, Sophia Robison, "A Study of Delinquency among Jewish Children in New York City," pp. 535–41.

[22] Kobrin, Puntil, and Peluso, *op. cit.*

[23] Harold Finestone, "A Comparative Study of Reformation and Recidivism among Italian and Polish Adult Male Criminal Offenders" (Ph.D. Dissertation, University of Chicago, 1964).

been considerable. As early as 1929, Shaw and his associates—following Thomas and Znaniecki[24] and Cooley[25]—had attributed the concentration of delinquency in the blighted areas of larger cities to the disintegration of the community as a unit of social control.[26] This interpretation seems particularly appropriate to the *early years* of settlement of immigrant groups in the city, whether these be European immigrants to this country, or native-born Negroes, as discussed above.[27] It seems less appropriate to an understanding of patterns of crime and delinquency —and the control of these phenomena—which develop following initial settlement with its attendant disorganization. It should be noted that the period of disorganization—or lack of stable organization—may be quite prolonged, as seems particularly to be the case for American Negroes, whose peculiar history in this country has led to the lack of well-developed community leadership and stable institutions—a situation which now appears to be changing, as noted above.

It was in 1943—a year after first publication of *Urban Areas* —that William Foote Whyte's classic study of "The Social Structure of an Italian Slum" was published.[28] Whyte studied "Cornerville," a district in Boston which, by many criteria,

[24] W. I. Thomas and F. Znaniecki, *The Polish Peasant in Europe and America* (New York: Knopf, 1927).

[25] C. H. Cooley, *Social Organization* (New York: Scribners, 1909).

[26] Clifford R. Shaw *et al.*, *Delinquency Areas* (Chicago: University of Chicago Press, 1929).

[27] Robison notes that the Jews in New York City at one time had much higher rates of delinquency than at present, and Thrasher describes gangs of Jewish boys in Chicago at an earlier period in the Jewish settlement in these cities. See Robison, *op. cit.,* and F. M. Thrasher, *The Gang* (Chicago: University of Chicago Press, 1927; abridged, 1963). In addition to the "traditional" aspects of immigrant cultures to which Toby draws attention, it is clear that the circumstances of immigration to this country have an important bearing on the types of problems with which immigrants are confronted and the types of adjustments they make. See, e.g., the discussion of different immigrant communities in R. E. Park and J. Miller, *Old World Traits Transplanted* (Chicago: University of Chicago Press, 1925).

[28] William Foote Whyte, *Street Corner Society: The Social Structure of an Italian Slum* (Chicago: University of Chicago Press, 1943). Articles from this study had begun to appear somewhat earlier, but too early to have had much impact on Shaw and McKay's work. See William Foote Whyte, "Corner Boys: A Study of Clique Behavior," *American Journal of Sociology,* March, 1941, pp.

appeared to be disorganized. Conventional institutions of the larger society apparently were ineffective in preventing poverty and physical deterioration, crime, delinquency, corruption, and vice. Yet "Cornerville" had "a complex and well-established organization of its own," consisting of organizational forms which were internally structured and related to one another, through "a hierarchy of personal relations based upon a system of reciprocal obligations."[29] Corner groups, the racket (largely "numbers" and other forms of gambling), the police, politics, the church, and "old country" ties all conformed to the pattern —a pattern of organization, sometimes implicit and apparently unconscious, at other times quite explicit, but always real in the lives of the people of Cornerville.

Although Whyte was not the first to discover organizational forms in the slum, his documentation of their nature was more systematic, and his impact on subsequent theoretical formulations and research effort was especially significant.[30] It became apparent that what appeared from the perspective of the larger society to be disorganization, or lack of organization, might from another perspective be quite organized, but ineffectively so from the perspective of the larger society. The theoretical impact of this point was extended by Kobrin[31] and later elaborated by Cloward[32] and by Cloward and Ohlin.[33]

647–64; and "The Social Role of the Settlement House," *Applied Anthropology,* October–December, 1941, pp. 14–19.

[29] Whyte, *Street Corner Society,* p. 272.

[30] In his Preface to the original edition Whyte acknowledged his debt to Lincoln Steffens, whose "autobiography first suggested to me that it would be possible to find out about some of the things that are discussed in this book" (p. xii). See also, Edwin H. Sutherland's account of the development of the theory of differential association in which he adopted the phrasing "differential social organization" rather than "social disorganization" on the grounds that the delinquent group clearly was organized; in Albert Cohen, Alfred Lindesmith, and Karl Schuessler, *The Sutherland Papers* (Bloomington, Ind.: Indiana University Press, 1956), p. 21.

[31] Kobrin, *op. cit.*

[32] Richard A. Cloward, "Illegitimate Means, Anomie, and Deviant Behavior," *American Sociological Review,* April, 1959, pp. 164–76.

[33] Cloward and Ohlin, *op. cit.*

Referring to "Varieties of Delinquency Areas," Kobrin comments that "the culture of delinquency areas and specific group patterns of delinquency in these areas may be regarded as in large part determined by the character of the interaction between the conventional and the criminal value systems. . . . Delinquency areas exhibit important differences in the degree to which integration between the conventional and criminal value systems is achieved."[34] By "integration" Kobrin refers to the firm establishment of relationships by the carriers of conventional and criminal values toward the achievement of commonly desired goals such as making money, or the exercise of political power. Integrated areas are characterized by systematic and organized criminal activity. Participants, and especially leaders, in such enterprise not only seek power through legitimate political processes but seek status in the social structure of the larger community by participation also in church activities, fraternal organizations, and the like. In such areas, delinquency tends to be rationalized and contained. Excesses of violence and destruction are avoided. Juveniles come to "recognize the potentialities for personal progress in the local society through success in delinquency" (p. 658). In acquiring and demonstrating the proper delinquent skills, juveniles may be "noted and valued by adult leaders in the rackets who are confronted, as are the leaders of all income-producing enterprises, with problems of the recruitment of competent personnel" (p. 658).[35]

By way of contrast, the polar extreme of the integrated area is the area in which violative behavior is frequent—and so criminal adult models exist to legitimize delinquent behavior by juveniles—but criminal and conventional value systems "are in extreme and open opposition to one another." As a consequence, delinquency in areas of this type tends to be "unrestrained by controls originating *at any point* in the adult social structure" and "to acquire a wild, untrammelled character" (pp. 658–59).

[34] Kobrin, *op. cit.*, p. 657.

[35] For a recent discussion of the manner in which these problems are handled by the most notorious of organized criminal enterprises, see Robert T. Anderson, "From Mafia to Cosa Nostra," *American Journal of Sociology,* November, 1965, pp. 302–10.

xxxvii INTRODUCTION TO REVISED EDITION

The community conditions conducive to the second type "are frequently produced by drastic changes in the class, ethnic, or racial characteristics of its population. Such transitions . . . tend to devitalize the older institutions of the area, and to introduce a period during which institutional and other controls are at a minimum. During these interim periods the bearers of conventional culture . . . are without the customary institutional machinery, and therefore in effect partially demobilized with reference to the diffusion of their value system" (p. 658).

Theoretically and empirically, delinquency areas are expected to range along a continuum between these extremes. Kobrin sees integration as a dynamic process and suggests one of the mechanisms by which it occurs, noting that the emergence of group norms among persistent violators often is "accompanied by regularized and dependable accommodations with such representatives of the wider society as police and politicians."

Cloward considerably extends the notion of integration between criminal and conventional elements in the community and, with Ohlin, develops more fully the theoretical relationship between such integration and patterns of juvenile delinquency. Basic to this formulation is Merton's fomulation of categories of behavior or role adaptations which emerge from the disjunction between cultural goals and socially structured opportunity.[36] Merton summarizes these adaptations as forms of conformity, innovation, ritualism, retreatism, and rebellion. Whereas certain forms of crime and delinquency can be conceptualized in other categories, that which is classified as innovation is most clearly related to the variables with which Merton is concerned. And, though examples may be found ranging the entire social class spectrum,[37] it is at the lower end of the socioeconomic scale that Merton locates "the greatest pressure toward deviation" (p. 144).

[36] As elaborated in Robert K. Merton, "Social Structure and Anomie," and "Continuities in the Theory of Social Structure and Anomie," *Social Theory and Social Structure* (rev. ed.; Glencoe, Ill.: Free Press, 1957), Chapters IV and V.

[37] See, e. g., Daniel Bell, "Crime as an American Way of Life," *Antioch Review,* Summer, 1953, pp. 131–54; Edwin Sutherland, *White Collar Crime* (New York: Dryden Press, 1949).

The status of unskilled labor and the consequent low income cannot readily compete *in terms of established standards of worth* with the promises of power and high income from organized vice, rackets, and crime [p. 145].

Indeed, Al Capone represents "the triumph of amoral intelligence over morally prescribed 'failure,' when the channels of vertical mobility are closed or narrowed *in a society which places a high premium on economic affluence and social ascent for all its members*" (p. 146).

To this formulation, Cloward adds the further variable of "differentials in availability of illegitimate means, noting that "several sociologists have alluded to such variations without explicitly incorporating this variable in a theory of deviant behavior."[38] Thus are joined the anomie and cultural transmission traditions, for the latter long had appreciated the importance for transmission of criminal values of the integration of different age levels of offenders in the community, of acceptance by those who were skilled in the necessary techniques and who could tutor the fledgling criminal who aspired to become professional.[39] Cloward insists that the term "illegitimate means" subsumes "both *learning structures* and *opportunity structures.*" His discussion suggests the importance for these matters of such factors as age, sex, ethnicity, kinship, and social class, all of which are to some degree documented in the research literature. By his introduction of the concept of illegitimate means Cloward extends the causal mechanism described by Merton, and soon after, with Ohlin, the general framework was applied to the problem of accounting for the emergence and maintenance of delinquent subcultures.[40]

[38] Cloward, *op. cit.*

[39] See Cloward's discussion, *ibid.*; also Edwin Sutherland, *The Professional Thief* (Chicago: University of Chicago Press, 1937); Shaw *et al., Delinquency Areas;* Shaw, *The Jack-Roller;* Frank Tannenbaum, *Crime and the Community* (Boston: Ginn & Co., 1938).

[40] Cloward and Ohlin, *op. cit.* DeFleur's recent work in Cordoba, Argentina, finds that delinquent subcultures such as those described in the United States have not emerged in that city. Both the ecology of delinquency and study of incarcerated offenders suggest that delinquency in Cordoba is primarily instrumental rather than expressive. Learning and opportunity structures for delinquency are quite different in Cordoba than in U.S. cities, and patterns of delinquency reflect these differences. The importance of cross-cultural study is empha-

Cloward notes the relatively independent development of the "anomie" and "cultural transmission" traditions of sociological concern with deviant behavior.[41] Readers of the first edition of *Urban Areas* doubtless have wondered at the absence in it of reference to Merton's now classic article, "Social Structure and Anomie," published some four years prior to *Urban Areas*, in 1938.[42] In his comment on the Shaw and McKay–Jonassen exchange, Toby argued that Merton's theory might help to bridge the gap between parties to this controversy, on the grounds that by their role in placing groups in the social structure, ethnic traditions were influential in producing anomie (as manifested in crime and delinquency).[43]

Shaw and McKay clearly were not unaware of the cultural and structural differences which formed the bases for these formulations. In Chapter VII and in the concluding chapter of the original edition (now Chapter XIII), their "general theoretical framework within which community data are interpreted" approaches very closely the Merton formulation concerning anomie, as it relates to crime and delinquency, and the later work of Kobrin, Cloward and Ohlin:

. . . it is assumed that the differentiation of areas and the segregation of population within the city have resulted in wide variation of opportunities in the struggle for position within our social order. The groups in the areas of lowest economic status find themselves at a disadvantage in the struggle to achieve the goals idealized in our civilization. These differences are translated into conduct through the general struggle for those economic symbols which signify a desirable position in the larger social order. Those persons who occupy a disadvantageous position are involved in a conflict between the goals assumed to be attainable in a free society and those actually

---

sized by these findings. See Lois B. DeFleur, "Delinquent Gangs in Cross-Cultural Perspective: The Case of Cordoba," *Journal of Research in Crime and Delinquency,* January, 1967, pp. 132–41; "A Cross-Cultural Comparison of Juvenile Offenders and Offenses: Cordoba, Argentina, and the United States," *Social Problems,* Spring, 1967, pp. 483–92; "Ecological Variables in the Cross-Cultural Study of Delinquency," *Social Forces,* June, 1967, pp. 556–70.

[41] Cloward, *op. cit.,* p. 164.

[42] Robert K. Merton, "Social Structure and Anomie," *American Sociological Review,* October, 1938, pp. 672–82.

[43] Toby, "Comment on the Jonassen-Shaw and McKay Controversy."

attainable for a large proportion of the population. It is understandable, then, that the economic position of persons living in the areas of least opportunity should be translated at times into unconventional conduct, in an effort to reconcile the idealized status and their practical prospects of attaining this status. Since, in our culture, status is determined largely in economic terms, the differences between contrasted areas in terms of economic status become the most important differences. Similarly, as might be expected, crimes against property are most numerous [pp. 180–81].

. . . the existence of a system of values supporting criminal behavior becomes important as a factor in shaping individual life-patterns, since it is only where such a system exists that the person through criminal activity may acquire the material goods so essential to status in our society and at the same time increase, rather than lose, his prestige in the smaller group system of which he has become an integral part [p. 183].

Theirs was the task primarily of documenting the social distribution of delinquency and of mapping the general process of cultural transmission. This they did superbly and on a massive scale. Others have followed, to isolate conceptually and empirically particular components of this process and mechanisms by which particular types of delinquency occur in communities and groups. These formulations tend to be more abstract than those of Shaw and McKay—whether they are more adequate to the phenomena to be explained remains largely an unsettled issue. Later empirical inquiries, for example, have failed to establish the superiority of anomie formulations over those of Shaw and McKay in interpretation of ecological correlates of crime and delinquency.[44] Typological thinking continues to be regarded as a hopeful method of ordering the complexity of delinquent behavior, but the suggested typologies have stood up only moderately well under empirical scrutiny.[45]

[44] See, e.g., Chilton, *op. cit.*; Karl Schuessler and Gerald Slatin, "Sources of Variation in U.S. City Crime, 1950 and 1960," *Journal of Research in Crime and Delinquency,* July, 1964, pp. 127–48.

[45] See, e.g., Irving Spergel, *Racketville, Slumtown, Haulburg: An Exploratory Study of Delinquent Subcultures* (Chicago: University of Chicago Press, 1964); H. Bloch and A. Niederhoffer, *The Gang: A Study in Adolescent Behavior* (New York: Philosophical Library, 1958); James F. Short, Jr., Ray A. Tennyson, and Kenneth I. Howard, "Behavior Dimensions of Gang Delinquency," *American Sociological Review,* June, 1963, pp. 411–28; Paul Lerman, "Argot, Symbolic Deviance and Subcultural Delinquency," *American Sociological Review,* April, 1967, pp. 209–24.

Some may wonder that Shaw and McKay did not hit upon the notion of "delinquent subcultures," since, with Thrasher,[46] they were responsible for a large portion of the data upon which contemporary formulations rest. Although they referred to delinquency "as a powerful competing way of life" in high-rate areas of the city (p. 164), it remained for Cohen to introduce the notion of the delinquent subculture. Cohen portrays the delinquent subculture as a collectively arrived at solution for status problems of some working-class males, as a type of reaction-formation against conventional middle-class values by those who are especially disadvantaged with respect to them.[47] It was perhaps because Shaw and McKay saw delinquency as such a normal part of community life, as play more than problem-solving, that the subcultural point of view was not developed in their work.[48] Other proposals describing and attempting to account for youth subcultures have followed.[49] Most knowledgeable observers agree that these constitute real advances, but their efficacy, in terms of explanatory power, is by no means clear. It is clear that there are variations in the patterns of group behavior—both delinquent and nondelinquent—and that these variations are in very complex ways related to the nature of local community structure and culture, including learning and opportunity structures[50] and social class culture,[51] to within-

[46] Thrasher, *op. cit.*

[47] Albert K. Cohen, *Delinquent Boys* (Glencoe, Ill.: Free Press, 1955).

[48] Henry D. McKay, "The Neighborhood and Child Conduct," *The Annals of the American Academy of Political and Social Science,* January, 1949, pp. 32–41, reprinted in *Cities and Society: The Revised Reader in Urban Sociology,* ed. Paul K. Hatt and Albert J. Reiss, Jr. (Glencoe, Ill.: Free Press, 1957), pp. 815–25.

[49] *Ibid.*; see also, Cloward and Ohlin, *op. cit.*; Albert K. Cohen and James F. Short, Jr., "Research in Delinquent Subcultures," *Journal of Social Issues,* 1958, pp. 20–37; Spergel, *op. cit.*; Bennett M. Berger, "Adolescence and Beyond," *Social Problems,* Spring, 1963, pp. 394–408.

[50] Cloward and Ohlin, *op. cit.*; also Kobrin, Puntil, and Peluso, *op. cit.*; Rivera and Short, *op. cit.*; Ramon J. Rivera and James F. Short, Jr., "Occupational Goals: A Comparative Analysis," in *Juvenile Gangs in Context,* ed. Malcolm W. Klein (Englewood Cliffs, N.J.: Prentice-Hall, 1967), pp. 70–90.

[51] See especially Walter B. Miller, "Lower Class Culture as a Generating Milieu of Gang Delinquency," *Journal of Social Issues,* 1958, pp. 5–19.

and between-group processes[52] and to characteristics of the individuals who compose these groups.[53] Later research has begun to describe these variations and to specify more precisely the nature of these factors and processes. The state of knowledge is such, however, that it seems likely that later formulations concerning these matters will undergo greater change as a result of future research than will the interpretations of the general process of cultural transmission advanced by Shaw and McKay.

The point is not that nothing more has been learned—for the field has been much enriched with new theories and data—rather, that the foundation laid by Shaw, McKay, and others not only has stood the test of time but remains of vital significance for contemporary research and theory and for programs oriented to delinquency control.

CONCLUSIONS

In conclusion, a note on the direction of future research seems appropriate, together with a brief discussion of changes made for this edition of the book.

Future research will, I believe, focus much more than does the present study on the impact on youth of mass media of communications, particularly as related to mass entertainment, fashion, and values and practices related to them—not so much as "causes" of crime and delinquency as the means by which youth in many parts of the world are stimulated to participate in common fads, fashions, and causes, and in some cases to react against them. I have been chided recently, as a representative of sociologists in this country, by a young French anthropologist who accuses us of ignoring the factor which he believes is paramount to understanding youth throughout the world, viz.,

---

[52] See especially Albert J. Reiss, Jr., "The Social Integration of Queers and Peers," *Social Problems,* Fall, 1961, pp. 102–20; Muzafer Sherif and Carolyn W. Sherif, *Reference Groups* (New York: Harper & Row, 1964); Short and Strodtbeck, *op. cit.*; Leon R. Jansyn, Jr., "Solidarity and Delinquency in a Street Corner Group," *American Sociological Review,* October, 1966, pp. 600–614; Malcolm Klein and Lois Crawford "Groups, Gangs, and Cohesiveness," *Journal of Research in Crime and Delinquency,* January, 1967, pp. 63–75.

[53] Robert A. Gordon, "Social Level, Social Disability, and Gang Interaction," *American Journal of Sociology,* July, 1967, pp. 42–62; Short and Strodtbeck, *op. cit.*, Chapter 10.

"Americanization," here and abroad. Jean Monod sees the behavior of the Parisian street gangs he studied as a reaction
against this "uniformization" of youth culture brought on by
American motion pictures and rock-and-roll music, and their
British counterparts.[54] He sees similar influences at work in
other parts of the world, on both sides of iron and bamboo "cur-
tains," in developing as well as in highly developed countries.[55]

The point, in the present context, is that the technology of
communication and transportation has changed vastly in the
past quarter of a century. The impact on youth also is vastly
different—not so much in the degree to which youngsters are or
are not intimately informed concerning illegal enterprises (see
Shaw and McKay's comments on page 173), as in terms of the
role of this technology in creating identity of youth among
themselves, stimulating fads and fashions and their attendant
markets, and reactions to these, perhaps as suggested by Monod.
It has seemed to me, on the one hand, that at least a few of the
youth subcultures which have acquired a "deviant" label in this
country might be considered, *in part,* as reactions against the
mass, particularly as represented by highly commercially promoted fads and fashions, e.g., various "beat" groups, Haight-
Ashbury and the new East Village Scene, and perhaps some
groups of the "Hell's Angels" type.[56] We have reports from
Europe, on the other hand, that many of those who get into
trouble with the law as a result of their participation in "riots"
related to the appearance of entertainment idols tend to have
previous delinquency records.[57] Leaders of such expressive

[54] Jean Monod, "Juvenile Gangs in Paris: Toward a Structural Analysis,"
Journal of Research in Crime and Delinquency, January, 1967, pp. 142–65.

[55] Variation in delinquent subcultures such as those noted by Monod in Paris,
DeFleur in Cordoba, and by numerous investigators in this country may be due,
in part, to variations in exposure of youth to mass media, as well as to general
levels of technological and economic development. Cf. *ibid.*; DeFleur, *op. cit.*;
Cloward and Ohlin, *op. cit.*; Cohen and Short, *op. cit.*

[56] See "Youth: The Hippies," *Time,* July 7, 1967, pp. 18–22; see also, Hunter S.
Thompson, *Hell's Angels* (New York: Random House, 1967).

[57] United Nations General Report by Wolf Middendorff, *New Forms of Juvenile Delinquency: Their Origin, Prevention and Treatment,* Second United Nations Congress on the Prevention of Crime and the Treatment of Offenders (London, 8–20 August 1960).

crowds turned to action apparently are especially likely to have previous records. I know of no such studies in this country. In any case, one does not know whether the findings results from the behavior of the youngsters primarily, or of the police who view them as troublemakers. Again, the point is not so much that the mass media are significantly related to juvenile delinquency—or to broader categories of deviancy—but that the media are dynamic forces in modern life, and we do not know enough about their relation to a variety of forms of behavior.

In part as a result of the changing technologies referred to above, it seems likely that non-slum communities today are less consistent in presenting to the child a homogeneous set of "constructive and restraining influences," "cultural standards and a wholesome social life," than Shaw and McKay, and others of the Old Chicago School, were wont to assume.[58] Since youngsters and communities in "better" social and economic circumstances were not studied with the intensity which was focused on the slum we cannot be certain of the interpretation even in the earlier period. Certainly the *stability* of middle-class communities is less today than formerly. Again, we simply know too little to be certain in our interpretations. Recent empirical work suggests that lower- and middle-class delinquency differ a great deal in patterns and that each is closely related to its own class cultural context.[59]

In the meantime, the present volume brings up-to-date the fact that rates of apprehension for the types of behavior which arouse the community to official action through its law enforcement machinery remain highest in blighted inner-city areas. Mr. McKay continues the task of "filling-in" empirical gaps created by the necessity to extrapolate from inadequate data, as is evidenced by his new chapters and by other research cited earlier in this Introduction.

Several chapters and Burgess' Introduction to the first edition of the book have been eliminated for this presentation. These include the earlier Part IV, consisting of chapters by research

[58] Shaw and McKay, *Social Factors*, p. 111.

[59] See selections in Edmund W. Vaz (ed.), *Middle-Class Juvenile Delinquency* (New York: Harper & Row, 1967); cf. Miller, *op. cit.*

workers on other cities: "Five Cities of the Pacific Northwest," by Norman S. Hayner; "Evansville, Indiana," by Paul G. Cressey; "Peoria, Illinois," by Clarence W. Schroeder; "Omaha, Nebraska," by T. Earl Sullenger; "Baltimore, Maryland," by Earl R. Moses; and "Minneapolis and St. Paul, Minnesota," by Calvin F. Schmid. In each case, the conclusion is reached that the distribution of delinquency is "fundamentally similar to that in other American cities."[60] Chapters on "Columbus, Ohio," "Birmingham, Alabama," and on "Little Rock, Arkansas, and Denver, Colorado," also were eliminated. Readers wishing more detailed information are referred to these chapters in the original edition.

The study remains largely a detailed investigation of Chicago, so long an important "laboratory" for sociologists. Mr. McKay's new chapters add considerably to this great tradition. Consideration of other cities is important, however, because it establishes in some measure both the generality and the limitations of the patterns more extensively documented for Chicago.

The final chapter of the original edition (now Chapter XIII) was a summing-up of the theoretical position developed by Shaw and McKay and a "progress report" of the Chicago Area Project. The Area Project was conceived and developed by Shaw largely on the basis of the research which went into the early monographs.[61] He devoted the greater part of his last twenty-three years to this effort, while McKay continued primarily to pursue research interests. This division of labor was quite compatible to the two men. Shaw was, above all, a man of action, and his mission in life became the Area Project. McKay was and is the contemplative scholar, the confirmed skeptic, persistent and unrelenting in his pursuit and analysis of data relevant to a point or a principle. The combination worked well. The importance of research was never lost on those who became associated with the Area Project. Indigenous workers and leaders often became indigenous researchers, with all the advantages

[60] Quoting from Hayner's chapter in the original edition, p. 386.

[61] Shaw et al., Delinquency Areas; Shaw and McKay, Social Factors; Shaw, The Jack-Roller; C. R. Shaw and M. E. Morre, The Natural History of a Delinquent Career (Chicago: University of Chicago Press, 1931).

and at least some of the disadvantages which this implies. Burgess and Bogue have noted that "as a strong supporter of the personal document and life history approach to sociological research . . . [Shaw] was a central figure in the stormy controversy over 'qualitative versus quantitative' research methods, yet his organization calmly turned out more statistical research on sociological topics than most of his critics."[62] It was McKay and those working with him who were responsible for the statistical output. We have learned much from the continuing efforts of this organization.[63]

ADDENDUM: THE CHICAGO AREA PROJECT AS A
SOCIAL MOVEMENT

The full story of the Chicago Area Project has never been told, and it may now be beyond recapture. Evaluation, in any case, is extremely difficult. I have left unaltered the original version of the final chapter, but a brief addendum seems appro-

[62] Ernest W. Burgess and Donald J. Bogue (eds.), *Contributions to Urban Sociology* (Chicago: University of Chicago Press, 1964), p. 591.

[63] In addition to the present volume and the several articles and books previously cited, see Clifford Shaw, *Brothers in Crime* (Chicago: University of Chicago Press, 1938); Solomon Kobrin, "Sociological Aspects of the Development of a Street Corner Group: An Exploratory Study," *American Journal of Orthopsychiatry,* October, 1961, pp. 685–702; Brahm Baittle, "Psychiatric Aspects of the Development of a Street Corner Group: An Exploratory Study," *American Journal of Orthopsychiatry,* October, 1961, pp. 703–12; Solomon Kobrin, "The Chicago Area Project—A 25-Year Assessment," *Annals of the American Academy of Political and Social Science,* March, 1959, pp. 19–29; Solomon Kobrin and Harold Finestone, *Drug Addiction among Young Persons in Chicago,* A Report of a Study Conducted by the Illinois Institute for Juvenile Research and The Chicago Area Project, issued October, 1953; Harold Finestone, "Cats, Kicks and Color," *Social Problems,* July, 1957, pp. 3–13; Harold Finestone, "Narcotics and Criminality," *Law and Contemporary Problems,* Winter, 1957, pp. 60–85; Helen MacGill Hughes (ed.), *The Fantastic Lodge: The Autobiography of a Girl Drug Addict* (Boston: Houghton Mifflin, 1961); Gary Schwartz and Don Merten, "The Language of Adolescence: An Anthropological Approach to the Youth Culture," *American Journal of Sociology,* March, 1967, pp. 453–68. Many unpublished papers have resulted from this work, and some are reported only in a preliminary way. Good examples are Henry D. McKay and Solomon Kobrin, "Nationality and Delinquency," and Henry D. McKay, "Report on the Criminal Careers of Male Delinquents in Chicago," in *Juvenile Delinquency and Youth Crime,* pp. 107–13. Both of these projects represent long-term interests of great importance. A more lengthy version of the Careers paper will be published separately by the President's Commission on Law Enforcement and Administration of Justice.

priate. In it, I hope to set the stage for further historical and sociological inquiry concerning the Chicago Area Project.

Recent information concerning the Chicago Area Project may be obtained from a number of sources.[64] On July 1, 1957, the field services personnel—community organizers and consultants to local citizens—were transferred from the staff of the Sociological Services of the Institute for Juvenile Research to the Illinois Youth Commission. Thus was effected the separation of the "action" and "research" aspects of the Chicago Area Project.

Sorrentino's discussion of "The Chicago Area Project after 25 Years" contains the following brief paragraph:[65]

Clifford Shaw's death in August 1957 was an irreplaceable loss. However, he left a legacy of ideas and practices which serve to inspire his associates, and the thousands of residents and workers in local communities throughout the nation. The Chicago Area Project, therefore, continues as a truly fitting living memorial to an outstanding social scientist, a humanitarian in the truest sense of that term, and *a great leader of a significant social movement*. [Italics mine.]

The remainder of this Addendum will sketch the background and the nature of this social movement.

The background is this book and related research—chiefly by Shaw and McKay and their associates; it is Clifford Shaw as a person and how he interpreted the human condition; and it is the people of the Area Project and the communities which they constituted. Shaw had been a probation and parole officer before he became a research sociologist at the Institute for Juvenile Research. His experiences with youthful and adult offenders affected him deeply and set his inquiring mind to work on the nature of their problems. He was convinced of the essential humanity of these young men and impressed and dismayed by their detachment from conventional groups. He saw in the experiences of his charges that this detachment was a two-way process, of youngsters drifting away from conventional groups

---

[64] Illinois Youth Commission, *Data Book on Community Committees Affiliated with the Chicago Area Project, 1963–1964*; Kobrin, "The Chicago Area Project—A 25-Year Assessment"; Anthony Sorrentino, "The Chicago Area Project after 25 Years," *Federal Probation*, June, 1959, pp. 40–45.

[65] Sorrentino, *op. cit.*, p. 41.

and institutions into playgroups and into gangs where delinquency became a way of life, and of rejection of the offender—
particularly the convicted offender—by conventional society.
He saw, too, the gulf between residents of slum communities and
the larger society—a gulf complicated by varied cultural backgrounds and poverty, but stemming largely from the relative
powerlessness of these people. In the current lexicon, he was
concerned with the problem of alienation, and he attributed
alienation in large part to powerlessness. Crime and delinquency, and social disorganization, were in turn complex products of
alienation and the forces related to it. His experience and personal philosophy, and the later studies, converged on the strate-
gy of reaching youngsters in the setting of their natural groups
and of organizing communities for acceptance and guidance of
potential and actual offenders, by more effective utilization of
their energies and of the community's resources.

The data upon which the Area Project was based resulted, as
Kobrin has noted, from a combination of ecological and social
psychological studies. The ecological are documented most fully
in this volume. Their interpretation, particularly as found in
Chapters VII, XIII, and XVI, rests heavily on extremely detailed case investigations such as appear in *The Jack-Roller, The
Natural History of a Delinquent Career*, and *Brothers in Crime*,
and briefly in Chapter VII. The point of view developed from
the latter type of study may be summarized in the propositions
that

... delinquency in most cases [is] the product of ... [a] simple and direct
process of social learning

and

... delinquency in the slum areas of our cities reflects the strivings of boys
in a social rather than an antisocial direction.[66]

Kobrin has summarized succinctly the theory on which the
Area Project program is based:

... taken in its most general aspect, delinquency as a problem in the modern metropolis is principally a product of the breakdown of the machinery
of spontaneous social control. The breakdown is precipitated by the cata-

---

[66] Kobrin, *op. cit.*, p. 21.

clysmic pace of social change to which migrants from a peasant or rural background are subjected when they enter the city. In its more specific aspects, delinquency was seen as adaptive behavior on the part of the male children of rural migrants acting as members of adolescent peer groups in their efforts to find their way to meaningful and respected adult roles essentially unaided by the older generation and under the influence of criminal models for whom the inner city areas furnish a haven.[67]

Shaw was one of the first—perhaps *the* first—to see the relevance and the potential of the deeply imbedded American tradition of local autonomy and organization, self-help and self-determination, for the problems of slum dwellers. He was aware that this tradition would have to be accommodated to countervailing forces of political and economic centralization and bureaucratization, and he had the political acumen to realize that this problem could be resolved only in the course of unfolding and unforeseeable events. In the meantime he was able to harness the mystique of the democratic ethos to enable many to begin opening doors on the corridors of power, and to open some of these doors himself, in the service of the enterprise.[68]

The history of the Area Project cannot be understood without reference to an additional factor. This factor was Shaw's missionary zeal. His classroom presence was a rich combination of "hard data" and case materials, humanitarian ideology and political reality, but above all of service in a cause—the cause of political and social self-determination by local neighborhoods and communities. It seemed clear as one listened to him in the classroom or engaged him in private conversation that this was more than scientific interest or pedagogical technique—more even than humanitarian service. It was Shaw's "calling," and he served it well.

Shaw's zeal was infectious. He was a charismatic leader possessed of great personal charm and persuasiveness. This was, in effect, the manner in which he "led" the Chicago Area Project—not directly, through the exercise of power, but "behind the scenes," through his influence on professionals recruited to the

[67] *Ibid.*, p. 22.

[68] I am indebted to Solomon Kobrin for discussions in private conversation and correspondence relative to many of these points.

work, on indigenous leaders in small groups in local neighborhoods, and on others with influence in the power structure of
Chicago and the state. He regarded as an article of faith the
importance and the integrity of local groups with local leadership dedicated to the solution of local problems. His role, and
the role of other professionals, was to provide local leaders the
expertise necessary to organize their communities more effectively for delinquency prevention, the rehabilitation of offenders, and the solution of other problems determined to be of
importance by these communities. It was also to provide a
bridge to the power structure and the economy of the larger
community. Shaw's leadership—both intellectual and charismatic—thus was not of the local community committees, and
therefore not of the bulk of the large numbers of people touched
by the movements. Leadership at this level was left to others,
with the active encouragement, financial assistance, and expertise of Shaw and his associates. Great autonomy was given
local committees. Kobrin observes in passing that "some of the
economic and political leadership of these communities did not
always fit philistine specifications of respectability, and that on
this score the Area Project program came under criticism during
its early days."[69] Despite such criticism, and despite occasional
decisions regarded as unsound by the Area Project staff, the
autonomy of this local committee was respected.

Shaw did not covet personal power. He was guided instead by
a personal ideology of great compassion and faith in the efficacy
of the research with which he had been associated and in the
principle of self-determination by local communities.

The image implied in the Area Project conception of the delinquency problem is that man tends always to organize his behavior in the service of his
human identity. To what extent this view is supported by the research of
Shaw and his associates, and to what extent the research proceeded from
this view is, of course, a difficult question to answer. The fact remains,
however, that from the beginning the Area Project program rested on a
conception of human nature which was optimistic concerning the prevention
of delinquency and the rehabilitation of the delinquent.[70]

[69] Kobrin, *op. cit.*, p. 23.   [70] *Ibid.*, p. 22.

This optimism, and Shaw's charisma, were reflected—and continue to be reflected—in meetings of the Community Committees. Here ideology, rather than the data of past or present research, sustains the movement in the absence of "hard" data on effectiveness. Annual meetings and reports of Community Committees tell of activities and of participation in them, of cases in which the work of the Committees has been successful in "rehabilitating" a youngster or an adult, of organizational success in achieving an objective—building a facility, launching a program, forcing or finagling a concession from the City Fathers. Shaw's name is mentioned frequently in these meetings and reports—as the man whose research and vision were responsible for the Area Project.[71]

The autonomy of individual Community Committees and their responsiveness to variations in local conditions have resulted in great variety among them in terms of organization, goals, and in motivation for participation by individuals. Kobrin has noted that these variations are related to the degree of local community structure and stability. Finestone's study, and informal observation, suggests that there are important ethnic variations, also, e.g., in the role played by the Church and by both nuclear and extended family relationships in the rehabilitation of juvenile and adult offenders.[72] Indeed, the character of the entire movement in any particular community may be greatly affected by such factors as the nature of relationships between an Area Project staff worker and the local parish priest, or the ethnicity of the priest and of the membership of the local Community Committee.

Despite such variation, the Area Project has a central core, of ideology and organization, and its analysis as a social movement appears to be appropriate. A part of the general humani-

---

[71] As this is being written, notice arrives of a memorial service observing the tenth anniversary of the death of Clifford R. Shaw at Joseph Bond Chapel, University of Chicago Quadrangle. The service is under the auspices of the Chicago Federation of Community Committees.

[72] Finestone, *op. cit.*; see also Harold Finestone, "Reformation and Recidivism among Italian and Polish Criminal Offenders," *American Journal of Sociology,* May, 1967, pp. 575–88.

tarian movement of the nineteenth century and of the elaboration of special services to offenders and their families which developed as part of that movement, it was based also on dissatis-
faction with the form taken by some of these services and with
certain features of urban life. The "enemy" of the movement
was apathy of local residents to their own problems, and "out-
siders," including "professionals," who attempted to "do for"
local communities rather than giving aid to but vesting power in
these communities.

The character of Community Committees has changed with
the passage of time—with changed populations in some communities and with changing social conditions generally. It has
changed, also, inevitably, with institutionalization of the movement. Among the more important changes influencing the Area
Project are those which have occurred among social work and
others of the "helping professions." Rapid strides have been
made, particularly in social work, toward professionalization, on
the one hand, and toward a rationale for "reaching out" to persons and groups who, for one reason or another, do not avail
themselves of traditional agency-centered service.[73] During this
period, also, welfare services have become "big business," and
competition for the welfare dollar—from both public and private sources—has become both more intense and more professional in character.[74]

Professionalization of social work at first had the effect of
removing social work services from those apparently most in
need of them—among adults, the indigent, the isolated, and the
alienated; among youngsters, the most aggressive and predatory
of groups. For as social workers retreated behind institutional
walls and waited for referrals in much the same manner as
physicians and dentists, these people simply did not come unless
forced to do so by court or other referral with authority. When
they did come they found often that social workers were sym-

[73] *Reaching the Unreached,* New York City Youth Board, 1952.

[74] For enlightened discussion of these and other developments in social welfare,
see Harold L. Wilensky and Charles N. Lebeaux, *Industrial Society and Social
Welfare* (New York: Free Press of Glencoe, 1958).

pathetic and sincere, but alien to—or at least not a part of—the local community, with all its class and ethnic connotations. It was to these concerns that the Area Project was most responsive, with its insistence on the autonomy and the viability of indigenous community organization and leadership.

During this same quarter of a century, social work also "discovered" indigenous leadership, and the gap today between Area Project philosophy and social work practice in this respect appears to have lessened considerably. One important intervening step in this process has been the widespread adoption of "street gang" or "detached" work as a means of controlling the depredations of delinquent gangs and redirecting their energies to constructive purposes. Efforts of this type, involving personal contact by adults with gangs in their natural habitat—on the street, in neighborhood hangouts, wherever they might be—began more than a century ago.[75] It was the Area Project, however, which first carried out such activity on a systematic and sustained basis. They did so, utilizing indigenous young men as workers with gangs, as part of larger programs of local community organizations. The social work profession, and most agencies, sought as gang workers trained social workers rather than indigenous adults. There is much current debate and little evidence concerning the proper training of gang workers. Differences between the Area Project and professional social work in this respect are greater in philosophy than in practice, in part because of a shortage of trained social workers for such positions. There is evidence from social-work and nonsocial-work programs alike that gang workers today are working more closely with and relying more heavily upon indigenous community leadership, including youth leadership, than previously has been the case in such programs.[76] This *rapprochement* appears to result primarily from increased movement of social-work and

[75] See, for example, the discussion in Irving Spergel, *Street Gang Work: Theory and Practice* (Reading, Mass.: Addison-Wesley, 1966), pp. xiv–xvii.

[76] See, for example, *ibid.*; Charles N. Cooper, "The Chicago Y.M.C.A. Detached Workers: Current Status of an Action Program," in Malcolm W. Klein and Barbara G. Myerhoff (eds.), *Juvenile Gangs in Context: Theory Research and Action* (Englewood Cliffs, N.J.: Prentice-Hall, 1967).

other agencies toward the Area Project model, and, again, it is related to the shortage of trained social workers for gang work. Increasingly, trained or experienced gang workers are coming to serve as supervisors or consultants to indigenous gang leaders, former gang leaders, and local adults who perform direct services with gangs.

Increased experimentation with the use of clients and former clients, and of indigenous persons in the "helping professions," coupled with the impetus provided by such federal programs as the "War on Poverty," is likely to result in even greater *rapprochement* between these competing philosophies and practices concerning delinquency control by means of work with gangs and with larger forces at work in shaping the nature of local communities.[77]

Thus, important aspects of the *problem* faced by the Area Project have changed, and a part of its *mission* has been accomplished. Systematic study of these changes would constitute an important contribution to the sociology and history of community organization and welfare effort, and to the study of social movements.

The combination of research and social action represented by Shaw and McKay and many of their associates, and by the Institute for Juvenile Research and the Chicago Area Project, is rare, indeed. We are much the richer, in data and theory, and in practical knowledge, as a result of these efforts. It is an honor and a pleasure to "introduce" them to a society which needs to be reminded, and to new scholars who will build upon them.

[77] The participation of indigenous leadership and organization has been a cornerstone—albeit a controversial one—of the Community Action Program of the "War on Poverty." See Frank Riessman, "Self-Help among the Poor: New Styles of Social Action," *Trans-Action,* September–October, 1965, pp. 32–37.

PART I

CHAPTER I

INTRODUCTION

DURING the past century many studies have been made which indicate that the incidence of officially recorded delinquency and crime varies from one locality to another. One such study, *Delinquency Areas*, was published in 1929 by the authors and their colleagues.[1] This monograph reported a study of the distribution of the home addresses of approximately 60,000 male individuals in Chicago who had been dealt with by the school authorities, the police, and the courts as actual or alleged truants, delinquents, or criminals. It was clearly demonstrated in this report that the rates of all three groups varied widely among the local communities in the city. The low-income communities near the centers of commerce and heavy industry had the highest rates, while those in outlying residential communities of higher economic status were more or less uniformly low.

The present volume brings the delinquency data for Chicago up to date, provides comparative data for several other large American cities, and includes much new material on the differential characteristics of local communities with varying rates of delinquents. Specifically, in this volume an attempt is made further to explore the following questions in regard to the ecology of delinquency and crime in American cities:

1. To what extent do the rates of delinquents and criminals show similar variations among the local communities in different types of American cities?

2. Does recidivism among delinquents vary from community to community in accordance with rates of delinquents?

3. To what extent do variations in rates of delinquents correspond to demonstrable differences in the economic, social, and

[1] Clifford R. Shaw, Frederick Zorbaugh, Henry D. McKay, and Leonard S. Cottrell, *Delinquency Areas* (Chicago: University of Chicago Press, 1929).

3

cultural characteristics of local communities in different types of cities?

4. How are the rates of delinquents in particular areas affected over a period of time by successive changes in the nativity and nationality composition of the population?

5. To what extent are the observed differences in the rates of delinquents between children of foreign and native parentage due to a differential geographic distribution of these two groups in the city?

6. Under what economic and social conditions does crime develop as a social tradition and become embodied in a system of criminal values?

7. What do the rates of delinquents, when computed by local areas for successive periods of time, reveal with respect to the effectiveness of traditional methods of treatment and prevention?

8. What are the implications, for treatment and prevention, of wide variations in rates of delinquents in different types of communities?

It is not assumed that this study will provide an answer to all of these questions. Certain facts are presented, however, which are useful in analyzing the nature of the problem of delinquency in urban communities and which have definite implications for the development of control techniques. Although it long has been recognized that the social conditions in low-income areas are such as to give rise to delinquency among a disproportionately large number of boys and young men, this fact has not been given the attention which its importance warrants in the development of therapeutic and preventive programs. It is hoped that the data in this volume will help to serve this purpose by focusing attention upon the need for broad programs of social reconstruction and community organization. It would appear from the findings of this study that successful treatment of the problem of delinquency in large cities will entail the development of programs which seek to effect changes in the conditions of life in specific local communities and in whole sections of the city. Diagnosis and supervision of individual offenders probably will not be sufficient to achieve this end. As Plant suggests:

The effects of social institutions upon the personality—those ways in which the cultural pattern in one or another way affects the working out of the individual's problem—are of only academic importance unless we can in one way or another alter the environment to meet the needs that appear.[2]

REGIONAL AND COMMUNITY VARIATIONS IN RATES
OF DELINQUENCY AND CRIME

As previously indicated, many studies of variation in the incidence of delinquency and crime in relation to different social and cultural backgrounds have been published during the past century. In the earliest of these studies, attention was focused primarily upon differences in rates of delinquency and crime among cities or large districts within a given country. These were followed by studies showing that such differences obtained also among local areas, communities, or neighborhoods within the corporate limits of large cities.

Among the very early ecological studies of crime were those made by Guerry in France and reported in his *Essai sur la statistique morale de la France* in 1833. In this study Guerry computed crime rates for the 86 departments of France.[3] These rates were based upon the number of persons accused of crime during the period 1825–30, inclusive. The variations in rates were marked. The number of persons accused of crime against the person varied from 1 out of 2,199 inhabitants in Corse, to 1 out of 37,014 in Creuse, with an average for all 86 departments of 1 out of 17,085 inhabitants. The number of persons accused of crimes against property varied from 1 out of 1,368 inhabitants in Seine, to 1 out of 20,235 inhabitants in Creuse, with an average of 1 out of 6,031 for all departments.[4]

---

[2] James S. Plant, M.D., *Personality and the Cultural Pattern* (New York: Commonwealth Fund, 1937), p. 234.

[3] André Michel Guerry, *Essai sur la statistique morale de la France* (Paris, 1833).

[4] The maps and tables prepared by Guerry were reproduced and discussed by Henry Lytton Bulwer in his work on *France, Social, Literary, and Political* (3d ed.; London: Richard Bentley, 1836), I, 169–210.

Other pertinent studies made in France include H. Joly, *La France criminelle* (Paris, 1891), and Gabriel Tarde, *Penal Philosophy*, trans. Rapelje Howell (Boston, 1912).

During the early part of the past century numerous statistical and government reports were published which indicated that the number of known criminals in relation to the population varied widely among the counties of England and Wales. As early as 1839 Rawson reported that the relative number of criminals was five times greater in certain counties than in others.[5] Twenty-three years later Mayhew published a rather exhaustive study of delinquency and crime in England.[6] Among other things this study included a series of maps showing the incidence of criminality and various types of crime by counties. In certain counties the incidence of criminality was almost four times as great as in other counties. The number of crimes per 10,000 inhabitants in the total population ranged from 26.1 to 7.1 in the 41 counties of England and Wales.

In addition to the numerous studies showing the variations in the incidence of criminality by towns and counties in England and Wales, similar comparisons were made between districts within particular counties. In 1856 John Glyde published a study showing the relative number of criminals in the 17 poor law unions in Suffolk County, England. The ratio between the number of criminals and the population ranged from 1 in 1,344 to 1 in 464 inhabitants for the 17 districts. Wide variations in the incidence of delinquency were also noted between the urban and rural dis-

[5] W. Rawson, "An Inquiry into the Statistics of Crime in England and Wales," *Journal of the Statistical Society of London*, II (1839), 334–44.

[6] Henry Mayhew, *London Labor and the London Poor* (London, 1862), IV, 455.

For similar studies reported during this early period see S. Redgrave, "Abstract of Criminal Tables for England and Wales," *Journal of the Statistical Society of London*, I (1838), 231–45; F. G. P. Neison, "Statistics of Crime in England and Wales for the Years 1834–1844," *ibid.*, XI (1848), 140–65; Joseph Fletcher, "Moral and Educational Statistics of England and Wales," *ibid.*, pp. 344–66, and *ibid.*, XII (1849), 189–336; W. M. Tartt, "Report on Criminal Returns," *ibid.*, XX (1857), 365–77; Mary Carpenter, "Importance of Statistics to the Reformatory Movement, with Returns from Female Reformatories," *ibid.*, pp. 33–40; J. Thackray Bunce, "On the Statistics of Crime in Birmingham, as Compared with Other Large Towns," *ibid.*, XXVIII (1865), 518–26; James T. Hammick, "On the Judicial Statistics of England and Wales, with Special Reference to the Recent Returns Relating to Crime," *ibid.*, XXX (1867), 375–426; and Leone Levi, "A Survey of Indictable and Summary Jurisdiction Offenses in England and Wales, 1857–1876," esp. IX, "Locality of Crime," *ibid.*, LXIII (1880), 423–56.

tricts and between different cities in the same county. Glyde concluded his report by stating that "as tables of crime for all England include counties of various degrees of criminality, so does the average for the county of Suffolk include districts, towns, and villages of opposite moral tendencies as developed by their criminal aspects."[7]

Lombroso and Niceforo, to mention only two of the early Italian students, found that both the number of criminals per unit of population and the incidence of certain types of crimes varied widely from one city to another and from one province to another. Niceforo, in a study of criminality in the island of Sardinia, found that the ratio between the number of cases of robbery and extortion and the total population ranged widely among the districts of the island.[8] With reference to the incidence of criminality in various parts of Italy, Lombroso stated:

In every part of Italy, almost in every province, there exists some village renowned for having furnished an unbroken series of special delinquents. Thus, in Liguria, Lerice is proverbial for swindlers, Campofreddo and Masson for homicides, Pozzolo for highway robberies. In the province of Lucca, Capannori is noted for its assassinations, and Carde in Piedmont for its field thefts. In southern Italy, Soro, Melfi, and St. Fele have always had their bandits since 1860, and the same is true of Partinico and Monreale in Sicily. . . . . But the most famous of all is the village of Artena in the province of Rome. . . . . It is to be noted that in Sicily brigandage is almost exclusively confined to that famous valley of the Conca d'Oro.[9]

Similar data are presented for Austria and Germany by Aschaffenburg. In summarizing the data for Germany he states:

While in the whole of Germany there were 1104 convicted persons to every 100,000 persons of punishable age, the number of such convicts in the government districts was: Oppeln 1860, Bromberg 1842, Gumbinnen 1746, Bremen 1732, The Palatinate 1657, Danzig 1541, Upper Bavaria 1528, Königsberg 1526, Marienwerd 1522, Lower Bavaria 1484, Posen 1424, and Mannheim 1211. On the other hand, Schaumburg-Lippe had only 419, and Waldeck 439 convictions. Waldeck offers an excellent opportunity for com-

---

[7] "Locality of Crime in Suffolk," *Journal of the Statistical Society of London*, XIX (1856), 102.

[8] Alfredo Niceforo, *La Delinquenza in Sardegna* (Palermo, 1897).

[9] Cesare Lombroso, *Crime: Its Causes and Remedies* (New York: Little, Brown & Co., 1911), pp. 23–24.

parison with a section containing approximately the same number of inhabitants. In 1890 Waldeck had a population of 38,986, Pirmasens 38,327. In Waldeck there were annually 172 convictions, while in Pirmasens there were 885![10]

Systematic studies of the relative incidence of delinquency in local districts within cities are, for the most part, of more recent development than the more general studies referred to in the previous pages, although the close association between conditions prevailing in particular districts within the city and the incidence of delinquency was emphasized in the very earliest investigations of the problem of delinquency. Throughout the early official reports and investigations of crime in London frequent reference is made to the so-called "low neighborhoods" in which delinquents and criminals were found in disproportionately large numbers. As early as 1840 Allison, in his *Principles of Population*, stated:

If any person will walk through St. Giles', the crowded alleys of Dublin, or the poorer quarters of Glasgow by night, he will meet with ample proof of these observations; he will no longer wonder at the disorderly habits and profligate enjoyments of the lower orders; his astonishment will be, not that there is so much, but that there is so little crime in the world. The great cause of human corruption in these crowded situations is the contagious nature of bad example and the extreme difficulty of avoiding the seductions of vice when they are brought into close and daily proximity with the younger part of the people. Whatever we may think of the strength of virtue, experience proves that the higher orders are indebted for their exemption from atrocious crime or disorderly habits chiefly to their fortunate removal from the scene of temptation; and that where they are exposed to the seductions which assail their inferiors, they are noways behind them in yielding to their influence. It is the peculiar misfortune of the poor in great cities that they cannot fly from these irresistible temptations, but that, turn where they will, they are met by the alluring forms of vice, or the seductions of guilty enjoyment. It is the experienced impossibility of concealing the attractions of vice from the younger part of the poor in great cities which exposes them to so many causes of demoralization. All this proceeds not from any unwonted or extraordinary depravity in the character of these victims of licentiousness, but from the almost irresistible nature of the temptations to which the poor are exposed. The rich, who censure their conduct, would in all probability yield as rapidly as they have done to the influence of similar causes. There

[10] Gustav Aschaffenburg, *Crime and Its Repression* (New York: Little, Brown & Co., 1913), p. 43.

is a certain degree of misery, a certain proximity to sin, which virtue is rarely able to withstand, and which the young, in particular, are generally unable to resist. The progress of vice in such circumstances is almost as certain and often nearly as rapid as that of physical contagion.[11]

Emphasis upon the influences of "low neighborhoods" was again indicated in the writings of Henry Mayhew in 1862. He states:

There are thousands of neglected children loitering about the low neighborhoods of the metropolis, and prowling about the streets, begging and stealing for their daily bread. They are to be found in Westminster, Whitechapel, Shoreditch, St. Giles', New Cut, Lambeth, the Borough, and other localities. Hundreds of them may be seen leaving their parents' homes and low lodging-houses every morning, sallying forth in search of food and plunder. They are fluttering in rags and in the most motley attire. Some are orphans and have no one to care for them; others have left their homes and live in lodging-houses in the most improvident manner, never thinking of to-morrow; others are sent out by their unprincipled parents to beg and steal for a livelihood; others are the children of poor but honest and industrious people, who have been led to steal through the bad companionship of juvenile thieves. Many of them have never been at a day-school nor attended a Sunday school, and have had no moral or religious instruction. On the contrary, they have been surrounded by the most baneful and degrading influences, and have been set a bad example by their parents and others with whom they came in contact, and are shunned by the honest and industrious classes of society. . . . .

These juvenile thieves are chiefly to be found in Lucretia Street, Lambeth; Union Street, Borough Road; Gunn Street, and Friars Street, Blackfriars Road; also at Whitechapel, St. Giles's, Drury Lane, Somers Town, Anderson Grove, and other localities. . . . .

The chief sources whence our pickpockets spring are from the low lodging-houses—from those dwellings in low neighborhoods, where their parents are thieves, and where improvident and drunken people neglect their children, such as Whitechapel, Shoreditch, Spitalfields, New Cut, Lambeth, the Borough, Clerkenwell, Drury Lane, and other localities. . . . .[12]

These early observations received statistical confirmation in Burt's study of juvenile delinquency in London in 1925.[13] In this

[11] Archibald Allison, *The Principles of Population and the Connection with Human Happiness* (Edinburgh: Wm. Blackwood & Son, 1840), II, 76–78.

[12] Mayhew, *op. cit.*, IV, 273, 278, 304.

[13] Cyril Burt, *The Young Delinquent* (London: D. Appleton & Co., 1925), pp. 67–90.

study Burt secured the address of each boy and girl reported as an industrial school case during the years 1922 and 1923, and calculated the ratio between the number of cases in each electoral area in London and the total number of children on the rolls of the council's schools. The ratio for the several areas ranges from 0.42 to 0.0, while the average for the city as a whole is 0.14. The map for the entire city indicates that the areas having the highest rates (0.25 and upward) are located adjacent to the central district of London, while those having the lowest rates (0.05 and less) are located in the outlying sections near the periphery of the city. It is interesting to observe, also, that the "low neighborhoods," which were regarded by the early students as the chief source of delinquency, fall within the areas having the highest rates of delinquency. Furthermore, these areas of delinquency correspond rather closely to the poverty areas revealed in the earlier study by Charles Booth.[14]

After the turn of the century many students became interested in the ecological study of delinquency in American cities. In 1912 Breckinridge and Abbott published a study showing the geographic distribution of cases of juvenile delinquency in the city of Chicago. They utilized for this purpose the cases of boys and girls brought before the Juvenile Court of Cook County on petitions alleging delinquency during the years 1899–1909. Among other things they prepared a map showing the location of the homes of these children. This map indicated that a disproportionately large number of the cases were concentrated in certain districts of the city. In this connection they state:

A study of this map makes possible several conclusions with regard to "delinquent neighborhoods." It becomes clear, in the first place, that the region from which the children of the court chiefly come is the densely populated West Side, and that the most conspicuous centers of delinquency in this section have been the congested wards which lie along the river and the canals. . . . .

. . . . The West Side furnished the largest quota of delinquency across the river. These are chiefly the Italian quarter of the Twenty-Second Ward on the North Side; the First and Second Wards, which together include the

[14] *Life and Labor in London* (London, 1891), Vol. II, Appen., "Showing Map of London Poverty by Districts."

district of segregated vice and a portion of the so-called "black belt" of the
South Side; and such distinct industrial communities as the districts near
the steel mills of South Chicago and near the stockyards.[15]

It should be noted that this study did not relate the number of
delinquents to the population in the various districts of the city.
While the distribution map served to localize the problem of delinquency and to show the absolute number of cases in the various
districts, rates by geographic units were not computed. Hence, it
was not possible to conclude from this study that the observed
concentration of cases was due to anything other than a greater
density of population in these areas. Since the publication of the
findings of Breckinridge and Abbott, studies have been carried on
in which the rate of delinquents (ratio between the number of delinquents and the appropriate population group) has been used as
a basis for comparisons among unit areas within the city.

In 1915 Ernest W. Burgess, under the direction of Professor
F. W. Blackmar, conducted a survey of social conditions in Lawrence, Kansas. This survey included a study of the geographic
distribution of alleged delinquent children for the city as a whole,
the absolute number of delinquents in the various districts, and
the rates of delinquents for the several areas. Both the number of
cases and the rates of delinquents show wide variations among the
several areas. The ratio between the number of alleged delinquent
children and the total population aged 5–16 years varied from
8.36 to 0.82 for the 6 wards of the city. In this connection Burgess
states:

The significant fact to be gathered from the records of the children of
Lawrence is the large proportion of juvenile delinquents in the entire child
population in the fourth ward. One child out of every twelve children five
and over, but under seventeen years old, appeared in the juvenile court in
the two-year period studied. If this proportion were maintained for a twelve-
year period, comprising the age groups between five and seventeen, the pre-
sumption is that at least one-half of the children in the fourth ward would
have appeared before the juvenile judge before reaching seventeen years.
Since the proportion of juvenile delinquency in the fourth ward is three times
as large as that in any other ward, the conclusion naturally follows that certain factors are at work here which are absent elsewhere in Lawrence. . . . .

[15] Sophonisba P. Breckinridge and Edith Abbott, *The Delinquent Child and the
Home* (New York: Russell Sage Foundation, 1912), pp. 150–53.

The low percentages of delinquency in wards 5 and 6, in North Lawrence, is to be accounted for by the semi-rural character of the community, with its opportunities for play, and by the distance from the industrial and business part of the community. . . . .[16]

Two years after the publication of the Lawrence survey R. D. McKenzie conducted a general study of Columbus, Ohio. In addition to showing the actual geographic distribution of the homes of delinquent children, this study also included rates of delinquents by wards, along with certain indexes of neighborhood situations and an intensive study of a local community. The rate of delinquency, which in this study represented the ratio between the number of delinquents and the number of registered voters, ranged from 1.66 to 0.35 for the 16 wards of the city.[17]

During recent years additional studies of the ecology of delinquency and crime have been made in a number of American cities.[18] All of these revealed rather wide variations in the rates

[16] F. W. Blackmar and E. W. Burgess, *Lawrence Social Survey* (Lawrence: University of Kansas, 1917), pp. 71-72.

[17] *The Neighborhood: A Study of Local Life in the City of Columbus, Ohio* (Chicago: University of Chicago Press, 1923).

[18] The following is a partial list of these studies: (a) Irwin W. Halpern, John N. Stanislaus, and Bernard Botein, *A Statistical Study of the Distribution of Adult and Juvenile Delinquents in the Boroughs of Manhattan and Brooklyn* (New York: Polygraphic Co. of America, 1934); Norman S. Hayner, "Delinquency Areas in the Puget Sound Region," *American Journal of Sociology*, Vol. XXXIX; Calvin F. Schmid, *Social Saga of Two Cities* (Minneapolis: Minneapolis Council of Social Agencies, 1937); R. Clyde White, "The Relation of Felonies to Environmental Factors in Indianapolis," *Social Forces*, Vol. X; J. B. Lottier, "Distribution of Criminal Offenses in Metropolitan Regions," *Journal of Criminal Law and Criminology*, Vol. XXIX; Herman Adler, Frances Cahn, and Johannes Stuart, *The Incidence of Delinquency in Berkeley, 1928-32* (Berkeley: University of California Press, 1934); Donald Trauger, L. Kral, and W. Rauscher, *Social Analysis of Des Moines* (Des Moines: Iowa State Planning Board, 1935); Vernon E. Keye, "Survey of Juvenile Delinquency in Evanston, Illinois" (Work Projects Administration Report, 1940); Emil Frankel, "New Brunswick Delinquency Areas Study" (Work Projects Administration Report, 1936); Donald R. Taft, "Testing the Selective Influence of Areas of Delinquency," *American Journal of Sociology*, XXXVIII, 1933; M. C. Elmer, "Maladjustment of Youth in Relation to Density of Population," *Proceedings of the American Sociological Society*, Vol. XXII; Howard Whipple Green, *Population Characteristics by Census Tracts, Cleveland, Ohio* (Cleveland: Plain Dealer Pub. Co., 1931); Sophia M. Robison, *Can Delinquency Be Measured?* (New York:

of delinquency by local areas. In some instances attention was focused almost exclusively upon variations in rates among areas while in others the rates were correlated with indexes of varying community backgrounds. In general, these studies support the findings reported in the authors' earlier publication, *Delinquency Areas*.[19] Brief reports of a few of these studies are included in this volume.

It may be observed that some of the studies presented are not of recent date. This fact does not detract from their theoretical value, since the primary interest is in the study of the relationship between the community and delinquency. A study completed ten years ago may serve this purpose as adequately as a current one. Whenever possible, data representing different periods of time have been utilized as a means of studying long-time trends in the relationship between volume of delinquency and local community characteristics.

In this attempt to analyze the variations in rates of delinquents by geographic areas in American cities a variety of statistical data are utilized for the purpose of determining the extent to which differences in the economic and social characteristics of local areas parallel variations in rates of delinquents. The methods employed include spot maps, statistical tables showing the rates of delinquents and economic and social variables computed for large zones

Columbia University Press, 1936); H. D. Shelden, "Problems in the Statistical Study of Juvenile Delinquency," *Metron*, XII, 1934; E. Franklin Frazier, *The Negro Family in Chicago* (Chicago: University of Chicago Press, 1933), pp. 204–19; William J. Ellis, *Delinquency Areas in Essex County Municipalities* (New Jersey Department of Institutions and Agencies, Trenton, 1938); Clarence W. Schroeder, *Delinquency in Peoria* (Peoria, Illinois: Bradley Polytechnic Institute, 1939); Edwin H. Sutherland, "Ecological Survey of Crime and Delinquency in Bloomington, Indiana," Indiana University, 1937; J. B. Maller, *Maladjusted Youth* (Report of the Children's Court Jurisdiction and Juvenile Delinquency Committee [Legislative Document No. 75 (1939), 201 pages]); J. B. Maller, *Juvenile Delinquency in the State of New York* (Report of the Children's Court Jurisdiction and Juvenile Delinquency Committee [Legislative Document No. 62 (1940), 115 pages]); Kimball Young, John L. Gillin, Calvert L. Dedrick, *The Madison Community* ("University of Wisconsin Studies," No. 62 [Madison: University of Wisconsin, 1934]); and W. Wallace Weaver, *West Philadelphia: A Study of Natural Social Areas* (Ph.D. thesis, University of Pennsylvania, 1930).

[19] *Op. cit.*

and classes of areas, zero-order correlations, and, in a few instances, higher-order correlations. While these maps and statistical data are useful in locating different types of areas, in differentiating the areas where the rates of delinquency are high from areas where the rates are low, and in predicting or forecasting expected rates, they do not furnish an explanation of delinquent conduct. This explanation, it is assumed, must be sought, in the first place, in the field of the more subtle human relationships and social values which comprise the social world of the child in the family and community. These more distinctively human situations, which seem to be directly related to delinquent conduct, are, in turn, products of larger economic and social processes characterizing the history and growth of the city and of the local communities which comprise it.

In this study the Chicago delinquency data are dealt with in a much more detailed manner than in the other cities for which data are presented. All of chapters ii–vii (Part II) are concerned with Chicago. These give a description of the growth and configuration of the city; the geographic distribution of delinquents and criminals, rates of infant mortality, tuberculosis, and insanity; and indexes of the variations in the economic, social, and cultural characteristics of local areas for which rates of delinquency have been computed.

Chapters viii through xii (Part III) comprise studies prepared by the authors on the distribution of delinquency in five cities or metropolitan areas which include a total of 24 separate municipalities. Although a few series of delinquent girls are included in certain of these studies, the primary emphasis has been placed upon ecological aspects of delinquency among males. Chapter xiii (Part IV) includes a summary of the findings, an interpretation in terms of a general theory, and a brief discussion of some of the implications of these studies for treatment and prevention. Chapters xiv through xvi (Part V) were prepared especially for this edition. They update data on delinquents and commitments in Chicago and bring to bear new data on Chicago suburbs.

PART II

CHAPTER II

GROWTH OF CHICAGO AND DIFFERENTIATION
OF LOCAL AREAS

C HICAGO is a large industrial and commercial city located
on the western shore of Lake Michigan near its southern
extremity. It is the second largest city in the United
States and the largest included in this study. Within a period of a
little over a century it has grown from a small town, with a population of about 200 and an area of $2\frac{1}{2}$ square miles, to a great
industrial metropolis, with a population of over 3,300,000 people
and a corporate area of 211 square miles, extending some 25 miles
along the lake front and from 8 to 10 miles inland.

During its growth a differentiation of areas has taken place
within Chicago. Even a casual observation reveals that certain
districts are occupied largely by industry and others used exclusively for residential purposes; that certain areas are occupied by
persons of low economic status and others by the very rich; and
that certain neighborhoods are characterized by a native white
population, and others by the foreign born, whose dominant lan-
guages are still those of the Old World. It is generally known, also,
that among areas in the city there are wide differences in the rates
of truants, of delinquents, and of adult criminals, as well as in disease and mortality rates and other indexes of well-being. More
subtle are the differences in standards and cultural values, in community organization, and in the nature of social life; but that they
exist there can be no question.

Why do these variations exist? Why has the city assumed this
configuration, with this particular distribution of poverty and
wealth and of racial and national groups? Why are there such
wide differences in standards and cultural values among areas
within the city?

This volume is based on the assumption that the best basis for
an understanding of the development of differences among urban

areas may be gained through study of the processes of city growth. Areas acquire high delinquency rates neither by chance nor by design but rather, it is assumed, as an end-product of processes in American city life over which, as yet, man has been able to exercise little control. This elaboration of the differentiation of areas in city growth is presented, then, as a frame of reference, a basis for analysis of the problem of delinquency not only in relation to the processes of urban expansion but also in relation to the whole complex of urban life.

In the present chapter an effort will be made (1) to outline and describe the processes of growth involved in the differentiation of areas in large cities; (2) to analyze the growth and expansion of Chicago with reference to these processes; and (3) to present some evidence of this differentiation, with the characteristics of the different types of areas resulting.

PROCESSES OF CITY GROWTH

The general processes of growth underlying segregation and differentiation of areas within cities have long been the subject of investigation by students of urban life. Professor Robert E. Park and others have pointed out the general character of these processes, noting that every American city of the same class tends to reproduce in the course of its expansion all the different types of areas and that these tend to exhibit, from city to city, very similar physical, social, and cultural characteristics, leading to their designation as "natural areas."[1]

In his description of the processes of radial expansion Professor E. W. Burgess has advanced the thesis that, in the absence of opposing factors, the American city tends to take the form of concentric zones.[2] Zone I in this conceptual scheme is the central business and industrial district; Zone II, the "zone in transition," or slum area, in the throes of change from residence to business and industry; Zone III, the zone of workingmen's homes; Zone IV, the

[1] Robert E. Park and E. W. Burgess, *The City* (Chicago: University of Chicago Press, 1925).

[2] Ernest W. Burgess (ed.), *The Urban Community* (Chicago: University of Chicago Press, 1926).

residential zone; and Zone V, the outer commuters' zone, beyond the city limits. The same general pattern of areas tends to appear in any major industrial center, even though such a "center" may be on the outskirts of a large city. This ideal or schematic construction furnishes a frame of reference from which the location and characteristics of given city areas may be studied at any moment, as well as the changes that take place as time goes on. In a growing city, zones are continuously expanding, which means that each inner zone must invade[3] the next beyond. The result of this process is observable in our large cities, where the central business and industrial areas, now largely uninhabited except by a transient population, at one time included within their limits all gradations of areas in the city.

The starting-point for a discussion of the processes of expansion and differentiation within the city, as indicated above, is the concentration of industry and commerce, especially the configuration including the central business district. Even if the city were not growing, and its internal organization were assumed to be static, the residential neighborhoods adjacent to industrial and commercial areas would be considered, no doubt, physically less desirable than those farther removed. This would be true especially of residential areas near the central business district, for in most cities these are the sections built up first in the development of the city and for that reason are characterized by the oldest homes. Generally speaking, the largest proportion of new dwellings are to be found in the outlying sections of any city, while the areas with the most old dwellings are close to the points of early settlement.

More directly, the presence of either industrial or commercial districts affects the desirability of adjacent residential areas, making life in them less pleasant, according to prevailing standards. The smoke and soot from heavy industrial plants soon render near-by residential structures dirty and ugly in appearance. Noise from factory machinery may be distracting; and the odors of certain industries, notably slaughtering and rendering, are often very disagreeable. These conditions, together with the fact that they

[3] The terms "invade" and "invasion" are here used in their technical ecological sense, meaning to "encroach upon."

soon become associated with undesirable social status, would tend to create wide differences in the distribution of areas even if the basic structure of the city were permanently fixed.

In an expanding city these differences among areas are exaggerated because invasion or the threat of invasion from inner-city areas results in more active deterioration, with subsequent demolition of the structures in those sections adjacent to industry and commerce. As the city grows, the areas of commerce and light industry near the center encroach upon areas used for residential purposes. The dwellings in such areas, often already undesirable because of age, are allowed to deteriorate when such invasion threatens or actually occurs, as further investment in them is unprofitable. These residences are permitted to yield whatever return can be secured in their dilapidated condition, often in total disregard of the housing laws, until they are demolished to make way for new industrial and commercial structures. Even if invasion has not taken place, these processes are evident when the area is zoned for purposes other than residence.

The same general trends are seen in residential districts adjacent to outlying industrial centers. The distinctions may not be so noticeable, the dwellings so old, or the threat of invasion so active; yet the sections closest to industry are, in general, considered least desirable.

When residential areas are being invaded or threatened by invasion, there is apparently little possibility of reconstruction without public subsidy. The physical undesirability of these areas and the ever present prospect of change in land use make it improbable that any first-class residences will be constructed from private funds without the enactment of some special protective legislation.[4] The result is that persons living in these areas move out as soon as possible. The general effect of this process has been the gradual evacuation of the central areas in all large

[4] Legislation in Illinois in 1941, authorizing privately financed neighborhood redevelopment corporations with limited condemnation powers, has been termed by planning experts as the "first effective attack on the slum problem undertaken in any large city." These experts are confident that "the tide of decentralization can be turned." The question of rentals within reach of low-income groups, however, remains unanswered, constituting the main 'argument for federal low-rent housing.

American cities, leading to the expression frequently heard: "The city is dying at its heart."

The differentiation of areas within the city on the basis of physical characteristics is co-ordinate with a segregation of the population on an economic basis. The relentless pressure of economic competition forces the group of lowest economic status into the areas which are least attractive, because there the rents are low, while the economically most secure groups choose higher-rental residential communities, most of which are near the periphery of the city. Between these two extremes lie communities representing a wide variety of economic levels.

This segregation according to the distribution of economic goods implies also a distribution of the population on an occupational and vocational basis. The persons in those occupations which command the lowest wages—the unskilled and service occupations—are forced to live in the areas of lowest rents, while those in the professions and the more remunerative occupations are concentrated in the more attractive sections of the city.

The segregation of population on an economic and occupational basis results, in turn, in the segregation of racial and nativity groups if, within these groups, different economic levels are represented. In northern industrial cities the group of lowest economic status has, until recently, comprised the most recent immigrants. This fact has resulted in the concentration of the foreign born in areas of lowest economic status and, conversely, in the concentration of native whites in the areas of higher economic status; but this separation does not mean that a given group of their descendants are permanently segregated, when the distinction is based on cultural differences only. The national groups which comprise the foreign born in one era may prosper and move; or they may follow their grown children, most of whom are native born, into outlying areas. Their places are taken by newer immigrant groups, who in turn are replaced by still more recent arrivals, and so on, as long as immigration continues. The result tends to be that, while the segregation of the foreign born in the areas of lowest economic status persists, the nationality groups predominating change from decade to decade. Similarly, the native white population living in areas of high economic status are, at any given time, the descendants of those who constituted the bulk of the foreign born in previous generations.

This segregation of population groups on an economic basis does not always proceed in the manner described, because it may be complicated by conditions which serve as barriers to the free movement of population within the city. In northern cities, barriers of racial prejudice and established custom have prevented the Negroes, the group now in the least advantageous position economically, from occupying certain low-rent areas, into which they otherwise would have been segregated by the economic process, and from moving outward into communities of their choice when economically able to do so. As a result, many have been restricted to neighborhoods which have most of the characteristics of inner-city areas but where often the rentals are disproportionately high, partly because of increased congestion and the resulting demand for homes. In southern cities the segregation of the Negro and white population corresponds in general to differences in economic status but is sustained by more elaborate caste mores and taboos.

THE GROWTH AND EXPANSION OF CHICAGO

An effort will next be made to trace the processes of city growth as they have operated in the city of Chicago and to describe briefly the characteristics of the areas differentiated.

The original plot of Chicago, surveyed about 1830, contained roughly $\frac{1}{2}$ square mile of territory, centered about the forks of the Chicago River. This area was extended to approximately 1 square mile in 1833 and to $2\frac{1}{2}$ square miles in 1835, when the town of Chicago was incorporated. Geographically, the site of Chicago was low and swampy but so level that elevation has been a negligible factor in determining the direction of metropolitan expansion. Two geographic barriers have been important, however—Lake Michigan and the Chicago River.

An effect of Lake Michigan is seen in the fact that the central business district is located on the lake shore—geographically not in the center of the city. The study of the growth of Chicago, diagramed schematically in terms of concentric circles, is at once modified, therefore, to a study in terms of semicircles. The Chicago River, likewise, has been significant both because it has interfered with transportation along the diagonals from the point of original settlement and the present business center and because early in the history of Chicago heavy industry was concentrated along the two branches of the river. This development was accompanied by the location of groups of industries in the areas surrounding this industrial section along the river, while high-class residential districts developed north, south, and west of the central business district.

The internal pattern of Chicago was determined largely by the section lines of the government survey. Dividing the city into square-mile areas, these lines have become the important streets which extend throughout the city from north to south and from east to west, tending to facilitate transportation and, consequently, to accelerate radial expansion along those arterial routes running at right angles and to retard radial expansion in those areas at oblique angles to the streets of the central business district. This basic tendency has been lessened somewhat by the presence of diagonal streets to the northwest and southwest, which originally were Indian trails and later became plank roads leading to Chicago from outlying suburbs.

The growth of Chicago is revealed by the changes between decennial census years. In 1840, 10 years after the original town was plotted, the population numbered 4,470. The population expanded nearly six times between 1840 and 1850, two and one-half times between 1850 and 1860, and nearly three times between 1860 and 1870. It reached 500,000 in 1880, 1,000,000 by 1900, and was well over 2,000,000 by 1910. The rate of increase between 1910 and 1920 was 23.6 per cent; between 1920 and 1930, 24.8 per cent; and between 1930 and 1940, 0.6 per cent. The drop in the rate of increase between 1930 and 1940 is due in part to the fact that during this period the areas of most rapid growth were outside the political boundaries of the city.

The territorial expansion corresponded roughly to population increase. In 1889, when Chicago comprised 44 square miles, an area of 126 square miles was annexed at one time, quadrupling the area of the city and increasing the number of square miles within the political boundaries to 170. This area included Kenwood, Hyde Park, South Chicago, Pullman, and many other small towns, as well as much unoccupied territory. From that time to the present, annexations have been relatively small but have increased the total city area to 211 square miles. Although some of the land within the political boundaries is as yet unpopulated, the metropolitan area extends far beyond these boundaries in every direction and includes many contiguous cities and towns located chiefly along transportation lines toward the north, south, and west.

In the course of this expansion, marked changes have taken place in the character of some sections of the city. This is especially true around the central business district, where early residential areas have been invaded by industrial and commercial developments and have therefore been extended farther and farther out from the center. Similarly, single-family dwellings have been replaced by the characteristic two-flat dwellings in many neighborhoods or by large apartment houses along the important transportation routes. Exclusive residential districts of single homes are now to be found only in the outlying districts and in the suburbs.

The general configuration of Chicago resulting from growth and expansion within the limits set by Lake Michigan, the Chicago River, checkerboard streets, and the early distribution of industry is outlined in Map 1, which shows the areas either occupied by or zoned for industrial and residential purposes.

Today the central business district covers much of the area included in the city as incorporated in March, 1837. This district of approximately 10.6 square miles has primarily a hotel and transient population near its center, but on the outer edge the land is in transition from residential to industrial and commercial uses. This change has not progressed at the same rate in all parts of the area. In some places light industrial plants, business houses, and garages have replaced dwelling-houses almost completely, while in other parts the land still is used primarily for residential pur-

MAP 1

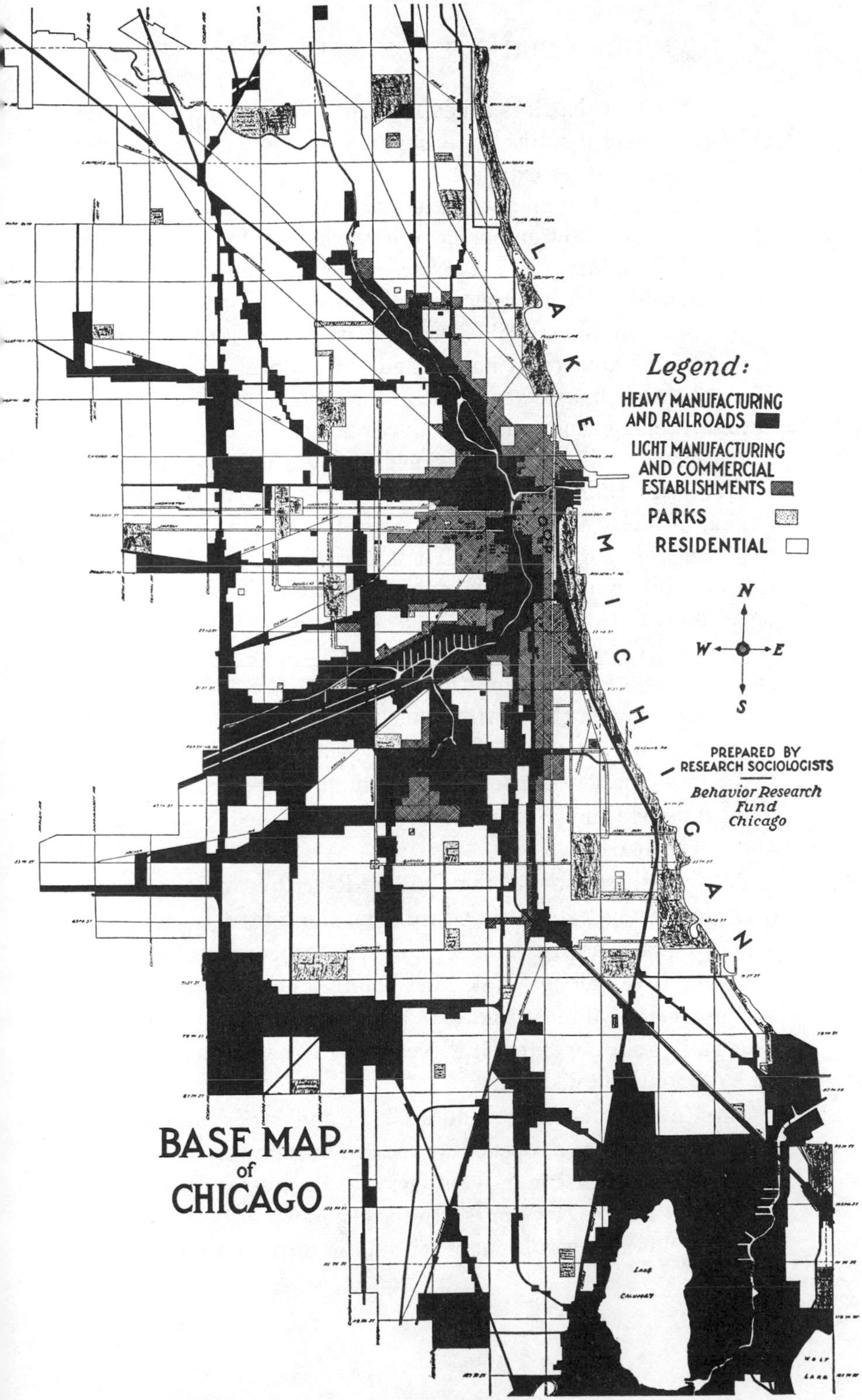
BASE MAP of CHICAGO
LAKE MICHIGAN
Legend:
HEAVY MANUFACTURING AND RAILROADS
LIGHT MANUFACTURING AND COMMERCIAL ESTABLISHMENTS
PARKS
RESIDENTIAL
N
W
E
S
PREPARED BY RESEARCH SOCIOLOGISTS
Behavior Research Fund Chicago

Zoning Map of Chicago

poses. The fact that it is zoned for light industry and commerce, however, makes it subject to occupancy for these uses as the central business district expands.

While practically all of the exclusive residential neighborhoods of early Chicago now are included in the areas either zoned for or occupied by industry and commerce, one small area on the Near North Side has withstood successfully the threats of industrial and commercial invasion. This district, occupied by large residences and exclusive apartment houses and known locally as the "Gold Coast," stands in vivid contrast to the adjoining areas of deteriorated dwellings and industrial development.

In contrast with the areas zoned for light industry and commerce, located for the most part in a semicircle surrounding the central business district, the districts of heavy industry in Chicago are widely distributed. They tend to be located at points strategic for industrial development because of natural advantages, such as the lake, trunk lines of railroads, or abundance of cheap land. The most extensive industrial areas in Chicago lie along the two forks of the Chicago River. The areas zoned for heavy industry on the North Branch extend some 4 miles northwest from the central business district, while the southern extension follows the south fork to the city limits, after broadening out to include the Union Stock Yards and the so-called "central manufacturing district."

Between these forks of the Chicago River lie two large industrial areas which extend westward from the central business district along railroad trunk lines. These, in turn, are intersected by industrial areas along trunk lines running north and south, so that in a very real sense the Near West Side, the Near Southwest Side, and, to a lesser extent, the Near Northwest Side are bounded by industrial establishments.

The Union Stock Yards and affiliated industries, clearly indicated on Map 1, were opened in 1863. The site was chosen both because of its industrial advantages and because at that time it was far outside the city limits. In the general annexation of 1889, however, this area was brought within the corporate boundary of the city, so that today the Union Stock Yards occupy a position not far from the geographic center of the city.

The South Chicago steel-mill center and the industrial centers indicated by the large areas zoned for industry in the southeastern section were also originally outside the city limits. South Chicago, located on Lake Michigan at the mouth of the Calumet River, was founded almost as early as Chicago, and for several decades remained an independent city. Although annexed to Chicago in 1889, it is still a more or less independent commercial and industrial center. The town of Pullman, located just west of Lake Calumet, likewise was annexed in 1889 and, like South Chicago, has retained its name and essential industrial characteristics. Much of the remaining area zoned for industry in the Calumet district at present is unoccupied waste land. Similarly, on the Southwest Side, the large sections marked in solid black on Map 1 are zoned for, but not yet occupied by, industrial establishments.

EVIDENCES OF DIFFERENTIATION RESULTING FROM CITY GROWTH

Demolition of Substandard Housing.—Evidence of physical change and deterioration in Chicago within the general framework of the industrial configuration is seen first in the high proportion of buildings in certain districts which have been condemned either for demolition or for repair. Map 2, showing the location of dilapidated or dangerous buildings demolished as of December, 1935, reveals that a large proportion of these buildings are adjacent to the central business district. It is within this district, known sociologically as an "area in transition," that the change in land use has been most rapid.

Increase and Decrease of Population.—Indirect evidence of the processes of invasion and differentiation in Chicago is seen in the decrease of population in areas adjacent to industry and commerce and the increase in outlying areas. In a rapidly growing city it is natural that a large number of areas should be increasing in population. For purposes of differentiating among communities it is much more significant that, even while the city of Chicago

MAP 2

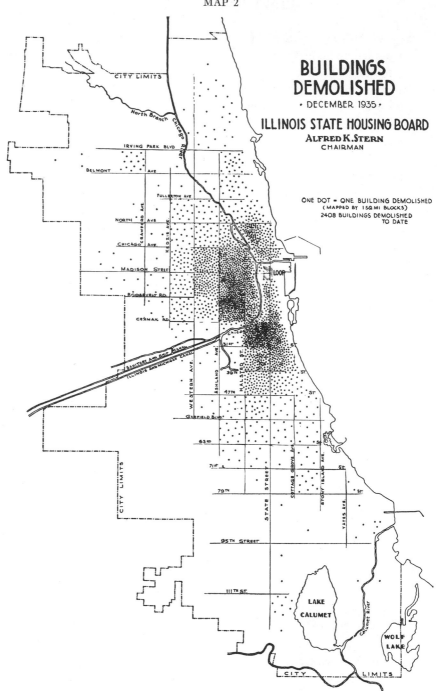

DISTRIBUTION OF DEMOLISHED BUILDINGS, CHICAGO, 1935

was growing at a very rapid rate, large areas constantly were being depopulated.

Between 1920 and 1930, a period of rapid growth, there were great changes in the distribution of the population in Chicago. The percentage of increase or decrease of population for this period in each of the 113 areas[5] into which the city was divided is shown in Map 3. It will be noted that the areas of decreasing population, delimited by heavy shading, almost completely surround the central business district, while practically all of the areas of rapid increase are near the periphery. Between these two extremes there is a continuous variation. The areas of greatest decrease in population are near the center. Beyond, in order, are the areas where there was a small decrease, then a small increase, then a substantial increase, and finally, at the city's periphery, a zone where the increase was very great. It is this continuum rather than the division into areas of decreasing and increasing population that is significant in showing the essential nature of the processes of city growth.

From Table 1 and Map 3 it will be seen that the population in 10 square-mile areas decreased more than 20 per cent between 1920 and 1930, and that in 26 additional areas the drop was between 1 and 20 per cent. The decrease reveals the fact of expansion more vividly when analyzed in conjunction with the rates of increase and decrease of population for the previous and subsequent decades. Between 1910 and 1920 the population decreased in 23 square-mile areas; while between 1930 and 1940, a period of comparatively slight growth in total city population, a drop occurred in 68 out of the 140 square-mile areas. It will be noted

[5] These areas represent the basic units into which the city of Chicago was divided for the presentation of rates of delinquents and other data based on the 1920 census. In the more densely populated sections of the city these are square-mile areas bounded on all four sides by the section lines of the government survey. In the more sparsely settled outlying areas, it was necessary, in many instances, to combine two or more contiguous square-mile areas until a minimum population base was secured. For the earliest delinquency series further combinations in the outlying areas reduced the number of areas to 106. For 1930 data many of the larger, more populous outlying areas were redivided, and the total number of areas increased to 140. Although some of these units contain more than 1 square mile, they will be referred to throughout this study as "square-mile areas."

MAP 3

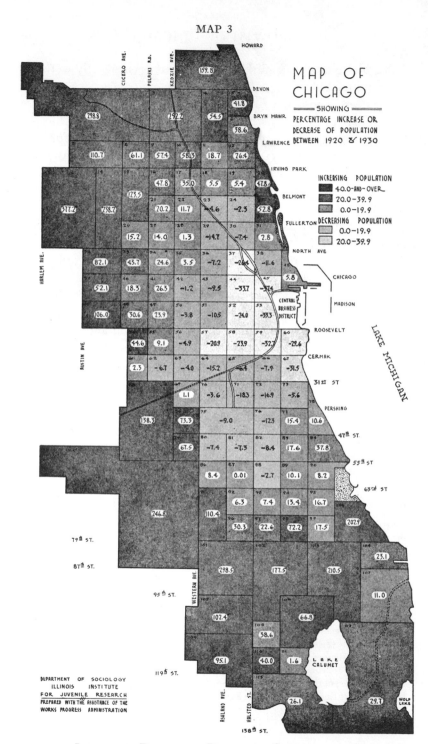

INCREASE OR DECREASE OF POPULATION, CHICAGO, 1920-30

that the outward movement from the 36 areas that decreased in population between 1920 and 1930 reduced the proportion of the total population in these areas from 40.0 per cent in 1920 to 27.7 per cent in 1930 and to 25.3 per cent in 1940.

This change in population in the different areas of Chicago establishes the rapidity with which the population is being evacuated from the center of the city. As the areas near the central business district are taken over for industry and commerce, the depopulated district extends farther and farther outward from

TABLE 1

PERCENTAGE OF CITY POPULATION, 1920, 1930, 1940, FOR SQUARE-MILE AREAS GROUPED BY PERCENTAGE OF POPULATION INCREASE OR DECREASE BETWEEN 1920 AND 1930

ERCENTAGE INCREASE OR DECREASE IN POPULATION 1920–30	NUMBER OF SQUARE-MILE AREAS	PERCENTAGE OF CITY POPULATION		
		1920	1930	1940
Decreasing:				
20–39..........	10	11.8	6.9	5.9
0–19..........	26	28.2	20.8	19.4
Increasing:				
0–19..........	28	29.0	25.4	25.9
20–39..........	15	11.6	11.9	12.6
40 and over......	34	19.4	35.0	36.2

the Loop; and new residential areas, characterized by very rapid growth of population, are pushed back to the city limits or into the suburbs beyond. On a smaller scale a similar process can be noted in the areas adjacent to each of the major outlying industrial centers.

Although the continuous decrease in population in the inner-city areas indicates a great drop in the number of persons per acre in these areas, this should not be interpreted to mean that there has been any increase in the number of rooms per family or decrease in the number of persons per room. It indicates rather that certain areas are being depopulated as they are abandoned for residential purposes, and either are allowed to remain unoccupied or are taken over for industrial or commercial use.

Segregation of Population on an Economic Basis.—The segregation of groups of low economic status into areas of physical deterioration and decreasing population is clearly indicated when rates of increase and decrease of population are related to indexes of economic status, such as percentage of families on relief, home ownership, median rentals, and occupation. These relationships as of 1930 and 1920 are presented in Table 2.

Families on Relief.—Economic segregation in Chicago is likewise indicated by Map 4, which shows the percentage of families on relief in 1934 in each of the 140 square-mile areas. These rates are based on the 115,132 families reported by the Illinois Emergency Relief Commission to be receiving relief and on the total number of families as given in the 1930 census. The range in the percentage of families on relief is from 1.4 in square mile 121 to 55.9 in square mile 87. The median is 10.6, and the percentage for the city 13.7.

It will be noted from Map 4 that the areas with the highest percentage of families on relief are the areas of physical deterioration and decreasing population. The lowest percentages, on the other hand, are found in the outlying and newer districts of the city, where the population is increasing and where there is comparatively little deterioration. Between these two extremes the gradations correspond closely with the gradations in the physical characteristics of the areas as already presented. A notable exception to this tendency is seen in certain Negro areas, where the rate of families on relief is high but where the population is increasing, probably as a result of the restrictions to free movement of Negro population into other areas.

Median Rentals.—Another index of economic status is presented in Map 5, which shows for 1930 the median equivalent monthly rental for each of the 140 areas. These rentals are based on the monthly rentals and home values as presented in the 1930 federal census, in relation to the total number of homes in each square mile.[6] From Map 5 it will be seen that the areas of lowest

---

[6] The computation of the median rental on the basis of the total number of homes was necessary both because in some areas only a small proportion of the homes was rented and because the rented homes often were not representative of the area.

[Footnote continued on page 36]

TABLE 2

ECONOMIC SEGREGATION BY AREAS GROUPED ACCORDING
TO INCREASE OR DECREASE OF POPULATION
1930 AND 1920

1930

Percentage Increase or Decrease of Population 1920–30	Percentage of Families on Relief 1934	Median Rental 1934	Median Rental 1930	Percentage of Families Owning Homes 1930	Percentage of Families Having Radios 1930
Decreasing:					
20–39 (27.5)*.......	30.0	$16.59	$22.72	16.6	34.2
0–19 (7.9)*.......	23.3	18.71	35.32	27.2	42.9
Increasing:					
0–19 (9.2)*.......	16.2	30.05	56.18	23.8	61.2
20–39 (28.4)*.......	8.6	35.85	62.94	27.6	71.5
40 and over (124.2)*	6.1	41.90	70.62	41.4	76.5

1920

Percentage Increase or Decrease of Population 1910–20	Rate of Dependent Families 1921	Percentage of Families Owning Homes 1920	Type of Occupation, 1920			
			Percentage Manufacturing	Percentage Domestic and Personal Service	Percentage Clerical	Percentage Professional
Decreasing:						
20–39 (32.5)*.......	3.2	12.2	50.6	8.6	6.2	2.3
0–19 (8.4)*.......	1.9	17.9	51.8	6.3	8.1	2.3
Increasing:						
0–19 (10.0)*.......	1.1	25.6	48.2	4.7	12.2	3.4
20–39 (29.9)*.......	0.5	28.9	46.8	5.0	13.9	5.0
40 and over (87.5)*..	0.4	32.2	39.4	5.9	14.2	6.1

* Percentages for class as a whole.

MAP 4

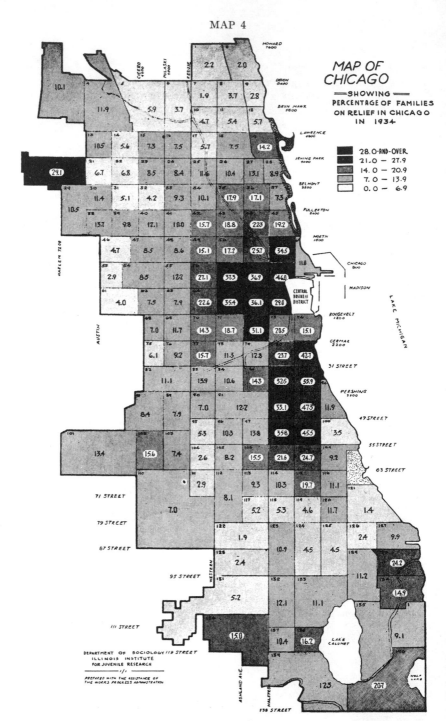

FAMILIES ON RELIEF, CHICAGO, 1934

MAP 5

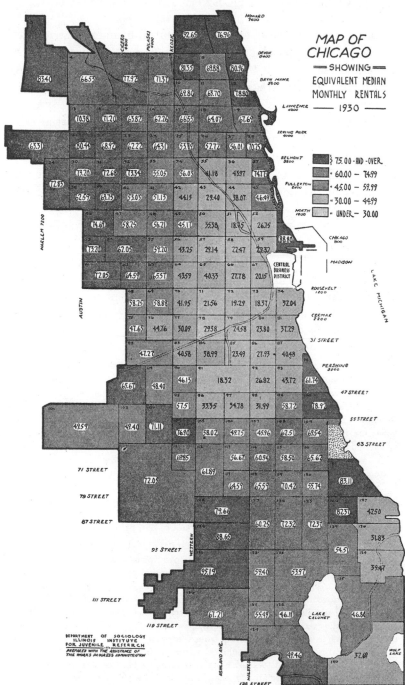

MEDIAN RENTALS, CHICAGO, 1930

rentals are concentrated around the central business district and the industrial areas along the two forks of the Chicago River. Outside these inner-city areas and in the South Chicago industrial district are the areas of slightly higher rents. In general, the rentals are successively higher as one moves outward from the central business district or away from the heavy industrial centers. With the exception of several Negro areas, where the rentals are disproportionately high, the configuration presented by the variations in median rentals corresponds closely with the variation in the percentage of families on relief as presented in Map 4.

Occupation Groups.[7]—Other evidence of economic segregation is to be seen in the differential distribution of occupation groups. These data are included in Table 2. They indicate that a disproportionate number of industrial workers are concentrated in the areas of physical deterioration and decreasing population, and a disproportionate number of professional and clerical workers in outlying residential communities, where the population is in-

---

There are probably some inherent errors in these data on monthly rentals. In apartment houses, for example, rentals usually included heat, water, and janitor service, whereas none of these is included in the rental of single homes. These differences may be even greater in furnished-apartment areas where all furnishings, and sometimes gas and light, are included in the rent. It was for the purpose of compensating for these variations that the monthly rentals for homes owned were calculated at 1 per cent of the total value.

These median rentals, calculated from the 1930 federal census, are approximately twice as high as the rentals in the same areas from the Civil Works Administration census for 1934, and it is probable that even these 1934 median rentals are higher than the median rent actually paid. However, for our purpose these variations are not important. We are interested in rentals as indications of the differences among areas rather than in the absolute amount of rent paid.

[7] The federal census of 1920 includes the best data for this analysis, since it was a census of occupations, whereas the census of 1930 was a census of gainful workers by industrial groups, in which "all persons whose services are employed in a given industry are classified under that industry." Even the general divisions of occupations used in 1920 are, in several instances, too general to serve as an adequate basis for a study of the differential distribution of occupations. Manufacturing includes, for example, the executives, superintendents, and technicians as well as the unskilled personnel. While it is obvious that, from the point of view of the study of economic segregation, executives should be separated from unskilled workers, these classifications can be used to show general tendencies, because the number of executives and managers is relatively small, as compared with the number of laborers.

creasing most rapidly. Since these occupational groups reflect variations in economic status, the facts constitute further evidence of economic segregation.

Segregation of Racial and Nationality Groups as a Product of Economic Segregation.—The segregation of population on an economic and occupational basis in American society brings about, in turn, a segregation of racial and nativity groups. Throughout most of the history of Chicago the groups of lowest economic status—that is, the foreign born and, more recently, the Negroes—have been concentrated in the areas of physical deterioration and low rentals. On the other hand, the native white population has been centered in the outlying communities, for collectively this group has a higher economic status. Together, the foreign-born and Negro groups furnish a large proportion of the unskilled industrial workers and a comparatively small proportion of the professional and clerical groups. The foreign born have been concentrated, therefore, in the areas adjacent to industrial establishments not only because it is economical and convenient for these workers to live closer to their work but also because they often cannot afford to live elsewhere. The same distribution among low-rent areas would probably characterize the Negroes were it not for the fact that racial barriers prevent their movement into many such areas and, in effect, operate to raise rents in the Negro area.

This segregation of population on an economic basis is again clearly indicated in Table 3. Especially noticeable is the concentration of Negro population in the areas where more than 21 per cent of the families are on relief. This concentration was not so apparent in 1920, when the highest proportion of Negro population was found in the areas with intermediate rates of dependent families, based on number receiving relief from private charities.

Concentration of Most Recent Immigrants and Migrants.—As indicated by the previous discussion, those nationality groups which represent the newest immigration constitute the largest proportion of the population in areas adjacent to the central business and industrial districts, while the so-called "older immigrant groups" are more widely dispersed. If citizenship is taken as an indication, more positive evidence of the segregation of the newest immigrants is to be seen in the differential distribution of the alien population, both in 1930 and in 1920. These variations in

TABLE 3

DISTRIBUTION OF RACIAL AND NATIVITY GROUPS BY AREAS
GROUPED ACCORDING TO RELIEF AND DEPEND-
ENCY RATES, 1930 AND 1920

	1930		
Percentage of Families on Relief 1934	Percentage Foreign-born and Negro Heads of Families	Percentage Negroes in Total Population	Percentage Foreign Born in White Population
28.0 and over (39.2)*...	78.5	38.1	32.9
21.0–27.9 (23.8)*...	62.5	15.7	29.5
14.0–20.9 (16.9)*...	59.4	3.9	32.4
7.0–13.9 (9.8)*...	46.7	0.3	27.1
0.0– 6.9 (3.8)*...	33.5	0.2	20.8

	1920		
Rates of Dependent Families 1921	Percentage Foreign-born and Negro Heads of Families	Percentage Negroes in Total Population	Percentage Foreign Born in White Population
2.0 and over (2.8)*.....	80.2	5.4	43.8
1.5–1.9 (1.7)*.....	71.9	3.5	37.8
1.0–1.4 (1.2)*.....	67.2	11.3	35.6
0.5–0.9 (0.7)*.....	54.5	1.6	29.2
0.0–0.4 (0.1)*.....	42.6	2.2	24.0

* Percentage for class as a whole.

the proportion of aliens in the white population are presented in Table 4. This table indicates that the areas of lowest economic status are occupied not only by the highest proportion of foreign born in the white population but also by the highest proportion of aliens in the foreign-born white population 21 years of age and over. The range in 1930 was from 15.9 per cent in the areas of lowest economic status to 3.8 per cent in the areas of highest status.

TABLE 4

DISTRIBUTION OF MOST RECENT IMMIGRANTS IN CHICAGO
BY AREAS GROUPED ACCORDING TO RELIEF AND
DEPENDENCY RATES, 1930 AND 1920

1930

Percentage of Families on Relief 1934	Percentage Foreign Born in White Population	Percentage Aliens in Foreign-born White Population 21 Years and Over	Percentage Aliens 21 Years and Over in White Population 21 and Over
28.0 and over (39.2)*....	32.9	30.5	15.9
21.0–27.9 (23.8)*...	29.5	27.3	12.6
14.0–20.9 (16.9)*...	32.4	25.6	12.6
7.0–13.9 (9.8)*...	27.1	19.7	7.9
0.0– 6.9 (3.8)*...	20.8	13.0	3.8

1920

Rates of Dependent Families 1921	Percentage Foreign Born in White Population	Percentage Aliens in Foreign-born White Population 21 Years and Over	Percentage Aliens 21 Years and Over in White Population 21 and Over
2.0 and over (2.8)*.....	43.8	41.1	28.7
1.5–1.9 (1.7)*.....	37.8	32.8	19.6
1.0–1.4 (1.2)*.....	35.6	26.9	15.0
0.5–0.9 (0.7)*.....	29.2	22.6	10.1
0.0–0.4 (0.1)*.....	24.0	16.5	5.4

* Percentage for class as a whole.

In his study of the Negro family Frazier similarly found the most recent Negro migrants to the city concentrated in the most deteriorated sections of the Negro areas. He states:

Although nearly four-fifths of all the Negroes in Chicago were born in the South, the proportion of southern-born inhabitants in the population diminishes as one leaves those sections of the Negro community nearest the heart of the city. It is in those zones just outside of the Loop where decaying residences and tottering frame dwellings presage the inroads of industry and business that the southern migrant is able to pay the cheap rents that landlords are willing to accept until their property is demanded by the expanding business area.[8]

The results of this process of segregation in Chicago as of 1930 are revealed in Map 6, which shows nativity and race of family heads. In those census tracts where a predominant number of the heads of families were foreign born, the leading nationality group is indicated.[9]

On this map the areas in solid black are those predominantly occupied by Negroes. Since only the numerically dominant group is indicated in each area, it should be remembered that there are Negroes in many of the other tracts in the city. This is especially true on the Near North Side, where large numbers of Negro families are to be found.

Several facts are immediately apparent from Map 6. In the

[8] E. Franklin Frazier, *The Negro Family in Chicago* (Chicago: University of Chicago Press, 1932), pp. 98–100.

[9] The effects of a large European immigration on Chicago over a long period of time and of a more recent migration of Negroes are shown in an analysis of the composition of the population. In 1930, 92.3 per cent of the population were white, 6.9 per cent were Negro, and 0.8 per cent were classified as "other races." At the time, 24.9 per cent of the population were foreign born, 39.4 per cent were classified "native white of foreign or mixed parentage," and 29.9 per cent as "native white of native parentage."

Since 1900, significant population changes have taken place. One trend indicating migration of Negroes to Chicago is the increase in the proportion of Negroes in the total population from 2.0 per cent in 1910 to 6.9 per cent in 1930. Another trend is a decrease in the foreign born in the total population from 35.7 to 24.9 per cent, while the percentage classified "native white of native parentage" increased from 20.4 in 1910 to 27.9 in 1930. In spite of this transition, in 1930 the foreign born and the children of the foreign born constituted 69.8 per cent of the total white population in the city. In 1940, 91.7 per cent of the population were white and 8.3 per cent non-white.

Of the foreign-born white, 17.8 per cent were born in Poland; 3.2 per cent in Germany; 13.0 per cent in Russia and Lithuania; 8.8 per cent in Italy; 7.8 per cent in Sweden; 6.5 per cent in the Irish Free State and North Ireland; and 5.8 per cent in Czechoslovakia.

MAP 6

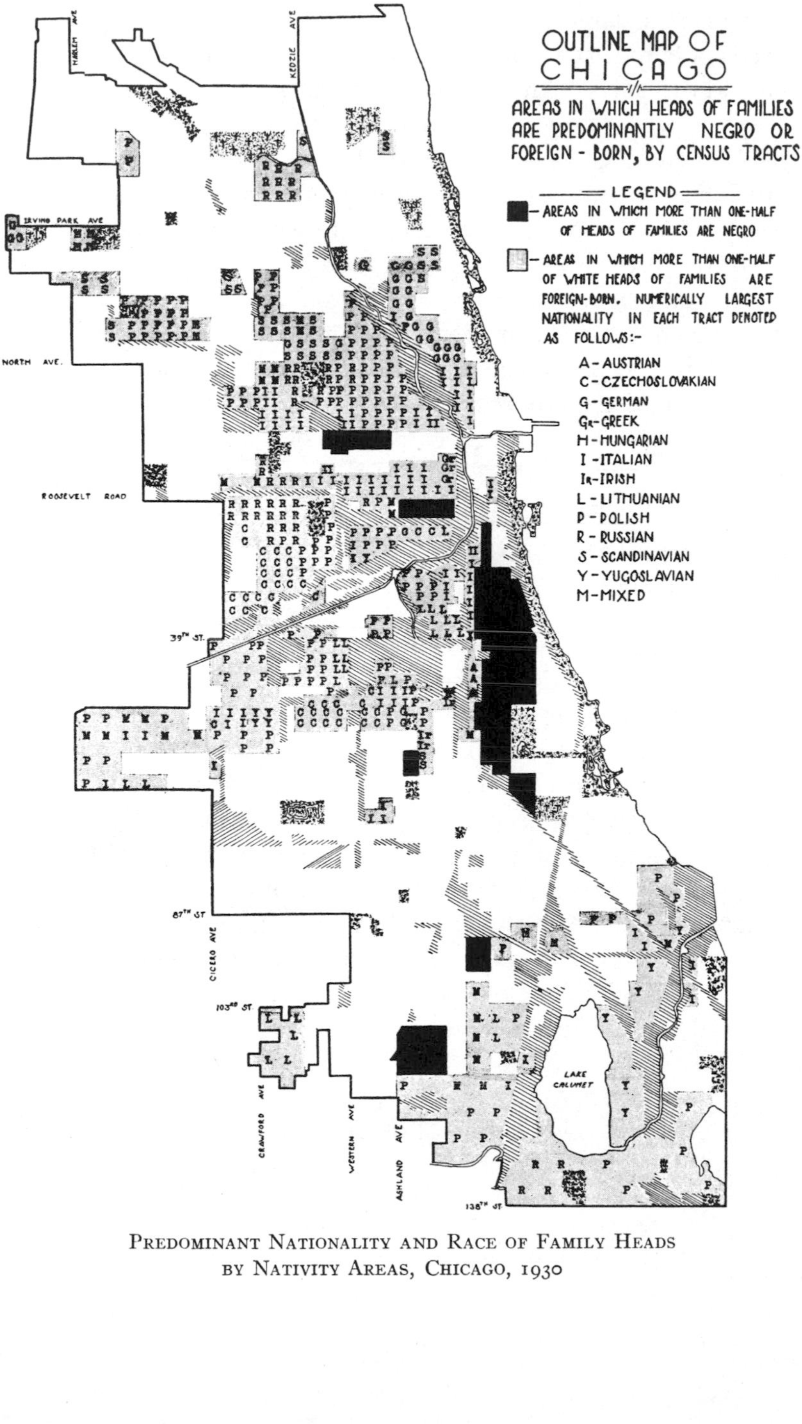

OUTLINE MAP OF
CHICAGO

AREAS IN WHICH HEADS OF FAMILIES
ARE PREDOMINANTLY NEGRO OR
FOREIGN - BORN, BY CENSUS TRACTS

LEGEND

- AREAS IN WHICH MORE THAN ONE-HALF
OF HEADS OF FAMILIES ARE NEGRO

- AREAS IN WHICH MORE THAN ONE-HALF
OF WHITE HEADS OF FAMILIES ARE
FOREIGN-BORN. NUMERICALLY LARGEST
NATIONALITY IN EACH TRACT DENOTED
AS FOLLOWS:-

A - AUSTRIAN
C - CZECHOSLOVAKIAN
G - GERMAN
Gr - GREEK
H - HUNGARIAN
I - ITALIAN
Ir - IRISH
L - LITHUANIAN
P - POLISH
R - RUSSIAN
S - SCANDINAVIAN
Y - YUGOSLAVIAN
M - MIXED

THATCHER AVE.
KEDZIE AVE.
IRVING PARK AVE
NORTH AVE.
ROOSEVELT ROAD
39TH ST.
87TH ST.
CICERO AVE
103RD ST.
CRAWFORD AVE
WESTERN AVE
ASHLAND AVE
138TH ST.
LAKE CALUMET

PREDOMINANT NATIONALITY AND RACE OF FAMILY HEADS
BY NATIVITY AREAS, CHICAGO, 1930

first place, a large proportion of tracts where the foreign-born heads of families constitute the predominant group are clustered around the city's point of original settlement or are distributed in the areas where heavy industry has been located. Secondly, symbols designating the country of birth of the foreign-born heads of families show that in some instances large areas are dominated by one national group and that the most recent immigrants are concentrated in the least desirable sections of the city.

This map represents the distribution of racial and national groups as of 1930, but it does not even suggest the nature of the process that brings about this segregation—the continuous succession of national groups in these immigrant areas. Similar maps for earlier decades would reveal a more decided concentration of foreign born, but the nationalities included would be different.[10] In short, nationality groups have succeeded one another in the areas of lowest economic status, while the concentrations of older immigrant groups are now to be found beyond the inner-city areas. Each new nationality group was segregated into the low-rent areas during the period of its adjustment to the New World. As they have moved out, their places have been taken by other newcomers from abroad until recent years, when part of this inner-city area has been occupied by the newly migrated Negro people.

Thus, in the process of city growth, areas within Chicago have been differentiated in such a way that they can be distinguished from one another by their physical or economic characteristics or, at any given moment, by the composition of the population. Associated with these differences and with the more subtle variations in the attitudes and values which accompany them are found marked variations in child behavior. These are reflected in differential rates of delinquents, as presented in subsequent chapters.

[10] Paul F. Cressey, "The Succession of Cultural Groups" (Ph.D. dissertation, Department of Sociology, University of Chicago, 1930).

CHAPTER III

DISTRIBUTION OF MALE JUVENILE DELIN-
QUENTS IN CHICAGO

THIS chapter is concerned with the geographic distribution of delinquent or alleged delinquent boys and the manner in which rates of delinquent boys vary from area to area in the city of Chicago. Questions pertaining to the total number of such boys in the city at any given time or to the trend in the total number during a given period of years are extraneous to the primary purpose of this discussion. The data presented serve as a means of indicating the pattern of distribution of delinquency in the city and the extent to which this pattern has changed or remained constant during a period of forty years. As an initial step in this study it is important to make clear the sense in which the term "delinquency" is used.

Definitions.—The term "male juvenile delinquent," as used in the studies reported in this volume, refers to a boy under 17 years of age[1] who is brought before the Juvenile Court, or other courts having jurisdiction, on delinquency petition; or whose case is disposed of by an officer of the law without a court appearance. "Alleged delinquent" is the more accurate term, since it sometimes happens that charges are not sustained. Legally, a boy is not a delinquent until he is officially known to have violated some provision of the law as currently interpreted. Only in terms of this official definition can the data here presented be considered as an enumeration of male juvenile delinquents.

Several different types of series will be analyzed in the following pages—school truants, alleged delinquents as above defined, and repeated offenders or recidivists—representing in various degrees of inclusiveness boys who have been dealt with either by the juvenile police officers or by the court. Although these are official cases only, it is assumed that their utility in differentiating areas

[1] The age limits vary in the cities studied.

43

44   JUVENILE DELINQUENCY AND URBAN AREAS

extends beyond the limits of the legal definition. Many boys commit serious offenses, yet are not apprehended. In recent years there has been a tendency to extend the term "delinquent" to include all boys engaging in the type of activities which, if known, would warrant action by official agencies. The White House Conference of 1930 adopted as its definition of delinquency: "Any such juvenile misconduct that might be dealt with under the law." In the present volume the term "delinquent" will be restricted to those boys dealt with officially, while those defined as delinquent according to the more inclusive use of the term will be referred to as boys engaging in "officially proscribed activity." The data presented here, therefore, may be considered as a sample or index, but not as a complete enumeration, of the total number of boys engaging in officially proscribed activity in any given area.

The total amount of officially proscribed activity in a community, recorded and unrecorded, and the number of children involved are, of course, difficult to estimate and practically impossible to measure exactly at the present time.[2] This fact underscores the need for a workable index—data which are available

[2] Sophia M. Robison (see Sophia Moses Robison, *Can Delinquency Be Measured?* [New York: Columbia University Press, 1936]) suggests that a measure of the amount of delinquency should include cases of "delinquent behavior" from the files of private agencies, in addition to official cases. In a New York series which she presents, these unofficial cases comprise 11.3 per cent of the total number. But it appears that their addition does not answer the questions associated either with measurement or with the development of an index. A series based on both official and private cases is still not an enumeration of delinquents as legally defined, nor is it a complete enumeration of all boys engaging in activity similar to that engaged in by official delinquents; for the latter would include, in addition to recorded cases, the unrecorded offenders known to workers in social agencies, schools, churches, recreation centers, and the like, as well as those known only to neighbors, friends, parents, and playmates.

Neither is there reason to believe that all recorded cases would constitute a better *index* of total delinquent behavior (number of individuals engaging in delinquent behavior) than is furnished by official cases only. In fact, a new problem is created when cases from private agencies are included, since definitions of the term "delinquent" are known to vary among public and private agencies. Thus, in a case record the concept "delinquency" may be used in connection with personality problems or with reference to behavior more or less common to all boys, which might be of no interest to the police even if brought to their attention.

Even if it is assumed that cases from private agencies are comparable to official cases, it is yet to be established that their inclusion improves the index.

with the series of events inaccessible to direct measurement. Such an index may be also a sample or incomplete enumeration of the whole, as are the data of this volume. Where two or more series of official delinquents exhibit close geographical association and covariance, even though separated in time by 10, 20, or 30 years and regardless of changes in nativity or nationality composition of the population, it seems reasonable to consider any one of them as a probable index of the more inclusive universe—the total number of boys within the area engaging in officially proscribed activity.

It is not possible to test conclusively the validity of any of the indexes of proscribed activity presented in this volume, since there is no satisfactory measure of such activity or complete enumeration of those who engage in it. Experience in various Chicago communities, however, furnishes a basis for confidence that the official cases do constitute an adequate and useful indication of the relative numbers of boys engaging in similar activity in various types of urban areas.

It is necessary, finally, to distinguish "officially proscribed activity," as above defined, from the still broader category of "problem behavior," including mischief, aggression, and personality problems of the type which often bring about a child's referral to a behavior clinic or other agency. The authors do not feel that rates of delinquents based on official cases can be used as indexes of this type of behavior. It is entirely probable that, in spite of overlapping, the distribution of these problem cases is quite different from the distribution of boys who are officially delinquent or who engage in activity similar to that engaged in by official delinquents.

The present series of data, then, are offered as fairly accurate measures of the relative numbers of delinquents living in contrasted types of areas in the cities studied, and also as probable indexes of the total number of boys engaging in officially proscribed activity within these communities.

Series Studied.—Traditionally, police arrests, court appearances, and convictions have been used to indicate the amount of adult crime. In the present study of the distribution of juvenile delinquents throughout the city it was possible to secure variations of each of these types of data; but, since conviction is not a juvenile court concept, commitments were substituted. The data fall into three groups: (1) series of alleged delinquents brought before the Juvenile Court on delinquency petition; (2) series of delinquents committed by the Juvenile Court to correctional institutions; and (3) series of alleged delinquents dealt with by police probation officers with or without court appearance.

Probably any one of these series would serve to establish the facts of distribution and variation in rates of official delinquents, because in no one of them are any apparent selective factors operating which would seriously distort this geographic distribution. Yet there are many advantages in using all three. In the first place, the three types of series will present the facts more adequately than would any one type alone, since the whole range of cases, from arrests through commitments, will be represented. Secondly, findings based upon the three will be more conclusive and convincing than those based upon a single index, provided, of course, that the findings are uniform and consistent. Finally, comparison of the findings of the police and commitment series with the findings of the juvenile court series will serve to check the validity of the latter as an index of the total number of boys engaging in officially proscribed activity.

In this Chicago study the distribution of delinquents, based upon juvenile court cases and commitments, will be presented for periods roughly centered about 1900, 1920, and 1930; and series of police cases, for three different years around 1930. These studies of the distribution of delinquents at different periods of time afford a basis for comparisons and for analysis of long-time trends and processes that could not be made for a single period. Likewise it will be possible to compare the rates of delinquents in the same areas at different periods, not only in those areas which show significant variations either in physical and economic characteristics or in the nationality and racial composition of the population, but also in those where there has been comparatively little change. This comparison furnishes a basis for an evaluation of the relative importance of physical and economic conditions, as contrasted with race and nationality, in relation to delinquency.

Under each type of series, in turn, the data representing different periods of time will be considered. Series of boys appearing in the Juvenile Court will be presented first; these will be followed by series of those committed by the Juvenile Court to correctional schools; and these, in turn, by cases dealt with by the police probation officers. As to time sequence, the most recent series will be presented first and the earliest series last. The manner of arrangement, the periods covered, and the number of individuals included in each series are indicated in the following outline:

A. Distribution of alleged delinquents brought before the Juvenile Court of Cook County
  1. A series of 8,411 alleged delinquent boys brought into the Juvenile Court during the 7-year period 1927–33
  2. A series of 8,141 alleged delinquent boys brought into the Juvenile Court during the 7-year period 1917–23
  3. A series of 8,056 alleged delinquent boys brought into the Juvenile Court during the 7-year period 1900–1906
  4. Comparisons among Series 1, 2, and 3
B. Distribution of delinquents committed by the Juvenile Court of Cook County to correctional schools
  1. A series of delinquents committed by the Juvenile Court during the 7-year period 1927–33
  2. A series of delinquents committed by the Juvenile Court during the 7-year period 1917–23
  3. A series of delinquents committed by the Juvenile Court during the 7-year period 1900–1906
  4. Comparisons among Series 1, 2, and 3
C. Distribution of alleged delinquent boys dealt with by the police probation officers
  1. A series of alleged delinquents dealt with by police probation officers during the year 1931
  2. A series of alleged delinquents dealt with by police probation officers during the year 1927
  3. A series of alleged delinquents dealt with by police probation officers during the year 1926
  4. Recreation survey study
  5. Comparisons among Series 1, 2, and 3

The relationship between the number of individuals in the above series and the number of years included will be more evi-

48 JUVENILE DELINQUENCY AND URBAN AREAS

dent if the instrumentalities employed in dealing with the problem of delinquency in Chicago are briefly described. Likewise,
this discussion should furnish a basis for analyzing the problems
involved in the use of series of cases extending over a period of
years, as compared with those for a single year.

In Chicago all boys who are arrested or who come to the attention of the police for investigation are dealt with by juvenile police
probation officers, one of whom is assigned to each police district
in the city. The individuals dealt with by these officers comprise
our police series and include, as would be expected, some boys
guilty of serious offenses, many guilty of lesser offenses, and also
those held only for investigation, for identification, or for some
other reason. On the average, about 85 per cent of the cases dealt
with by the police probation officer are disposed of by him without court action, while the remaining 15 per cent are taken before
the Juvenile Court on petitions alleging delinquency. The fact
that such a large percentage of the boys are dealt with without
court action does not mean that these boys are not delinquent.
It suggests, rather, that the police probation officer, who has
broad discretionary power, has decided that they should not be
taken into court, either because they are too young, because they
are first offenders, because the offenses with which they are
charged do not appear to him to be serious, or for other reasons
best known to himself. The 15 per cent taken to court are, presumably, either those who have committed the most serious offenses, who are recidivists, or who for any other reason are assumed by the officers to present serious problems.

The Juvenile Court, in turn, ultimately commits to training or
correctional schools somewhere between one-quarter and one-half
of the boys against whom delinquency petitions have been filed.
These boys are, for the most part, guilty of serious delinquencies,
and most of them are recidivists.[3] The numerical relationship
between this group, the boys who are brought before the Juvenile
Court, and the boys dealt with by the police probation officers

---

[3] The number of individuals committed to institutions at the time of first appearance in court is comparatively small. Most boys are committed for subsequent offenses.

This means that, of every 30 boys dealt with by the police probation officers, 5 are taken to court on delinquency petition and 2 are
ultimately committed by the court to correctional institutions.

Because of Chicago's size, a rather large sample of cases is
needed. Just what the minimum could be is not known, but from
experience it seems that series including several thousand individuals show the facts of distribution most clearly. The number of
individuals dealt with by the police probation officers in a single
year approaches 10,000; a year, therefore, was taken as a unit in
the police series. It is evident, however, that the number of boys
taken to court in a year would not furnish an adequate sample.
Accordingly, the three juvenile court series were based on the
boys brought to court on delinquency petition during a 7-year
period. Similarly, the commitment series cover 7-year periods.
Logically, the latter should extend over a longer period than the
juvenile court series, since fewer boys are included. In this study,
however, the same periods were used for both, with the result that
the commitment series contain fewer cases than either the juvenile
court or the police series.

In the calculation of rates of delinquents the basic assumption
as to population is the same in a series extending over several
years as in a series for a single year. The population for any given
area, although stated in the census volumes as the population for
a year, is actually the population as of the census date only. Thus,
the 1930 population is the population as of April 1, 1930, the only
day on which the exact population of an area is known, and the
only day, therefore, for which exact rates of delinquents might be
calculated. Since it is impossible to calculate rates of delinquents
for this one day, an assumption must be made as to the average
population in a given period. If the population is changing very
little, it can be assumed that at any other day, month, year, or
period of years it will be about the same as on the day of enumeration. For a changing population, adjustments can be made if the
rate of increase or decrease is known.

Since the same assumptions as to the constancy of population
are made for a month, a year, or a period of years, the period of

time covered by a series of cases is not important, providing the date of the known population is near the midyear of the series. The only advantage in a short period is that there is less probability of change in the rate of population growth or decline in local areas. On the other hand, there are advantages in having rates of delinquents for series covering a longer period of time. In this study, rates are calculated for series covering from 1 to 7 years; accordingly, the reader can make his own comparisons and draw his conclusions as to the advantages and disadvantages of each time interval.

A. THE DISTRIBUTION OF ALLEGED DELINQUENTS BROUGHT
BEFORE THE JUVENILE COURT OF COOK COUNTY

1. THE 1927–33 JUVENILE COURT SERIES

Series Studied.—These 8,411 different alleged male delinquents were brought before the Juvenile Court of Cook County from Chicago on petitions alleging delinquency during the 7-year period between January 1, 1927, and December 31, 1933. They are all separate individuals, as duplications from year to year, as well as within the separate years, have been eliminated from the series.

Distribution of Delinquents.—Map 7 shows the distribution by place of residence of the 8,411 different male delinquents. Each dot represents the home address of one delinquent boy; only one dot was used for each individual, regardless of the number of times he appeared in court from any area.[4]

Upon inspection, Map 7 reveals some very interesting characteristics. It will be observed immediately that there are areas of marked concentration of delinquents, as compared with other areas where the dots are widely dispersed. These concentrations are most obvious immediately north and northwest of the Loop along the North Branch of the Chicago River, in the areas some distance south of the Loop along State Street, and in the areas immediately outside and extending westward from the northern part of the Loop. In addition to these major concentrations, lesser

[4] These home addresses were plotted by street and number on a large base map of the city of Chicago, on which all streets are shown, and then copied on the outline map reproduced.

MAP 7

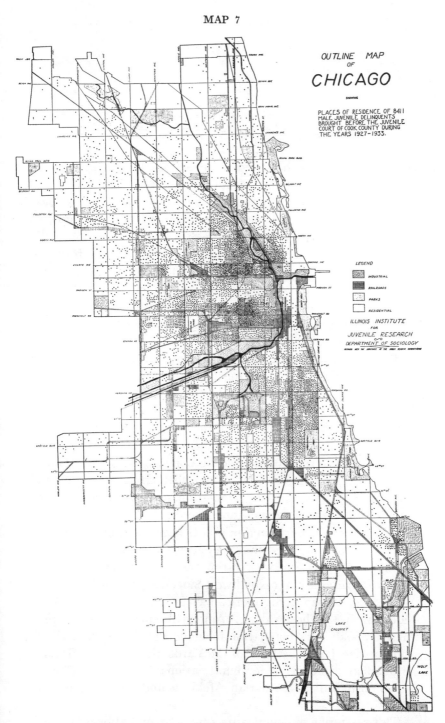

OUTLINE MAP
OF
CHICAGO
SHOWING

PLACES OF RESIDENCE OF 8411
MALE JUVENILE DELINQUENTS
BROUGHT BEFORE THE JUVENILE
COURT OF COOK COUNTY DURING
THE YEARS 1927-1933.

LEGEND

INDUSTRIAL

RAILROADS

PARKS

RESIDENTIAL

ILLINOIS INSTITUTE
FOR
JUVENILE RESEARCH
AND
DEPARTMENT OF SOCIOLOGY

DISTRIBUTION OF MALE JUVENILE DELINQUENTS, CHICAGO, 1927–33

52   JUVENILE DELINQUENCY AND URBAN AREAS

clusters of dots will be noted in several outlying areas, in the Back of the Yards and the South Chicago steel-mill districts.

This distribution of delinquents is closely related to the location of industrial and commercial areas and to the composition of the population. In the first place, as has already been noted, the areas of heaviest concentration are, in general, not far from the central business district, within or near the areas zoned for light industry or commerce. As one moves outward, away from these areas into the residential communities, the cases are more and more scattered until, near the periphery of the city, they are, in general, widely dispersed.

The concentrations of delinquents not adjacent to the central business district are, for the most part, near outlying heavy industrial areas, especially along the two branches of the Chicago River and in the Stock Yards and South Chicago districts. Comparison of the distribution map in turn with Maps 3, 4, and 5[5] reveals further that the alleged delinquents are concentrated mainly in areas characterized by decreasing population and low rentals, with high percentages of families on relief. Here, too, industrial workers predominate. The population in these neighborhoods was, during 1927–33, largely foreign born, with high proportions of recent arrivals, aliens, and migrants from the rural South.

As to national heritage, the area of concentration of delinquents on the Near North Side was, during the period covered, predominantly Italian; the lower Northwest Side, mainly Polish; the Near West Side, Italian and American Negro; and the Lower West Side, chiefly Czechoslovakian. Among the more outlying areas, the Humboldt Park population included Poles, Swedes, Italians, and Russian Jews; the Back of the Yards district was Polish and Lithuanian; while the predominant nationalities in South Chicago were Polish, Italian, Hungarian, Mexican, and Yugoslavian. (See Map 6.)

This scattering of delinquents among many national groups is characteristic of each of the three periods studied, though the proportions in each nationality vary. The groups producing the most alleged delinquents are, in every instance, those most re-

[5] See chap. ii.

result of the ongoing processes of American city life.

In order to compare the number of delinquents by areas and to relate this number in each instance to the population of the same age and sex, the city was divided into 140 areas.[6] Most of these are square miles, bounded on all four sides by the section lines of the government survey. In some instances, where much of the territory was occupied by industry or where, for other reasons, the population was sparse, it was necessary to combine several contiguous square-mile areas. In our discussion, however, these units, regardless of size, will be referred to as "square-mile areas."

When the distribution of the 8,411 delinquents is analyzed in terms of these 140 square-mile areas, wide differences are evident. In each of 3 areas there are more than 300 delinquents, while 8 have more than 150 each. At the other extreme, there is 1 area from which only 3 delinquents were taken to court, 15 with fewer than 10, and 25 with fewer than 15 delinquents. Moreover, the actual difference in concentration is greater than these comparisons suggest, since many areas with large numbers of delinquents have less residential space and population than those with fewer. The theoretical significance of these facts is at least twofold. First, they reveal the wide variation in distribution; second, they indicate, quite apart from density of population, the differential probability of a boy's having contact with other delinquent boys in the same area or of observing their activities.

Rates of Delinquents.—Map 8 shows the rates of delinquents in each of the 140 square-mile areas. These rates represent the number of alleged delinquents taken to the Juvenile Court from each area during 1927–33, per hundred of the aged 10–16 male population in that area as of 1930. It should be borne in mind that the 7-year rate here presented is less than the sum of 7 yearly rates, since all duplications have been eliminated.

The range in this series is from 0.5 to 18.9. The median is 2.5 and the rate for the city as a whole, 4.2. Three of the 140 areas have rates above 17.0, and 14 below 1.0. Similarly, there are 12

---

[6] Rates were computed also for 60 local communities and 120 subcommunities. They reveal approximately the same variations as the rates for square-mile areas.

MAP 8

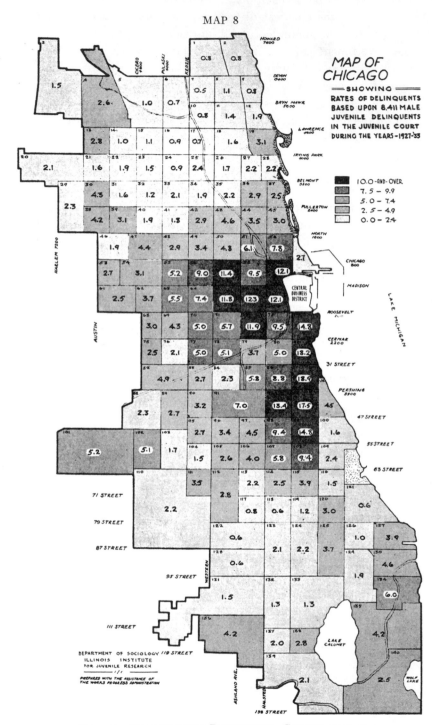

RATES OF MALE JUVENILE DELINQUENTS, CHICAGO, 1927–33

areas where the rates are more than 10.0, and 50 where they are less than 2.5. This comparison brings out two fundamental facts, namely, that there are wide differences among areas and that the number of areas with low rates far exceeds the number where they are high. The areas with the highest rates are located directly south of the central business district, and the areas with the next highest rates north and west of the Loop. At the other extreme, low rates of delinquents will be noted in many of the outlying areas.

Most of the areas characterized by high rates of delinquents, as well as by a concentration of individual delinquents, are either in or adjacent to areas zoned for industry and commerce. This is true not only for areas close to the central business district but also for outlying areas, such as those near the Stock Yards, the South Chicago steel mills, and other industrial sections. On the other hand, the areas with low rates are, for the most part, those zoned for residential purposes.

Between the center of the city and the periphery the rates, on the whole, show a regular decrease. There are, of course, deviations from this general tendency. In some outlying sections there are areas of high rates, especially in the Stock Yards and Southwest manufacturing districts and adjacent to the South Chicago steel mills. On the other hand, not all areas close to the central business district have high rates. Area 60, for example, located just north of the Loop and including the "Gold Coast," has a rate of 2.7; and Areas 37 and 45, not far to the north, have comparatively low rates. It may be noted, however, that the physical and social characteristics of these areas differ from those of the surrounding areas.

One apparent exception to the general tendency of the rates to decrease from the center of the city outward may be noted south of the central business district, between Areas 74 and 115. Here the highest rates are in the second, third, and fourth areas (81, 87, and 93). When rates were calculated separately for the Negro and white delinquents in these areas, however, it was found that both decreased uniformly, in contrast to the combined rate. The rates for white boys, calculated necessarily on small samples, fol-

56   JUVENILE DELINQUENCY AND URBAN AREAS

lowed with some irregularities the common radial pattern, ranging from 13.4 in Area 74, the highest rate, to 2.5 in Area 115. The
corresponding range for Negro delinquents was from 21.2 in the
first area south of the Loop to 6.0 in the seventh area. This drop
is significant because it shows that the rates of delinquents for
Negro boys, although somewhat higher than those for the whites,
exhibit similarly wide variations among different communities.

It was for the purpose of reducing the fluctuations resulting
from chance that square-mile areas were selected for the presentation of rates of delinquents, in place of the smaller census tracts
into which the city of Chicago is divided. There are, however,
some advantages in considering the rates of delinquents by census
tracts or even by smaller units. In an area as large as a square
mile there may be many different types of neighborhoods. On the
other hand, it is difficult to ascertain whether the variations in
rates in the smaller areas within a square mile represent actual
differences which would be sustained by subsequent studies or
whether they are purely chance variations.

In order to illustrate the variations for small units within
square-mile areas, rates are presented for the census tracts combined in the construction of three areas. These variations are
given in Table 5. The variations in Area 2, as shown in the table,
are proportionately great, but they are not significant, since the
sample of delinquents on which they were based was very small.

Square-mile Area 51 is relatively homogeneous, since rates for
the tracts within it do not vary widely from the rate for the area
as a whole. The critical ratio for the most widely separated rates
in this area is 1.66.

There is reason to believe that in Area 97, however, the rates in
the north half are significantly higher than in the south half. This
is supported by the fact that the critical ratio of the rate in one of
the tracts in the north half and the rate in a tract in the south
half is 3.42. The critical ratio of the rate of delinquents in the
entire north half of this square mile (6.2) and the rate in the south
half (2.6) is 4.34.

These data indicate that, in some instances at least, the differences between rates of delinquents within areas are statistically

be said to conform, in a general way, to those for the square-mile areas; but, as indicated above, they exhibit some variation and irregularities, both because they reflect actual differences among local neighborhoods and because of the chance fluctuations due to small samples. The rates by square miles smooth out some of these variations, give a more general picture of the delinquency situation; and reveal more clearly the general trends and tendencies. Rates for successively larger areas smooth the picture more and more and present with increasing clarity the general trends.

TABLE 5

RATES OF DELINQUENTS FOR CENSUS
TRACTS INCLUDED IN AREAS
2, 51, AND 97

Area 2	Area 51	Area 97
0.0	5.0	2.1
0.3	5.5	2.1
0.4	6.1	3.0
0.4	6.6	5.1
0.5	7.2	6.0
1.1	9.5	6.7
1.3		6.7
1.4		7.0

This is clearly indicated in the zone rates presented at the end of this section. It should be evident from this discussion that rates both of delinquents calculated for small areas and of those for large areas have their advantages and disadvantages and that the size of area best suited to the calculation of rates depends upon the purposes for which the calculations are made.

It should be noted that on the South Side of Chicago the rates of delinquents decrease to a low point about 7 or 8 miles from the central business district and that beyond this point, as in South Chicago and the Pullman industrial districts, they are noticeably higher. From the standpoint of city growth these South Chicago areas are independent centers, not related to the radial expansion of Chicago proper. They may be said, therefore, to confirm the radial pattern, being, in effect, secondary industrial and business

MAP 9

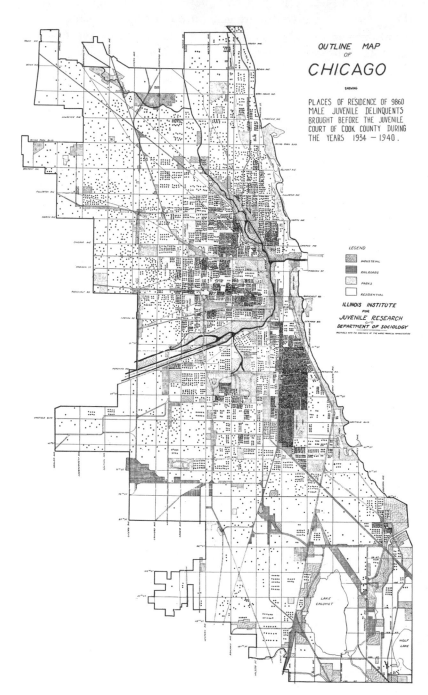

OUTLINE MAP
OF
CHICAGO

SHOWING

PLACES OF RESIDENCE OF 9860
MALE JUVENILE DELINQUENTS
BROUGHT BEFORE THE JUVENILE
COURT OF COOK COUNTY DURING
THE YEARS 1934 — 1940.

LEGEND

INDUSTRIAL

RAILROADS

PARKS

RESIDENTIAL

ILLINOIS INSTITUTE
FOR
JUVENILE RESEARCH
C-10
DEPARTMENT OF SOCIOLOGY
PREPARED WITH THE ASSISTANCE OF THE WORKS PROGRESS ADMINISTRATION

DISTRIBUTION OF MALE JUVENILE DELINQUENTS, CHICAGO, 1934–40

centers—from each of which, in turn, the rates of delinquents tend to decrease as distance outward increases.

The 1934–40 Juvenile Court Series.—The most recent data available comprise a series of 9,860 Chicago boys brought before the Juvenile Court of Cook County during the 7-year period 1934–40. Map 9 presents the distribution of these alleged delinquents by census tracts, each dot being placed within the tract in which the boy's home was located, but not at the exact address. Rates have not been computed, as the necessary population totals, by age groups, of the 1940 census were as yet unavailable.

Map 9 reveals a configuration quite similar to that for the 1927–33 series, except for increased concentration in the deteriorated areas south of the Loop and more dispersion into the outlying sections to the north and west, reflecting, no doubt, the movement of population away from the city's center.

2. THE 1917–23 JUVENILE COURT SERIES

In the foregoing section the distribution of delinquents and the variation in rates for Chicago were studied by analyzing a series of cases brought into the Juvenile Court of Cook County during the years 1927–33 in relation to the 1930 census data. In the present section a similar series covering a period centered about the 1920 census will be presented. This series includes the 8,141 alleged male delinquents brought before the Juvenile Court of Cook County from Chicago on delinquency petition in the 7-year period 1917–23.

Series Studied and Types of Offenses.—The 1917–23 juvenile court series was secured in the same manner and from the same sources as the 1927–33 series. With the exception of the changes in the number of areas for which rates of delinquents were calculated, the data will be analyzed in the same way. Since no important change has taken place in the basic procedure of taking boys to the Juvenile Court, these boys also represent those charged by police probation officers with relatively serious offenses.

The nature of the offenses committed by these 8,141 individuals is indicated by the classification of the 12,029 petitions filed

29.4 per cent of the alleged offenses were burglary, 12.2 per cent larceny of automobiles, and 20.4 per cent petty stealing. These offenses, together with a total of 7.5 per cent for other stealing offenses, such as holdup, shoplifting, and purse-snatching, give a total of 69.5 per cent classified as "all stealing." The remaining 30.5 per cent included incorrigibility, 17.1 per cent; disorderly conduct, 4.4 per cent; and all sex offenses, 2.1 per cent. There can be little doubt that these boys were, on the whole, involved in serious delinquency.

In this series, 16.7 per cent of the boys were under 13 years of age, 12.7 per cent were 13, and 18.3 per cent were 14. The highest frequencies are in the 15- and 16-year age groups, these two comprising 51.9 per cent of the total.

Distribution of Delinquents.—Map 10 shows the distribution by place of residence of the 8,141 boys in this series. This map indicates that the distribution is very similar to that previously presented and that the areas of concentration coincide quite closely with similar areas on the 1927–33 map. The one distinctive difference is that the concentrations in the areas later occupied by Negroes are much less evident in the 1917–23 series. Otherwise, the areas of heavy concentration, as in the previous series, are adjacent to the central business and industrial districts and to certain outlying industrial centers, while the areas in which the dots are widely dispersed fall in the outlying sections of the city.

The distribution indicates that this series also presents very great geographical variations in the number of delinquents. One of the 113 square-mile areas contains 6 delinquents, while another contains 312. Four areas contain fewer than 10 delinquents each, while 5 contain more than 250 each. When the distribution is analyzed further, it is found that 11 areas contain fewer than 15 delinquents, and 18 fewer than 20 delinquents each. At the other extreme, a total of 7 areas contain more than 200 delinquents each, and 14 contain more than 150.

Rates of Delinquents.—The area rates for the present series are given on Map 11. These represent the number of boys brought to the Juvenile Court from each of the 113 square-mile areas during

MAP 10

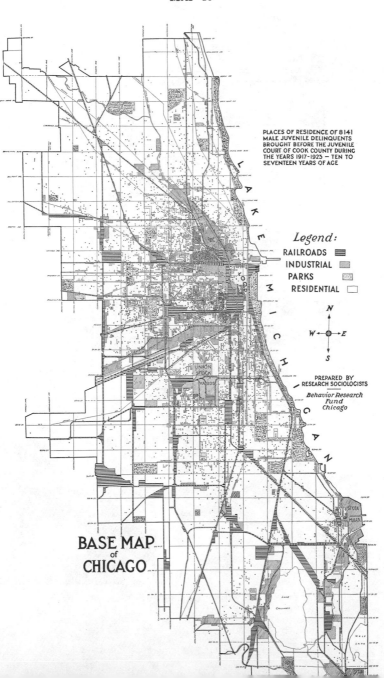

PLACES OF RESIDENCE OF 8141
MALE JUVENILE DELINQUENTS
BROUGHT BEFORE THE JUVENILE
COURT OF COOK COUNTY DURING
THE YEARS 1917-1923 — TEN TO
SEVENTEEN YEARS OF AGE

Legend:

RAILROADS

INDUSTRIAL

PARKS

RESIDENTIAL

N

W ←●→ *E*

S

PREPARED BY
RESEARCH SOCIOLOGISTS

*Behavior Research
Fund
Chicago*

UNION
STOCK
YARDS

STEEL
MILLS

BASE MAP
of
CHICAGO

LAKE MICHIGAN

LOOP

LAKE
CALUMET

MAP 11

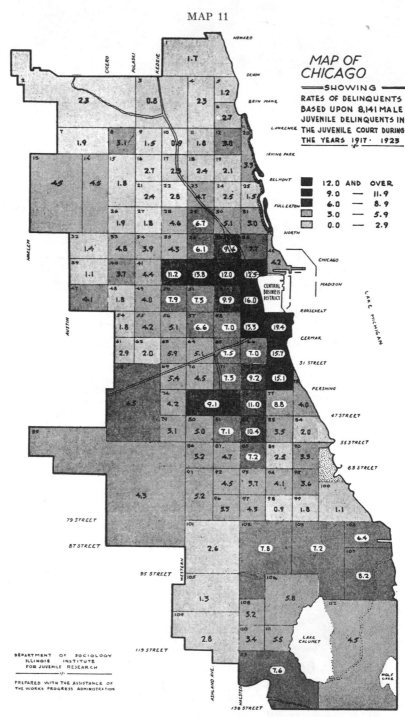

MAP OF
CHICAGO
━━━ SHOWING ━━━
RATES OF DELINQUENTS
BASED UPON 8,141 MALE
JUVENILE DELINQUENTS IN
THE JUVENILE COURT DURING
THE YEARS 1917 · 1923

	12.0 AND OVER
	9.0 — 11.9
	6.0 — 8.9
	3.0 — 5.9
	0.0 — 2.9

DEPARTMENT OF SOCIOLOGY
ILLINOIS INSTITUTE
FOR JUVENILE RESEARCH

PREPARED WITH THE ASSISTANCE OF
THE WORKS PROGRESS ADMINISTRATION

RATES OF MALE JUVENILE DELINQUENTS, CHICAGO, 1917–23

the 7-year period, per 100 of the aged 10–16 male population in each of these areas as of 1920. The range of rates is from 0.8 to 19.4; the median for the series is 4.3 and the rate for the city, 5.4. Three areas have rates of less than 1.0, and a total of 19 areas less than 2.0. At the other extreme, 4 areas have rates of 15.0 or over, and 8 areas of 12.0 or over. In other words, 8 areas have rates of delinquents that are more than twelve times as great as those in 3 other areas, and more than six times as great as the rates in 19 other areas.

Map 11 reveals variations in the rates of delinquents quite similar to those of the previous series. The range between high- and low-rate areas is not so great, however; and the areas with high rates of delinquents extend only about 4 miles south from the Loop in the present series, as compared with 6 or 7 miles in 1927–33.

3. THE 1900–1906 JUVENILE COURT SERIES

Series Studied and Types of Offenses.—Third in this sequence is the series of 8,056 male delinquents brought into the Juvenile Court of Cook County from Chicago during 1900–1906 (the first 7 years of the Juvenile Court's existence). By comparing this series with that for 1927–33 it will be possible to determine the extent to which variations in the rates correspond and the extent to which changes in rates can be related to changes in the physical or social characteristics of the local areas.

The age distribution of the boys in the 1900–1906 series indicates that, on the whole, they were a little younger than those in the more recent series. At that time the upper age limit in the Juvenile Court was 15 instead of 16, and a somewhat larger number of boys were under 10 years of age (6.1 per cent). The highest frequencies were in ages 13, 14, and 15. With regard to offenses, it seems probable that some boys were taken to court in these earlier years on charges for which no petitions would be filed by the police probation officers at the present time. This is indicated both by the fact that the number of cases in court was greater in proportion to the population than at present and by the fact that the classification of offenses indicated a somewhat higher proportion of less serious charges.

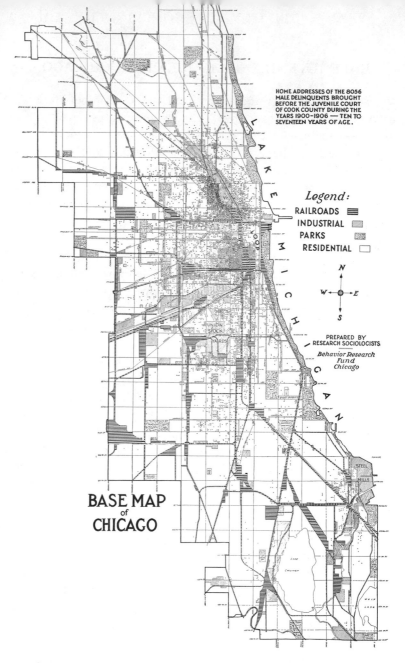

HOME ADDRESSES OF THE 8056
MALE DELINQUENTS BROUGHT
BEFORE THE JUVENILE COURT
OF COOK COUNTY DURING THE
YEARS 1900-1906 — TEN TO
SEVENTEEN YEARS OF AGE.

Legend:
RAILROADS
INDUSTRIAL
PARKS
RESIDENTIAL

N
W ← → E
S

PREPARED BY
RESEARCH SOCIOLOGISTS

*Behavior Research
Fund
Chicago*

BASE MAP
of
CHICAGO

LAKE MICHIGAN

UNION
STOCK
YARDS

STEEL
MILLS

LAKE
CALUMET

WOLF
LAKE

DISTRIBUTION OF MALE JUVENILE DELINQUENTS, CHICAGO, 1900–1906

MALE JUVENILE DELINQUENTS IN CHICAGO   65

Distribution of Delinquents.—Map 12 shows the distribution by home address of the 8,056 boys brought to court in the 7-year period 1900–1906. In this series, as in those previously discussed, it will be noted that a preponderance of the delinquent boys lived either in areas adjacent to the central business and industrial district or along the two forks of the Chicago River, Back of the Yards, or in South Chicago, with relatively few in other outlying areas.

While this series exhibits the same general configuration found in the others, there are two noticeable variations. First, the concentrations are somewhat more restricted and closer to the central business district and to the industrial centers than in the later series. This is to be expected, since many of the areas used for residential purposes in this early period have since been depopulated by expanding industry and commerce. Second, on this map there are relatively few delinquents in the areas east of State Street, south from the Loop. These areas, it will be remembered, contained many delinquents in the 1917–23 map and were also areas of heavy concentration in 1927–33.

Rates of Delinquents.—Map 13 shows the rates of delinquents in the 106 square-mile areas used for this 1900–1906 series. The population upon which these rates were calculated was secured by combining into 106 comparable areas the 1,200 enumeration districts of 1900 and the 431 census tracts of 1910 and computing the yearly increase or decrease of population in each. The population for the midyear of this series was then estimated from the aged 10–15 male population in 1910. The areas for which rates are presented are practically the same as those used in the 1917–23 juvenile court series, except that in 7 instances it was necessary to construct combinations of the 113 areas in order to secure a larger population in districts which were sparsely settled at that time.

The rates in this series range from 0.6 to 29.8. The median is 4.9 and the rate for the city as a whole 8.4. Four areas have rates of 20.0 and over; 7 have rates of 15.0 or over; and 12 have rates of 12.0 or over. At the other extreme, 3 areas have rates of less than 1.0, and 12 of less than 2.0.

MAP 13

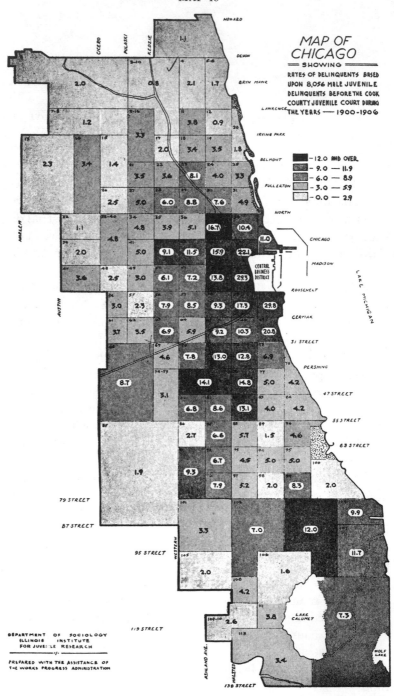

RATES OF MALE JUVENILE DELINQUENTS, CHICAGO, 1900–1906

Map 13 indicates that the variation in rates of delinquents is quite similar to the variations presented previously. The 4 areas with highest rates are all immediately adjacent to the Loop, and other high-rate areas are in the Stock Yards district and in South Chicago. The areas with low rates, on the other hand, are located, for the most part, near the city's periphery. As compared to rate maps for subsequent series, it can be seen that the areas with very high rates are somewhat more closely concentrated around the central business district. This is especially noticeable south from the Loop and east of State Street, where, after the first 2 miles, the rates of delinquents are below the average for the city as a whole.

4. COMPARISONS AMONG JUVENILE COURT SERIES (1927–33, 1917–23, AND 1900–1906)

Three methods will be employed to determine the extent to which the variations in rates of delinquents in the several time series correspond: (1) comparisons by zones, (2) area comparisons and correlations, and (3) extent of concentration.

Rates by Zones.—Rates of delinquents were calculated for each of 5 zones drawn at 2-mile intervals, with a focal point in the heart of the central business district. These rates were computed on the basis of the number of delinquents and the total aged 10–16 male population in each zone.[7]

It should be borne in mind that zone rates of delinquents are presented chiefly because of their theoretical value. They show the variations in rates more conceptually and idealistically than do the rates for smaller units. The number of zones used for this purpose is not important, as it is not assumed that there are actual zones in the city or sharp dividing lines between those presented. It is assumed, rather, that a more or less continuous variation exists between the rates of delinquents in the areas close to the center of the city and those outlying and that any arbitrary number of zones will exhibit this difference satisfactorily.

Inspection of the rate maps indicates that there are wide dif-

---

[7] When a square-mile area was divided by one of the concentric circles, the aged 10–16 population and the number of delinquents allocated to each zone corresponded to the proportion of the area which fell in each.

within each zone, just as there are among rates for census tracts within each square-mile area. These fluctuations do not greatly affect the general trend, however; in fact, it is because the zone rates eliminate the fluctuations evident for smaller areas and present the general tendencies that they are interesting and important.

Maps A, B, and C, Figure 1, show rates of delinquents by 5 complete zones, and also by the north and south halves of the city separately, for the three juvenile court series that have been presented. On the same figure are given the critical ratios between the rates in outer and inner zones, which are so great that clearly they could not be due to chance alone. The critical ratios for adjacent zones (not shown) are also statistically significant in every instance.

Area Comparisons and Correlations.—Of the 24 areas with the highest rates of delinquents in the 1927–33 series, 20 are among the 24 highest also in 1917–23. On the other hand, a few areas where significant changes took place in community characteristics show also marked changes in rates of delinquents. When the 1917–23 and 1927–33 rates are correlated by the 113 areas used for the earlier series the coefficient is found to be .70 ± .02. This coefficient is greatly reduced by the fact that the rates in 6 areas have changed so much that the points representing them fell entirely outside the line of scatter on the correlation sheet.

Most of the areas of high rates in the 1900–1906 series also correspond with those ranking highest in the two later series. Of the 12 highest in 1900–1906, 9 were among the 12 highest in 1927–33. Three of the 5 highest-rate areas in the latter series, but not in the former, are the same 3 found among the high-rate areas as of 1917–23. Although some new areas appear among those with high rates in the more recent series, it is significant to note that all 12 of the areas of highest rates in the 1900–1906 series are among the areas of high rates in 1927–33. Because of these areas, the correspondence between the series is even more clearly seen when comparisons involving a larger number of areas are made. Of the 25 areas with the highest rates of delinquents in the 1900–1906

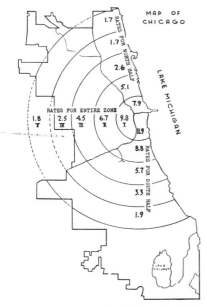

A. Zone rates of male juvenile delinquents, 1927–33 series

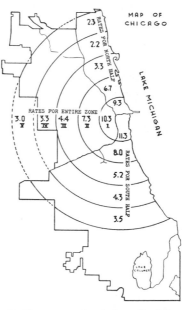

B. Zone rates of male juvenile delinquents, 1917–23 series

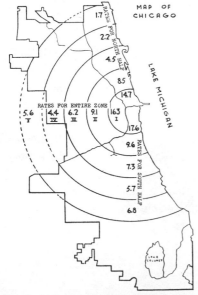

C. Zone rates of male juvenile delinquents, 1900–1906 series

CRITICAL RATIOS OF SELECTED ZONE RATES

Juvenile Court Series (Individuals)

Zones	Difference	Standard Error of the Difference	Critical Ratio
	A. 1927–33		
1 and 4.......	7.3	.301	24.2
1 and 5.......	8.0	.302	26.5
2 and 4.......	4.2	.142	29.6
2 and 5.......	4.9	.142	34.5
	B. 1917–23		
1 and 4.......	7.0	.293	23.9
1 and 5.......	7.3	.314	23.2
2 and 4.......	4.0	.162	24.7
2 and 5.......	4.3	.196	21.9
	C. 1900–1906		
1 and 4.......	11.9	.371	32.1
1 and 5.......	10.7	.467	22.9
2 and 4.......	4.7	.241	19.5
2 and 5.......	3.5	.371	9.4

series, 19 are included among the 25 highest in the 1917–23 series, and 18 among the 25 highest in 1927–33, even though these series are separated by approximately 2 and 3 decades, respectively. This is especially significant in view of the fact that the nationality composition of the population has changed completely in some of these neighborhoods.

A more general statement of the relationship is found when the rates in the 1900–1906 series are correlated with those for each of the other juvenile court series. To accomplish this, it was necessary to calculate rates in the two later juvenile court series for the same 106 areas used in the early series. The coefficient secured for 1900–1906 and 1917–23 was .85 ± .04, and that for 1900–1906 and 1927–33 was .61 ± .04. In the latter case the coefficient was reduced by the few values which fell far out of the line of scatter, indicating areas where considerable change had occurred.

These coefficients are remarkably high when it is recalled that the series are separated by about 20 and 30 years, respectively. They reveal that, in general, the areas of high rates of delinquents around 1900 were the high-rate areas also several decades later. This consistency reflects once more the operation of general processes of distribution and segregation in the life of the city.

Extent of Concentration.—The distribution of delinquents in relation to male population 10–16 years of age for each of the three juvenile court series has been further analyzed by dividing the population into four equal parts on the basis of the magnitude of rates of delinquents, then calculating the percentage of the total number of delinquents and total city area for each population quartile, as shown in Table 6.

It is apparent that the quarter of the population living in the areas of highest rates occupied only 19.2 per cent of the geographic area of the city in the 1927–33 series, 17.8 per cent in 1917–23, and 13.1 per cent in 1900–1906. Yet, in each instance this quarter of the population produced about one-half of the delinquents.

When the delinquents in each series, in turn, are divided into four equal parts according to magnitude of rate of delinquents and the corresponding distribution of population and city area is analyzed, the concentration of delinquents is again clearly evident (see Table 7).

TABLE 6

PERCENTAGE OF DELINQUENTS AND OF CITY AREA FOR QUARTILES
OF MALE POPULATION AGED 10–16, WHEN AREAS ARE RANKED
BY RATE OF DELINQUENTS: THREE JUVENILE COURT SERIES

QUARTILES OF POPULATION	PERCENTAGE OF DELINQUENTS			PERCENTAGE OF CITY AREA		
	1927–33	1917–23	1900–1906	1927–33	1917–23	1900–1906
Upper one-fourth, in high-rate areas......	54.3	46.1	47.3	19.2	17.8	13.1
Second one-fourth.....	23.9	27.3	26.6	19.4	24.8	12.1
Third one-fourth......	14.6	17.7	17.4	32.3	27.1	21.7
Lower one-fourth, in low-rate areas.......	7.2	8.9	8.7	29.1	30.3	53.1

TABLE 7

PERCENTAGE OF MALE POPULATION AGED 10–16 AND OF CITY AREA FOR
QUARTILES OF DELINQUENTS WHEN AREAS ARE RANKED BY RATE
OF DELINQUENTS: THREE JUVENILE COURT SERIES

QUARTILES OF DELINQUENTS	PERCENTAGE OF POPULATION			PERCENTAGE OF CITY AREA		
	1927–33	1917–23	1900–1906	1927–33	1917–23	1900–1906
Upper one-fourth, from high-rate areas......	7.7	10.9	10.6	5.5	6.0	3.7
Second one-fourth.....	13.8	12.1	16.6	8.6	11.1	10.1
Third one-fourth......	24.3	29.0	24.1	22.0	27.4	17.8
Lower one-fourth, from low-rate areas.......	54.2	48.0	48.7	63.9	55.5	68.4

Table 7 shows that the upper quarter of the delinquents, living in high-rate areas, represented only 7.7 per cent of the population in the 1927–33 series, 10.9 per cent as of 1917–23, and 10.6 per cent in 1900–1906; and occupied respectively only 5.5, 6.0, and 3.7 per cent of the total city area. At the opposite extreme, the one-fourth of the delinquents in the areas of lowest rates came

in 1927–33, 48 per cent of the population and 55.5 per cent of the area a decade earlier, and 48.7 per cent of the population and 68.4 per cent of the area in 1900–1906.

This section is concerned with the least inclusive enumeration of delinquent boys in Chicago, namely, those committed to correctional institutions by the Juvenile Court of Cook County. Three series will be presented: (1) the 1927–33 commitment series, (2) the 1917–23 commitment series, and (3) the 1900–1906 commitment series.

As has been noted, roughly two-fifths of the boys taken to the Juvenile Court on delinquency petition are ultimately committed to correctional institutions. Since these series cover the same periods as the juvenile court delinquency series, it follows that they will contain only about two-fifths as many boys. On the other hand, these boys committed to institutions are the most serious delinquents known to the court. Most of them are recidivists, since few boys are committed on their first appearance, and some have served time previously in institutions for delinquents.

The graphic presentation of these commitment series will be limited to rate maps and zone maps.

1. THE 1927–33 COMMITMENT SERIES

This series includes 2,593 individuals committed by the Juvenile Court to correctional institutions during the 7-year period 1927–33. The majority of these boys had committed serious offenses and were recidivists. With respect to age they were, on the whole, somewhat above the average for boys appearing in the Juvenile Court.

Distribution.—When distributed by home address, wide areal variations are found in the number of committed delinquents. There were 7 areas from which more than 90 boys were committed. At the other extreme, no delinquents were committed from 3 areas, and 1 boy only from each of 9 others, while not more than 2 boys were committed from each of 19 areas.

MALE JUVENILE DELINQUENTS IN CHICAGO   73

Rates.—Map 14 shows the rate of committed delinquents in each of the 140 areas. These are 7-year rates, as were those in the corresponding juvenile court series, and calculated by the same method, on the basis of the same population. They represent in each area, therefore, the number of boys committed in a 7-year period per 100 of the aged 10–16 male population as of 1930. To distinguish them from the rates of juvenile court delinquents, these will be referred to as "rates of commitments" or "rates of committed delinquents."

Although the separate rates in this series are low because of the relatively small number of committed delinquents, the variation is even greater than in the juvenile court series. The range is from 0.0 to 9.2, the median is 0.7, and the rate for the city as a whole is 1.3. Three areas have rates of 7.0 or over, and 6 of 5.0 or over. At the other extreme, 3 areas have rates of 0.0, and 12 of 0.1 or less.

Map 14 reveals the same general configuration that was found in the juvenile court series. The areas with highest commitment rates surround the Loop and extend directly south, with relatively high rates also in the Stock Yards areas, near the Southwest manufacturing district, and in South Chicago. Low-rate areas, on the other hand, are to be noted in the outlying districts.

2. THE 1917–23 COMMITMENT SERIES

The second series of committed delinquents includes the 2,639 Chicago boys committed to institutions by the Juvenile Court of Cook County during the 7-year period 1917–23. Since the boys in this series appeared in the 1917–23 juvenile court series and were committed, they include the most serious delinquents known to the court for this period.

Distribution.—When these committed delinquents were tabulated on the basis of the 113 areas into which the city was divided for this series, it was found that there were 3 areas from each of which more than 50 boys had been committed, 6 with 1 commitment, and 14 with less than 5 commitments each.

Rates.—When rates of committed delinquents were calculated, it was found that the range extended from 0.1 to 6.9. The median

MAP 14

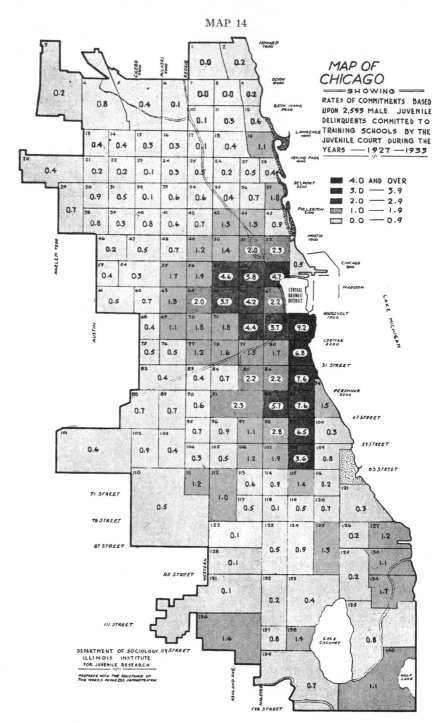

RATES OF COMMITTED DELINQUENTS, CHICAGO, 1927–33

area rate for the series is 1.2, and the rate for the city 1.8. Four areas have rates of 5.0 or over, and 17 of 3.0 or more; while at the lower end of the range 14 areas have rates under 0.5, and 46 of less than 1.0. Map 15 shows clearly that the geographic distribution and variation of rates in this series closely resemble the two series previously presented.

3. THE 1900–1906 COMMITMENT SERIES

This series includes the 3,224 boys committed to correctional schools during the first 7 years of the existence of the Juvenile Court (1900–1906), out of the total number included in the corresponding juvenile court series.

Distribution.—When distributed by home address, wide variations were found among the 106 areas into which Chicago was divided for this early series. More than 150 boys were committed from each of 3 areas, and more than 100 from each of 8. At the other extreme, only 3 boys were committed from each of 8 areas, and 2 from each of 4; while 10 areas showed 1 commitment each, and 2 areas none.

Rates.—The rates of committed delinquents range from 0.0 to 12.5, the median is 1.7, and the rate for the city as a whole 3.4. Six areas have rates under 0.5, and 26 under 1.0. Four areas, on the other hand, have rates above 9.0, and 10 above 6.0. Map 16 shows the configuration.

4. COMPARISONS AMONG COMMITMENT SERIES

The extent to which the variations in rates of committed delinquents correspond for the three time series will be stated in terms of zone comparisons, area comparisons and correlations, and extent of concentration.

Rates by Zones.—Since the rates in these three series of committed delinquents are based on smaller samples than were those for the juvenile court delinquency series, the variations are somewhat less regular. When zone rates are calculated, however, these irregularities are smoothed out and the general trends revealed. As Maps *A*, *B*, and *C*, Figure 2, show, these trends based on juvenile court commitments correspond closely to the trends based on rates of all individuals brought before the court (see Fig. 1).

MAP 15

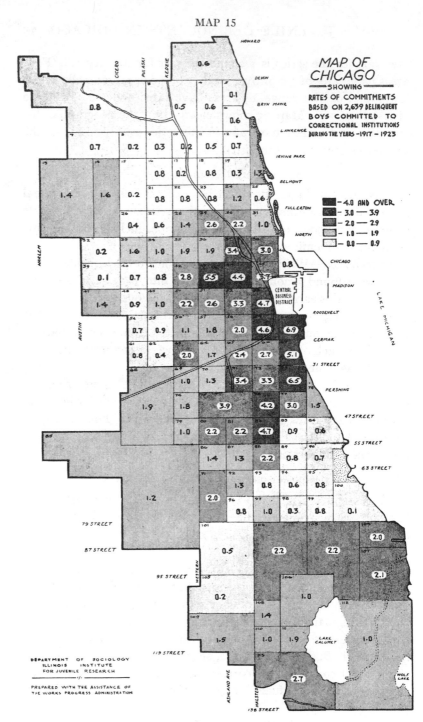

RATES OF COMMITTED DELINQUENTS, CHICAGO, 1917–23

MAP 16

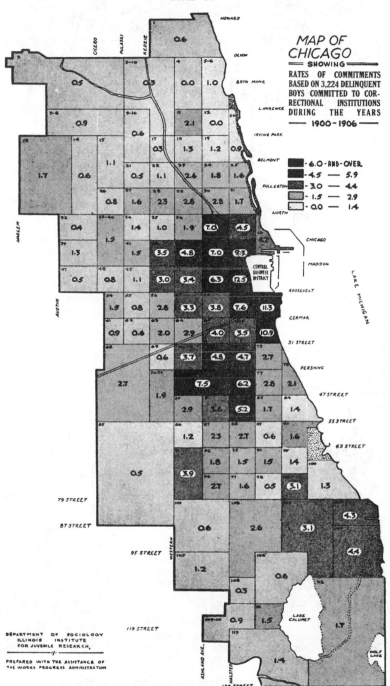

MAP OF
CHICAGO
═ SHOWING ═
RATES OF COMMITMENTS
BASED ON 3,224 DELINQUENT
BOYS COMMITTED TO COR-
RECTIONAL INSTITUTIONS
DURING THE YEARS
─ 1900-1906 ─

- 6.0 - AND - OVER
- 4.5 — 5.9
- 3.0 — 4.4
- 1.5 — 2.9
- 0.0 — 1.4

RATES OF COMMITTED DELINQUENTS, CHICAGO, 1900–1906

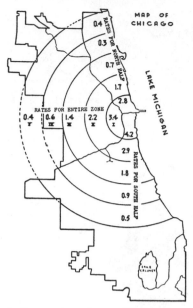

A. Zone rates of committed delinquents, 1927–33 series

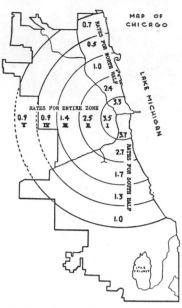

B. Zone rates of committed delinquents, 1917–23 series

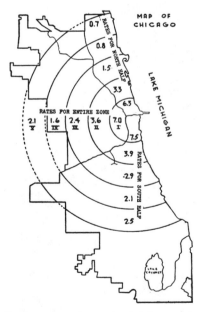

C. Zone rates of committed delinquents, 1900–1906 series

CRITICAL RATIOS OF SELECTED ZONE RATES
Commitment Series

Zones	Difference	Standard Error of the Difference	Critical Ratio
	A. 1927–33		
I and 4.......	2.8	.182	15.4
I and 5.......	3.0	.182	16.5
2 and 4.......	1.6	..080	20.0
2 and 5.......	1.8	.079	22.8
	B. 1917–23		
I and 4.......	2.6	.176	14.8
I and 5.......	2.6	.186	14.0
2 and 4.......	1.6	.095	16.8
2 and 5.......	1.6	.113	14.2
	C. 1900–1906		
I and 4.......	5.4	.250	21.6
I and 5.......	4.9	.306	16.0
2 and 4.......	2.0	.151	13.2
2 and 5.......	1.5	.233	6.4

FIG. 2.—Zone maps for three series of committed delinquents

In the 1927–33 series the city rates vary from 3.4 in Zone I to 0.4 in Zone V, a decrease of 88 per cent, as compared with a drop of nearly 75 per cent in the 1917–23 series and of 70 per cent for the 1900–1906 data.

The zone rates for the north and south halves of the city also exhibit variations corresponding to those in the broader delinquency series. As indicated previously, the South Chicago industrial district constitutes a new locus from which, in turn, analysis might be made on a zonal basis.

Area Comparisons and Correlations.—The same general configuration of rates is seen for 1900–1906 as has been noted for the two other series. The most important difference is in the areas south from the Loop. In 1900–1906, it will be seen, only the first 2 areas to the south are characterized by high rates; whereas in the 1917–23 series the rates are high in the first 4 areas, and in 1927–33 these areas of high rates extend southward 6 or 7 miles.

When the 1917–23 and 1927–33 series are compared, it is found that of the 25 areas with the highest rates in the former series, 20 are included among the 25 highest a decade later. As in the juvenile court delinquency series, 3 of the 5 areas among the highest in 1927–33, but not in the earlier series, are areas where marked changes in community characteristics have occurred.

When the rates of delinquents in the 113 areas of the 1917–23 series are correlated with the corresponding rates for 1927–33, $r = .74 \pm .03$. For 1927–33 and 1900–1906, by 106 areas, the coefficient is $.66 \pm .04$; and for 1917–23 and 1900–1906 it is $.81 \pm .02$.

Extent of Concentration.—The concentration of committed delinquents in each series has been analyzed by ranking the areas by rate of committed delinquents, then dividing the aged 10–16 male population into four equal parts and computing the proportion of total committed delinquents and of city area for each population quartile (see Table 8).

It will be noted that more than half of the committed delinquents in each of the three series come from the quarter of the population living in areas of highest rates, although these constitute less than one-fifth of the total city area. At the other extreme, the quarter of the population in lowest-rate areas produced 7.3 per cent of the committed delinquents in 1900–1906, 7.2 per cent in the 1917–23 series, and only 4.3 per cent during 1927–33.

TABLE 8

PERCENTAGE OF COMMITTED DELINQUENTS AND OF CITY AREA FOR QUAR-
TILES OF MALE POPULATION AGED 10–16, WHEN AREAS ARE RANKED BY
RATE OF COMMITTED DELINQUENTS: THREE COMMITMENT SERIES

QUARTILES OF POPULATION	PERCENTAGE OF COMMITTED DELINQUENTS			PERCENTAGE OF CITY AREA		
	1927–33	1917–23	1900–1906	1927–33	1917–23	1900–1906
Upper' one-fourth, in high-rate areas......	62.1	51.1	50.2	18.3	19.6	9.1
Second one-fourth.....	22.1	27.1	25.8	21.2	18.1	12.9
Third one-fourth......	11.5	14.6	16.7	30.8	33.1	26.0
Lower one-fourth, in low-rate areas.......	4.3	7.2	7.3	29.7	29.2	52.0

TABLE 9

PERCENTAGE OF MALE POPULATION AGED 10–16 AND OF CITY AREA FOR QUAR-
TILES OF COMMITTED DELINQUENTS WHEN AREAS ARE RANKED BY RATE
OF COMMITTED DELINQUENTS: THREE COMMITMENT SERIES

QUARTILES OF COMMITTED DELINQUENTS	PERCENTAGE OF POPULATION			PERCENTAGE OF CITY AREA		
	1927–33	1917–23	1900–1906	1927–33	1917–23	1900–1906
Upper one-fourth, from high-rate areas......	5.5	9.1	9.6	4.3	6.2	4.4
Second one-fourth.....	10.6	15.0	15.3	6.8	10.8	4.7
Third one-fourth......	21.7	22.0	24.0	14.3	15.0	12.5
Lower one-fourth, from low-rate areas.......	62.2	53.9	51.1	74.6	68.0	78.4

This concentration is again evident when the total number of committed boys in each series is divided into quartiles according to rate of committed delinquents and the corresponding percentages of population and of city area are computed (see Table 9).

It will be seen from Table 9 that the one-fourth of the committed boys living in high-rate areas represented less than 10 per cent of the population and 7 per cent of the city area, in each time series. On the other hand, the one-fourth in lowest-rate areas came from more than 51 per cent of the population and 68 per cent or over of the city area. Both tables show the greatest concentration in the 1927–33 series.

C. THE DISTRIBUTION OF POLICE ARRESTS

The third, and most inclusive, basic enumeration of delinquents or alleged delinquents and index of the number of boys engaged in officially proscribed activity in Chicago includes all boys dealt with by the juvenile police probation officers, one of whom is assigned to each police station. Most of the boys charged with delinquencies are brought to the attention of these officers, who decide whether the boy is to be dismissed with a warning or taken into court. In considering the seriousness of the offenses charged, it should be borne in mind that in some court systems all the boys in these series would be taken to court, although in Chicago only about 15 per cent have delinquency petitions filed against them.

Since no permanent official record is made of these police cases, it has not been possible to study their distribution over widely separated periods of time. The following series, however, will be presented: (1) the 1931 police series, (2) the 1927 police series, and (3) the 1926 police series. These series will be analyzed in less detail than those preceding, as it is necessary only to determine the extent to which the findings agree.

I. THE 1931 POLICE SERIES

This series includes the boys whose names and addresses appeared in the records of the police probation officers during 1931. They were, as a group, somewhat younger than the boys taken into court, about 30 per cent being under 13 years. A rough classification of the offenses charged indicates that stealing; shoplifting; snatching pocketbooks; stealing automobiles; breaking into stores, residences, or factories; and similar offenses accounted for approximately half the total. The remaining half of the boys were charged with a variety of offenses, including truancy from home, assault, malicious mischief, destruction of property, trespassing, manslaughter, and sex immorality.

Distribution.—When these cases were plotted by home address, the resulting configuration was quite similar to that in the 1927–33 juvenile court series (see Map 7). Analysis on the basis of 140 square-mile areas shows that 2 areas contain over 300, and 13 areas over 200, boys each. At the other extreme, fewer than 20 boys appear in each of 18 areas.

Rates.—Rates of police arrests were likewise calculated, by areas, on the basis of the 1930 aged 10–16 male population. These are 1-year rates and may be conveniently thought of as the percentage of all boys who were arrested during the year. The range of rates is from 0.5 to 19.4. The city rate is 5.4, and the median 4.0. The rate map for this series has been omitted because it closely resembles those previously presented.

Zone rates.—The variation in police cases from the center of the city outward is indicated by zone rates calculated for the same zones used in the other series. These are shown in Figure 3, *A*. Here, again, regular decreases in the rates are to be noted as distance from the Loop increases, for the two halves of the city considered separately and for both together. As in the other series, the South Side rates are considerably higher than those for corresponding zones on the North Side.

2. THE 1927 POLICE SERIES

The second police series comprises the 8,951 boys who appeared in the records of the police probation officers during 1927. With respect to age and offense, these boys were not widely different from those in the 1931 series. Approximately 55 per cent were charged with some form of stealing.

Distribution.—The configuration resulting from the plotting of these cases on the map by home address is similar to that in the other series. Of the 113 square-mile areas, 15 contained fewer than 10 arrested boys, as compared with 12 which contained over 250 each.

Rates.—A rate was calculated for each local area on the basis of the estimated aged 10–16 male population for 1927. The range of rates is from 0.0 to 21.8, the median being 3.4, and the city rate 4.9.

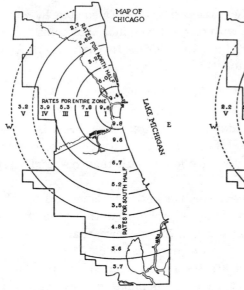

A. Zone rates of police arrests, 1931

B. Zone rates of police arrests, 1927

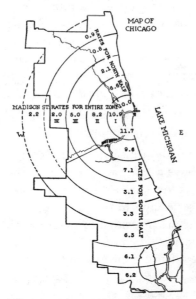

C. Zone rates of police arrests, 1926

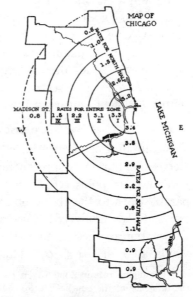

D. Zone rates of juvenile court police records, 1935

FIG. 3.—Zone maps for police-arrests series

Zone Rates.—As in the 1931 series, rates calculated by zones show a regular decrease, with one or two minor exceptions,[8] from the central business district outward, for the two halves of the city separately and for both together (see Fig. 3, *B*).

3. THE 1926 POLICE SERIES

The third police series includes the 9,243 individual Chicago boys whose names and addresses appeared in the records of the juvenile police probation officers during 1926. They correspond closely, as to age and type of offense, with the 1931 and 1927 series.

Distribution.—With regard to distribution by home address, the configuration in this series is likewise similar to that of the previous series. Of the 113 local areas, 12 contain fewer than 10 arrested boys each, whereas 14 areas have more than 200 each.

Rates.—Rates of police arrests were calculated by square-mile areas on the basis of the aged 10–16 population as estimated for 1926. The range of area rates is from 0.0 to 26.6, with a median of 3.4 and a city rate of 5.2. In each of 5 areas the rate is over 20.0, and in 5 additional areas it is between 15.0 and 20.0. At the other extreme, the rate is under 1.0 in 17 areas. In general, the distribution of high- and low-rate areas shows no noticeable variation from the series already presented.

Zone Rates.—The decrease in rates of police arrests from the center of the city outward is indicated by Figure 3, *C*.

4. RECREATION SURVEY STUDY

A computation of rates based on data furnished by the Chicago Recreation Survey,[9] representing boys whose names appear in the juvenile court police records for 1935, revealed a distribution comparable both to the above police series and to the juvenile court series already analyzed. Zone rates are presented in Figure 3, *D*. Correlation of these data with the 1927–33 rates of delinquents yields an *r* of .84 ± .02. This evidence from an independent

[8] The higher rate in Zone VI on the South Side, for all these series, indicates the influence of the South Chicago industrial district.

[9] *Private Recreation* ("Chicago Recreation Survey," Vol. III) (Chicago: Chicago Recreation Commission, 1938). This survey was conducted under the direction of Professor Arthur J. Todd, of Northwestern University.

source constitutes an additional index of delinquent activity in Chicago and tends to strengthen the conclusions drawn.

5. COMPARISONS AMONG POLICE SERIES

Correlation.—Nineteen of the 25 areas with highest rates in 1927 and 18 of the highest in 1926 are included among the first 25 in 1931. Correlation between the 1927 and 1931 series yields an *r* of .87 ± .01, and the corresponding correlation for 1926 and 1931 results in a coefficient of .83 ± .02. The correlation between the 1926 and 1927 series is much closer. The 12 areas of highest rates for these 2 years are the same, and the coefficient secured when the two series are correlated is .96 ± .005.

TABLE 10

PERCENTAGE OF POLICE ARRESTS AND OF CITY AREA FOR QUARTILES OF
MALE POPULATION AGED 10–16, WHEN AREAS ARE RANKED BY
RATE OF POLICE ARRESTS: THREE POLICE SERIES

QUARTILES OF POPULATION	PERCENTAGE OF POLICE ARRESTS			PERCENTAGE OF CITY AREA		
	1931	1927	1926	1931	1927	1926
Upper one-fourth, in high-rate areas......	49.0	58.9	59.8	18.6	20.2	23.9
Second one-fourth.....	25.7	26.2	26.1	20.5	35.4	25.8
Third one-fourth......	16.2	11.8	10.3	29.2	17.9	18.4
Lower one-fourth, in low-rate areas.......	9.1	3.1	3.8	21.7	20.5	31.9

Extent of Concentration in Juvenile Police Arrests.—The residential concentration of boys arrested by the police can be readily seen when their distribution is analyzed in relation to that of the total aged 10–16 male population. As in the previous series, the square-mile areas were arranged in rank order on the basis of the rate of police arrests. The population was then divided into four equal parts and the percentage of police arrests and of total city area was calculated for each population quartile (see Table 10).

Table 10 indicates to what extent the distribution of alleged delinquents arrested differs from that of the population. Thus, the one-fourth of the aged 10–16 male population living in the areas of highest rates produced 49.0 per cent of the delinquents in the

1931 series, 58.9 per cent in 1927, and 59.8 per cent in 1926; while
the one-fourth living in areas of lowest rates produced only 9.1,
3.1, and 3.8 per cent of the delinquents, respectively.

The absolute differences among percentages in these three series
should not be taken as proof of a trend in the distribution of delinquents. Such variations might be due to changes in policy in
some police districts, to the fact that the population base for the
1926 and 1927 series was estimated, or to a variety of other factors. The important point is that, in spite of minor variations, all
three series present the same general features.

TABLE 11

PERCENTAGE OF MALE POPULATION AGED 10–16 AND OF CITY AREA
FOR QUARTILES OF POLICE ARRESTS WHEN AREAS ARE RANKED
BY RATE OF POLICE ARRESTS: THREE POLICE SERIES

QUARTILES OF POLICE ARRESTS	PERCENTAGE OF POPULATION			PERCENTAGE OF CITY AREA		
	1931	1927	1926	1931	1927	1926
Upper one-fourth, from high-rate areas......	9.6	7.1	7.0	6.8	6.7	5.8
Second one-fourth.....	16.2	12.2	11.7	12.2	8.6	13.6
Third one-fourth......	24.6	19.1	18.1	20.5	17.6	17.4
Lower one-fourth, from low-rate areas.......	49.6	61.6	63.2	60.5	67.1	63.2

Table 11 shows the percentages of population and of city area
for each quartile of the delinquents when the latter are grouped
according to magnitude of the rate of police arrests. It will be
noted that the one-quarter of the delinquents from the highest-
rate areas represented only 9.6 per cent of the population in the
1931 series, 7.1 per cent in the 1927 series, and 7.0 per cent in the
1926 series; while the one-quarter of the delinquents in the low-
rate areas came from 49.6, 61.6, and 63.2 per cent of the population in the 1931, 1927, and 1926 series, respectively.

In each series, likewise, the upper one-fourth of the delinquents
came from less than 7 per cent of the total city area, while the
lower one-fourth represented more than 60 per cent of the city
area.

D. TYPES OF SERIES COMPARED

Up to this point the only correlations presented have been be-- tween series of the same general type—that is, between two juvenile court series or between one commitment series and another. Although these represent different periods, the correlations are sufficiently high to indicate that rates of delinquents in Chicago have remained relatively constant over a long period of time.

The present section concerns the relationship between the findings as revealed by the different types of series covering the same period of time. Correlation of the three juvenile court series with the corresponding commitment series yielded the following results:

1927–33　juvenile court series and
1927–33　commitment series............ $r = .97 \pm .01$

1917–23　juvenile court series and
1917–23　commitment series............ $r = .96 \pm .01$

1900–1906 juvenile court series and
1900–1906 commitment series............ $r = .97 \pm .01$

A close relationship is likewise indicated by the fact that 23 out of the 25 areas with highest rates in each juvenile court series are among the 25 highest also in the corresponding commitment series.

When the police series were correlated with contemporary juvenile court and commitment data, the following coefficients were secured:

1927–33 juvenile court series and
1931 police series....................... $r = .81 \pm .02$

1927–33 commitment series and
1931 police series....................... $r = .86 \pm .01$

1917–23 juvenile court series and
1927 police series....................... $r = .85 \pm .02$

1917–23 commitment series and
1927 police series....................... $r = .86 \pm .02$

1917–23 juvenile court series and
1926 police series....................... $r = .85 \pm .02$

1917–23 commitment series and
1926 police series....................... $r = .86 \pm .02$

Further comparisons are possible through analysis of the variations in zone rates for the several series. Here the rate in Zone I
in each series has been taken as a base, and the rates for successive zones are expressed as percentages of this base (see Table
12).

When proportionate values in Zone V are compared, it is clear
that rates for the three commitment series have decreased more

TABLE 12

RELATIVE RATES BY ZONES: JUVENILE COURT SERIES
COMMITMENT SERIES, AND POLICE SERIES
(Rate in Zone I = 100)

SERIES	ZONES				
	I	II	III	IV	V
Juvenile Court:					
1927–33..........	100	68.4	45.9	25.5	18.4
1917–23..........	100	70.1	42.7	32.0	29.1
1900–1906........	100	55.8	38.0	27.0	34.3
Commitment:					
1927–33..........	100	64.7	41.2	17.6	11.8
1917–23..........	100	71.4	40.0	25.7	25.7
1900–1906........	100	51.4	34.3	22.9	30.0
Police:					
1931.............	100	81.3	55.2	40.6	33.3
1927.............	100	78.8	43.4	24.2	22.2
1926.............	100	75.2	45.9	18.3	20.2

sharply than those for the corresponding juvenile court series.
The drop in rates for two of the three police series is also greater
than the decrease in the juvenile court series for 1927–33 and
1917–23.

On the basis of the above facts, several deductions as to the
relative usefulness of the different types of series can be made. It
is evident, first, that the findings in the three types are so similar
that any one of them might be used as an index of the others. The
juvenile court series, however, show somewhat less concentration
and variation in rates than either the police or commitment series.

They are less inclusive than the police series, yet not limited to the serious offenders comprising the committed group; and they presumably represent, therefore, a conservative sample of the boys engaging in officially proscribed activity throughout the city. It is the authors' conclusion that, where a single set of data must serve, juvenile court series may be used safely as an index of this broader universe.

CHAPTER IV

DISTRIBUTION OF OTHER COMMUNITY
PROBLEMS IN CHICAGO

JUVENILE delinquency is commonly thought of as indicating some degree of pathology within a community. It is by definition a departure from a behavior code or norm approved by the larger society, even when representing, for the child concerned, conformity to the standards of his immediate social group or groups. The conventional civic and law-enforcing bodies therefore consider delinquency a social problem requiring more or less constant attention to achieve any reduction in the rate.

Many other "problem" conditions might be listed, each representing a state of affairs considered undesirable by most citizens. These would include various forms of unemployment, dependency, misconduct, and family disorganization, as well as high rates of sickness and death. It may be asked: Do these other phenomena exhibit any correspondence among themselves and with rates of boys brought into court? In answering this question, five sets of data have been selected for comparison. Rates of school truants and of young adult offenders will be presented by communities, as well as rates of infant mortality, tuberculosis, and mental disorder.

Rates of School Truants.—Maps 17 and 18 show the distribution and rates of male school truants in the 140 square-mile areas in Chicago, based on the geographical distribution of 3,653 boys brought into the Juvenile Court of Cook County from Chicago on truancy petition during the 7-year period 1927–33 and on the aged 10–16 male population as of 1930. The range of area rates is from 0.0 to 11.4; the median is 1.1; and the rate for the city as a whole, 1.8.

It is evident from the general configuration shown that the variations in rates of truants are quite similar to those for delinquents. When the rates in this series are correlated with those

MAP 17

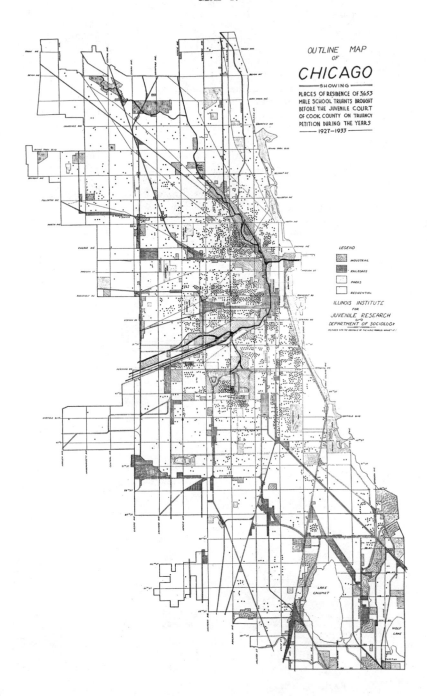

OUTLINE MAP
OF
CHICAGO
SHOWING
PLACES OF RESIDENCE OF 3,653
MALE SCHOOL TRUANTS BROUGHT
BEFORE THE JUVENILE COURT
OF COOK COUNTY ON TRUANCY
PETITION DURING THE YEARS
1927–1933

LEGEND
INDUSTRIAL
RAILROADS
PARKS
RESIDENTIAL

ILLINOIS INSTITUTE
FOR
JUVENILE RESEARCH
DEPARTMENT OF SOCIOLOGY

DISTRIBUTION OF SCHOOL TRUANTS (MALE), CHICAGO, 1927–33

MAP 18

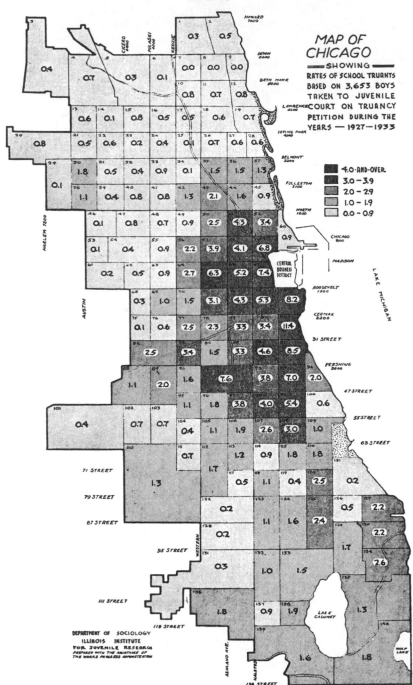

MAP OF
CHICAGO
═══ SHOWING ═══
RATES OF SCHOOL TRUANTS
BASED ON 3,653 BOYS
TAKEN TO JUVENILE
COURT ON TRUANCY
PETITION DURING THE
YEARS — 1927—1933

4.0-AND-OVER
3.0 – 3.9
2.0 – 2.9
1.0 – 1.9
0.0 – 0.9

DEPARTMENT OF SOCIOLOGY
ILLINOIS INSTITUTE
FOR JUVENILE RESEARCH
PREPARED WITH THE ASSISTANCE OF
THE WORKS PROGRESS ADMINISTRATION

RATES OF SCHOOL TRUANTS (MALE), CHICAGO, 1927–33

of delinquents in the 1927–33 juvenile court series, the coefficient is .89 ± .01. When the rates for a comparable series of school truants—5,159 boys brought into the Juvenile Court on truancy petition between 1917 and 1927—are correlated with the rates of delinquents in the 1917–23 series, the coefficient is .80 ± .02. If the correspondence noted is analyzed by classes of areas, the association is even more apparent. The comparison between these two rates of truants and the corresponding rates of delinquents and commitments is presented in Table 13.[1] Figure 4, *A* and *B*, shows graphically the relation between rates of truants and of delinquents.

Rates of Young Adult Offenders.—Rates of boys' court offenders were calculated for each of the 140 square-mile areas, representing the number of males 17–20 years of age brought into the Chicago Boys' Court[2] during the year 1938, per 100 boys of the same age in the area, as of 1934. These rates and the distribution on which they are based are shown on Maps 19 and 20. The range of rates is from 0.0 in Area 8 to 20.5 in Area 93, with 213 cases. The median is 2.5, and the rate for the city as a whole 3.6. As in most of

---

[1] The difference in the number of truants in the 1930 and 1920 series cannot be taken as a basis for the conclusion that there was less truancy in Chicago in 1930 than in 1920. At least two factors enter into this difference. First, the rates based on the 1920 census represent more years. Second, changes in administrative policy may result in variation in the proportion of school truants against whom petitions are filed. This problem of the absolute number of truants in the different series does not concern us here, since we are interested in an index of the distribution of truancy rather than in an attempt to measure this type of behavior.

[2] The Chicago Boys' Court has jurisdiction over male offenders 17–20 years of age. About 12 per cent of the individuals in this series were dealt with in the Automobile Court, another branch of the Municipal Court of Chicago. For our purposes, however, the series will be designated as the "boys' court series."

The distribution of young adult offenders can be studied more profitably than the distribution of older criminals. Most of the boys included in the two series of boys' court offenders were living in their own homes with their families at the time they were brought to court. Their distribution, therefore, represents quite accurately the area in which they became offenders, or, in terms of probability, the areas where boys are most likely to become adult offenders. In contrast, the distribution of older criminals does not represent necessarily the areas in which the criminal behavior is developed. If they have been successful in the criminal world, they may live in the better residential communities; if not, they may be segregated in rooming-houses or areas of homeless men.

MAP 19

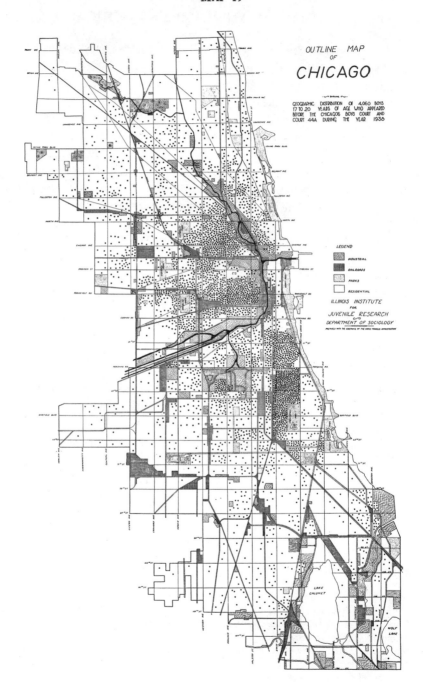

OUTLINE MAP
OF

CHICAGO

GEOGRAPHIC DISTRIBUTION OF 4,060 BOYS
17 TO 20 YEARS OF AGE WHO APPEARED
BEFORE THE CHICAGO'S BOYS COURT AND
COURT 44A DURING THE YEAR 1938

LEGEND

INDUSTRIAL
RAILROADS
PARKS
RESIDENTIAL

ILLINOIS INSTITUTE
FOR
JUVENILE RESEARCH
AND
DEPARTMENT OF SOCIOLOGY

DISTRIBUTION OF BOYS' COURT OFFENDERS, CHICAGO, 1938

the delinquency series, the distribution is sharply skewed, with
the value of the median rate close to the lower end of the range
and with very high rates in a relatively small number of areas.
For the most part, the areas with high rates are those in which
rates of delinquents and school truants also are high.

TABLE 13

RATES OF MALE JUVENILE DELINQUENTS AND
COMMITMENTS FOR AREAS GROUPED BY RATE
OF TRUANTS: 1927–33 AND 1917–23 JUVENILE
COURT SERIES

Rates of Truants 1927–33	Rate of Delinquents 1927–33	Rate of Commitments 1927–33
4.0 and over (5.4)*......	11.4	4.1
3.0–3.9 (3.4)*......	7.0	2.5
2.0–2.9 (2.3)*......	5.1	1.4
1.0–1.9 (1.5)*......	3.0	0.9
0.0–0.9 (0.5)*......	2.1	0.5

Rates of Truants 1917–27	Rate of Delinquents 1917–23	Rate of Commitments 1917–23
8.0 and over (10.1)*.....	11.9	4.1
6.0–7.9 (6.5)*.....	8.6	3.0
4.0–5.9 (4.5)*.....	7.0	2.2
2.0–3.9 (3.0)*.....	5.5	1.7
0.0–1.9 (1.1)*.....	2.9	0.8

* Rate for class as a whole.

When these boys' court rates are correlated with rates of delinquents in the 1927–33 juvenile court series, the coefficient is
.90 ± .01. A comparable series of rates, based on 6,398 male offenders charged with more serious types of misconduct and
brought before the Boys' Court during the years 1924–26, were
correlated with the rates of delinquents in the 1917–23 series.
This coefficient is .90 ± .01.

Similarity in distribution is again indicated when the boys'
court rates are correlated with the rates of truants. Correlation

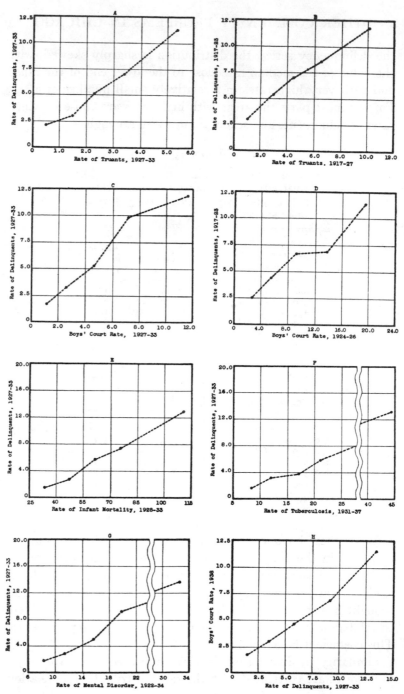

FIG. 4.—Relationship between rates of juvenile delinquents and other community problems.

MAP 20

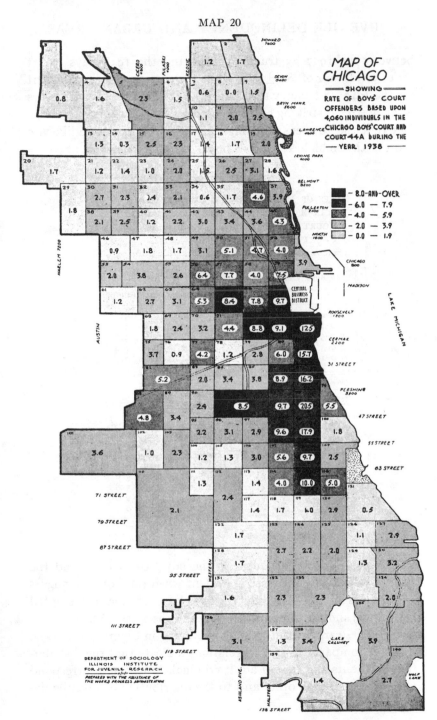

RATES OF BOYS' COURT OFFENDERS, CHICAGO, 1938

between the 1927–33 truancy series and the 1938 boys' court series yields an r of .84 ± .02, while the corresponding coefficient for the 1917–27 truancy series and the 1924–26 boys' court series is .95 ± .01. A striking correspondence in this series is seen in the fact that the 16 areas with highest rates of truants are likewise those with the highest rates of boys' court offenders.

TABLE 14

RATES OF MALE JUVENILE DELINQUENTS AND OF
SCHOOL TRUANTS FOR AREAS GROUPED BY BOYS'
COURT RATE: 1927–33 AND 1917–23 JUVENILE
COURT SERIES

Boys' Court Rates 1938	Rate of Delinquents 1927–33	Rate of Truants 1927–33
8.0 and over (11.7)*....	12.0	5.2
6.0–7.9 (7.2)*....	9.9	4.1
4.0–5.9 (4.7)*....	5.3	2.6
2.0–3.9 (2.7)*....	3.2	1.4
0.0–1.9 (1.3)*....	1.7	0.5

Boys' Court Rates 1924–26	Rate of Delinquents 1917–23	Rate of Truants 1917–27
16.0 and over (19.7)*....	11.2	8.6
12.0–15.9 (13.9)*....	6.8	5.6
8.0–11.9 (9.2)*....	6.5	3.8
4.0– 7.9 (5.6)*....	4.3	2.0
0.0– 3.9 (2.8)*....	2.5	0.9

* Rate for class as a whole.

The close association between the boys' court rates and the rates of delinquents likewise is evident when rates of delinquents and truants are calculated for the five classes of areas represented on Map 19 and for comparable classes in the 1924–26 boys' court series. These are presented in Table 14 and in Figure 4, C and D.

These comparisons and correlations indicate that the distribution of truants and that of adult criminals in Chicago correspond very closely to each other and to the distribution of juvenile delinquents.[3] As will be shown in chapter v, a large proportion of the school truants against whom petitions are filed subsequently become juvenile delinquents, and a good proportion of the delinquents have at some time in their career been truants. Just as truancy may be an indication of the beginning of a delinquent career, so a delinquent career often is the training school for adult crime.

Infant Mortality.—Rates of infant mortality, tuberculosis, and insanity or mental disorder in Chicago are not available for the 140 areas used for presentation of the delinquency data. Rates of infant mortality and mental disorder will be presented by 119 subcommunities, for which rates of delinquents also have been calculated (1927–33).[4] The distribution of tuberculosis, in turn, will be considered by larger local community areas.

The similarity in the distribution of infant mortality and of delinquency can be seen on Map 21. These infant mortality rates represent the number of infant deaths per 1,000 live births during the period 1928–33.[5] The range is from 25.7 to 167.2. The median is 49.8, and the rate for the city as a whole 55.3. It will be noted

[3] Possibly the best index of the delinquency-producing potentialities of any area is to be secured from a combination of several sets of rates. The multiple correlation regression equation with four variables was found to be:

$$X_1 = -0.666 + 0.917X_2 + 0.403X_3 + 0.117X_4,$$
$$S_{1.234} = 1.202,$$

where X_1 is the rate of delinquents (Map 8), X_2 the rate of truants (Map 18), X_3 the rate of boys' court offenders (Map 20), and X_4 the rate of families on relief (Map 4).

In Area 64, for example, the expected rate would be

$$2.7 \times 0.917 + 5.3 \times 0.403 + 22.6 \times 0.117 - 0.666 = 6.6 .$$

The observed rate for this area as given on Map 8 is 7.4, which in this instance is greater than the computed rate of 6.6.

[4] These "subcommunities" represent combinations of census tracts widely used for statistical purposes. They are somewhat homogeneous in population, nationality, and economic status. Data are not shown for the Loop area because the population base is not adequate for the calculation of rates. This reduces the number of subcommunities from 120 to 119.

[5] Data from Philip M. Hauser, "Differential Fertility, Mortality, and Net Reproduction in Chicago, 1928–33" (unpublished Ph.D. dissertation, Department of Sociology, University of Chicago, 1938).

MAP 21

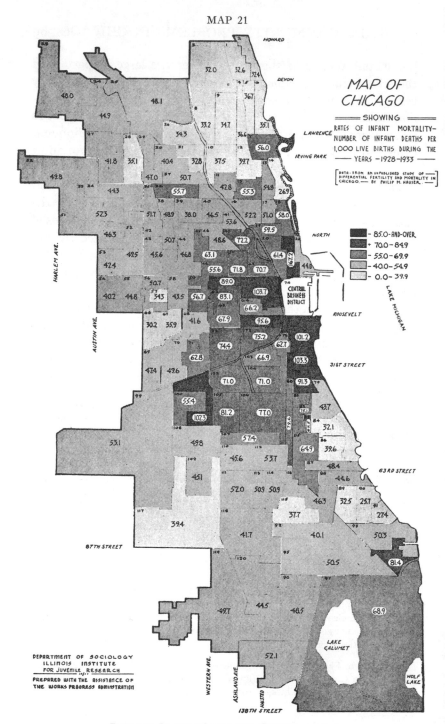

RATES OF INFANT MORTALITY, CHICAGO, 1928–33

that the areas of highest infant mortality correspond, with a few exceptions, to the areas of high rates of delinquents. When the rates of delinquents in the 119 subcommunities are correlated with these rates of infant mortality, the coefficient is .64 ± .04. This correlation is reduced materially by the disproportionately high rates of infant mortality in Subcommunities 21 and 101, where the presence of institutions for homeless mothers and children affects sharply the rates of infant deaths.[6]

When rates of delinquents are computed for the five classes of areas based on infant mortality rates, the general correspondence between these two variables is again evident. These data are presented in Table 15 and in Figure 4, *E*.

TABLE 15

RATES OF DELINQUENTS FOR AREAS GROUPED
ACCORDING TO RATE OF INFANT
MORTALITY

Rates of Infant Mortality 1927–33	Rate of Delinquents 1927–33
85.0 and over (*111.7*)*.................	12.9
70.0–84.9 (*75.9*)*.................	7.4
55.0–69.9 (*61.6*)*.................	5.8
40.0–54.9 (*47.6*)*.................	2.7
Under 40.0 (*34.3*)*.................	1.6

* Rate for class as a whole.

Rates of Tuberculosis.—The distribution of cases and rates of tuberculosis for 60 community areas are presented on Maps 22 and 23.[7] These rates represent the average number of tuberculosis cases reported annually for each of the 60 communities for the years 1931–37, inclusive, per 100,000 population in the area as of 1934. The range of rates is from 6.3 in Area 45 to 78.6 in Area 33–35. The median is 11.3, and the rate for the city as a whole 16.9.

The general configuration shown on Map 23 corresponds quite closely to the pattern of rates of delinquents for the same areas.

[6] Omission of Subcommunity 21 raises the coefficient to .75 ± .03.

[7] Source: *Health Data Book* of the City of Chicago (published by the Chicago Board of Health and the Tuberculosis Institute of Chicago and Cook County, 1939). Seventy-five Chicago communities have been regrouped into a total of 60, by combining each of 15 communities having a small population with the one adjacent.

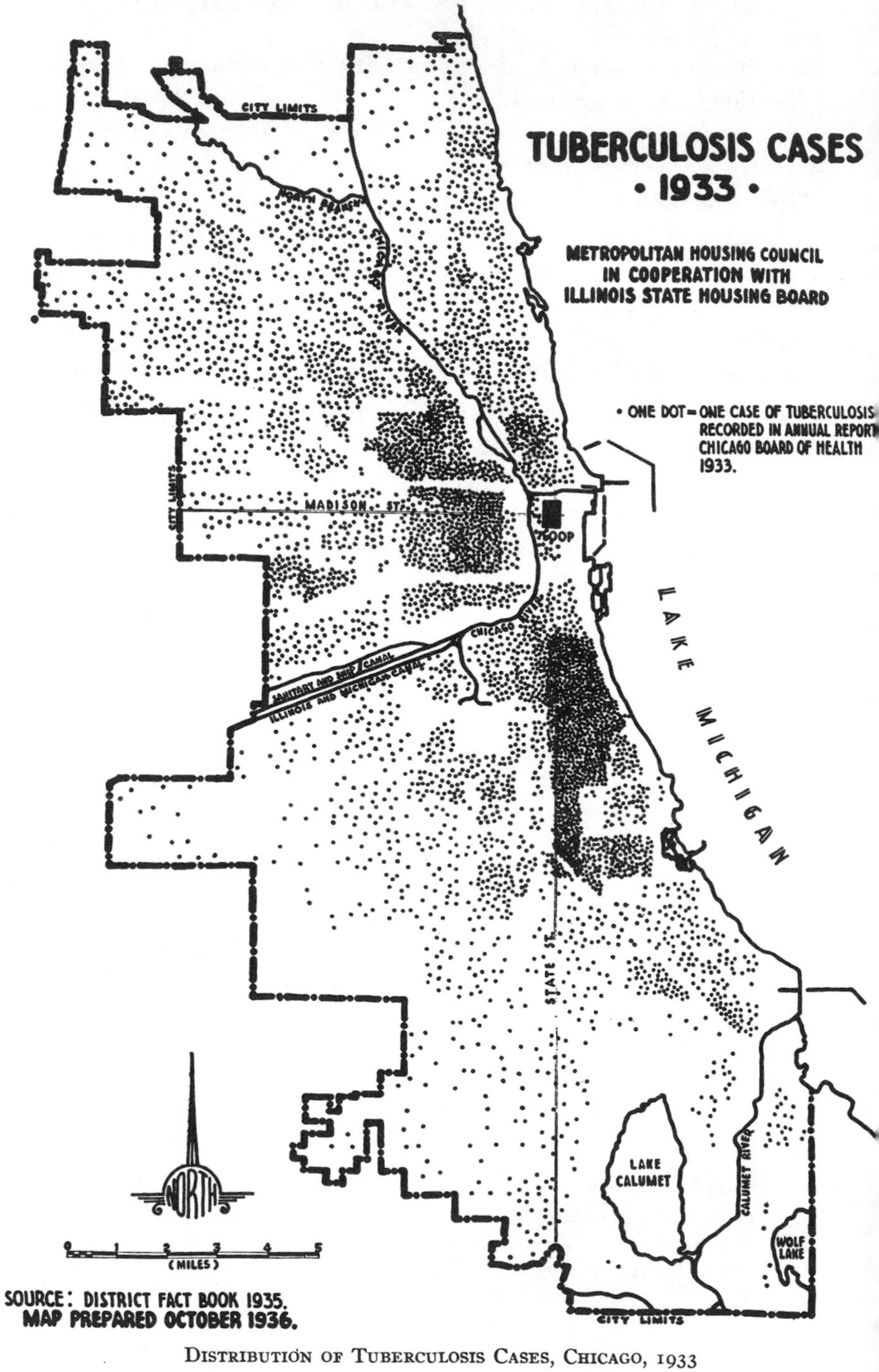

MAP 22

TUBERCULOSIS CASES
· 1933 ·

METROPOLITAN HOUSING COUNCIL
IN COOPERATION WITH
ILLINOIS STATE HOUSING BOARD

· ONE DOT = ONE CASE OF TUBERCULOSIS
RECORDED IN ANNUAL REPORT
CHICAGO BOARD OF HEALTH
1933.

SOURCE: DISTRICT FACT BOOK 1935.
MAP PREPARED OCTOBER 1936.

DISTRIBUTION OF TUBERCULOSIS CASES, CHICAGO, 1933

MAP 23

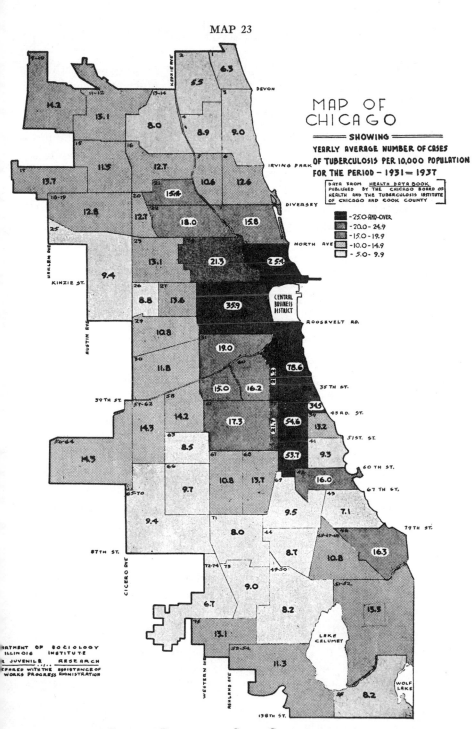

RATES OF TUBERCULOSIS CASES, CHICAGO, 1931–37

When rates of delinquents in these 60 areas are correlated with the yearly average rates of tuberculosis, the coefficient is .93 ± .01. The generally close correspondence between the two is made clear by the data presented in Table 16 and Figure 4, *F*.

Rates of Mental Disorder.—The rates of insanity or mental disease presented on Map 24 are based on the 34,864 cases admitted to state and private hospitals during the years 1922–34 as presented by Faris and Dunham.[8] They represent the number of cases in each subcommunity for the entire 13-year period, per 100,000 population 15 years of age and over. The range of rates

TABLE 16

RATES OF DELINQUENTS FOR AREAS GROUPED
ACCORDING TO RATE OF TUBERCULOSIS

Rates of Tuberculosis 1931–37	Rate of Delinquents 1927–33
25.0 and over (44.7)*	13.1
20.0–24.9 (21.4)*	5.9
15.0–19.9 (16.8)*	3.9
10.0–14.9 (12.4)*	3.1
5.0– 9.9 (8.4)*	1.7

* Rate for class as a whole.

in this series is from 6.2 in Area 23 to 64.9 in Area 74. The median is 11.3, and the rate for the city as a whole 13.1. It will be noted from Map 24 that the general configuration of these rates corresponds quite closely with that of the delinquency map. When these rates of mental disorder in the 119 subcommunities are correlated with rates of delinquents (1927–33 juvenile court series) in the same areas, the coefficient is .72 ± .03.[9] The covariance is presented in Table 17 and in Figure 4, *G*.

Social Phenomena by Zones.—Rates by mile zones for delinquents, truants, boys' court cases, infant mortality, tuberculosis, and mental disorder are presented in Table 18. Covariance among these variables by zones is closer than that for any other data presented. It will be noted that there is not a single instance

[8] Robert E. L. Faris and H. Warren Dunham, *Mental Disorders in Urban Areas* (Chicago: University of Chicago Press, 1939), p. 192.

[9] Omission of Subcommunities 21 and 61, which fall far out of the line of scatter, raises this coefficient to .83 ± .02.

MAP 24

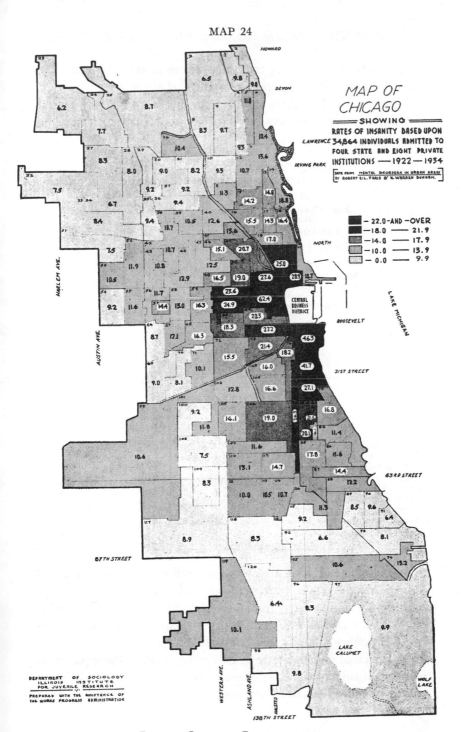

RATES OF INSANITY, CHICAGO, 1922–34

in which they do not vary together. These relationships are presented graphically in Figures 24 and 25, chapter vi.

On the basis of the facts presented in this chapter it is clear that delinquency is not an isolated phenomenon. Instead, it is found

TABLE 17

RATES OF DELINQUENTS FOR AREAS GROUPED
ACCORDING TO RATE OF MENTAL
DISORDER

Rates of Mental Disorder 1922–34	Rate of Delinquents 1927–33
22.0 and over (32.7)*.................	13.7
18.0–21.9 (19.9)*.................	9.2
14.0–17.9 (15.7)*.................	5.0
10.0–13.9 (11.5)*.................	2.9
Under 10.0 (8.4)*.................	1.9

* Rate for class as a whole.

TABLE 18

SOCIAL DATA BY ZONES

COMMUNITY PROBLEMS	ZONES				
	I	II	III	IV	V
Rates of delinquents, 1927–33....	9.8	6.7	4.5	2.5	1.8
Rates of truants, 1927–33.......	4.4	3.1	1.7	1.0	0.7
Boys' court rates, 1938..........	6.3	5.9	3.9	2.6	1.6
Rates of infant mortality, 1928–33	86.7	67.5	54.7	45.9	41.3
Rates of tuberculosis, 1931–37...	33.5	25.0	18.4	12.5	9.2
Rates of mental disorder, 1922–34	32.0	18.8	13.2	10.1	8.4
Rates of delinquents, 1917–23...	10.3	7.3	4.4	3.3	3.0
Rates of truants, 1917–27.......	8.2	5.0	2.1	1.5	1.4
Boys' court rates, 1924–26.......	15.8	11.8	6.2	4.4	3.9
Rates of adult criminals, 1920...	2.2	1.6	0.8	0.6	0.4

to be closely associated, area by area, with rates of truancy, adult crime, infant mortality, tuberculosis, and mental disorder, as representative community problems. The data suggest that similar variations would be revealed for other types of "problem" conditions if further analysis were undertaken.

No attempt will be made at this point to relate these phenomena to existing physical, economic, and social characteristics of the areas differentiated in the process of city growth. However, a close association is visually apparent when Maps 17–24 are compared with those of chapter ii; and, since a significant relationship is found between rates of delinquents and these community characteristics (physical, economic, and social), it may safely be assumed that other problems highly correlated with rates of delinquents, such as those discussed in this chapter, are, in fact, similarly associated with neighborhood conditions.

CHAPTER V

TRUANCY, RECIDIVISM, AND COMMITMENT

TO THIS point, the present study has been concerned only with social backgrounds and with the distribution of individual offenders, regardless of the number of times each may have appeared in court. In the present chapter court appearances and commitments will be analyzed by areas, in relation to rates of individual delinquents. The relationship between rate of delinquents and the percentage of truants who became delinquent will also be explored. If these several variables were consistently proportionate to one another in the different sections of the city, the inclusion of the data would add nothing to the picture already presented. But a preliminary analysis by five zones reveals differentials, for inner-city and outlying areas, in the proportion of truants who became delinquent, the number of court appearances per individual, and the proportion of delinquents committed.

Table 19 shows that, with a single exception, the downward trend in the proportion of truants who became delinquent, from the first to the fifth zone, is consistent for both time series. Table 20, based on three juvenile court delinquency series, shows a marked range in ratio of cases (court appearances) to individual delinquents. For Zone I (1927–33) the number of cases is 1.46 times higher than the number of delinquents, while for Zone V the corresponding ratio is 1.28. In other words, each 100 delinquents in the first, or inner, zone appeared in court a total of 146 times during 1927–33, as compared with 128 court appearances for each 100 in Zone V. Similar variations are revealed for the 1917–23 and the 1900–1906 series. Between the extremes, in all three series, the ratios in Zone II, III, and IV present fairly smooth gradations.

Table 21 shows that for each time series the ratio of commitments to individual delinquents also decreased from the inner to

TABLE 19

TRUANTS WHO BECAME DELINQUENT, BY ZONES*
TWO TRUANCY SERIES

SERIES	ZONES				
	I	II	III	IV	V
1927–33: Number of truants (T)........	465	1,358	928	424	225
Number of truant delinquents (TD).....................	209	611	409	159	75
Ratio TD/T.............	.45	.45	.44	.38	.33
1917–23: Number of truants...........	477	964	524	232	122
Number of truant delinquents..	273	555	282	117	49
Ratio TD/T.............	.57	.58	.54	.50	.40

* These 5 zones do not include the entire city area; therefore, the totals of the figures given are slightly less in each case than the city totals.

TABLE 20

INDIVIDUAL DELINQUENTS AND DELINQUENCY CASES, BY ZONES
THREE JUVENILE COURT DELINQUENCY SERIES

SERIES	ZONES				
	I	II	III	IV	V
1927–33: Individual delinquents (ID)....	1,014	2,876	2,384	1,079	575
Delinquency cases (DC).......	1,476	4,138	3,361	1,403	736
Ratio DC/ID............	1.46	1.43	1.41	1.30	1.28
1917–23: Individual delinquents........	1,246	2,973	1,953	968	403
Delinquency cases...........	1,986	4,526	2,754	1,335	561
Ratio DC/ID.......'....	1.59	1.52	1.41	1.39	1.37
1900–1906: Individual delinquents........	2,146	3,195	1,552	536	261
Delinquency cases...........	3,478	4,788	2,217	756	398
Ratio DC/ID............	1.62	1.50	1.42	1.39	1.54

the outer zone. Here, again, it must be noted that the significant finding is the trend from zone to zone rather than the absolute variation in percentage of boys committed.

This preliminary analysis by zones indicates the need for a more thorough exploration of the manner in which the several sets of data under consideration vary together in different types of local areas. Accordingly, areas have been grouped not by geo-

TABLE 21

INDIVIDUAL DELINQUENTS AND INDIVIDUALS COMMITTED, BY
ZONES: THREE JUVENILE COURT DELINQUENCY SERIES

SERIES	ZONES				
	I	II	III	IV	V
1927–33:					
Individual delinquents (*ID*)....	1,014	2,876	2,384	1,079	575
Individuals committed (*IC*)....	357	954	726	274	140
Ratio *IC/ID*...........	.35	.33	.31	.25	.24
1917–23:					
Individual delinquents........	1,246	2,973	1,953	968	403
Individuals committed........	425	1,031	623	272	117
Ratio *IC/ID*...........	.34	.34	.32	.27	.27
1900–1906:					
Individual delinquents........	2,146	3,195	1,552	536	261
Individuals committed........	921	1,277	593	200	96
Ratio *IC/ID*...........	.42	.40	.39	.36	.38

graphical position, as for the zonal analysis, but into classes based on rate of delinquents.[1] Since rates of delinquents are known to correlate highly with measures of social and economic status, this is in effect a socioeconomic classification as well. The degree of association among the variables will be expressed in terms of average relationship, determined by the method of least squares—a method which makes it possible to estimate, within limits set by the S_y, or standard error of estimate, the amount of behavior of a given type which may be expected in a given area, on the basis of facts already ascertained.

[1] Thus, all areas with rates of delinquents between 0.0 and 0.9 fall in the first class interval, regardless of location, and so on.

The following outline should prove helpful in distinguishing the relationships between the several series of data to be considered.

I. Truancy series[2]
  A. Rate of delinquents and percentage of juvenile court truants who became delinquent, 1927–33 series (Fig. 5 and Table 22)
  B. Rate of delinquents and percentage of juvenile court truants who became delinquent, 1917–23 series (Fig. 6 and Table 23)

II. Delinquency series[3]
  A. Comparison for Chicago as a whole: juvenile careers of truant and nontruant delinquents, 1927–33 and 1917–23 series (Table 24)
  B. The 1927–33 juvenile court series
    1. Rate of delinquents and percentage of delinquents who became recidivists (Figs. 7 and 8; Tables 25 and 26)
    2. Rate of delinquents and average number of times recidivists appeared in court (Figs. 9 and 10; Tables 27 and 28)
    3. Rate of delinquents and percentage of delinquents committed (Figs. 11 and 12; Tables 29 and 30)
  C. The 1917–23 juvenile court series
    1. Rate of delinquents and percentage of delinquents who became recidivists (Figs. 13 and 14; Tables 31 and 32)
    2. Rate of delinquents and average number of times recidivists appeared in court (Figs. 15 and 16; Tables 33 and 34)
    3. Rate of delinquents and percentage of delinquents committed (Figs. 17 and 18; Tables 35 and 36)
    4. Rate of delinquents and percentage of 1920 delinquents arrested as adult criminals (Fig. 19 and Table 37)
  D. The 1906–1906 juvenile court series
    1. Rate of delinquents and percentage of delinquents who became recidivists (Fig. 20 and Table 38)
    2. Rate of delinquents and average number of times recidivists appeared in court (Fig. 21 and Table 39)
    3. Rate of delinquents and percentage of delinquents committed (Fig. 22 and Table 40)

[2] The basic data here are the records of a series of 3,653 boys first brought into court on truancy petition from 1927 to 1933 (already presented in chap. iv above) and a corresponding series for 1917–23.

[3] These three series comprise boys first brought into court on delinquency petition during the periods specified. For full description see chap. iii. In the present chapter the totals in the 1927–33 delinquency and commitment series differ slightly from those presented in chap. iii. The difference in the former resulted from the location of 16 additional cases in a recheck of official records. The difference in the total number of individuals in the commitment series resulted from a minor change in the definition of a commitment.

I. TRUANCY SERIES

A. 1927–33 SERIES

It has long been known that a considerable proportion of school truants become delinquent. During 1927–33 a total of 3,653 Chicago boys were brought into the Juvenile Court of Cook County on truancy petition. Of this number, 1,566, or 42.9 per cent, appeared as delinquents on other occasions also.[4]

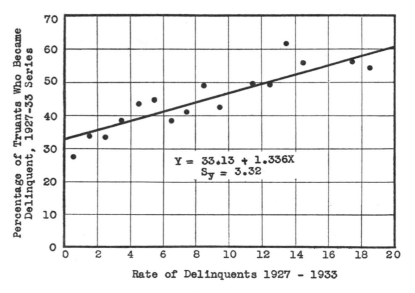

$$Y = 33.13 + 1.336X$$
$$S_y = 3.32$$

FIG. 5

To determine the relationship between truancy and delinquency in various types of urban neighborhoods, the percentages of truants who became delinquent before passing the juvenile court age were plotted on a scatter diagram, by the 16 classes of areas used for the 1927–33 delinquency series[5] (see Fig. 5). Rate of delinquents was the independent variable. A linear curve was

[4] In most cases, though not in all, these boys were taken to court as truants prior to their appearance as delinquents.

[5] Since there were no areas with delinquency rates of 10, 15, and 16, the areas all fell into 16 classes.

then fitted to these values by the method of least squares.[6] Data on which the curve is based are given in Table 22.

Inspection of the curve indicates that, on the average, 34.9 per cent of all juvenile court truants became delinquent in areas with

TABLE 22

Truants Who Became Delinquent, 1927–33 Juvenile
Court Truancy Series

Area Rates of Delinquents	Number of Truants	Number of Truant Delinquents	Percentage of Truant Delinquents	
			Observed*	Computed†
0.0– 0.9	73	20	27.4	34.9
1.0– 1.9	198	67	33.8	36.1
2.0– 2.9	455	151	33.2	37.3
3.0– 3.9	361	137	38.0	38.5
4.0– 4.9	487	211	43.3	39.7
5.0– 5.9	382	171	44.8	41.0
6.0– 6.9	147	57	38.8	42.2
7.0– 7.9	234	96	41.0	43.4
8.0– 8.9	78	38	48.7	44.6
9.0– 9.9	236	100	42.4	45.8
11.0–11.9	371	180	48.5	48.2
12.0–12.9	210	102	48.6	49.4
13.0–13.9	55	34	61.8	50.6
14.0–14.9	92	51	55.4	51.8
17.0–17.9	117	66	56.4	55.5
18.0–18.9	157	85	54.1	56.7
Total	3,653	1,566	42.9	42.9

* Value plotted at mid-point of class interval, Fig. 5.
† Value on the regression line at mid-point of class interval, Fig. 5.

rates of delinquents under 1.0. In areas where the latter rates were between 18 and 19, however, the corresponding percentage was 56.7. It may be said, then, that unless social conditions in Chicago change markedly, approximately 22 more of each 100

[6] In fitting this curve, the values for the 16 classes were weighted according to the number of truants in each class, since there was wide variation among the classes and since several values were based on extremely small samples. The same procedure was followed in fitting each of the curves subsequently presented in this chapter. Similarly, the S_y has been computed for the weighted values. Its use for any other set of values, therefore, is limited.

truants of the city might be expected to become delinquent during a given period in the areas of highest rates of delinquents than in those ranking low.

B. 1917–23 SERIES

A similar tabulation for 1917–23 shows that, of the 2,515 Chicago boys appearing in court on truancy petition during this 7-year period, 1,382, or 55 per cent, also were delinquent before

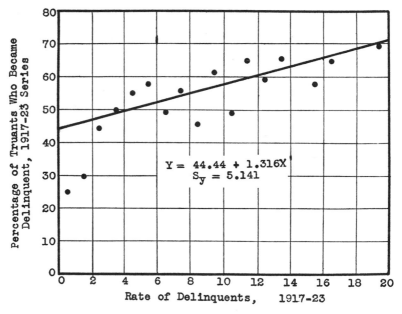

$$Y = 44.44 + 1.316X$$
$$S_y = 5.141$$

FIG. 6

they passed the juvenile court age. The percentage of truants who became delinquent in 17 classes of areas (grouped on the basis of rate of delinquents, 1917–23) was calculated and plotted as before, with rate of delinquents as the independent variable; and a linear curve was fitted. The data are given in Table 23. From Figure 6 it will be observed that the average percentage of truants who became delinquent was 45.1 in lowest-rate areas, and 70.1 in those with rates between 19 and 20. This means that, on the average, and assuming relatively unchanged conditions, 25 more truants of every 100 might be expected to become delinquent during a given period in the high-rate areas than in those where the rates are low, on the basis of these data.

It will be noted that there is a marked consistency between the results for the two series, separated in time by a full decade. A definite tendency has been shown for relatively more truants to

TABLE 23

TRUANTS WHO BECAME DELINQUENTS, 1917–23
JUVENILE COURT TRUANCY SERIES

AREA RATES OF DELINQUENTS	NUMBER OF TRUANTS	NUMBER OF TRUANT DELINQUENTS	PERCENTAGE OF TRUANT DELINQUENTS	
			Observed	Computed
0.0– 0.9	8	2	25.0	45.1
1.0– 1.9	64	19	29.7	46.4
2.0– 2.9	110	49	44.5	47.7
3.0– 3.9	128	63	49.2	49.0
4.0– 4.9	296	163	55.1	50.4
5.0– 5.9	154	89	57.8	51.7
6.0– 6.9	259	126	48.6	53.0
7.0– 7.9	524	290	55.3	54.3
8.0– 8.9	82	38	46.3	55.6
9.0– 9.9	318	194	61.0	56.9
10.0–10.9	39	19	48.7	58.3
11.0–11.9	67	43	64.2	59.6
12.0–12.9	129	76	58.9	60.9
13.0–13.9	155	102	65.8	62.2
15.0–15.9	124	71	57.3	64.8
16.0–16.9	39	25	64.1	66.2
19.0–19.9	19	13	68.4	70.1
Total	2,515	1,382	55.0	55.0

become delinquent in the inner-city areas and in those character-ized by high rates of delinquency, wherever they may be found, than in the low-rate areas.

II. DELINQUENCY SERIES

Analysis of the truancy series just presented reveals that the proportion of truants becoming delinquents varied with the type of community situation as reflected in rate of delinquents. Next to be considered are the three basic juvenile court series—boys brought into court on delinquency petition for the first time, including both truant and nontruant groups. Here the purpose is to determine, through analysis of the subsequent juvenile careers of these boys, the relation between type of community situation and proportion of delinquents who became recidivists, the number of times recidivists appeared in court, and the proportion of delinquents committed to institutions, both for the city as a whole and by local areas.

A. COMPARISONS FOR CHICAGO, 1927–33 AND 1917–23

The question at once arises: Are truant delinquents more likely than the nontruants to reappear in court on delinquency petition, and are there significant differences between the two groups

TABLE 24

RECIDIVISTS, COURT APPEARANCES, AND COMMITMENTS, BY TRUANT
AND NONTRUANT DELINQUENTS, FOR CHICAGO: 1927–33
AND 1917–23 JUVENILE COURT SERIES

DELINQUENTS	PERCENTAGE OF RECIDIVISTS*		AVERAGE NUMBER OF COURT APPEARANCES (RECIDIVISTS)*		PERCENTAGE COMMITTED	
	1927–33†	1917–23‡	1927–33	1917–23	1927–33	1917–23
Total.......	29.3	29.4	2.36	2.63	30.2	32.4
Truants........	34.4	53.1	2.34	2.85	51.4	48.7
Nontruants.....	28.2	24.5	2.37	2.53	25.3	29.1

* Appearances on truancy petition are not included in these tabulations. One possible explanation for the difference between the two series is the increasing tendency of the court to use the Chicago Parental School as a place of commitment. Since boys can be committed to this institution only on truancy petition, the delinquency petition was in some cases arbitrarily amended to a truancy petition, reducing the number of court appearances for alleged delinquency. The extent of operation of this factor is unknown.

† Total number of delinquents, 8,427.

‡ Total number of delinquents, 8,141.

with respect to their subsequent careers? An affirmative answer is indicated by the data summarized in Table 24, for the city as a whole, for 1927–33 and 1917–23.

Table 24 shows that, for the city as a whole, a higher percentage of truant delinquents were recidivists, approximately one-third in 1927–33 and one-half in 1917–23 reappearing in the juvenile court on delinquency petition, as compared with roughly one-fourth of the nontruants in both periods. The probability of a delinquent's becoming a recidivist, therefore, is considerably greater in Chicago if he has also been before the court as a truant. No significant differences are revealed between truant and non-

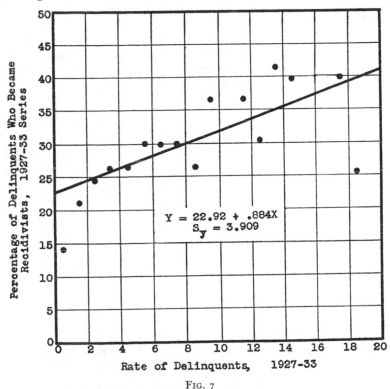

$$Y = 22.92 + .884X$$
$$S_y = 3.909$$

Rate of Delinquents, 1927-33

FIG. 7

truant recidivists as to average number of court appearances (see Table 24, n. *). With respect to the third comparison—percentage committed to institutions—it will be noted that the rate of commitment was more than twice as high for truant as for non-truant delinquents in 1927–33. The difference is less marked for the 1917–23 data.

B. THE 1927-33 JUVENILE COURT SERIES

Recidivism.—In relating area rates of delinquents and percentage of delinquents who became recidivists, for 1927–33, interesting contrasts are revealed among local areas. The 8,427 individual delinquents were grouped into 16 classes, according to rate of delinquents, and the proportion becoming recidivists computed for each class. The resulting values were plotted, with rate of delinquents as the independent variable, and a linear curve was then fitted to these values (see Fig. 7 and Table 25).

TABLE 25

DELINQUENTS WHO BECAME RECIDIVISTS, FOR AREAS
GROUPED BY RATE OF DELINQUENTS, 1927–33
JUVENILE COURT SERIES

AREA RATES OF DELINQUENTS	NUMBER OF DELINQUENTS	NUMBER OF RECIDIVISTS	PERCENTAGE OF RECIDIVISTS	
			Observed*	Computed†
0.0– 0.9........	141	20	14.18	23.36
1.0– 1.9........	512	108	21.09	24.24
2.0– 2.9........	1,062	259	24.39	25.13
3.0– 3.9........	881	230	26.11	26.01
4.0– 4.9........	1,101	290	26.34	26.89
5.0– 5.9........	934	275	29.44	27.78
6.0– 6.9........	229	67	29.26	28.66
7.0– 7.9........	431	126	29.23	29.55
8.0– 8.9........	156	42	26.92	30.43
9.0– 9.9........	596	219	36.74	31.31
11.0–11.9.......	897	328	36.57	33.08
12.0–12.9........	454	139	30.62	33.97
13.0–13.9........	188	78	41.49	34.85
14.0–14.9........	238	95	39.92	35.73
17.0–17.9........	289	115	39.79	38.39
18.0–18.9........	318	81	25.47	39.27
Total........	8,427	2,472	29.33	29.33

* Value plotted at mid-point of class interval, Fig. 7.
† Value on regression line at mid-point of class interval, Fig. 7.

Figure 7 and Table 25 show that in the areas having high rates of delinquents twice as many delinquents became recidivists as in those with low rates and that, on the average, throughout the city, for the period studied, recidivism increased with rate of delinquents. Since recidivism is particularly frequent among truant delinquents, it may be expected that their presence in the series will exert considerable influence on the variation in the relation-

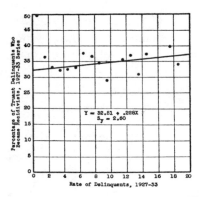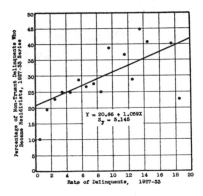

$$Y = 32.51 + .228X$$
$$S_y = 2.60$$

$$Y = 20.66 + 1.059X$$
$$S_y = 5.145$$

FIG. 8

TABLE 26

TRUANT AND NONTRUANT DELINQUENTS WHO BECAME RECIDIVISTS
FOR AREAS GROUPED BY RATE OF DELINQUENTS
1927–33 JUVENILE COURT SERIES

AREA RATES OF DELINQUENTS	NUMBER OF DELINQUENTS		NUMBER OF RECIDIVISTS		PERCENTAGE OF RECIDIVISTS			
					Observed		Computed	
	Truant	Non-truant	Truant	Non-truant	Truant	Non-truant	Truant	Non-truant
0.0– 0.9...	14	127	7	13	50.0	10.2	32.6	21.2
1.0– 1.9...	55	457	20	88	36.4	19.3	32.9	22.2
2.0– 2.9...	162	900	54	205	33.3	22.8	33.1	23.3
3.0– 3.9...	164	717	53	177	32.3	24.7	33.3	24.4
4.0– 4.9...	215	886	70	220	32.6	24.8	33.5	25.4
5.0– 5.9...	172	762	57	218	33.1	28.6	33.8	26.5
6.0– 6.9...	53	176	20	47	37.7	26.7	34.0	27.5
7.0– 7.9...	93	338	34	92	36.6	27.2	34.2	28.6
8.0– 8.9...	35	121	12	30	34.3	24.8	34.4	29.7
9.0– 9.9...	93	503	27	192	29.0	38.2	34.7	30.7
11.0–11.9...	199	698	71	257	35.7	36.8	35.1	32.8
12.0–12.9...	108	346	40	99	37.0	28.6	35.4	33.9
13.0–13.9...	42	146	13	65	31.0	44.5	35.6	35.0
14.0–14.9...	59	179	22	73	37.3	40.8	35.8	36.0
17.0–17.9...	58	231	23	92	39.7	39.8	36.5	39.2
18.0–18.9...	82	236	28	53	34.1	22.5	36.7	40.2
Total....	1,604	6,823	551	1,921	34.4	28.2	34.4	28.2

ship noted. To determine the extent of this influence, the percentages of truant and nontruant delinquents who became recidivists have been related separately to rates of delinquents, in the 16 classes of areas already described (see Fig. 8 and Table 26). Here the geographical variation and the range from low- to high-rate areas are again emphasized, particularly for the truant recidi-

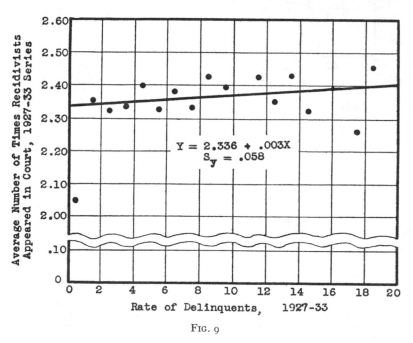

FIG. 9

vists. On the average, 10 more of every 100 truant delinquents became recidivists than of nontruant delinquents, in low-rate areas. The difference is much less marked in areas of high rates. It would seem that truancy is more frequently a precursor of recidivistic delinquency in areas where the rates of delinquents are comparatively low. The trend is the same, however, in both cases.

Court Appearances.—Next to be considered is the relationship between rates of delinquents and the number of appearances recidivists make in court. The average number of court appearances per recidivist was calculated for each class interval, the resulting values plotted, and a linear curve fitted (see Fig. 9 and

Table 27). Inasmuch as all recidivists appear in court at least twice, the significant figures here which indicate variation are those following the decimal point.

It is apparent that the average number of court appearances varies directly with rates of delinquents. In other words, recidi-

TABLE 27

COURT APPEARANCES OF RECIDIVISTS, FOR AREAS GROUPED
BY RATE OF DELINQUENTS, 1927–33
JUVENILE COURT SERIES

AREA RATES OF DELINQUENTS	NUMBER OF RECIDIVISTS	NUMBER OF COURT APPEARANCES	AVERAGE NUMBER OF COURT APPEARANCES	
			Observed	Computed
0.0– 0.9	20	41	2.05	2.34
1.0– 1.9	108	254	2.35	2.34
2.0– 2.9	259	600	2.32	2.34
3.0– 3.9	230	538	2.34	2.35
4.0– 4.9	290	696	2.40	2.35
5.0– 5.9	275	640	2.33	2.35
6.0– 6.9	67	160	2.39	2.36
7.0– 7.9	126	294	2.33	2.36
8.0– 8.9	42	102	2.43	2.36
9.0– 9.9	219	524	2.39	2.37
11.0–11.9	328	794	2.42	2.37
12.0–12.9	139	327	2.35	2.38
13.0–13.9	78	189	2.42	2.39
14.0–14.9	95	220	2.32	2.38
17.0–17.9	115	260	2.26	2.39
18.0–18.9	81	199	2.46	2.39
Total	2,472	5,838	2.36	2.36

vists from high-rate areas reappear in court more frequently than do those from low-rate areas. Since the sample here is small, the relationship can be more clearly shown by grouping all areas into three classes, according to rate of delinquents, and computing the percentage of recidivists appearing in court three times or more for each class. In the low-rate areas (rates of delinquents 0.0–2.9) 25 per cent of all recidivists appeared three times or more, as compared with 27.8 per cent for those where the rates were highest. The percentage with three court appearances shows little variation

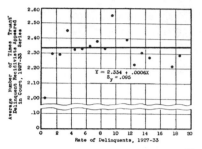
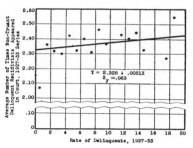

FIG. 10

TABLE 28

COURT APPEARANCES OF TRUANT AND NONTRUANT RECIDIVISTS
FOR AREAS GROUPED BY RATE OF DELINQUENTS
1927–33 JUVENILE COURT SERIES

AREA RATES OF DELINQUENTS	NUMBER OF RECIDIVISTS		NUMBER OF COURT APPEARANCES		AVERAGE NUMBER OF COURT APPEARANCES			
					Observed		Computed	
	Truant	Non-truant	Truant	Non-truant	Truant	Non-truant	Truant	Non-truant
0.0– 0.9...	7	13	14	27	2.00	2.08	2.33	2.33
1.0– 1.9...	20	88	46	208	2.30	2.36	2.34	2.34
2.0– 2.9...	54	205	124	476	2.30	2.32	2.34	2.34
3.0– 3.9...	53	177	130	408	2.45	2.31	2.34	2.35
4.0– 4.9...	70	220	163	533	2.33	2.42	2.34	2.35
5.0– 5.9...	57	218	133	507	2.33	2.33	2.34	2.36
6.0– 6.9...	20	47	47	113	2.35	2.40	2.34	2.36
7.0– 7.9...	34	92	81	213	2.38	2.32	2.34	2.37
8.0– 8.9...	12	30	28	74	2.33	2.47	2.34	2.37
9.0– 9.9...	27	192	69	455	2.56	2.37	2.34	2.38
11.0–11.9...	71	257	170	624	2.39	2.43	2.34	2.39
12.0–12.9...	40	99	89	238	2.23	2.40	2.34	2.39
13.0–13.9...	13	65	30	159	2.31	2.45	2.34	2.40
14.0–14.9...	22	73	50	170	2.27	2.33	2.34	2.40
17.0–17.9...	23	92	51	209	2.22	2.27	2.34	2.42
18.0–18.9...	28	53	64	135	2.29	2.55	2.35	2.42
Total....	551	1,921	1,289	4,549	2.34	2.37	2.34	2.37

from low-rate to high-rate areas; but significantly more appeared four and five times in the high-rate areas (rates 6.0 and over). Evidently there are a disproportionate number of repeaters in these high-rate neighborhoods.

Figure 10 and Table 28 present the same data for truant and nontruant recidivists. Here the range of computed values on the

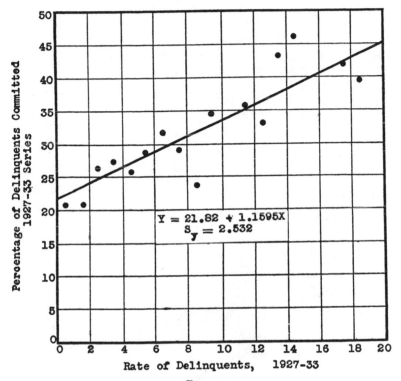

FIG. 11

curve is markedly greater for the nontruants than for the truants, but the direction of change is the same for both.

Commitments.—To conclude the analysis of this 1927–33 series, data on commitment to correctional institutions will be analyzed, in relation to rate of delinquents. Proceeding as above, the percentage of delinquents committed was calculated for each of the 16 class intervals, the values plotted, and a linear curve fitted to the weighted values (see Fig. 11 and Table 29). The range in expected values here (indicating average relationship) is from 22.4 in areas with low rates of delinquents to 43.3 in areas of high rates—an increase of 93.3 per cent. This means that, on the average, under similar conditions, the expectation would be that about 20 more of each 100 delinquents would be committed in areas of high rates, as compared with areas where the rates are low.

TABLE 29

DELINQUENTS COMMITTED, FOR AREAS GROUPED BY RATE OF
DELINQUENTS, 1927–33 JUVENILE COURT SERIES

AREA RATES OF DELINQUENTS	NUMBER OF DELINQUENTS	NUMBER COMMITTED	PERCENTAGE COMMITTED	
			Observed	Computed
0.0– 0.9.........	141	29	20.57	22.40
1.0– 1.9.........	512	105	20.51	23.56
2.0– 2.9.........	1,062	280	26.37	24.72
3.0– 3.9.........	881	239	27.13	25.88
4.0– 4.9.........	1,101	284	25.79	27.04
5.0– 5.9.........	934	266	28.48	28.20
6.0– 6.9.........	229	73	31.88	29.36
7.0– 7.9.........	431	125	29.00	30.52
8.0– 8.9.........	156	37	23.72	31.68
9.0– 9.9.........	596	204	34.23	32.84
11.0–11.9.........	897	316	35.23	35.16
12.0–12.9.........	454	151	33.26	36.32
13.0–13.9.........	188	81	43.09	37.48
14.0–14.9.........	238	110	46.22	38.64
17.0–17.9.........	289	122	42.21	42.12
18.0–18.9.........	318	125	39.31	43.28
Total.........	8,427	2,547	30.22	30.22

Figure 12 and Table 30 indicate the differential results for truant, as compared with nontruant, delinquents. Here, again, a greater range in the computed values is seen for the nontruant delinquents—from 18.2 per cent committed in lowest-rate areas to 37.6 per cent where the rates are highest. This suggests that about 19 more in every 100 nontruant delinquents, on the average, would be expected to be committed in the highest-rate areas than in lowest-rate areas, as compared with 15 more in each 100 truant delinquents.

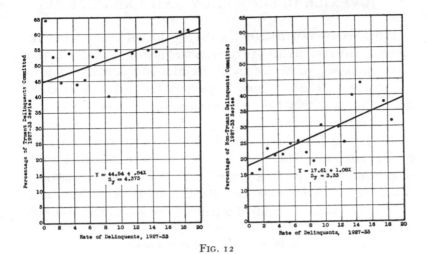

$$Y = 44.54 + .84X \qquad S_y = 4.373$$

$$Y = 17.61 + 1.08X \qquad S_y = 3.33$$

Rate of Delinquents, 1927-33

Percentage of Truant Delinquents Committed 1927-33 Series

Percentage of Non-Truant Delinquents Committed 1927-33 Series

Fig. 12

TABLE 30

TRUANT AND NONTRUANT DELINQUENTS COMMITTED, FOR AREAS
GROUPED BY RATE OF DELINQUENTS, 1927–33
JUVENILE COURT SERIES

| AREA RATES OF DELINQUENTS | NUMBER OF DELINQUENTS | | NUMBER COMMITTED | | PERCENTAGE COMMITTED | | | |
| | | | | | Observed | | Computed | |
	Truant	Non-truant	Truant	Non-truant	Truant	Non-truant	Truant	Non-truant
0.0– 0.9...	14	127	9	20	64.3	15.7	45.0	18.2
1.0– 1.9...	55	457	29	76	52.7	16.6	45.8	19.2
2.0– 2.9...	162	900	72	208	44.4	23.1	46.6	20.3
3.0– 3.9...	164	717	88	151	53.7	21.1	47.5	21.4
4.0– 4.9...	215	886	94	190	43.7	21.4	48.3	22.5
5.0– 5.9...	172	762	78	188	45.3	24.7	49.2	23.6
6.0– 6.9...	53	176	28	45	52.8	25.6	50.0	24.6
7.0– 7.9...	93	338	51	74	54.8	21.9	50.8	25.7
8.0– 8.9...	35	121	14	23	40.0	19.0	51.7	26.8
9.0– 9.9...	93	503	51	153	54.8	30.4	52.5	27.9
11.0–11.9...	199	698	107	209	53.8	29.9	54.2	30.0
12.0–12.9...	108	346	63	88	58.3	25.4	55.0	31.1
13.0–13.9...	42	146	23	58	54.8	39.7	55.9	32.2
14.0–14.9...	59	179	32	78	54.2	43.6	46.7	33.3
17.0–17.9...	58	231	35	87	60.3	37.7	59.2	36.5
18.0–18.9...	82	236	50	75	61.0	31.8	60.1	37.6
Total....	1,604	6,823	824	1,723	51.4	25.3	51.4	25.3

It has been shown that, for the 1927–33 juvenile court series, recidivism and commitment to correctional institutions have a definite relationship to type of social situation as reflected by rate of delinquents. Relatively more boys from the high-rate areas reappear in court; they have a higher average number of court appearances; and they are more frequently committed by the court to institutions than those whose homes are in areas characterized by low rates of delinquents. The data indicate, too, that a disproportionately large percentage of truants became delinquent, as compared with nontruants, and that truants are more frequently recidivists and are committed oftener, especially in the high-rate areas.

C. THE 1917–23 JUVENILE COURT SERIES

A consistency in the relationship between certain variables and rates of delinquents for one 7-year period has been demonstrated. The next step is to present data from an earlier period, to determine whether the above results hold true also for a disparate time series.

During the 1917–23 period, 8,141 boys were brought before the Juvenile Court on delinquency petition. Rate of delinquents having been computed for each square-mile area, the areas were next grouped into 17 classes, on the basis of rate of delinquents. To determine the relation of recidivism, court appearances, and commitment to area of residence, each variable was related to rate of delinquents, and a linear curve fitted by the method of least squares. The data were subdivided also into truant and nontruant groups, each of which was related separately to rate of delinquents, by the same method.

Figures 13–18 and Tables 31–36 present the results of this analysis, which parallels that for the 1927–33 series.

Figures 13–18 and Tables 31–36 reveal a positive relationship in every instance between rates of delinquents in the 1917–23 series and the variables under consideration. As in the 1927–33 series, the percentage of delinquents who were recidivists, the average number of times recidivists appeared in court, and the percentage of delinquents committed to correctional institutions increased, on the average, as rates of delinquents rose. It was found, too, that the truant delinquents produced a greater propor-

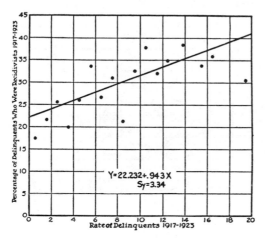

FIG. 13

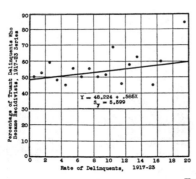

FIG. 14

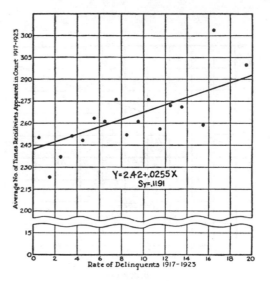

FIG. 15

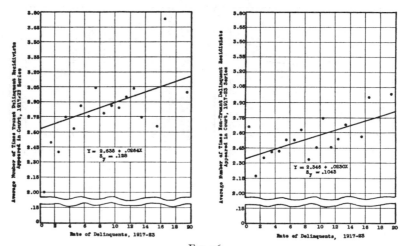

FIG. 16

128

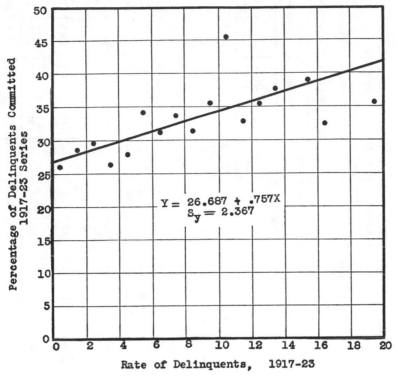

$$Y = 26.687 + .757X$$
$$S_y = 2.367$$

Rate of Delinquents, 1917-23

FIG. 17

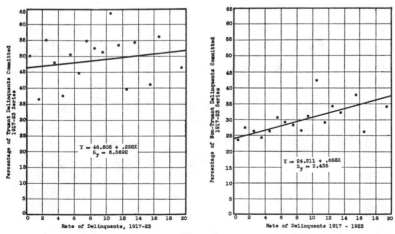

$$Y = 46.605 + .258X$$
$$S_y = 6.5692$$

Rate of Delinquents, 1917-23

$$Y = 24.211 + .658X$$
$$S_y = 2.435$$

Rate of Delinquents 1917 - 1923

FIG. 18

TABLE 31

DELINQUENTS WHO BECAME RECIDIVISTS, FOR AREAS GROUPED BY RATE OF DELINQUENTS, 1917–23 JUVENILE COURT SERIES

AREA RATES OF DELINQUENTS	NUMBER OF DELINQUENTS	NUMBER OF RECIDIVISTS	PERCENTAGE OF RECIDIVISTS	
			Observed	Computed
0.0– 0.9	23	4	17.4	22.7
1.0– 1.9	263	57	21.7	23.7
2.0– 2.9	481	123	25.6	24.6
3.0– 3.9	552	110	19.9	25.5
4.0– 4.9	1,172	306	26.1	26.5
5.0– 5.9	527	177	33.6	27.4
6.0– 6.9	828	220	26.6	28.4
7.0– 7.9	1,535	477	31.1	29.3
8.0– 8.9	225	48	21.3	30.3
9.0– 9.9	811	264	32.6	31.2
10.0–10.9	135	51	37.8	32.1
11.0–11.9	277	89	32.1	33.1
12.0–12.9	347	121	34.9	34.0
13.0–13.9	410	158	38.5	35.0
15.0–15.9	343	116	33.8	36.9
16.0–16.9	117	42	35.9	37.9
19.0–19.9	95	29	30.5	40.6
Total	8,141	2,392	29.4	29.4

TABLE 32

TRUANT AND NONTRUANT DELINQUENTS WHO BECAME RECIDIVISTS FOR AREAS GROUPED BY RATE OF DELINQUENTS 1917–23 JUVENILE COURT SERIES

AREA RATES OF DELINQUENTS	NUMBER OF DELINQUENTS		NUMBER OF RECIDIVISTS		PERCENTAGE OF RECIDIVISTS			
					Observed		Computed	
	Truant	Non-truant	Truant	Non-truant	Truant	Non-truant	Truant	Non-truant
0.0– 0.9	2	21	1	3	50.0	14.3	48.5	19.5
1.0– 1.9	19	244	10	47	52.6	19.3	49.1	20.3
2.0– 2.9	49	432	29	94	59.2	21.8	49.7	21.0
3.0– 3.9	63	489	30	80	47.6	16.4	50.3	21.7
4.0– 4.9	163	1,009	74	232	45.4	23.0	50.9	22.4
5.0– 5.9	89	438	50	127	56.2	29.0	51.4	23.1
6.0– 6.9	126	702	63	157	50.0	22.4	52.0	23.9
7.0– 7.9	290	1,245	159	318	54.8	25.5	52.6	24.6
8.0– 8.9	38	187	19	29	50.0	15.5	53.2	25.3
9.0– 9.9	194	617	100	164	51.5	26.6	53.8	26.0
10.0–10.9	19	116	13	38	68.4	32.8	54.4	26.8
11.0–11.9	43	234	20	69	46.5	29.5	54.9	27.5
12.0–12.9	76	271	44	77	57.9	28.4	55.5	28.2
13.0–13.9	102	308	64	94	62.7	30.5	56.1	28.9
15.0–15.9	71	272	32	84	45.1	30.9	57.3	30.4
16.0–16.9	25	92	15	27	60.1	29.3	57.9	31.1
19.0–19.9	13	82	11	18	84.6	22.0	59.6	33.2
Total	1,382	6,759	734	1,658	53.1	24.5	53.1	24.5

TABLE 33

COURT APPEARANCES OF RECIDIVISTS, FOR AREAS GROUPED BY RATE OF DELINQUENTS, 1917–23 JUVENILE COURT SERIES

AREA RATES OF DELINQUENTS	NUMBER OF RECIDIVISTS	NUMBER OF COURT APPEARANCES	Observed	Computed
0.0– 0.9	4	10	2.50	2.43
1.0– 1.9	57	127	2.23	2.46
2.0– 2.9	123	292	2.37	2.48
3.0– 3.9	110	276	2.51	2.51
4.0– 4.9	306	750	2.48	2.53
5.0– 5.9	177	466	2.63	2.56
6.0– 6.9	220	575	2.61	2.59
7.0– 7.9	477	1,317	2.76	2.61
8.0– 8.9	48	121	2.52	2.64
9.0– 9.9	264	688	2.61	2.66
10.0–10.9	51	141	2.76	2.69
11.0–11.9	89	228	2.56	2.71
12.0–12.9	121	329	2.72	2.74
13.0–13.9	158	428	2.71	2.76
15.0–15.9	116	300	2.59	2.81
16.0–16.9	42	136	3.24	2.84
19.0–19.9	29	87	3.00	2.92
Total	2,392	6,280	2.63	2.63

TABLE 34

COURT APPEARANCES OF TRUANT AND NONTRUANT RECIDIVISTS FOR AREAS GROUPED BY RATE OF DELINQUENTS 1917–23 JUVENILE COURT SERIES

AREA RATES OF DELINQUENTS	NUMBER OF RECIDIVISTS Truant	NUMBER OF RECIDIVISTS Non-truant	NUMBER OF COURT APPEARANCES Truant	NUMBER OF COURT APPEARANCES Non-truant	Observed Truant	Observed Non-truant	Computed Truant	Computed Non-truant
0.0– 0.9	1	3	2	8	2.00	2.67	2.65	2.36
1.0– 1.9	10	47	25	102	2.50	2.17	2.67	2.38
2.0– 2.9	29	94	70	222	2.41	2.36	2.70	2.40
3.0– 3.9	30	80	82	194	2.73	2.43	2.73	2.43
4.0– 4.9	74	232	195	564	2.64	2.43	2.75	2.45
5.0– 5.9	50	127	144	322	2.88	2.54	2.78	2.47
6.0– 6.9	63	157	174	401	2.76	2.55	2.81	2.50
7.0– 7.9	159	318	482	835	3.03	2.63	2.83	2.52
8.0– 8.9	19	29	53	68	2.79	2.34	2.86	2.54
9.0– 9.9	100	164	287	401	2.87	2.45	2.89	2.57
10.0–10.9	13	38	37	104	2.85	2.74	2.91	2.59
11.0–11.9	20	69	59	169	2.95	2.45	2.94	2.61
12.0–12.9	44	77	133	196	3.02	2.55	2.97	2.63
13.0–13.9	64	94	176	252	2.75	2.68	2.99	2.66
15.0–15.9	32	84	85	215	2.66	2.56	3.04	2.70
16.0–16.9	15	27	56	80	3.73	2.96	3.07	2.73
19.0–19.9	11	18	33	54	3.00	3.00	3.15	2.80
Total	734	1,658	2,093	4,187	2.85	2.53	2.85	2.53

TABLE 35

DELINQUENTS COMMITTED, FOR AREAS GROUPED BY RATE OF DELINQUENTS, 1917–23 JUVENILE COURT SERIES

AREA RATES OF DELINQUENTS	NUMBER OF DELINQUENTS	NUMBER COMMITTED	PERCENTAGE COMMITTED	
			Observed	Computed
0.0– 0.9	23	6	26.1	27.1
1.0– 1.9	263	74	28.1	27.8
2.0– 2.9	481	140	29.1	28.6
3.0– 3.9	552	148	26.8	29.3
4.0– 4.9	1,172	327	27.9	30.1
5.0– 5.9	527	179	34.0	30.9
6.0– 6.9	828	260	31.4	31.6
7.0– 7.9	1,535	512	33.4	32.4
8.0– 8.9	225	70	31.1	33.1
9.0– 9.9	811	290	35.8	33.9
10.0–10.9	135	61	45.2	34.6
11.0–11.9	277	91	32.9	35.4
12.0–12.9	347	123	35.4	36.2
13.0–13.9	410	154	37.6	36.9
15.0–15.9	343	132	38.5	38.4
16.0–16.9	117	38	32.5	39.2
19.0–19.9	95	34	35.8	41.4
Total	8,141	2,639	32.4	32.4

TABLE 36

TRUANT AND NONTRUANT DELINQUENTS COMMITTED, FOR AREAS GROUPED BY RATE OF DELINQUENTS, 1917–23 JUVENILE COURT SERIES

AREA RATES OF DELINQUENTS	NUMBER OF DELINQUENTS		NUMBER COMMITTED		PERCENTAGE COMMITTED			
					Observed		Computed	
	Truant	Non-truant	Truant	Non-truant	Truant	Non-truant	Truant	Non-truant
0.0– 0.9	2	21	1	5	50.0	23.8	46.7	24.5
1.0– 1.9	19	244	7	67	36.8	27.5	47.0	25.2
2.0– 2.9	49	432	27	113	55.1	26.2	47.3	25.9
3.0– 3.9	63	489	30	118	47.6	24.1	47.5	26.5
4.0– 4.9	163	1,009	61	266	37.4	26.4	47.8	27.2
5.0– 5.9	89	438	45	134	50.6	30.6	48.0	27.8
6.0– 6.9	126	702	56	204	44.4	29.1	48.3	28.5
7.0– 7.9	290	1,245	159	353	54.8	28.4	48.5	29.1
8.0– 8.9	38	187	20	50	52.6	26.7	48.8	29.8
9.0– 9.9	194	617	99	191	51.0	31.0	49.1	30.5
10.0–10.9	19	116	12	49	63.2	42.2	49.3	31.1
11.0–11.9	43	234	23	68	53.5	29.1	49.6	31.8
12.0–12.9	76	271	30	93	39.5	34.3	49.8	32.4
13.0–13.9	102	308	55	99	53.9	32.1	50.1	33.1
15.0–15.9	71	272	29	103	40.8	37.9	50.6	34.4
16.0–16.9	25	92	14	24	56.0	26.1	50.9	35.1
19.0–19.9	13	82	6	28	46.2	34.1	51.6	37.0
Total	1,382	6,759	674	1,965	48.7	29.1	48.7	29.1

tion of recidivists, appeared in court more frequently, and were somewhat more often committed to correctional institutions, as compared with the nontruants. The positive relation with rates of delinquents held true also for these subgroups, although in the percentage of truant delinquents who became recidivists and those

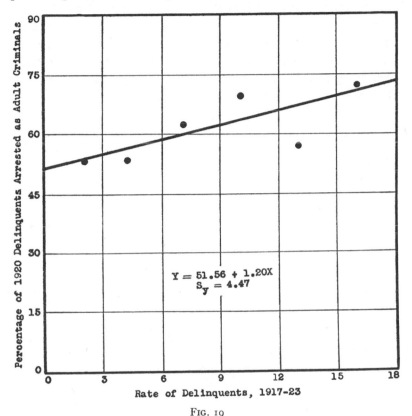

FIG. 19

committed to institutions the variation found among classes of areas was not so great as for the series as a whole.

In addition to the facts above summarized, evidence was obtained indicating how frequently juvenile delinquents go on to careers of adult crime. A follow-up study was made, through official records, of the subsequent careers of a one-third sample of all Chicago boys brought into the Juvenile Court of Cook County on delinquency petition during 1920. The proportion of these delinquents who appeared in court as adult offenders through 1938 was related to the rate of delinquents in each area[7] (1917–23 series) by the method of least squares, and a linear curve was fitted. The data are presented in Table 37 and Figure 19.

The outstanding fact is that during the period covered, three-fifths of the boys reappeared in court as adult offenders. Here again, however, a striking variation is seen among types of areas, 70.7 per cent of the delinquents from high-rate areas, on the average, being arrested as adults, in comparison with 53.9 per cent from areas where the rates were low.

TABLE 37

DELINQUENTS ARRESTED AS ADULT CRIMINALS, FOR AREAS GROUPED
BY RATE OF DELINQUENTS: ONE-THIRD SAMPLE
OF 1920 JUVENILE COURT SERIES

AREA RATES OF DELINQUENTS	NUMBER OF DELINQUENTS*	NUMBER ARRESTED AS ADULTS†	PERCENTAGE ARRESTED	
			Observed	Computed
0.0– 2.9 (2.0)‡....	28	15	53.6	53.9
3.0– 5.9 (4.2)‡ ..	119	64	53.8	56.6
6.0– 8.9 (7.1)‡...	136	85	62.5	60.1
9.0–11.9 (10.0)‡...	56	39	69.8	63.5
12.0–14.9 (13.0)‡...	42	24	57.1	67.1
15.0 and over (16.0)‡...	18	13	72.2	70.7
Total.............	399	240	60.2	60.2

* This comprises a one-third sample of the Chicago boys brought into the Juvenile Court on delinquency petition during 1920.
† For offenses more serious than traffic violations.
‡ Value plotted, Fig. 19 (rate for class as a whole).

D. THE 1900–1906 JUVENILE COURT SERIES

Since data on percentage of truants who became delinquent for the period 1900–1906 were not available, the analysis of this series is limited to three considerations, namely: the percentage of delinquents who became recidivists, the average number of times recidivists appeared in court, and the percentage of delinquents committed.

The 8,056 individuals brought before the court on delinquency

[7] Because of the relatively small sample (399 individuals) the size of the class interval was increased, the first class including all areas with rates of delinquents under 3.0, and so on.

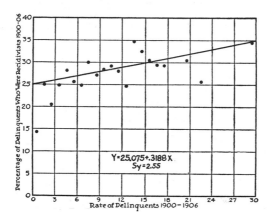

FIG. 20

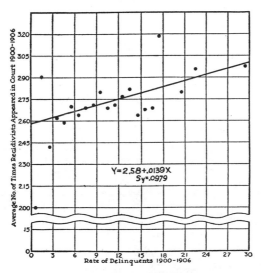

FIG. 21

petition during these years represented 106 square-mile areas. These areas were grouped into 21 classes according to rate of delinquents. Rates in the series ranged from 0.6 to 29.3. Each variable under consideration (rates of recidivism and commitment and average number of court appearances) was then related to rate of delinquents, a linear curve being fitted by the method of

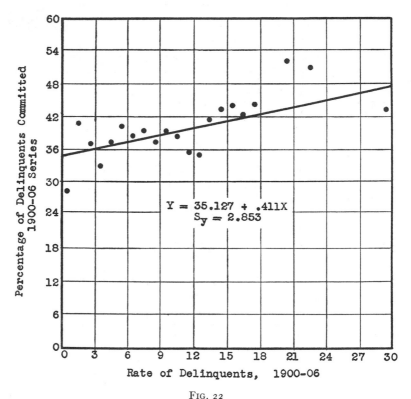

$$Y = 35.127 + .411X$$
$$S_y = 2.853$$

FIG. 22

least squares. Figures 20, 21, and 22 and Tables 38, 39, and 40 present the results of this analysis.

On the basis of the foregoing analysis for the 1900–1906 series, it can be concluded, as for the 1917–23 series, that in the areas of highest rates of delinquents a larger percentage of delinquents became recidivists, the recidivists reappeared in court more frequently, and relatively more delinquents were committed. These phenomena are all closely related.

TABLE 38

DELINQUENTS WHO BECAME RECIDIVISTS, FOR AREAS GROUPED BY RATE OF DELINQUENTS, 1900–1906 JUVENILE COURT SERIES

AREA RATES OF DELINQUENTS	NUMBER OF DELINQUENTS	NUMBER OF RECIDIVISTS	PERCENTAGE OF RECIDIVISTS	
			Observed	Computed
0.0– 0.9	7	1	14.3	25.2
1.0– 1.9	44	11	25.0	25.5
2.0– 2.9	147	26	20.5	25.9
3.0– 3.9	378	94	24.9	26.2
4.0– 4.9	337	95	28.2	26.5
5.0– 5.9	408	105	25.7	26.8
6.0– 6.9	557	138	24.8	27.2
7.0– 7.9	503	151	30.0	27.5
8.0– 8.9	780	211	27.1	27.8
9.0– 9.9	691	196	28.4	28.1
10.0–10.9	421	123	29.2	28.4
11.0–11.9	461	129	28.0	28.7
12.0–12.9	243	60	24.7	29.1
13.0–13.9	724	252	34.8	29.4
14.0–14.9	335	109	32.5	29.7
15.0–15.9	357	109	30.5	30.0
16.0–16.9	486	143	29.4	30.3
17.0–17.9	270	79	29.3	30.7
20.0–20.9	184	56	30.4	31.6
22.0–22.9	192	49	25.5	32.3
29.0–29.9	551	189	34.3	34.5
Total	8,056	2,326	28.9	28.9

TABLE 39

COURT APPEARANCES OF RECIDIVISTS, FOR AREAS GROUPED BY RATE OF DELINQUENTS 1900–1906 JUVENILE COURT SERIES

AREA RATES OF DELINQUENTS	NUMBER OF RECIDIVISTS	NUMBER OF COURT APPEARANCES	AVERAGE NUMBER OF COURT APPEARANCES	
			Observed	Computed
0.0– 0.9	1	2	2.00	2.58
1.0– 1.9	11	32	2.91	2.60
2.0– 2.9	26	63	2.42	2.62
3.0– 3.9	94	246	2.62	2.63
4.0– 4.9	95	246	2.59	2.64
5.0– 5.9	105	284	2.70	2.66
6.0– 6.9	138	364	2.64	2.67
7.0– 7.9	151	406	2.69	2.68
8.0– 8.9	211	572	2.71	2.70
9.0– 9.9	196	540	2.80	2.71
10.0–10.9	123	331	2.69	2.73
11.0–11.9	129	349	2.71	2.74
12.0–12.9	60	166	2.77	2.75
13.0–13.9	252	711	2.82	2.77
14.0–14.9	109	288	2.64	2.78
15.0–15.9	109	292	2.68	2.80
16.0–16.9	143	384	2.69	2.81
17.0–17.9	79	252	3.19	2.82
20.0–20.9	56	157	2.80	2.87
22.0–22.9	49	145	2.96	2.89
29.0–29.9	189	564	2.98	2.99
Total	2,326	6,403	2.75	2.75

SUMMARY

In conclusion, it may be said that the one salient fact constantly reappearing in the evidence assembled for three separate juvenile court series, covering more than 30 years, is the dispropor-

TABLE 40

DELINQUENTS COMMITTED, FOR AREAS GROUPED
BY RATE OF DELINQUENTS, 1900–1906
JUVENILE COURT SERIES

AREA RATES OF DELINQUENTS	NUMBER OF DELINQUENTS	NUMBER COMMITTED	PERCENTAGE COMMITTED	
			Observed	Computed
0.0– 0.9.........	7	2	28.6	35.3
1.0– 1.9.........	44	18	40.9	35.7
2.0– 2.9.........	127	47	37.0	36.2
3.0– 3.9.........	378	123	32.5	36.6
4.0– 4.9.........	337	125	37.1	37.0
5.0– 5.9.........	408	164	40.2	37.4
6.0– 6.9.........	557	214	38.4	37.8
7.0– 7.9.........	503	198	39.4	38.2
8.0– 8.9.........	780	290	37.2	38.6
9.0– 9.9.........	691	270	39.1	39.0
10.0–10.9.........	421	162	38.5	39.4
11.0–11.9.........	461	165	35.8	39.9
12.0–12.9.........	243	85	35.0	40.3
13.0–13.9.........	724	302	41.7	40.7
14.0–14.9.........	335	146	43.6	41.1
15.0–15.9.........	357	157	44.0	41.5
16.0–16.9.........	486	205	42.2	41.9
17.0–17.9.........	270	119	44.1	42.3
20.0–20.9.........	184	96	52.2	43.6
22.0–22.9.........	192	98	51.0	44.4
29.0–29.9.........	551	238	43.2	47.3
Total.........	8,056	3,224	40.0	40.0

tionate amount of recidivism occurring in those sections of the city where the rates of delinquents are highest. The regularity and uniformity of appearance of these phenomena are impressive. Not only average number of court appearances but also the proportion of delinquent boys committed to correctional institutions throughout the city for all series likewise vary disproportionately with rates of delinquents. Moreover, relatively more delinquents in the high-rate areas are later arrested as adult criminals. Clearly, the factors which send a larger percentage of boys into court from certain areas tend also to return a higher proportion of these same boys as they mature. Furthermore, these data establish the fact that the variation among areas in number of offenses is considerably greater than the variation in rates computed upon the basis of individual offenders.

CHAPTER VI

DELINQUENCY RATES AND COMMUNITY CHARACTERISTICS

THE question has been asked many times: What is it, in modern city life, that produces delinquency? Why do relatively large numbers of boys from the inner urban areas appear in court with such striking regularity, year after year, regardless of changing population structure or the ups and downs of the business cycle? In preceding chapters different series of male juvenile delinquents were presented which closely parallel one another in geographical distribution although widely separated in time, and the close resemblance of all these series to the distribution of truants and of adult criminals was shown. Moreover, many other community characteristics—median rentals, families on relief, infant mortality rates, and so on—reveal similar patterns of variation throughout the city. The next step would be to determine, if possible, the extent to which these two sets of data are related. How consistently do they vary together, if at all, and how high is the degree of association?

Where high zero-order correlations are found to exist uniformly between two variables, with a small probable error, it is possible and valid to consider either series as an approximate index, or indicator, of the other. This holds true for any two variables which are known to be associated or to vary concomitantly. The relationship, of course, may be either direct or inverse. In neither case, however, is there justification in assuming, on this basis alone, that the observed association is of a cause-and-effect nature; it may be, rather, that both variables are similarly affected by some third factor. Further analysis is needed. Controlled experimentation is often useful in establishing the degree to which a change in one variable "causes" or brings about a corresponding change in the other. In the social field, however, experimentation is difficult. Instead, it is often necessary to rely upon refined statistical techniques, such as partial correlation, which, for certain types of data, enable the investigator to measure the effects of one factor while holding others relatively constant. By the method of successive redistribution, also, the influence of one or more variables may be held constant. Thus, it is possible to study the relationship between rates of delinquents and economic status for a single nationality group throughout the city or for various nationality groups in the same area or class of areas. This process may be extended indefinitely, subject only to the limitations of the available data. In the analysis to be presented, both of the latter methods have been used in an attempt to determine how much weight should be given to various more or less influential factors.

Several practical considerations prevent the neat and precise statistical analysis which would be desirable. The characteristics studied represent only a sampling of the myriad forms in which community life and social relationships find expression. The rate of delinquents must itself be thought of as an imperfect enumeration of the delinquents and an index of the larger number of boys engaging in officially proscribed activities. Not only will there be chance fluctuations in the amount of alleged delinquency from year to year, but the policy of the local police officer in referring boys to the Juvenile Court, the focusing of the public eye upon conditions in an area, and numerous other matters may bring about a change in the index without any essential change in the underlying delinquency-producing influences in the community or in the behavior resulting therefrom. If the infant mortality rates or the rates of families on relief are looked upon as indexes of economic status or of the social organization of a community, it is obvious that they can be considered only very crude indicators at best. The perturbing influence of other variables must always be considered.

Certain exceptional conditions are known to limit the value of other variables chosen as indicators of local community differentiation. Median rental has been used widely because of its popularity as an index of economic status, although in Chicago such an index is far from satisfactory when applied to areas of colored population. The Negro is forced to pay considerably higher rents than the whites for comparable housing; thus his economic level is made to appear higher on the basis of rental than it actually is. Similarly, rates of increase or decrease of population are modified in Negro areas by restrictions on free movement placed upon the Negro population. Thus, in certain areas the population is increasing where it normally would be expected to decrease if there were no such barriers. Likewise, the percentage of families owning homes is not entirely satisfactory as an economic index in large urban centers, where many of the well-to-do rent expensive apartments. It is, however, an indication of the relative stability of population in an area.

Correlation of series of rates based on geographical areas is further complicated by the fact that magnitude of the coefficient is influenced by the size of the area selected. This tendency has been noted by several writers,[1] but no satisfactory solution of the problem has been offered. If it be borne in mind that a correlation of area data is an index of geographical association for a particular type of spatial division only, rather than a fixed measure of functional relationship, it will be apparent that a change in area size changes the meaning of the correlation. Thus, an r of .90 or above for two series of rates calculated by square-mile areas indicates a high degree of association between the magnitudes of the two rates in most of the square miles but does not tell us the exact degree of covariance for smaller or larger areas.

With these limitations clearly in mind, a number of correlation coefficients and tables of covariance are presented. The statistical data characterizing and differentiating local urban areas may be grouped under three headings: (1) physical status, (2) economic status, and (3) population composition. These will be considered, in turn, in relation to rates of delinquents.

---

[1] See, e.g., C. E. Gehlke and K. Biehl, "Certain Effects of Grouping upon the Size of the Correlation Coefficient in Census Tract Material," *Journal of the American Statistical Association, Proceedings*, XXIX, Suppl. (March, 1934), 169–70.

The location of major industrial and commercial developments, the distribution of buildings condemned for demolition or repair, and the percentage increase or decrease in population by square-mile areas were presented in chapter ii as indications of the physical differentiation of areas within the city. Quantitative measures of the first two are not available, but inspection of the distribution maps shows clearly that the highest rates of delinquents are most frequently found in, or adjacent to, areas of heavy industry and commerce. These same neighborhoods have the largest number of condemned buildings. The only notable exception to this generalization, for Chicago, appears in some of the areas south of the central business district.

There is, of course, little reason to postulate a direct relationship between living in proximity to industrial developments and becoming delinquent. While railroads and industrial properties may offer a field for delinquent behavior, they can hardly be regarded as a cause of such activities. Industrial invasion and physical deterioration do, however, make an area less desirable for residential purposes. As a consequence, in time there is found a movement from this area of those people able to afford more attractive surroundings. Further, the decrease in the number of buildings available for residential purposes leads to a decrease in the population of the area.

Population Increase or Decrease.—Increase or decrease of population and rates of delinquents, by square-mile areas, do not exhibit a linear relationship. A relatively slight difference in rate of decrease of population, or of rate of increase for areas where the increase is slight, is generally associated with a considerable change in rates of delinquents; while for large differences in rates of increase of population, where increase is great, there is little or no consistent difference in rates of delinquents. Thus, areas increasing more than 70 per cent show no corresponding drop in rates of delinquents, although the relationship is clear up to this point. An adequate measure of the degree of association between rates of delinquents and rates of population change must take into account the curvilinearity of the relationship. Accordingly, the correlation ratio, η, has been used.[2] When the rates of delinquents in the 1927–33 juvenile court series are thus correlated with the percentage increase or decrease of population between 1920 and 1930, by the 113 square-mile areas for which 1920 data are available, with rates of delinquents as the dependent variable, the correlation ratio, η_{yx}, is found to be .52. For the 1917–23 series of delinquents and the percentage increase or decrease of population from 1910 to 1920, with rates of delinquents again the dependent variable, η_{yx} is .69. (In both these calculations all population increases above 200 per cent were counted as 200.)

The sharp drop in the degree of association between the two series from one decade to the next is very largely due, no doubt, to the rapid increase during this period of the population in the colored district, where rates of delinquents were high. These were the only areas of significantly increasing population which also had high rates of delinquents. Conversely, some of the largest outlying areas, which show a marked growth in population, contain within them small areas near industrial developments where the population is decreasing and where a corresponding concentration of delinquents appears.

The general correspondence between rates of delinquents and population increase or decrease, by five classes of areas grouped according to population change, is presented in Table 41. The classes correspond to the five shadings on Map 3. For comparison, rates of delinquents based on the 1917–23 data are shown for five classes of areas grouped on the basis of population increase or decrease between 1910 and 1920.

It will be noted that in both these comparisons the highest rates of delinquents are in the classes of areas where the decrease in

---

[2] In each instance the percentage increase or decrease of population will be taken as the independent, or X, variable; and the rate of delinquents as the dependent, or Y, variable. In other words, the regression of rates of delinquents (Y) on increase or decrease of population (X) will be considered. This will be indicated by the symbol η_{yx}.

population is most rapid and that both indicate a consistent decrease in rates of delinquents with increasing population. The variation for the 1927–33 juvenile court series is from 9.5 to 2.0, while for the 1917–23 series it is from 9.7 to 3.4. These variations are presented graphically in Figure 23, *A* and *B*.

TABLE 41

RATES OF DELINQUENTS FOR AREAS GROUPED ACCORDING TO PERCENTAGE INCREASE OR DECREASE OF POPULATION: 1927–33 AND 1917–23

Percentage Increase or Decrease of Population, 1920–30		Rate of Delinquents 1927–33
Decreasing:		
20–39	(27.5)*...................	9.5
0–19	(7.9)*.................	6.3
Increasing:		
0–19	(9.2)*.................	4.1
20–39	(28.4)*.................	3.0
40 and over	(124.2)*.................	2.0

Percentage Increase or Decrease of Population, 1910–20		Rate of Delinquents 1917–23
Decreasing:		
20–39	(32.5)*.................	9.7
0–19	(8.4)*.................	8.6
Increasing:		
0–19	(10.0)*.................	5.3
20–39	(29.9)*.................	4.0
40 and over	(87.5)*.................	3.4

* Percentage for class as a whole.

These correlation ratios and tables establish the fact that there is a similarity between the pattern of distribution of delinquency and that of population growth or decline. The data do not establish a causal relationship between the two variables, however. The fact that the population of an area is decreasing does not impel a boy to become delinquent. It may be said, however, that decreasing population is usually related to industrial invasion of an area and contributes to the development of a general situation conducive to delinquency.

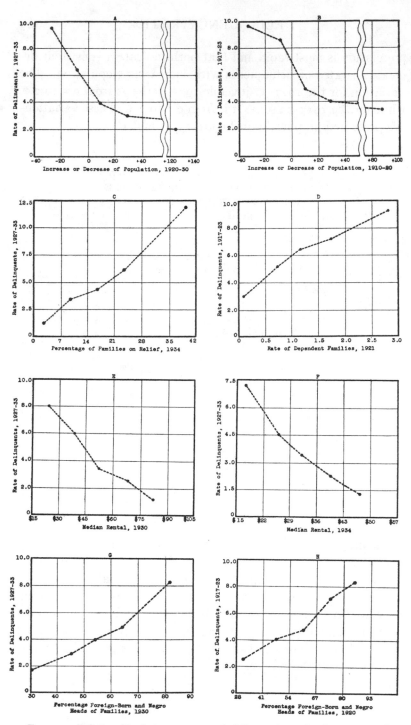

FIG. 23.—Relationship between rates of delinquents and other community characteristics.

INDEXES OF ECONOMIC STATUS IN RELATION
TO RATES OF DELINQUENTS

Percentage of Families on Relief.—When the rates of delinquents
in the 1927–33 series are correlated with percentages of families
on relief in 1934, by 140 square-mile areas, the coefficient is
.89 ± .01. The extent and nature of the correspondence between

TABLE 42

RATES OF DELINQUENTS AND OF JUVENILE COURT
COMMITMENTS, FOR AREAS GROUPED BY PER-
CENTAGE OF FAMILIES ON RELIEF OR DEPEND-
ENT: 1927–33 AND 1917–23 SERIES

Percentage of Families on Relief, 1934	Rate of Delinquents 1927–33	Rate of Commitments 1927–33
28.0 and over (*39.2*)*....	11.7	4.3
21.0–27.9 (*23.8*)*....	6.1	1.9
14.0–20.9 (*16.9*)*....	4.3	1.4
7.0–13.9 (*9.8*)*....	2.9	0.7
0.0– 6.9 (*3.8*)*....	1.4	0.3

Rates of Dependency 1921	Rate of Delinquents 1917–23	Rate of Commitments 1917–23
2.0 and over (*2.8*)*....	9.2	3.2
1.5–1.9 (*1.7*)*....	7.1	2.5
1.0–1.4 (*1.2*)*....	6.4	2.2
0.5–0.9 (*0.7*)*....	5.1	1.5
0.0–0.4 (*0.1*)*....	2.9	0.8

* Percentage for class as a whole.

these two variables in Chicago are further indicated by the general
comparison shown in Table 42 with rates of commitments added.
Comparable data for the 1917–23 series are presented for classes
of areas grouped by 1921 dependency rates.[3]

The smooth variation in rates of delinquents with variation in
the percentage of families on relief and rates of family dependency
is presented graphically in Figure 23, *C* and *D*.

[3] The rates of dependency are based upon a study made by Professor Erle Fiske
Young and Faye B. Karpf, showing the total number of families receiving financial
aid from the United Charities and the Jewish Charities.

Median Rentals.—It is apparent from inspection, also, that there is a generally close association between equivalent monthly rentals and rates of delinquents. The areas of lowest rentals as of 1930 correspond quite closely with those of high rates of delinquents, and vice versa, though the relationship is not entirely linear. The zero-order coefficient obtained when median rentals

TABLE 43

RATES OF DELINQUENTS AND OF JUVENILE COURT COMMITMENTS
FOR AREAS GROUPED BY MEDIAN RENTAL (140 SQUARE-
MILE AREAS AND 60 COMMUNITIES), 1927–33 SERIES

Median Rentals, 1930 (140 Square-Mile Areas)	Rate of Delinquents 1927–33	Rate of Commitments 1927–33
$75.00 and over ($82.88)*..........	1.1	0.2
60.00–$74.99 (67.56)*..........	2.5	0.6
45.00– 59.99 (52.72)*..........	3.4	1.2
30.00– 44.99 (38.60)*..........	6.0	2.9
Under $30.00 (23.91)*..........	8.0	3.9

Median Rentals, 1934 (60 Community Areas)	Rate of Delinquents 1927–33	Rate of Commitments 1927–33
$43.00 and over ($47.49)*..........	1.2	0.3
36.00–$42.99 (40.13)*..........	2.2	0.6
29.00– 35.99 (32.43)*..........	3.3	1.4
22.00– 28.99 (26.77)*..........	4.5	2.3
Under $22.00 (17.31)*..........	7.2	3.5

* Rental for class as a whole.

and rates of delinquents in the 140 square-mile areas are correlated is −.61 ± .04. The areas deviating most from the general trend are the South Side neighborhoods, where, as a result of special conditions, previously discussed, the relationship between income and rentals is not the same as for the rest of the city. It is interesting in this connection, however, that when the predominantly Negro areas are considered separately, the median rentals are seen to vary inversely with rates of delinquents, just as they do in the white areas. When logarithms of rates of delinquents are plotted against median rentals, the regression is nearly linear, the coefficient being $-.71 \pm .03$ for the 140 areas.

The association between rentals and rates of delinquents is further indicated when rates of delinquents are calculated for the five classes of areas shown on Map 5 (chap. ii). For comparison, the same delinquency data were used to compute rates for classes of areas grouped according to median rentals, by communities instead of by square-mile areas, from the Chicago census of 1934. The results are presented in Table 43.

The data of Table 43 indicate that the rate of delinquents in the lowest rental class is more than seven times as high as that in the highest rental class, when the 1930 data are used, and six times as high when the calculations are based on the 1934 census by larger community areas. These relationships are presented graphically in Figure 23, E and F.

Home Ownership.—The relationship between families on relief and rates of delinquents, as has been shown, is positive and linear. Median rentals and home ownership, on the other hand, are both inversely related to delinquency; but in the latter case, now to be considered, the relationship is not linear. The correlation ratio has therefore been used. When the 1927–33 rates of delinquents are correlated with the percentage of families owning their homes, in the 140 square-mile areas, as of 1930, the correlation ratio, η, is $-.49$. Similarly, when the 1917–23 rates are correlated with the percentage of families owning homes in 1920, η is $-.47$. Both these correlations are naturally reduced by the low rates of home ownership in some apartment-house areas, where the rates of delinquents are also low. They are high enough, however, to indicate that, generally speaking, low rates of home ownership and high rates of delinquents tend to appear together throughout Chicago.

The general association of home ownership with rates of delinquents is clearly evident when the latter are calculated for classes of areas grouped on the basis of the rates of home ownership, as shown on Map 25. Table 44 shows the rates of delinquents for these five classes of areas and for similar classes as of 1920.

MAP 25

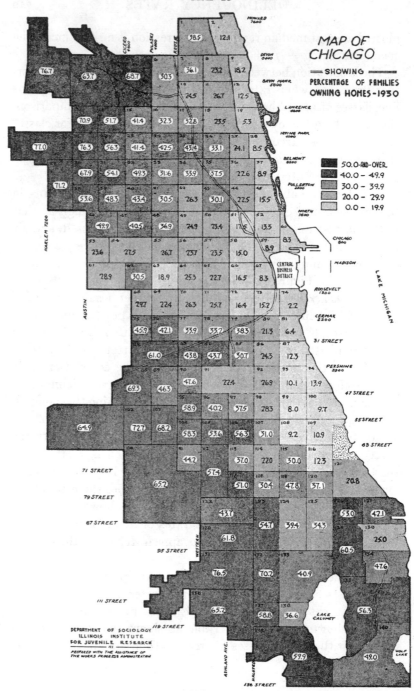

HOME OWNERSHIP, CHICAGO, 1930

As indicated previously, the association appears to be closer when rates of delinquents are compared with each of these variables for five general classes of areas than when the correlations are based on the 140 smaller areas into which the city has been divided for the purpose of this study. This is especially true of the relation between rates of delinquents and percentages of home-owning families. The latter measure is no doubt, at the same time,

TABLE 44

RATES OF DELINQUENTS FOR AREAS GROUPED
BY PERCENTAGE OF FAMILIES OWNING
HOMES: 1927–33 AND 1917–23 SERIES

Percentage of Families Owning Homes, 1930		Rate of Delinquents 1927–33
Under 20	(12.0)*	7.6
20–29.9	(24.3)*	5.1
30–39.9	(33.8)*	3.0
40–49.9	(44.4)*	2.5
50 and over	(62.7)*	2.3

Percentage of Families Owning Homes, 1920		Rate of Delinquents 1917–23
Under 15	(9.9)*	7.7
15.0–24.9	(20.0)*	6.6
25.0–34.9	(30.0)*	4.4
35.0–44.9	(38.8)*	3.2
45.0 and over	(56.2)*	3.8

* Percentage for class as a whole.

an indication of economic level, of the desirability status of an area, and of mobility. When the correlation ratio is calculated for the 140 areas, the coefficient is reduced greatly by the fact that many apartment areas are characterized both by low rates of delinquents and by low rates of home ownership. It will be noted, however, that the inverse relationship between the two phenomena is almost perfect when the data are treated in the five general classes. In this case, it is the trend alone which is clear, since actual differences within the areas are obscured.

Before closing the discussion of economic characteristics in relation to delinquency, it is necessary to ask: What is the meaning of the facts assembled? In view of the marked degree of covariance throughout the city, it is easy to postulate a causal relationship between economic level and rates of juvenile delinquents. The correlation between rates of families on relief and rates of delinquents (indicated by an r of .89 $\pm$ .01) suggests that, where the percentage of dependent families is high, one may confidently expect also a high delinquency rate; yet the former is not in itself an *explanation* of the latter. There was little or no change in the rate of delinquents for the city as a whole from 1929 to 1934, when applications for assistance were mounting daily and the rates of families dependent on public and private relief increased more than tenfold. This would seem to indicate that the relief rate is not itself causally related to rate of delinquents. The patterns of distribution for both phenomena during these years, however, continued to correspond. Rentals, relief, and other measures of economic level fluctuate widely with the business cycle; but it is only as they serve to differentiate neighborhoods from one another that they seem related to the incidence of delinquency. It is when the rentals in an area are low, *relative to other areas in the city*, that this area selects the least-privileged population groups. On the other hand, rates of delinquents, of adult criminals, of infant deaths, and of tuberculosis, for any given area, remain relatively stable from year to year, showing but minor fluctuations with the business cycle. A rise or fall in one is usually accompanied by a corresponding change in the others, as shown in chapter iv, and apparently indicates a change in the relative status of the local area itself.

POPULATION COMPOSITION IN RELATION TO RATES OF DELINQUENTS

In Chicago, as in other northern industrial cities, as has been said, it is the most recent arrivals—persons of foreign birth and those who have migrated from other sections of this country— who find it necessary to make their homes in neighborhoods of low economic level. Thus the newer European immigrants are found concentrated in certain areas, while Negroes from the rural South and Mexicans occupy others of comparable status. Neither of these population categories, considered separately, however, is

suitable for correlation with rates of delinquents, since some areas
of high rates have a predominantly immigrant population and
others are entirely or largely Negro. Both categories, however,
refer to groups of low economic status, making their adjustment
to a complex urban environment. Foreign-born and Negro heads
of families will therefore be considered together,[4] in order to study
this segregation of the newer arrivals, on a city-wide scale.

Percentage of Foreign-born and Negro Heads of Families.—When
the rates of delinquents in the 1927–33 series are correlated with
the percentage of foreign-born and Negro heads of families as of
1930, by 140 square-mile areas, the coefficient is found to be .60 ±
.03. Similarly, when the 1917–23 delinquency data are correlated
with percentages of foreign-born and Negro heads of families for
1920, by the 113 areas into which the city was divided for that
series, the coefficient is .58 ± .04.

When rates of delinquents are calculated for the classes of areas
shown on Map 26, wide variations are found between the rates in
the classes where the percentage of foreign-born and Negro heads
of families is high and in those where it is low. These data are
presented in Table 45 and in Figure 23, *G* and *H*. Since the number of foreign-born heads of families in the population decreased
and the number of Negroes increased between 1920 and 1930, the
total proportions of foreign-born and Negro heads of families in
each class do not correspond. The variation with rates of delinquents, however, remains unchanged.

While it is apparent from these data that the foreign born and
the Negroes are concentrated in the areas of high rates of delinquents, the meaning of this association is not easily determined.
One might be led to assume that the relatively large number of
boys brought into court is due to the presence of certain racial or
national groups were it not for the fact that the population composition of many of these neighborhoods has changed completely,

---

[4] The categories "foreign born" and "Negro" are not compatable, since the
former group is made up primarily of adults, while the latter includes all members of
the race. The classification "heads of families" has been used, therefore, foreign-
born and Negro family heads being entirely comparable groupings. The census
classification "other races" has been included—a relatively small group, comprising Mexicans, Japanese, Chinese, Filipinos, etc.

MAP 26

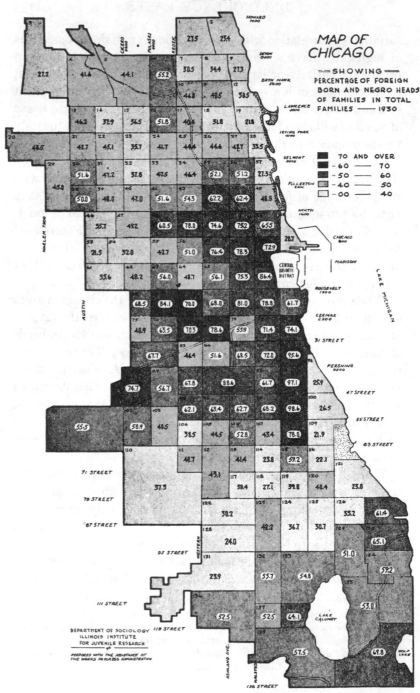

FOREIGN-BORN AND NEGRO HEADS OF FAMILIES, CHICAGO, 1930

without appreciable change in their rank as to rates of delinquents. Clearly, one must beware of attaching causal significance
to race or nativity. For, in the present social and economic system, it is the Negroes and the foreign born, or at least the newest
immigrants, who have least access to the necessities of life and
who are therefore least prepared for the competitive struggle. It
is they who are forced to live in the worst slum areas and who are
least able to organize against the effects of such living.

TABLE 45

RATES OF DELINQUENTS FOR AREAS GROUPED BY
PERCENTAGE OF FOREIGN-BORN AND NEGRO
HEADS OF FAMILIES: 1930 AND 1920

Percentage of Foreign-born and Negro Heads of Families, 1930	Rate of Delinquents 1927–33
70.0 and over (81.4)*..................	8.2
60.0–69.9 (64.5)*..................	4.8
50.0–59.9 (53.9)*..................	3.9
40.0–49.9 (45.5)*..................	2.8
Under 40.0 (30.0)*..................	1.7

Percentage of Foreign-born and Negro Heads of Families, 1920	Rate of Delinquents 1917–23
80.0 and over (85.3)*..................	8.4
67.0–79.9 (73.8)*..................	7.1
54.0–66.9 (60.2)*..................	4.6
41.0–53.9 (47.6)*..................	4.1
Under 41.0 (32.3)*..................	2.6

* Percentage for class as a whole.

In Chicago three kinds of data are available for the study of
nativity, nationality, and race in relation to rates of delinquents.
These data concern (1) the succession of nationality groups in the
high-rate areas over a period of years; (2) changes in the national
and racial backgrounds of children appearing in the Juvenile
Court; and (3) rates of delinquents for particular racial, nativity,
or nationality groups in different types of areas at any given moment. In evaluating the significance of community characteristics
found to be associated with high rates of delinquents, the relative weight of race, nativity, and nationality must be understood.
Therefore, a few basic tables from a more extended forthcoming

study will be presented, dealing, in order, with the three types of data referred to above.

Marked changes in population composition characterizing high-delinquency areas are indicated in Table 46, which shows for 8 inner-city areas[5] the variation, within the total foreign-born

TABLE 46

DISTRIBUTION OF NATIONALITIES IN THE FOREIGN-BORN
POPULATION AT INTERVALS FROM 1884 TO 1930, FOR
8 CHICAGO AREAS COMBINED*

COUNTRY OF BIRTH	PERCENTAGE IN TOTAL FOREIGN-BORN POPULATION FOR EIGHT AREAS			
	1884†	1898	1920	1930
Germany.............	46.2	35.9	7.2	6.2
Ireland...............	22.2	18.7	2.8	2.3
England and Scotland...	4.8	3.2	1.5	1.6
Scandinavia...........	16.9	19.8	2.4	2.0
Czechoslovakia........	3.5	6.2	2.8	2.8
Italy.................	0.4	2.4	21.6	25.5
Poland...............	2.6	4.2	29.2	34.0
Slavic countries........	0.1	2.2	19.6	14.0
All others............	3.3	7.4	12.9	11.6
Total............	100.0	100.0	100.0	100.0

* These have been areas of first immigrant settlement throughout the period studied.

† Area 91 is not included in computations for this column because in 1884 it was outside the boundaries of Chicago.

population, of percentages born in each specified country, between 1884 and 1930.[6]

It is readily evident from the data in Table 46 that the proportions of Germans, Irish, English-Scotch, and Scandinavians in the foreign-born population in 8 inner-city Chicago areas underwent, between 1884 and 1930, a decided decline (90.1 to 12.2 per cent); while the proportions of Italians, Poles, and Slavs increased. As

[5] These eight areas are 50, 52, 58, 66, 71, 79, 80, and 91.

[6] This tabulation includes most of the adult population, and consequently most of the parents of boys of juvenile court age. For example, in 1920, on the average, the fathers of 87 per cent of all boys 10–16 years of age in these areas were foreign born. The percentage of delinquent boys in the 8 areas in the same period whose fathers were foreign born was very nearly the same (83).

may be seen from a study of the rate maps representing the three juvenile court series, the 8 areas maintained, throughout these decades, approximately the same rates of delinquents relative to other areas. Some increased slightly in rank, others dropped slightly; but no trend in either direction was apparent. This is indicated roughly by the fact that the mean percentile ranks for the 8 areas, in the juvenile court series of 1927–33, 1917–23, and 1900–1906, were, respectively, 83, 85, and 85. It is significant, also, that when most families of a given nationality had moved out of these areas of first settlement, those who remained produced fewer delinquents than would be expected on the basis of their proportion in the population.

These 8 areas are but samples of the high-rate areas where changes in the population occurred. A similar analysis of any one of the inner-city areas in Chicago would no doubt reveal great changes in the nationality composition of the population, without discernible effect on the comparative status of the area as to rates of delinquents.

The second type of data available pertaining to the movement of national groups out of the high-rate areas is seen in Table 47,[7] which shows, over three decades, the changing proportion of delinquent boys whose fathers were born in each specified country.

Following the shift out of the areas of first settlement on the part of each older immigrant nationality, the proportion of their children among the boys of foreign parentage appearing in the Juvenile Court underwent a notable decline. Just as they were being replaced in their old areas of residence by more recent immigrants, so their sons were replaced in the dockets of the court by the sons of new arrivals. Further, no evidence exists which would indicate that the children of the nationalities disappearing from the court records are reappearing as children of the native-born children of the native-born descendants of these newcomers. The rates of delinquents in areas populated by these descendants re-

[7] From Clifford R. Shaw and Henry D. McKay, *Social Factors in Juvenile Delinquency*, Vol. II of *Report on the Causes of Crime*, National Commission on Law Observance and Enforcement, Report No. 13 (Washington, D.C.: U.S. Government Printing Office, 1931), p. 95.

main low, and in the Juvenile Court the proportion of boys born of native parents increases less rapidly than the proportion of native-parentage boys in the general population.

Further data dealing with the effect of nationality, nativity, and race on rates of delinquents are presented in Tables 48, 49, and 50. These indicate that the relatively higher rates found among the children of Negroes as compared with those of whites, the children of foreign-born as compared with those of native parents, and the

TABLE 47

PERCENTAGE DISTRIBUTION OF DELINQUENT BOYS BY COUNTRY OF
BIRTH OF THEIR FATHERS, FOR EACH FIFTH YEAR SINCE
1900, JUVENILE COURT OF COOK COUNTY

Country of Birth of Fathers	1900	1905	1910	1915	1920	1925	1930
United States:							
White...........	16.0	19.0	16.5	16.5	23.0	21.7	19.5
Negro...........	4.7	5.1	5.5	6.2	9.9	17.1	21.7
Germany..........	20.4	19.5	15.5	11.0	6.3	3.5	1.9
Ireland..........	18.7	15.4	12.3	10.7	6.1	3.1	1.3
Italy............	5.1	8.3	7.9	10.1	12.7	12.8	11.7
Poland...........	15.1	15.7	18.6	22.1	24.5	21.9	21.0
England and Scotland	3.4	3.0	2.5	2.6	0.9	0.7	0.6
Scandinavia.......	3.8	5.6	2.9	2.8	2.3	0.5	0.8
Austria..........	0.1	0.3	0.9	1.3	0.8	2.2	1.7
Lithuania.........	0.1	0.3	1.1	2.9	2.2	3.9	3.8
Czechoslovakia......	4.6	4.3	5.5	3.0	2.2	2.8	4.2
All others.........	8.0	4.5	11.8	10.8	9.1	9.8	11.8
Total..........	100.0	100.0	100.0	100.0	100.0	100.0	100.0

children of recent immigrant nationalities as compared with those of older immigrants may be attributed to the different patterns of distribution of these population groups within the city at a given time rather than to differences in the capacity of their children for conventional behavior.

The data in Tables 48, 49, and 50 support three related propositions. First, comparisons indicate that the white as well as the Negro, the native as well as the foreign born, and the older immigrant nationalities as well as the recent arrivals range in their rates of delinquents from the very highest to the lowest. While each population group at a given moment shows a concentration in certain types of social areas, and hence a characteristic magnitude in rate of delinquents, adequate samples of each may be found also in areas which, for them, are at the time atypical. Thus, as indicated in Table 48, rates for children of the foreign

TABLE 48

NUMBER AND RATES OF MALE JUVENILE DELINQUENTS, FOR NATIVITY
GROUPS, BY CLASSES OF AREAS GROUPED BY RATES OF
WHITE DELINQUENTS, 1927–33

AREA RATES OF WHITE DELINQUENTS	NATIVE WHITE OF NATIVE PARENTAGE (NWNP)			NATIVE WHITE OF FOREIGN OR MIXED PARENTAGE (NWFP)			PERCENTAGE BY WHICH RATE FOR NWFP EXCEEDS RATE FOR NWNP
	Boys Aged 10–16	Juvenile Delinquents	Rate of Delinquents	Boys Aged 10–16	Juvenile Delinquents	Rate of Delinquents	
0.0– 0.9.......	15,707	75	·0.48	14,684	78	0·.53	10.4
1.0– 1.9.......	17,428	225	1.29	23,218	364	1.57	21.7
2.0– 2.9.......	11,213	225	2.01	20,840	546	2.62	30.3
3.0– 3.9........	8,034	259	3.22	20,021	695	3.47	7.8
4.0– 4.9.......	4,082	167	4.09	11,567	514	4.44	8.6
5.0– 5.9.......	2,471	127	5.14	11,095	616	5.55	8.0
6.0– 6.9.......	1,739	81	4.66	6,805	467	6.86	47.2
7.0– 7.9.......	1,380	80	5.80	4,925	390	7.92	36.6
8.0– 8.9.......	505	44	8.71	1,935	162	8.37	− 3.9
9.0– 9.9.......	747	80	10.71	3,029	276	9.11	−14.9
10.0–10.9.......	401	32	7.98	1,656	182	10.99	37.7
11.0–11.9.......	418	50	11.96	1,739	193	11.10	− 7.2
12.0 and over....	308	46	14.94	2,654	410	15.45	3.4
City........	64,433	1,491	2.31	124,168	4,893	3.94	70.6
City (standardized)*..	64,433	2,080	3.23	124,168	4,537	3.65	13.0

* In this redistribution the racial and national groups in each class of areas were adjusted to correspond with their proportion in the city as a whole, as of 1930. The classes used were based on rates of white delinquents. However, standardization by areas grouped according to median rentals or other index of economic status would no doubt give approximately the same result.

born range from 0.53 to 15.45, and those for children of native whites from 0.48 to 14.94. Similarly, the rates for children of such diverse nationality groups as the Poles and the Italians, as well as for all other nationalities taken as a group, display a wide range. Racial comparisons present the same picture, although the variations are not so great. Data presented in Table 50 indicate that rates of delinquents among Negro children, as among whites, display wide variation. No racial, national, or nativity group exhibits a uniform, characteristic rate of delinquents in all parts of Chicago.

Second, within the same type of social area, the foreign born and the natives, recent immigrant nationalities, and older immi-

TABLE 49

RATES OF MALE JUVENILE DELINQUENTS FOR NATIVITY AND
NATIONALITY GROUPS, BY CLASSES OF AREAS GROUPED BY
RATES OF WHITE DELINQUENTS, 1927–33

AREA RATES OF WHITE DELINQUENTS	RATES OF DELINQUENTS					
	White	Native White of Native Parentage	Native White of Foreign or Mixed Parentage	Polish Origin	Italian Origin	All Other Native White of Foreign or Mixed Parentage
0.0– 0.9	0.50	0.48	0.53	0.53	0.89	0.52
1.0– 1.9	1.45	1.29	1.57	1.98	2.18	1.35
2.0– 2.9	2.41	2.01	2.62	2.97	4.08	2.24
3.0– 3.9	3.40	3.22	3.47	3.97	3.73	3.13
4.0– 4.9	4.35	4.09	4.44	5.22	5.36	3.75
5.0– 5.9	5.48	5.14	5.55	6.11	5.55	4.95
6.0– 6.9	6.41	4.66	6.86	7.34	7.95	5.77
7.0– 7.9	7.45	5.80	7.92	7.16	9.25	7.66
8.0– 8.9	8.44	8.71	8.37	9.43	8.30	7.87
9.0– 9.9	9.43	10.71	9.11	9.46	7.37	9.46
10.0–10.9	10.40	7.98	10.99	12.50	11.46	10.08
11.0–11.9	11.27	11.96	11.10	14.48	10.78	9.20
12.0 and over	15.40	14.94	15.45	11.68	18.40	11.76
City	3.38	2.31	3.94	4.58	7.06	2.95
City (standardized)*	3.53	3.23	3.65	3.99	4.29	3.23

* See Table 48, n., for standardization procedure.

grants produce very similar rates of delinquents. Those among the foreign born and among the recent immigrants who from 1927 to 1933 lived in physically adequate residential areas of higher economic status displayed low rates of delinquents, while, conversely, those among the native born and among the older immigrants who in that period occupied physically deteriorated areas of low economic status displayed high rates of delinquents. Negroes living in the most deteriorated and disorganized portions of the Negro community possessed the highest Negro rate of delinquents, just as whites living in comparable white areas showed the highest white rates.

Third, certain population groups with high rates of delinquents now dwell in preponderant numbers in those deteriorated and disorganized inner-city industrial areas where long-standing traditions of delinquent behavior have survived successive invasions of peoples of diverse origin. By "standardizing" their distribution—

TABLE 50

Number and Rates of Male Juvenile Delinquents, for Racial Groups, by Classes of Areas Grouped According to Rate of White Delinquents, 1927–33

Area Rates of Delinquents	White			Negro			Percentage by Which Rate for Negroes Exceeds Rate for Whites
	Boys Aged 10–16	Juvenile Delinquents	Rate of Delinquents	Boys Aged 10–16	Juvenile Delinquents	Rate of Delinquents	
0.0–3.9	120,642	2,461	2.04	574	42	7.32	258.8
4.0–7.9	50,095	2,387	4.76	1,065	181	17.00	257.1
8.0 and over	17,864	1,536	8.60	7,600	1,482	19.50	126.7
City	188,601	6,384	3.38	9,239	1,705	18.45	445.9
City (standardized)* . .	188,601	6,786	3.60	9,239	1,054	11.41	216.9

* See Table 48, n., for standardization procedure.

that is, creating a hypothetical proportionate redistribution of each nativity, racial, and nationality group throughout the city— it is possible to see the effect of the actual disproportionate concentration of each group at present in the high-rate areas. Table 48 indicates that such standardization reduces the delinquency rate for white children of foreign or mixed parentage from 3.94 to 3.65, and raises the rate for those of native white parentage from 2.31 to 3.23. It is interesting to note that in the unstandardized data the rate for foreign-parentage children in the city as a whole was 70.6 per cent greater than the city-wide rate for native-parentage children. Adjustment for disproportionate distribution of these two nativity groups reduced this excess to 13.0 per cent. The difficulty of securing areas which are uniform with reference to their social characteristics, however, renders the statistical correction sought in the use of the standardizing procedure only an approximate one at best. It is not valid, for example, to assume that the children of the foreign born residing in areas of predominantly native population live in exactly the same life-situation as do the children of native parents. Differences in status, values, and attitudes of associates are known to exist. If these differences could be statistically eliminated (an obvious impossibility), it is safe to assume that the difference in rate between these two nativity groups would approach zero.

Standardization with reference to parental nationality, as indicated in Table 49, lowers the Italian rate from 7.06 to 4.29 and the Polish rate from 4.58 to 3.99, while raising the rate of the "all others" group from 2.94 to 3.23. Similarly, Table 50 suggests the extent to which the Negro rate is a function of concentration in high-rate areas. Standardization here reduces the Negro rate from 18.45 to 11.41 and raises the white rate from 3.38 to 3.60.

It appears to be established, then, that each racial, nativity, and nationality group in Chicago displays widely varying rates of delinquents; that rates for immigrant groups in particular show a wide historical fluctuation; that diverse racial, nativity, and national groups possess relatively similar rates of delinquents in similar social areas; and that each of these groups displays the effect of disproportionate concentration in its respective areas at a given time. In the face of these facts it is difficult to sustain the contention that, by themselves, the factors of race, nativity, and nationality are vitally related to the problem of juvenile delinquency. It seems necessary to conclude, rather, that the significantly higher rates of delinquents found among the children of Negroes, the foreign born, and more recent immigrants are closely related to existing differences in their respective patterns of geographical distribution within the city. If these groups were found in the same proportion in all local areas, existing differences in the relative number of boys brought into court from the various groups might be expected to be greatly reduced or to disappear entirely.

It may be that the correlation between rates of delinquents and foreign-born and Negro heads of families is incidental to relationships between rates of delinquents and apparently more basic social and economic characteristics of local communities. Evidence that this is the case is seen in two partial correlation coefficients computed. Selecting the relief rate as a fair measure of economic level, the problem is to determine the relative weight of this and other factors. The partial correlation coefficient between rate of delinquents and percentage of families on relief, holding constant the percentage of foreign-born and Negro heads of families, in the 140 areas, is .76 ± .02. However, the coefficient for rates of delinquents and percentage of foreign-born and Negro heads of families, when percentage of families on relief is held constant, is only .26 ± .05. It is clear from these coefficients, therefore, that the percentage of families on relief is related to rates of delinquents in a more significant way than is the percentage of foreign-born and Negro heads of families.

It should be emphasized that the high degree of association between rates of delinquents and other community characteristics, as revealed in this chapter, does not mean that these characteristics must be regarded as causes of delinquency, or vice versa. Within certain types of areas differentiated in city growth, these phenomena appear together with such regularity that their rates are highly correlated. Yet the nature of the relationship between types of conduct and given physical, economic, or demographic characteristics is not revealed by the magnitude either of zero-order or partial correlation coefficients, or of other measures of association.

A high degree of association may lead to the uncritical assumption that certain factors are causally related, whereas further analysis shows the existing association to be entirely adventitious. This is apparently the case with the data on nativity, nationality, and race above presented. That, on the whole, the proportion of foreign-born and Negro population is higher in areas with high rates of delinquents there can be little doubt; but the facts furnish ample basis for the further conclusion that the boys brought into court are not delinquent *because* their parents are foreign born or Negro but rather because of other aspects of the total

TABLE 51

RATE OF DELINQUENTS, INCREASE OR DECREASE OF POPULATION, ECONOMIC SEGREGATION, AND SEGREGATION BY RACE AND NATIVITY, FOR 2-MILE ZONES, 1927–33 JUVENILE COURT SERIES

COMMUNITY CHARACTERISTICS	ZONES				
	I	II	III	IV	V
Rate of delinquents, 1927–33....	9.8	6.7	4.5	2.5	1.8
Percentage increase or decrease of population, 1920–30.........	−21.3	−9.3	12.3	42.9	140.8
Economic segregation:					
Percentage of families on relief, 1934....................	27.9	24.0	14.8	8.6	5.9
Median rentals, 1930.........	$38.08	$36.51	$53.08	$65.38	$73.51
Median rentals, 1934.........	$21.45	$20.44	$29.42	$38.04	$42.52
Percentage of families owning homes, 1930..............	12.8	21.8	26.2	32.8	47.2
Percentage in domestic and personal services, 1930.........	14.0	9.1	7.7	7.1	4.7
Segregation by race and nativity:					
Percentage of foreign-born and Negro heads of families, 1930.	62.3	64.9	55.9	40.4	39.4
Percentage of Negroes and other races in total population, 1930	9.5	12.8	10.8	4.9	0.3
Percentage of foreign born in white population, 1930......	33.2	33.1	28.7	23.5	20.7
Percentage of aliens in foreign-born population 21 and over, 1930....................	32.9	27.6	20.0	15.4	14.9
Percentage of aliens in white population 21 and over, 1930.	15.0	14.2	8.7	5.0	4.5

situation in which they live. In the same way, the relationship between rates of delinquents and each associated variable should be explored, either by further analysis, by experimentation, or by the study of negative cases.

SUMMARY

Variations in Community Characteristics by Zones.—All data presented in this chapter have been tabulated for the same zones used in analyzing the delinquency materials. Table 51 and Figure

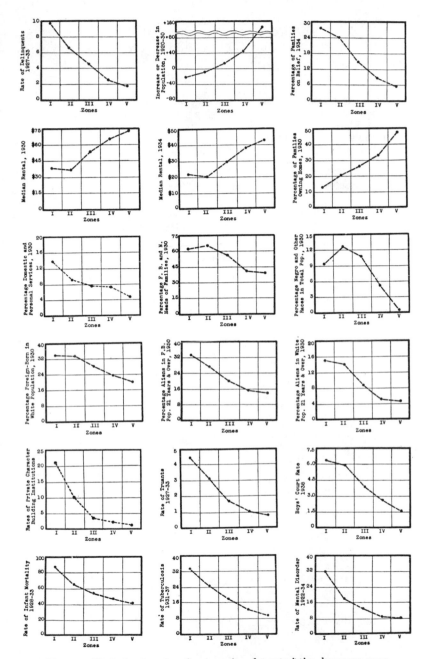

FIG. 24.—Variation in rates of community characteristics, by zones, 1930

24 bring together the phenomena associated with the 1927–33 juvenile court series, and Table 52 and Figure 25 present similar comparisons for the 1917–23 data.

TABLE 52

RATE OF DELINQUENTS, PERCENTAGE INCREASE OR DECREASE OF POPULA-
TION, ECONOMIC SEGREGATION, SEGREGATION BY RACE AND NATIVITY,
AND EMPLOYMENT BY TYPE OF INDUSTRY, FOR 2-MILE ZONES, 1917–23
JUVENILE COURT SERIES

COMMUNITY CHARACTERISTICS	ZONES				
	I	II	III	IV	V
Rate of delinquents, 1917–23.....	10.3	7.3	4.4	3.3	3.0
Percentage increase or decrease of population, 1910–20.........	−22.8	−2.2	35.3	71.0	124.4
Economic segregation:					
Rate of family dependency, 1921	3.0	1.7	0.6	0.4	0.3
Juvenile court dependency cases, 1917–23....................	1.7	1.2	0.7	0.5	0.4
Juvenile court mothers' pension cases, 1917–23.............	1.7	1.2	0.7	0.4	0.3
Percentage of families owning homes, 1920..............	11.9	17.5	25.6	31.9	43.6
Segregation by race and nativity:					
Percentage of foreign-born and Negro heads of families, 1920.	72.3	69.7	55.1	42.6	40.6
Percentage of Negroes in total population, 1920..........	2.5	8.3	4.3	1.6	0.4
Percentage of foreign born in white population, 1920......	41.0	37.5	30.1	23.6	22.6
Percentage of aliens in foreign-born population 21 and over, 1920....................	41.9	33.1	22.5	16.6	16.2
Percentage of aliens in white population 21 and over, 1920.	24.0	19.0	9.9	5.7	5.6
Employment by type of industry, 1920:					
Percentage manufacturing and mechanical................	46.6	50.2	43.3	39.3	40.3
Percentage clerical...........	6.7	9.5	13.0	15.8	15.5
Percentage professional services	3.4	3.2	4.4	5.7	6.4
Percentage domestic and personal services..............	10.3	7.2	5.3	4.1	3.3

It has been shown that, when rates of delinquents are calculated for classes of areas grouped according to rate of any one of a number of community characteristics studied, a distinct pattern appears—the two sets of rates in each case varying together.

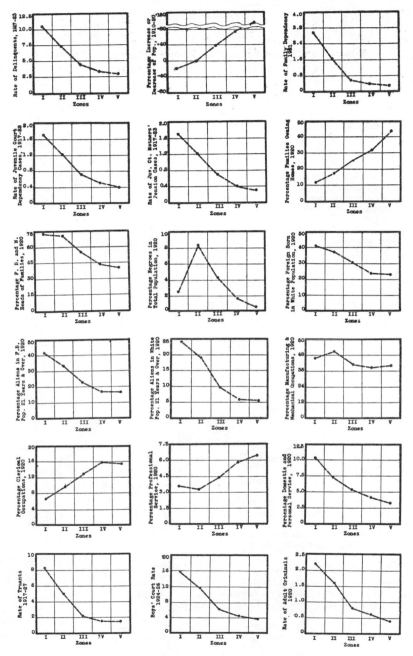

FIG. 25.—Variation in rates of community characteristics, by zones, 1920

TABLE 53

COMMUNITY CHARACTERISTICS, FOR AREAS GROUPED BY RATE OF DELINQUENTS: 1927–33 AND 1917–23 SERIES

COMMUNITY CHARACTERISTICS	RATES OF DELINQUENTS, 1927–33				
	0.0–2.4 (1.5)*	2.5–4.9 (3.5)*	5.0–7.4 (5.8)*	7.5–9.9 (9.0)*	10.0 and Over (13.5)*
Percentage increase or decrease of population, 1920–30†.........	59.7	28.6	−6.2	−14.0	−11.8
Median rental, 1930‡...........	$67.96	$54.83	$38.19	$35.58	$36.41
Percentage of families on relief, 1934‡......................	6.9	11.9	17.1	30.6	40.5
Percentage of families owning homes, 1930‡.................	35.9	32.0	27.5	17.5	14.9
Percentage of foreign-born and Negro heads of families, 1930‡.	37.8	50.5	51.8	69.3	81.9
Rate of truants, 1927–33‡.......	0.7	1.5	2.8	3.9	5.4
Rate of young adult offenders, 1938‡......................	1.7	3.0	4.6	6.9	11.5
Rate of infant mortality, 1928–34§	41.8	55.1	72.0	72.9	78.3
Rate of mental disorder, 1922–34§	9.4	12.5	19.0	26.9	23.6
Rate of tuberculosis, 1931–37‖ ...	9.9	13.2	19.7	27.8	64.6

COMMUNITY CHARACTERISTICS†	RATES OF DELINQUENTS, 1917–23				
	0.0–2.9 (2.0)*	3.0–5.9 (4.2)*	6.0–8.9 (7.1)*	9.0–11.9 (10.0)*	12.0 and Over (14.1)*
Percentage increase or decrease of population, 1910–20..........	67.9	43.4	−0.4	−10.4	−19.2
Percentage of families owning homes, 1920.................	33.6	28.4	22.7	16.8	10.0
Percentage of foreign-born and Negro heads of families, 1920...	43.9	52.4	68.4	75.5	77.6
Rate of truants, 1917–27........	0.9	2.0	5.1	7.6	9.8
Boys' court cases, 1924–26......	3.1	5.5	11.8	17.1	21.6
Juvenile court dependents, 1917–23..........................	0.3	0.7	1.1	1.6	2.4
Family dependency, 1921........	0.2	0.6	1.7	2.1	2.6

* Rate for class as a whole.   ‡ By 140 areas.   ‖ By 60 areas.
† By 113 areas.   § By 120 areas.

When values of these other community characteristics, in turn, are calculated for classes of areas grouped by rate of delinquents, the same consistent trends appear, as is seen in Table 53.

The data in this chapter indicate a high degree of association between rates of delinquents and other community character-istics when correlations are computed on the basis of values in square-mile areas or similar subdivisions, and a still closer gen-eral association by large zones or classes of areas. In the following chapters an attempt will be made to determine how the commu-nity conditions in question are related to delinquency—in short, to describe briefly the mechanisms and processes through which these conditions are translated into conduct.

CHAPTER VII

DIFFERENCES IN SOCIAL VALUES AND ORGANI-
ZATION AMONG LOCAL COMMUNITIES

I N THE previous chapter those areas of the city where the
rates of delinquents are high have been distinguished from
the low-rate areas in terms of physical, economic, and population characteristics. In the present chapter attention is focused
upon the more subtle differences in values, standards, attitudes,
traditions, and institutions. This discussion will be based upon
data already presented and also upon facts drawn from other
studies or from personal acquaintance with the communities under consideration.

DIFFERENTIAL SYSTEMS OF VALUES

In general, the more subtle differences between types of communities in Chicago may be encompassed within the general proposition that in the areas of low rates of delinquents there is more
or less uniformity, consistency, and universality of conventional
values and attitudes with respect to child care, conformity to law,
and related matters; whereas in the high-rate areas systems of
competing and conflicting moral values have developed. Even
though in the latter situation conventional traditions and institutions are dominant, delinquency has developed as a powerful
competing way of life. It derives its impelling force in the boy's
life from the fact that it provides a means of securing economic
gain, prestige, and other human satisfactions and is embodied in
delinquent groups and criminal organizations, many of which
have great influence, power, and prestige.

In the areas of high economic status where the rates of delinquents are low there is, in general, a similarity in the attitudes of
the residents with reference to conventional values, as has been
said, especially those related to the welfare of children. This is
illustrated by the practical unanimity of opinion as to the desir-

ability of education and constructive leisure-time activities and of the need for a general health program. It is shown, too, in the subtle, yet easily recognizable, pressure exerted upon children to keep them engaged in conventional activities, and in the resistance offered by the community to behavior which threatens the conventional values. It does not follow that all the activities participated in by members of the community are lawful; but, since any unlawful pursuits are likely to be carried out in other parts of the city, children living in the low-rate communities are, on the whole, insulated from direct contact with these deviant forms of adult behavior.

In the middle-class areas and the areas of high economic status, moreover, the similarity of attitudes and values as to social control is expressed in institutions and voluntary associations designed to perpetuate and protect these values. Among these may be included such organizations as the parent-teachers associations, women's clubs, service clubs, churches, neighborhood centers, and the like. Where these institutions represent dominant values, the child is exposed to, and participates in a significant way in one mode of life only. While he may have knowledge of alternatives, they are not integral parts of the system in which he participates.

In contrast, the areas of low economic status, where the rates of delinquents are high, are characterized by wide diversity in norms and standards of behavior. The moral values range from those that are strictly conventional to those in direct opposition to conventionality as symbolized by the family, the church, and other institutions common to our general society. The deviant values are symbolized by groups and institutions ranging from adult criminal gangs engaged in theft and the marketing of stolen goods, on the one hand, to quasi-legitimate businesses and the rackets through which partial or complete control of legitimate business is sometimes exercised, on the other. Thus, within the same community, theft may be defined as right and proper in some groups and as immoral, improper, and undesirable in others. In some groups wealth and prestige are secured through acts of skill and courage in the delinquent or criminal world, while in neighboring groups any attempt to achieve distinction in this manner would result in extreme disapprobation. Two conflicting systems of economic activity here present roughly equivalent opportunities for employment and for promotion. Evidence of success in the criminal world is indicated by the presence of adult criminals whose clothes and automobiles indicate unmistakably that they have prospered in their chosen fields. The values missed and the greater risks incurred are not so clearly apparent to the young.

Children living in such communities are exposed to a variety of contradictory standards and forms of behavior rather than to a relatively consistent and conventional pattern.[1] More than one type of moral institution and education are available to them. A boy may be familiar with, or exposed to, either the system of conventional activities or the system of criminal activities, or both. Similarly, he may participate in the activities of groups which engage mainly in delinquent activities, those concerned with conventional pursuits, or those which alternate between the two worlds. His attitudes and habits will be formed largely in accordance with the extent to which he participates in and becomes identified with one or the other of these several types of groups.

Conflicts of values necessarily arise when boys are brought in contact with so many forms of conduct not reconcilable with conventional morality as expressed in church and school. A boy may be found guilty of delinquency in the court, which represents the values of the larger society, for an act which has had at least tacit approval in the community in which he lives. It is perhaps common knowledge in the neighborhood that public funds are embezzled and that favors and special consideration can be received from some public officials through the payment of stipulated sums; the boys assume that all officials can be influenced in this way. They are familiar with the location of illegal institutions in the community and with the procedures through which such institutions are opened and kept in operation; they know where

[1] Edwin H. Sutherland has called this process "differential association." See E. H. Sutherland, *Principles of Criminology* (Chicago: J. B. Lippincott Co., 1939), chap. i.

stolen goods can be sold and the kinds of merchandise for which there is a ready market; they know what the rackets are; and they see in fine clothes, expensive cars, and other lavish expenditures the evidences of wealth among those who openly engage in illegal activities. All boys in the city have some knowledge of these activities; but in the inner-city areas they are known intimately, in terms of personal relationships, while in other sections they enter the child's experience through more impersonal forms of communication, such as motion pictures, the newspaper, and the radio.

Other types of evidence tending to support the existence of diverse systems of values in various areas are to be found in the data on delinquency and crime. In the previous chapter, variations by local areas in the number and rates of adult offenders were presented. When translated into its significance for children, the presence of a large number of adult criminals in certain areas means that children there are in contact with crime as a career and with the criminal way of life, symbolized by organized crime. In this type of organization can be seen the delegation of authority, the division of labor, the specialization of function, and all the other characteristics common to well-organized business institutions wherever found.

Similarly, the delinquency data presented graphically on spot maps and rate maps in the preceding pages give plausibility to the existence of a coherent system of values supporting delinquent acts. In making these interpretations it should be remembered that delinquency is essentially group behavior. A study of boys brought into the Juvenile Court of Cook County during the year 1928[2] revealed that 81.8 per cent of these boys committed the offenses for which they were brought to court as members of groups. And when the offenses were limited to stealing, it was found that 89 per cent of all offenders were taken to court as group or gang members. In many additional cases where the boy

[2] Clifford R. Shaw and Henry D. McKay, *Social Factors in Juvenile Delinquency*, Vol. II of *Report on the Causes of Crime*, National Commission on Law Observance and Enforcement, Report No. 13 (Washington, D.C.: U.S. Government Printing Office, 1931), pp. 191–99.

actually committed his offense alone, the influence of companions was, nevertheless, apparent. This point is illustrated in certain cases of boys charged with stealing from members of their own families, where the theft clearly reflects the influence and instigation of companions, and in instances where the problems of the boy charged with incorrigibility reveal conflicting values, those of the family competing with those of the delinquent group for his allegiance.

The heavy concentration of delinquency in certain areas means, therefore, that boys living in these areas are in contact not only with individuals who engage in proscribed activity but also with groups which sanction such behavior and exert pressure upon their members to conform to group standards. Examination of the distribution map reveals that, in contrast with the areas of concentration of delinquents, there are many other communities where the cases are so widely dispersed that the chances of a boy's having intimate contact with other delinquents or with delinquent groups are comparatively slight.

The importance of the concentration of delinquents is seen most clearly when the effect is viewed in a temporal perspective. The maps representing distribution of delinquents at successive periods indicate that, year after year, decade after decade, the same areas have been characterized by these concentrations. This means that delinquent boys in these areas have contact not only with other delinquents who are their contemporaries but also with older offenders, who in turn had contact with delinquents preceding them, and so on back to the earliest history of the neighborhood. This contact means that the traditions of delinquency can be and are transmitted down through successive generations of boys, in much the same way that language and other social forms are transmitted.

The cumulative effect of this transmission of tradition is seen in two kinds of data, which will be presented here only very briefly. The first is a study of offenses, which reveals that certain types of delinquency have tended to characterize certain city areas. The execution of each type involves techniques which must be learned from others who have participated in the same activity. Each involves specialization of function, and each has its own terminology and standards of behavior. Jack-rolling, shoplifting, stealing from junkmen, and stealing automobiles are examples of offenses with well-developed techniques, passed on by one generation to the next.

The second body of evidence on the effects of the continuity of tradition within delinquent groups comprises the results of a study of the contacts between delinquents, made through the use of official records.[3] The names of boys who appeared together in court were taken, and the range of their association with other boys whose names appeared in the same records was then analyzed and charted. It was found that some members of each delinquent group had participated in offenses in the company of other older boys, and so on, backward in time in an unbroken continuity as far as the records were available. The continuity thus traced is roughly comparable to that which might be established among baseball players through their appearance in official line-ups or regularly scheduled games. In baseball it is known that the techniques are transmitted through practice in back yards, playgrounds, sand lots, and in other places where boys congregate. Similarly in the case of delinquency traditions, if an unbroken continuity can be traced through formal institutions such as the Juvenile Court, the actual contacts among delinquents in the community must be numerous, continuous, and vital.

The way in which boys are inducted into unconventional behavior has been revealed by large numbers of case studies of youths living in areas where the rates of delinquents are high. Through the boy's own life-story the wide range of contacts with other boys has been revealed. These stories indicate how at early ages the boys took part with older boys in delinquent activities, and how, as they themselves acquired experience, they initiated others into the same pursuits. These cases reveal also the steps through which members are incorporated into the delinquent group organization. Often at early ages boys engage in malicious

[3] "Contacts between Successive Generations of Delinquent Boys in a Low-Income Area in Chicago" (unpublished study by the Department of Sociology, Illinois Institute for Juvenile Research, 1940).

mischief and simple acts of stealing. As their careers develop, they become involved in more serious offenses, and finally become skilled workmen or specialists in some particular field of criminal activity. In each of these phases the boy is supported by the sanction and the approbation of the delinquent group to which he belongs.

The manner in which the boy in the high-rate areas is exposed to delinquency values and assimilates them through his group contacts is most clearly revealed in autobiographical documents. To illustrate this process, short excerpts from the life-stories of three delinquents in widely separated sections of Chicago are presented, essentially as written.

CASE 1

My start as a delinquent was as many more fellows started. It started with playing hookey from school. Then I was shown how to get cookies, cakes, and a lot of other things that can make the day nice for a young truant. That was simple, the folks having credit at stores and paying every two weeks or month were the goats. I would go into the store and ask for whatever I wanted and when I got it all I had to say was put it on the bill, and walk out. When the time came for the bill to be payed it was all marked in with the regular purchases and nothing was said. From that it led to taking pennies from mother's purse, stealing junk from yards, etc. Then it started to be a habit of going through the brothers pockets while he was at work and taking change, a dime, fifteen cents, a quarter and sometimes more; it all depended on how much change was there. That served to give me enough courage to prowl a house when the opportunity came one day. I would have never did it alone but being with one of my pals that was different. That led to heaving coal and selling it, stealing pidgeons and sometimes chickens and selling them, also hanging around Hiesler and Junge bakery and crawling through windows and stealing cakes and cookies, and also stealing and selling bicycles. And so it went, always increasing the value of the theft, until it came up to where I was using a gun and had dropped most of the petty things and was going after some real dough.

My neighborhood at the time of my first delinquencies was not the worst nor either the best. The parents living in the neighborhood were respectable, and if there boys or girls were found or heard of doing any thing wrong they were taken care of. There were a lot of ways this was accomplished, for instance, a good paddling, well that came with all the remedys, then there was such a thing as making them stay in the house after supper and hit the hay early while the rest of his or her crowd was outside playing. Then there was another one, on Saturdays and Sunday afternoons every kid in the neighborhood went to the show but I know plenty of kids that didn't go all the time because they were caught, maybe stealing some little thing, playing hookey, or maybe even breaking a window on purpose.

As a whole, the people of the neighborhood were the right kind of people. They wanted and tried to the best of there knowledge, to keep there kids on the right path. They forbid them to go with the bad actors and punished them when they found out that they were together. In the meantime the folks of the bad actors were just as busy trying to straighten them out.

The feelings of these people is this. Each family thought, well if Jones kid is going bad, let him, thats his peoples lookout, but mines not if I can help it. What somebody elses kid did did not bother them as long as it did not involve there kid or property.

Like in nearly every neighborhood there was a bunch of us younger guys that no amount of beating could keep us going right for over a few hours. Then there was also the big gang, made up of older guys somewhere between 14 and 17 years of age. Then there was also the oldest bunch hanging around in front of the saloon. These guys were mostly men from about 21 to 35 mostly drunkards and who hardly ever worked but they never mixed outside of themselves. My nerve and gameness to get into anything that was going on got me in with this bunch and after getting pinched a couple of times and licking a few of the older lads, I was looked on as sort of a hero by the lads of my own class, and then I started hanging with these older guys steady.

When I first started stealing or at the time of my first delinquency my gang were all little young fellows of my own age more or less selfish as it seems to me now as I look back and of course they did a little bit of stealing but when they did whatever they got they kept to themselves very seldom dividing with anyone else. I was all together different, whatever I had, stolen, or bought, I allways split it. When I stole a few pennies it was spent in the company of my pals and they got as much of whatever I bought as I did. For being so bighearted of course they looked on me as a sort of a leader and thought I was a swell and clever guy to get away with things as I did. This also made me feel like a big guy and so I kept getting a little braver as I went along and kept doing bigger jobs.

After I was admitted to the older gang, through my nerve and gameness I was sort of a flunky. I was easy. They could get whatever I had and I'd do about everything they wanted me to, and not until I licked several of the younger members was I treated as a regular. After that, some other guy had to do the dirty work. I was still easy though, I gave away and let them talk me out of everything I had and nearly allways had to be the lead man. For instance, if a bicycle was standing on some porch it was me that was told to go up and get it and not wanting to be thought yellow I got it. After it was sold I might get a fourth of what I should have and I'd never say anything.

It was this way until after I started hanging with another gang for a while and then came back to hang with the old one again. I got into an argument with one of the new leaders of the gang and licked him and after that it was a toss up between me and the former as to who really was leader. After that I would hang with different gangs, once with this mob, another time with that, and every gang I hung with seemed to think I was the whole circus. I could fight and I would and I was an all around true badman, who wouldn't talk if pinched.

CASE 2

One day when I was about nine, we were caught by the gang that beat me up my first day home from the orphanage. They wanted us to join their gang. I saw we would get the worst of it, so I made a bargain with them. I told them to let James (my brother) alone, and if they did, I would join their gang. They wanted the both of us and I pleaded and begged. Finally, the leader, the fellow that gave me a beating, agreed. I made James promise he would say nothing to ma. The gang was about thirty strong. They would steal milk off porches, bread from bread boxes, steal from peddlers and take kids' lunch money from them. At first I just watched for them.

One day they said they would go out that night and break into peanut slots for the pennies. I told them I couldn't stay out that late, so we made a plan. We would start out about seven o'clock and be back before nine o'clock. Each man would be given a chance to show his mettle. We would travel in groups on each side of the street until we spotted a gum slot or peanut slot. Each of us had stones and pieces of rock in our pockets. The leader would be the first to break into the slot machine for pennies. He would take a hammer and knock in the back of the slot, at the same time holding his hat or cap, whatever he happened to be wearing at the time, so that the pennies would roll or slide right into it. We were on the side lines and in case the proprietor or someone tried to grab him we would let loose a barrage of stones that would slow him up and give whoever was doing the dirty work a chance to get away. Thus we were almost sure of getting what we were after.

When my turn came I wanted to back down. I was shaking like a leaf. They threatened to jump me, so I took the hammer and busted a machine which held gum balls. I was so nervous when I did the penny slot that I hit it in such a manner that I busted the glass with my elbow. I dropped the hammer and grabbed my cap which I had laid under the slot. When I got to the gang my cap held a mixture of glass, gum balls and pennies. My arm was numb, I must have hit my crazy bone. I must have collected thirty pennies, about a dozen gum balls, and some glass. The boys tapped me on the back and told me I did fine which made me feel good. We made about a dollar apiece almost every time. I would go home from these forages and give James a dime to keep his mouth shut. I would tell ma I was playing with the older boys. She believed me.

We got tired of slot machines. One of the boys hit on the idea of snatching purses. My first purse snatching was at the elevated station. I waited alongside the steps on the ground ready to grab the purse. Along came a woman up the steps. She must have been about forty years old. I waited breathlessly, not wanting even to breathe for fear my intended victim would hear it. She came up the stairs slowly. I got a bead on her purse, shot my hand in through the opening in the iron grill work, grabbed the purse, and was on my way. She must have been struck speechless, because I did not hear an outcry until I was about 200 feet from where I snatched the purse. I got away all right. My snatch was worth $37.00. We were not allowed to keep any trinkets or anything that was found in the purse and many times we threw away watches, rings, keys, photos, necklaces, good purses, pencils, and pens. The leader would never let us keep anything for fear we might get picked up and they would find something to incriminate us. It would be too bad as someone was bound to talk. Now that I think of it, this leader of ours was a pretty shrewd guy.

We snatched purses on elevated platforms. We got on the platforms by climbing the adjoining building to the roof, and going from the roof to the station platform. We would wait until a train came and then we would spot our victim. When the train started we would all three of us reach in through the open windows and grab a purse. We were highly successful, but could not play a station more than once. This we could not keep up for more than three days because everyone was on the alert and they had dicks planted on platforms. We were almost caught once and so found out about the dicks.

One evening another fellow and myself were on the D—— Station. We had climbed up an iron ladder. I grabbed a purse and a dick was on the other end of the same platform. The woman screamed and the dick was after me. I dropped the purse over the rail to the ladder. The dicks were not allowed to shoot at kids with short pants in those days, so I got away. We never worked that way any more. We snatched purses in the park by hiding in the bushes. When a lone woman came along and all was clear I would grab the purse and run through the bushes and over streets until I came to where the boys were waiting. We would hide in alleys, doorways, behind bill posters, and in any place where we could snatch a purse.

Then we started stealing from junk men. We would find a shed suitably located near an alley. We made sure the shed was nice and dark. Then we would wait for a junk man and one of the boys would go out and ask him if he wanted to buy some copper. The peddler would ask how much copper he had and the boy would say, "Plenty." The peddler would figure, "Well, here's where I gyp the kid," so he would come in and we would jump him and take his money. Then we would all run out and close the door. We could hear the peddler hollering for help. Many times we would almost split our sides laughing at the antics of the peddler when we jumped him. We got away with this for about two weeks until the peddlers smartened up. Many times while the rest of us had the peddler in the shed, rolling him, one or two of the boys would steal the horse and wagon, take it in the neighborhood and take out all the junk. Most of the boys would shoot dice with their money, but I used mine to go to the theatre with James and for candy and ice cream. That way James kept his mouth shut and we had a good time.

In the meantime I would play hookey from school and have one of the boys' older brothers write a note to the teacher stating that I was sick. I got away with this for a long time. We finally moved into a nice flat just across the street, but I still hung out with the same boys. Finally, one day I came home with about $30.00 and James got jealous and wanted to join the gang. I told him of the chances we were taking and promised him that some day we would work together, just him and I. This quieted him. I worked with the boys for about four months from my new address. Everyone liked me because I had guts and I finally became the leader's lieutenant. No one objected.

I suggested the idea of breaking into box cars and stealing merchandise. We would go up on the tracks, break the seals and carry out shoes, coats, dresses and anything we could get. One of the boys' older brothers would get rid of the stuff and give us some money. He probably gypped us out of plenty but we were content that we made a few dollars almost every night. Finally one night I had a falling out with the leader. He was a little bigger than I was, but I must have had a knack at using my fists and could take punishment. I beat him until he cried, "You win!" Then I was head man. The boys all liked me anyway. While fighting with the leader I must have been thinking about the time he beat me up when I got out of the orphans' home, because I really fought, not so much to win, but to get revenge and even the score. I sure went to town on his eyes and nose.

As I said before I was head man when I beat the leader. I took the boys to M—— Street and told everyone to steal something. Almost everyone did get something. We met under my uncle's back porch, hid our stuff, and went out for more. We stole shoes, caps, stockings, men's and women's watches, candy, cigars, cards, anything we could lay our hands on. When we got stuff we could not get rid of, we had one of the kids' brothers get rid of it. All the money was divided equally, of course. Now and then I "went south" with a few bucks. We had a lot of narrow escapes, and so I finally quit that gang.

I picked out two brothers to work with me—Rudy and Tom. Their bigger brother was a strong-arm artist, their mother and father made booze and bought bonds with the proceeds. All this I found out later. However, I took these two brothers with me because I liked them and they had more guts than any of the boys. I also added James to my gang and we started snatching purses ourselves. I had James watch for us while we did the work. He wanted to try it, but I made him do what I said. We made good, the four of us. Rudy and Tom liked dice and cards and they taught James and me all about it. All our money we used for playing cards, shooting dice, going to theatres, ice cream, candy, Riverview, and White City. Mostly we were in White City. We would take in everything at White City until our money gave out. We would then sneak on the L and go home. We always managed to get home about 9:00 or 10:00 P.M. We were bawled out, but that's all.

CASE 3

I can only remember the things I done since I was eleven years old. I was going to a school for crippled children. At eight oclock in the morning a bus would come and take me to school. They gave us our dinner there and brought us home at a quarter after three. When I got home I would eat supper and go to the corner and meet some of the kids in the neighborhood. Most of the people who lived there were poor. So we used to get a couple of coaster wagons and burlap-sacks and go down to the tracks and steal coal out of the freight car. Then we would take it home. We would go to get coal three or four times every night. On Saturdays we would go into the stock yards and chase cows or pigs. Some days we would go to Mr. G's stable and rent a horse and wagon to ride around with. When I was twelve I went to the hospital and was operated on. I had my ankle stiffened so I would walk straight. I laid in the hospital for eight or nine months. After I came home I walked on crutches for three months before I could use my leg. As soon as I could walk I went out with the boys and started stealing coal again. One day as I was getting coal I was caught. A detective took me into a railroad shanty and asked me where I lived and when I would not tell him, he went to the phone to call the police. I ran out of the shanty and he chased me, but I got away from him.

When I was fourteen my father died and we moved. I had one year of school to finish so I started to go to the school near where we lived. I was there about three weeks when I started to go with a lad by the name of William Jones. We called him Bill for short. He had a fancy for pigeons and rabbits. I started to go out nights and we would steal as high as 100 or 200 pigeons a week. We would sell them at fifty cents a pair. . . . .

We needed something to go to different neighborhoods with so we stole a couple of bicycles and put wire baskets on the handle bars to carry them in. We stole pigeons for about two years and then we quit. We started to go with a lot of lads who were breaking into schools. One day I was in the park with one of the lads, when one of the park officers arrested us. He had been told to watch in the park for the lad I was with. We were taken to the Juvenile home and they asked us a lot of questions about the schools. The lad I was with told them I was not with him and the other lads and they turned me loose. At the time I was arrested I was fifteen and was going to high school. I went there seven months and then I quit. Jones was working for a meat market and I decided I would go to work. I got myself a job in a electrical shop. It seemed the more money I got the more I wanted so I started to stealing cars and breaking into stores.

When I was sixteen I started to go out with the girls pretty steady and I had to have a lot of money. I would steal a car in the night time and the next day I would go to the high school and take some girls home. I would go there at a quarter after twelve and take two girls home. Then I would go home and eat dinner. After dinner I would wait until a quarter after two and go back to the high school and take two more home. After supper I would meet some of the gang and we would take a couple of girls out riding or to a show. I worked for the electrical shop for three months and was laid off. I went to work for another shop. I was getting eighteen dollars a week then. I was spraying and dipping baskets and it wasn't a very good job.

I started going with a different bunch of lads. We would steal cars and sell them. I use to get as high as $70.00 or $100.00 for one car. I never did know where one of the lads sold them. When we stole a car we had to give the car to him and he would take it and sell it and bring us the money the next day. The lads I was going with were a bunch of burglars and automobile thieves. We were soon taught by the older members of the gang not to ride in one stolen car more than 24 hours and not to ride in the neighborhood we stole it in. When a car is stolen it is never looked for until after twenty-four hours.

I was going with them for about six months. They were all caught one day except me. One of the lads was caught with a car and he turned stool pigeon. Five of them were sent to the Bridewell for ninety days and two were given six months. As I was the only one of the gang not in jail I had a hard time for ninety days sending my seven partners money for eats and cigarettes. You can just about imagine what the other lad who sent them there got, when they got out. As soon as they got out, we started stealing cars again.

A study recently completed[4] gives support both to the notion that there is frequent continuity between juvenile delinquency and adult crime and to the significance of group participation in the perpetuation of criminal activities. Through this study it has been shown that more than 60 per cent of all boys who appeared in the Juvenile Court of Cook County during 1920 were arrested as adults for offenses other than traffic violations in the 15 years subsequent to their initial court appearance. It was found also that the chances of a boy's continuing in adult crime were some-

[4] "Criminal Careers of Former Juvenile Delinquents" (unpublished study [mimeo.] by Department of Sociology, Illinois Institute for Juvenile Research, Chicago, 1941).

what greater if he appeared in court as a member of a group than they were if he appeared alone, and much greater if he had one or more delinquent brothers. Of the boys who had no brothers with official delinquency records, 56.5 per cent continued in adult crime, as compared with 72.0 per cent of those known to have one or more delinquent brothers.

Taken together, these studies indicate that most delinquent acts are committed by boys in groups, that delinquent boys have frequent contact with other delinquents, that the techniques for specific offenses are transmitted through delinquent group organization, and that in his officially proscribed activity the boy is supported and sustained by the delinquent group to which he belongs.

DIFFERENTIAL SOCIAL ORGANIZATION

Other subtle differences among communities are to be found in the character of their local institutions, especially those specifically related to the problem of social control. The family, in areas of high rates of delinquents, is affected by the conflicting systems of values and the problems of survival and conformity with which it is confronted. Family organization in high-rate areas is affected in several different ways by the divergent systems of values encountered. In the first place, it may be made practically impotent by the existing interrelationships between the two systems. Ordinarily, the family is thought of as representing conventional values and opposed to deviant forms of behavior. Opposition from families within the area to illegal practices and institutions is lessened, however, by the fact that each system may be contributing in certain ways to the economic well-being of many large family groups. Thus, even if a family represents conventional values, some member, relative, or friend may be gaining a livelihood through illegal or quasi-legal institutions—a fact tending to neutralize the family's opposition to the criminal system.

Another reason for the frequent ineffectiveness of the family in directing boys' activities along conventional lines is doubtless the allegiance which the boys may feel they owe to delinquent groups. A boy is often so fully incorporated into the group that it exercises more control than does the family. This is especially true in those neighborhoods where most of the parents are European-born. There the parents' attitudes and interests reflect an Old World background, while their children are more fully Americanized and more sophisticated, assuming in many cases the role of interpreter. In this situation the parental control is weakened, and the family may be ineffective in competing with play groups and organized gangs in which life, though it may be insecure, is undeniably colorful, stimulating, and enticing.

A third possible reason for ineffectiveness of the family is that many problems with which it is confronted in delinquency areas are new problems, for which there is no traditional solution. An example is the use of leisure time by children. This is not a problem in the Old World or in rural American communities, where children start to work at an early age and have a recognized part in the system of production. Hence, there are no time-honored solutions for difficulties which arise out of the fact that children in the city go to work at a later age and have much more leisure at their disposal. In the absence of any accepted solution for this problem, harsh punishment may be administered; but this is often ineffective, serving only to alienate the children still more from family and home.

Other differences between high-rate and low-rate areas in Chicago are to be seen in the nature of the existing community organization. Thomas and Znaniecki[5] have analyzed the effectively organized community in terms of the presence of social opinion with regard to problems of common interest, identical or at least consistent attitudes with reference to these problems, the ability to reach approximate unanimity on the question of how a problem should be dealt with, and the ability to carry this solution into action through harmonious co-operation.

Such practical unanimity of opinion and action does exist, on many questions, in areas where the rates of delinquents are low. But, in the high-rate areas, the very presence of conflicting systems of values operates against such unanimity. Other factors

[5] W. I. Thomas and Florian Znaniecki, *The Polish Peasant in Europe and America* (New York: Alfred A. Knopf, 1927), II, 1171.

hindering the development of consistently effective attitudes with reference to these problems of public welfare are the poverty of these high-rate areas, the wide diversity of cultural backgrounds represented there, and the fact that the outward movement of population in a city like Chicago has resulted in the organization of life in terms of ultimate residence. Even though frustrated in his attempts to achieve economic security and to move into other areas, the immigrant, living in areas of first settlement, often has defined his goals in terms of the better residential community into which he hopes some day to move. Accordingly, the immediate problems of his present neighborhood may not be of great concern to him.

Another characteristic of the areas with high rates of delinquents is the presence of large numbers of nonindigenous philanthropic agencies and institutions—social settlements, boys' clubs, and similar agencies—established to deal with local problems. These are, of course, financed largely from outside the area. They are also controlled and staffed, in most cases, by persons other than local residents and should be distinguished from indigenous organizations and institutions growing out of the felt needs of the local citizens. The latter organizations, which include American institutions, Old World institutions, or a synthesis of the two, are rooted in each case in the sentiments and traditions of the people. The nonindigenous agencies, while they may furnish many services and be widely used, seldom become the people's institutions, because they are not outgrowths of the local collective life. The very fact that these nonindigenous private agencies long have been concentrated in delinquency areas without modifying appreciably the marked disproportion of delinquents concentrated there suggests a limited effectiveness in deterring boys from careers in delinquency and crime.[6]

Tax-supported public institutions such as parks, schools, and playgrounds are also found in high-rate, as well as in low-rate, areas. These, too, are usually controlled and administered from

---

[6] Rates of private character-building institutions (representing the number of social settlements, boys' clubs, and Y.M.C.A.'s per 10,000 boys 10–16 years of age) decrease from Zones I to V as follows: 21.2, 10.2, 3.5, 2.3, 1.3.

without the local area; and, together with other institutions, they represent to the neighborhood the standards of the larger community. However, they may be actually quite different institutions in different parts of the city, depending on their meaning and the attitudes of the people toward them. If the school or playground adapts its program in any way to local needs and interests, with the support of local sentiment, it becomes a functioning part of the community; but, instead, it is often relatively isolated from the people of the area, if not in conflict with them. High rates of truants in the inner-city areas may be regarded as an indication of this separation.

These more subtle differences between contrasting types of areas are not assumed to be wholly distinct from the differences presented in quantitative form in earlier chapters. They are, no doubt, products or by-products of the same processes of growth which physically differentiate city areas and segregate the population on an economic basis. This economic segregation in itself, as has been said, does not furnish an explanation for delinquency. Negative cases are too numerous to permit such a conclusion. But in the areas of lowest economic status and least vocational opportunity a special setting is created in which the development of a system of values embodied in a social, economic, and prestige system in conflict with conventional values is not only a probability but an actuality.

The general theoretical framework within which all community data are interpreted will be fully stated in the concluding chapter. Briefly summarized, it is assumed that the differentiation of areas and the segregation of population within the city have resulted in wide variation of opportunities in the struggle for position within our social order. The groups in the areas of lowest economic status find themselves at a disadvantage in the struggle to achieve the goals idealized in our civilization. These differences are translated into conduct through the general struggle for those economic symbols which signify a desirable position in the larger social order. Those persons who occupy a disadvantageous position are involved in a conflict between the goals assumed to be attainable in a free society and those actually attainable for a large proportion of the population. It is understandable, then, that the economic position of persons living in the areas of least opportunity should be translated at times into unconventional conduct, in an effort to reconcile the idealized status and their practical prospects of attaining this status. Since, in our culture, status is determined largely in economic terms, the differences between contrasted areas in terms of economic status become the most important differences. Similarly, as might be expected, crimes against property are most numerous.

The physical, economic, and social conditions associated with high rates of delinquents in local communities occupied by white population exist in exaggerated form in most of the Negro areas. Of all the population groups in the city, the Negro people occupy the most disadvantageous position in relation to the distribution of economic and social values. Their efforts to achieve a more satisfactory and advantageous position in the economic and social life of the city are seriously thwarted by many restrictions with respect to residence, employment, education, and social and cultural pursuits. These restrictions have contributed to the development of conditions within the local community conducive to an unusually large volume of delinquency.

The problems of education, training, and control of children and youth are further complicated by the economic, social, and cultural dislocations that have taken place as a result of the transition from the relatively simple economy of the South to the complicated industrial organization of the large northern city. The effect of this transition upon social institutions, particularly the family, has been set forth in great detail in the penetrating studies of E. Franklin Frazier. In this connection he states:

During and following the World War, the urbanization of the Negro population was accelerated and acquired even greater significance than earlier migrations to cities. The Negro was carried beyond the small southern cities and plunged into the midst of modern industrial centers in the North. Except for the war period, when there was a great demand for his labor, the migration of the Negro to northern cities has forced him into a much more rigorous type of competition with whites than he has ever faced. Because of his rural background and ignorance, he has entered modern industry as a part of the great army of unskilled workers. Like the immigrant groups that have preceded him, he has been forced to live in the slum areas of northern cities. In vain social workers and others have constantly held conferences on the housing conditions of Negroes, but they have been forced finally to face the fundamental fact of the Negro's poverty. Likewise, social and welfare agencies have been unable to stem the tide of family disorganization that has followed as a natural consequence of the impact of modern civilization upon the folkways and mores of a simple peasant folk. Even Negro families with traditions of stable family life have been not unaffected by the social and economic forces in urban communities. Family traditions and social distinctions that had meaning and significance in the relatively simple and stable southern communities have lost their meaning in the new world of the modern city.

One of the most important consequences of the urbanization of the Negro has been the rapid occupational differentiation of the population. A Negro middle class has come into existence as the result of new opportunities and greater freedom as well as the new demands of the awakened Negro communities for all kinds of services. This change in the structure of Negro life has been rapid and has not had time to solidify. The old established families, generally of mulatto origin, have looked with contempt upon the new middle class which has come into prominence as the result of successful competition in the new environment. With some truth on their side, they have complained that these newcomers lack the culture, stability in family life, and purity of morals which characterized their own class when it graced the social pyramid. In fact, there has not been sufficient time for these new strata to form definite patterns of family life. Consequently, there is much confusion and conflict in ideals and aims and patterns of behavior which have been taken over as the result of the various types of suggestion and imitation in the urban environment.[7]

The development of divergent systems of values requires a type of situation in which traditional conventional control is either weak or nonexistent. It is a well-known fact that the growth of cities and the increase in devices for transportation and communication have so accelerated the rate of change in our society that the traditional means of social control, effective in primitive society and in isolated rural communities, have been weakened everywhere and rendered especially ineffective in large cities. Moreover, the city, with its anonymity, its emphasis on economic rather than personal values, and its freedom and tolerance, furnishes a favorable situation for the development of devices to im-

[7] *The Negro Family in the United States* (Chicago: University of Chicago Press 1939), pp. 484–86.

prove one's status, outside of the conventionally accepted and approved methods. This tendency is stimulated by the fact that the wide range of secondary social contacts in modern life operates to multiply the wishes of individuals. The automobile, motion pictures, magazine and newspaper advertising, the radio, and other means of communication flaunt luxury standards before all, creating or helping to create desires which often cannot be satisfied with the meager facilities available to families in areas of low economic status. The urge to satisfy the wishes and desires so created has helped to bring into existence and to perpetuate the existing system of criminal activities.

It is recognized that in a free society the struggle to improve one's status in terms of accepted values is common to all persons in all social strata. And it is a well-known fact that attempts are made by some persons in all economic classes to improve their positions by violating the rules and laws designed to regulate economic activity.[8] However, it is assumed that these violations with reference to property are most frequent where the prospect of thus enhancing one's social status outweighs the chances for loss of position and prestige in the competitive struggle. It is in this connection that the existence of a system of values supporting criminal behavior becomes important as a factor in shaping individual life-patterns, since it is only where such a system exists that the person through criminal activity may acquire the material goods so essential to status in our society and at the same time increase, rather than lose, his prestige in the smaller group system of which he has become an integral part.

[8] See Edwin H. Sutherland, "White Collar Criminality," *American Sociological Review*, V (February, 1940), 1–12.

PART III

CHAPTER VIII

PHILADELPHIA

THE study of Chicago revealed a significant relationship between the distribution of delinquent boys and the areas differentiated during the processes of city growth. Therefore, as an introduction to the study in each of the other cities to be presented, the history of the city's growth and development will be sketched, including a brief statement of the factors influencing the location of the original settlement and a description of the geographic characteristics of the site as related to the direction of the growth in area and in population as related to natural advantages or barriers. To these data will be added facts on total population, composition of the population, area, and other distinguishing urban characteristics.

Philadelphia, like Chicago, is a large city and an important industrial center. The points of contrast are more obvious, however. Philadelphia was, in its beginning, a city with a plan, which brings it into contrast with the early unplanned expansion of Chicago. It is an eastern seaport city and, from the point of view of our national life, an old historical city. Finally, Philadelphia represents in its growth not so much the expansion of a community outward from one center as it does a constellation of centers brought under one name by legislative enactment. Although these cities have grown together until their boundaries are no longer discernible, many have retained their identity as business and social centers much more than have the outlying sections of Chicago. These differences in location, history, and structural development imply differences in governmental and social institutions, as well as more subtle differences in culture and tradition. These are introduced, therefore, as new variables in the study of the distribution of juvenile delinquents.

THE GROWTH OF PHILADELPHIA

History.—Philadelphia is located at the junction of the Delaware and Schuylkill rivers about 100 miles from the Atlantic
Ocean by way of the Delaware. The site chosen for the city by
the settlers sent out by William Penn in 1682 was on the peninsula
between the Delaware and Schuylkill rivers about 5 miles above
their junction. The city, as originally laid out, extended from the
Delaware River on the east to the Schuylkill on the west, a distance of about 2 miles, and from Vine Street on the north to Cedar
Street on the south, about 1 mile.

Geographically, the land was an almost level plain cut through
by several small streams but without any restraining physical
barriers. To the south the land was also level, but somewhat
lower, being only slightly above sea-level near the junction of the
rivers. To the north of the original city, on the other hand, the
land which later was to become a part of Philadelphia was high
and rolling. Rising slowly on the Delaware River side, but more
abruptly along the Schuylkill, it reached a height of more than
400 feet above sea-level in the region where Germantown was to
be established a few years later. Likewise, on the west, the region
which was to become West Philadelphia was then rolling country
somewhat higher than the original city.

The street plan, carefully worked out, included High Street
(now Market), a wide street extending from river to river about
midway between the northern and southern boundaries of the new
city; and Broad Street, equally wide, running north and south. At
the intersection of these two streets, which marked the geographic
center of the corporate area, a large public square was laid out.
The assumption underlying the plan of the new city of Philadelphia was that there would be simultaneous developments in-
ward from each river, meeting at the square. But, although both
rivers were navigable, the fact that the Delaware was larger and
offered a longer water frontage at tidewater level made it so much
more attractive from the standpoint of navigation that the early
settlers preferred to remain near it. Consequently the city
grew, not east and west, as had been planned, but northward and
southward along the Delaware River front.

This early city was centered about High and Second streets, where the City Hall and markets were located. As the city grew, this center moved slowly westward until today the square at the intersection of Broad and Market streets, now called City Hall Square, may well be taken as the center of the downtown business district. Time has not detracted from the importance of Market Street; and Broad Street, for over a century outside the built-up area, now has become the leading north and south thoroughfare.

The original boundaries of Philadelphia remained unchanged for 172 years; and, as the corporate area was only 1 mile in length, the city soon spread beyond its boundaries along the Delaware River. Before the Revolutionary War, Southwark on the south and Northern Liberties on the north had been incorporated as separate districts. In 1811 Mease wrote that the settlement had "increased northward and southward of the original plot, upon the Delaware front, and now occupies a space nearly three miles in length north and south, while the buildings in the middle, where they are most extended, reach little more than a mile from the Delaware."[1]

The population continued to spread beyond the original boundaries; and, as the adjoining territory became populated, it was organized into corporate districts. Following Northern Liberties on the northeast, the following were incorporated: Spring Garden and Penn on the north, West Philadelphia on the west, and Moyamensing on the south. In 1850 the population of Philadelphia was 121,376, and that of the contiguous districts just enumerated 238,927, indicating that only about one-third of the area's population lived within the city limits.

Beyond these districts but within the present limits of the city were several other boroughs of considerable size and importance. Germantown, founded by Germans the year following the settlement of Philadelphia, was a city of 6,209 located on the high land to the northwest. Manayunk, with a population of 6,158, was located on the Schuylkill above the fall line. Frankford, with a population of 5,346, was near the Delaware, northeast of the city

[1] James Mease, *Picture of Philadelphia* (Philadelphia, 1811), pp. 24–25.

proper. In this same district were the smaller towns of White Hall, Bridesburg, and Aramingo.

In 1854 these cities, towns, and corporate districts were abolished and the boundaries of Philadelphia extended to the county lines by the state legislature. Thus, by a single act the corporate area of the city was increased about sixty-five times, or from the original 2 square miles to the present 129; and the population was increased from 121,376, the population of Philadelphia in 1850, to 408,462, the population of the county in the same year.

Although Philadelphia is an old city, it is obvious that its development into a great metropolis has been relatively recent. In 1790, 108 years after the first settlement, and 90 years after incorporation as a city, the population was only 28,522, and the population of the county 54,391. By 1860, the first census after the consolidation, the population was well over half a million, and by 1890 it had passed the million mark. The population of Philadelphia given by the census of 1920 was 1,823,779, and for 1930 it totaled 1,964,430. The rate of increase between 1920 and 1930 was 7.0 per cent.

The direction of greatest growth in Philadelphia has been northward. A fairly accurate picture of the way in which the city has spread is given by the distribution of population if the city is divided into Old Philadelphia, the original city; North and South Philadelphia, the areas between the rivers above and below the original city; and West Philadelphia, the name given to all of the area west of the Schuylkill. North Philadelphia contained in 1930 more than half of the population of the city, or 57.7 per cent. This northward development took two general directions—along the Delaware and northwest on the high ground along Wissahickon Creek.

Apart from these general movements, sections have been built up where local transportation made them desirable for residential purposes, and around industrial plants near rail or water transportation. The area of Old Philadelphia contains 2.9 per cent and South Philadelphia 18.3 per cent of the population. Growth to the south has been prevented by the limits of the area and the fact that land near the junction of the rivers is so low as to be undesirable for residential purposes. West Philadelphia contains 21.1 per cent of the population. Once across the Schuylkill, the growth extended westward beyond the city limits. The movement toward the southwest has been limited, however.

Although the present study of delinquency will be confined to the city proper, it is important to remember that many of the finest residential areas of Philadelphia are in the suburbs along the main thoroughfares outside the city. These suburbs, along with Camden, New Jersey, an industrial community located directly across the Delaware River from the center of the business district and representing the eastward growth, may all be thought of as part of the development of Greater Philadelphia.

Composition of the Population.—In 1930, 88.6 per cent of the population were recorded as white, and 11.3 per cent as Negro. Of the total white population, 69.7 per cent were native and 18.9 per cent foreign born. Of the white population, 42.8 per cent were natives of native parentage, 26.9 per cent natives of foreign parentage, and 9.0 per cent natives of mixed parentage. The predominating nationalities among the foreign-born white population were Russian and Italian, these two groups including, respectively, 22.0 and 18.5 per cent of the total foreign-born population. The predominating nationality throughout the life of the city has been the Irish, one-third of the foreign born being so classified in 1900.

MALE JUVENILE DELINQUENTS IN PHILADELPHIA

Cases of juvenile delinquents in Philadelphia up to 16 years of age are heard in the Juvenile Division of the Municipal Court. In this court a large number of informal complaints are disposed of unofficially by the probation staff. By this method many boys against whom only trivial complaints have been made are eliminated from the official court cases.

Series Studied and Types of Offenses.—For the present study, only boys brought to the court on petitions alleging delinquency were included. The series covers a 3-year period (1926–28) and includes 5,859 boys. For the most part, these boys fall within the age range from 9 to 15 years. The highest frequencies are in the thirteenth, fourteenth, and fifteenth years, which comprise, respectively, 16.3, 17.7, and 21.4 per cent of the total. Only 2.6 per cent of the boys were over 15 years of age. Of the total number, 48.2 per cent were charged with stealing, 14.5 per cent with running away from home, 11.7 per cent with destruction of property, and 8.5 per cent with truancy from school, while 6 per cent were incorrigible, 2.4 per cent were sex offenders, and 8.7 per cent were charged with other offenses.

Distribution.—The distribution of the 5,859 boys is indicated on Map 27. City Hall Square, at the intersection of Broad and Market streets, may be taken as the center of the main business district and, in the discussion, a focal point of the distribution of delinquents. The area surrounding City Hall Square, in which there are very few dots, indicates quite clearly the central business district, an area largely depopulated, with an especially small juvenile population. To the south of the old city a great concentration of dots will be noted, extending over most of the built-up sections of South Philadelphia. North of the old city an almost equally dense concentration appears, especially east of Broad Street. West of Broad Street there are more open spaces, with some very decided concentrations just north of Vine, the old city limits, and north and south from Girard College. Broad Street, like Market, is, for the most part, commercial rather than residential, so that the open spaces on either side of both North and South Market indicate absence of resident population.

It is interesting to observe that the concentrations of delinquency in the areas farther removed from the center of the city are located in districts which were either separate towns or cities prior to the consolidation of 1854. Decided clusters of dots will be noticed at Richmond, which was one of the corporate districts of Philadelphia, and at Bridesburg and Frankford—still, from many points of view, separate communities. Another cluster of dots will be observed farther up the river at Tacony. In North Central Philadelphia a cluster of dots is seen at Franklinville, southeast of Hunting Park, and another very decided concentration near Nicetown, directly west of Hunting Park. Further concentrations will

MAP 27

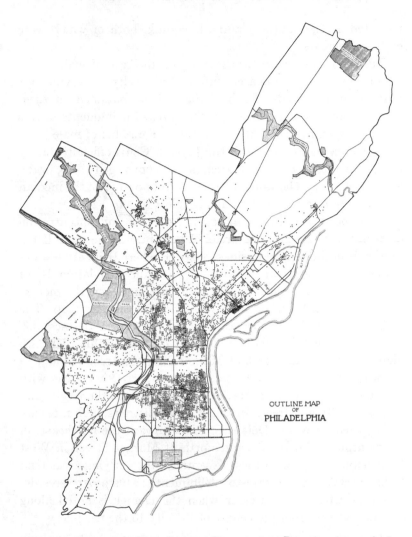

OUTLINE MAP
OF
PHILADELPHIA

DISTRIBUTION OF 5,859 MALE JUVENILE DELINQUENTS, PHILADELPHIA, 1926–38

be noted at Germantown and Manayunk, both of which were early settlements.

Rates of Delinquents.—Map 28 shows the rate of male delinquents in each of the 134 areas into which the city was divided for purposes of this study. Each of these areas contained, in 1927, 500 or more males aged 10–15.[2] The rates of delinquents in this series are 3-year rates; that is, they are the number of male juvenile delinquents brought into the Juvenile Court officially during the 3-year period, from each area, per 100 boys aged 10–15 in the area as of 1927. The range of rates is from 0 to 22.6, the median 4.7, and the rate for the city as a whole 5.6.

It will be observed that, in general, the areas of concentration of delinquents are also the areas of high rates. One notable exception is in the central business district, where there are few delinquents but high rates, since the juvenile population is, of course, very small. Outside of this district, however, the picture given by the distribution map is verified by the rate map. The highest rates are in the areas that include the central business district and incidentally all of the old city of Philadelphia. The two highest rates are just north of Market Street in Areas 6–4 and 5–15, with rates of 22.6 and 19.0, respectively. Other areas with very high rates are along Market Street, between the rivers, and just east of Broad Street. In the outlying districts, high rates are to be noted along the Delaware River toward the northeast, in Germantown, Manayunk, and north of Market Street in West Philadelphia. But, with these exceptions, the outlying areas tend to have relatively low rates of delinquents. This progressive decrease in rates becomes clear when the change is noted along streets that run from the center of the city to the periphery.

[2] These areas were constructed by combining school census blocks into larger areas until the desired population was secured. With one minor exception, the boundaries of the 10 large school districts into which Philadelphia is divided were retained. The prefix of the number assigned to each area indicates the school district in which it is located. The aged 10–15 male population in these 123 areas was calculated from the 1927 total aged 6–15 school population. In order to make this calculation as accurate as possible, the ratio of the aged 10–15 male population to the total school population was established separately for each of the 10 school districts. This ratio was then used in computing the aged 10–15 male population from the total aged 6–15 population in each of the areas within the several school districts.

MAP 28

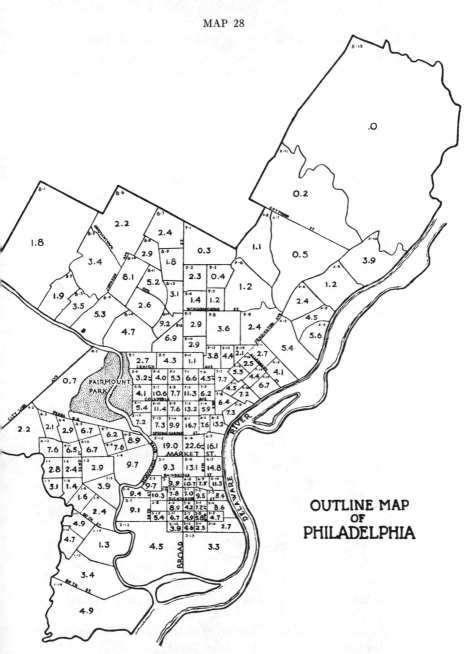

RATES OF MALE JUVENILE DELINQUENTS, PHILADELPHIA, BY AREAS

Rates by Zones.—The tendency of the rates of delinquents in Philadelphia to decrease from the center of the city outward is presented schematically on Map 29. These zones were constructed

MAP 29

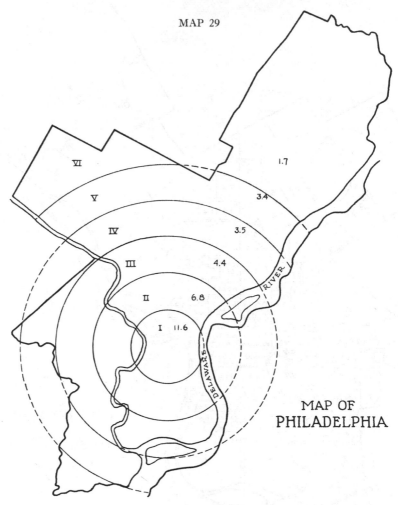

RATES OF MALE JUVENILE DELINQUENTS, PHILADELPHIA, BY ZONES

by taking a focal point at the corner of Broad and Market streets and drawing concentric circles at intervals of $1\frac{1}{2}$ miles. The rates were calculated in the same manner as were the rates in the

separate areas, and they represent the number of delinquents per
100 of the aged 10–15 male population in each zone. It is interesting that, in spite of the relatively high rates near some of the outlying centers, the zone rates decrease regularly from 11.6 in the
first zone to 1.7 in the last. In other words, nearly seven times as
many boys per 100 became delinquent in the areas within $1\frac{1}{2}$
miles of the center of the city as in the areas located more than 9
miles from this point.

Extent of Concentration. —In order to show more clearly the extent of concentration of the 5,856 delinquents in relation to the

TABLE 54

PERCENTAGE OF DELINQUENTS AND OF CITY AREA
FOR QUARTILES OF MALE POPULATION AGED
10–15, WHEN AREAS ARE RANKED BY RATE OF
DELINQUENTS

Quartiles of Population	Percentage of Delinquents	Percentage of City Area
Upper one-fourth, in high-rate areas............	46.6	9.4
Second one-fourth.......	28.1	10.1
Third one-fourth.........	17.2	23.9
Lower one-fourth, in low-rate areas............	8.1	56.6

distribution of population and the geographic area of Philadelphia,
the aged 10–15 male population was divided into four equal parts,
on the basis of the magnitude of the rates of delinquents, by ar-
ranging the 134 areas in a series from the area with the lowest
rate to that with the highest. The variation in the distribution of
delinquents and city area for these quartiles is indicated in Table
54.

When Table 54 is examined, the wide variation between the
percentages of delinquents from the upper and lower quarters of
the population is apparent. The high-rate areas containing the
upper one-quarter of the population include 46.6 per cent of the
delinquents and only 9.4 per cent of the geographic area of the
city. At the other extreme, the areas including the lower one-
quarter of the population contain only 8.1 per cent of the delinquents but 56.7 per cent of the city area.

Variations of similar significance are revealed when the 5,859 delinquents in turn are divided into four groups according to the magnitude of the area rates of delinquents. This is shown in Table 55.

It will be noted that the upper one-quarter of the delinquents are concentrated in 4.0 per cent of the city area and represent 10.8 per cent of the aged 10–15 male population, while the same number of delinquents in the areas with lowest rates are distributed over 79.2 per cent of the city area and represent 49.6 per cent of the population. When a division is made at the median,

TABLE 55

PERCENTAGE OF MALE POPULATION AGED 10–15 AND OF CITY AREA FOR QUARTILES OF DELINQUENTS WHEN AREAS ARE RANKED BY RATE OF DELINQUENTS

Quartiles of Delinquents	Percentage of Population	Percentage of City Area
Upper one-quarter, from high-rate areas........	10.8	4.0
Second one-quarter......	16.8	6.0
Third one-quarter.......	22.8	10.8
Lower one-quarter, from low-rate areas.........	49.6	79.2

it will be noted that the delinquents in the upper half represent less than three-tenths of the aged 10–15 male population and only one-tenth of the geographic area of the city.

COMMUNITY CHARACTERISTICS IN RELATION
TO RATES OF DELINQUENTS

It has been shown that there are wide variations in the rates of delinquents among areas in Philadelphia. In the present section, as in the study of Chicago, data will be presented which serve to differentiate the areas of high rates of delinquents from the areas of low rates and to indicate the nature of the processes of selection and distribution in city growth. Emphasis will be placed on the extent to which the characteristics of the areas differentiated in these processes are associated with delinquency rates in Philadelphia.

Since most of our indexes of community characteristics are calculated from data based on the 48 wards[3] into which the city is divided, rates of delinquents for the same series (1926–28) but calculated for wards, using the federal census population, will be presented. Map 30 shows the rates of delinquents in 44 ward areas in Philadelphia, calculated from the distribution presented on Map 27 and the aged 10–15 male population in each ward corrected to 1927, the midyear of the series.[4]

It will be noted that the 22 areas with rates of 7.0 or above are all in or near central Philadelphia, while the 18 areas with rates below 7.0 are all outside of this central district. It is evident, therefore, that, although the population for these rates was secured from another source, and the rates themselves are presented for areas with different boundaries, the general configuration is the same as that of Map 28. These differences in rates of delinquents indicate that there are probably fundamental variations between the communities adjacent to commerce and industry and the outlying residential communities. Many of these variations, as in Chicago, may be the result of the differentiation that has taken place as the city has expanded.

Physical Differentiation.—The evidence of these processes is clearly seen when the areas close to the central business district in Philadelphia are compared with outlying residential communities. The former, which include the original city, are all zoned for commerce and industry and are constantly undergoing a change to these uses. This invasion, or change in the use of land, is indicated by the population decrease in the central business and industrial district and the areas adjacent to it and by the demolition of buildings used for residential purposes within the same areas.

Increasing or Decreasing Population.—Map 31 shows the wards in Philadelphia where the population increased or decreased be-

---

[3] Because of the small population in some of the wards in central Philadelphia, it was necessary to make several combinations. Thus, Wards 3 and 4 were combined into one area, Wards 5 and 6 into another, Wards 7 and 8 into a third, and Wards 9 and 10 into a fourth area. In this way the 48 wards were reduced to 44. The regular ward numbers have been retained throughout, however.

[4] This estimate was based on the rate of increase or decrease of population in each ward between 1920 and 1930.

MAP 30

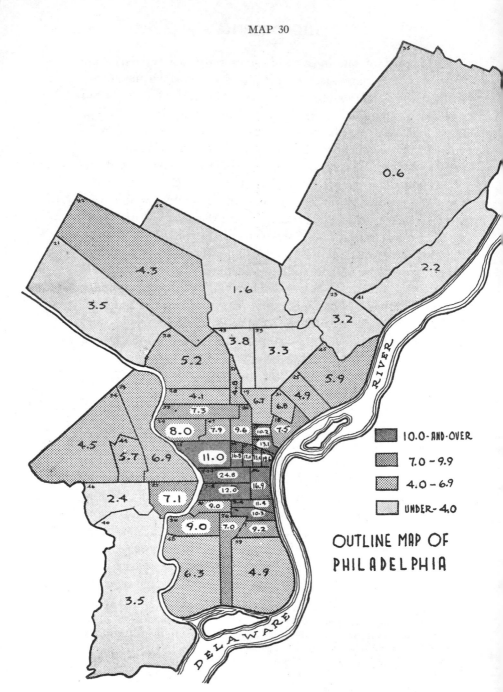

RATES OF MALE JUVENILE DELINQUENTS, PHILADELPHIA, BY WARDS

MAP 31

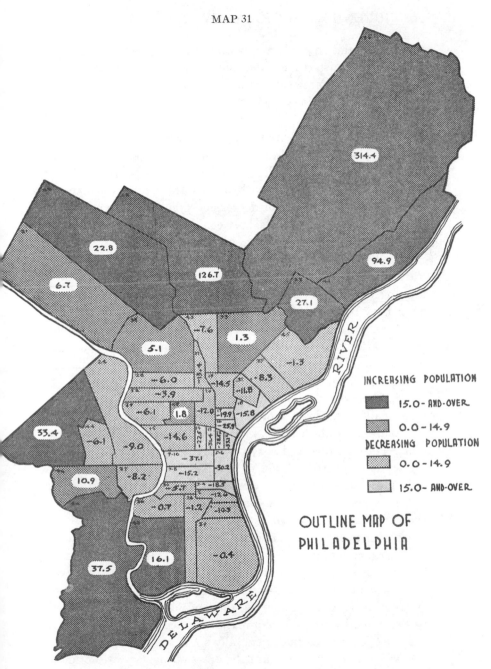

INCREASING POPULATION

15.0- AND-OVER

0.0 - 14.9

DECREASING POPULATION

0.0 - 14.9

15.0- AND-OVER

OUTLINE MAP OF
PHILADELPHIA

PERCENTAGE INCREASE OR DECREASE OF POPULATION, PHILADELPHIA, 1920–30

tween 1920 and 1930. It will be noted that the areas of greatest
decrease are clustered around the central business district and
that just beyond are other areas of decreasing population, while
the areas of population growth are those farthest from the business
center.

On Map 31, 11 areas are shown as decreasing more than 15 per
cent, while only 7 areas dropped as much as this between 1910 and
1920. Similarly, 20 areas decreased less than 15 per cent between
1920 and 1930, compared with only 9 areas between 1910 and
1920. In short, the area of decreasing population grew from 16
areas, representing 20 wards, between 1910 and 1920, to 31 areas,
representing 35 wards, in the succeeding decade. This comparison
reveals the nature of the process of growth in Philadelphia. As
the central business district has expanded, the rate of decrease in
the areas most centrally located has been accelerated, and new
areas have been added to those already decreasing. Evidence of
the fact that this process was not limited to the two decades under
consideration is found in the fact that the population of Old Philadelphia, now the central business district, decreased 26.5 per cent
between 1850 and 1910.

This process of depopulation and outward movement is evident
on a smaller scale in each of the outlying centers in Philadelphia.
An analysis of the change in population in the school census
blocks between 1920 and 1927 reveals that small areas of decreasing population surround each of the older outlying commercial and
industrial centers. These areas of decreasing population are
naturally concealed by the general trend in the wards in which
they are located.

In order to explore the relationship between increasing and decreasing population and rates of delinquents, these variables will
be correlated, first, by areas based on wards and, second, by combining the areas into groups according to rates of increase or decrease of population. Likewise, rates of increase or decrease will
be presented by zones for comparative purposes.

Inspection reveals that, generally speaking, the areas of greatest decrease in population are the areas of highest rates of delinquents, and vice versa. This apparent correspondence is borne

out by correlations. When the rates of delinquents in the 134 areas of Map 28 are correlated with the increase or decrease of population in these same areas, as calculated from the school census of 1927, r equals $-.51 \pm .043$.[5] When the rates of delinquents in the 44 ward areas are correlated with the percentage increase or decrease of population between 1920 and 1930, the value of r is $-.77 \pm .041$. The fact that the coefficient is much higher when calculated for a smaller number of areas indicates that the relationship between rates of delinquents and trend of population is general, admitting of frequent exceptions in specific small areas.

TABLE 56

RATES OF DELINQUENTS FOR AREAS GROUPED BY
PERCENTAGE INCREASE OR DECREASE
IN POPULATION

Percentage Increase or Decrease in Population, 1920–30	Rate of Delinquents
Decreasing:	
15.0 and over	13.1
0.0–14.9	6.9
Increasing:	
0.0–14.9	4.1
15.0 and over	3.4

The relationship may also be illustrated by calculating rates of delinquents for the four classes of areas represented on Map 31. These rates, given in Table 56, show the general association between increasing and decreasing population and rates of delinquents. This does not mean, of course, that the variables bear a causal relationship to one another.

Demolition.—Another indication of expansion in Philadelphia is seen in the demolition of residential buildings. A map prepared by the Philadelphia Housing Association shows, by wards, the number of persons dehoused through demolitions during 1923–27 and indicates that most of the buildings demolished were in or adjoining the central business district. Calculated upon the basis of the 1920 census, 7.5 per cent of the total population were de-

[5] When the rate of increase in the 3 areas with very high rates is assumed to be 60 per cent.

housed during this period in the 11 areas of greatest decrease of population, as indicated by the heaviest shading on Map 31. The largest population of persons dehoused was in or near the area of Old Philadelphia.

In contrast with the high percentage of persons dehoused in the central district, only 0.9 per cent of the population were dehoused in the areas decreasing less than 15 per cent and only 0.3 per cent in the areas of increasing population. In other words, 61.7 per cent of the persons dehoused lived in areas which decreased more than 15 per cent between 1920 and 1930, 29.8 per cent in areas which decreased less than 15 per cent, and 8.5 per cent in areas of increasing population.

Since the percentage of persons dehoused in five years was equal to more than half of the population decrease in the decade, in most of these central areas, it is evident that the decrease in population did not represent primarily a change in the net density of population per housing unit, but rather a drop in the number of buildings used for residential purposes. In these central areas few residences are replaced, so that with the invasion of industry and commerce decreasing population is inevitable. In the other areas of decreasing population there may have been a decrease in the net density, since the proportion of persons dehoused was relatively small.

It will be apparent that those areas with the highest percentages of persons dehoused are, in large part, the areas with the highest rates of delinquents. Demolition of residences is more heavily concentrated in central areas and shows greater variation between these and the outlying areas than does the distribution of delinquents, but the general association of these variables for the 44 ward areas is indicated by a coefficient of linear correlation of .72 ± .05. The percentage of persons dehoused is thus an index of other community characteristics, the areas in which this percentage ranks relatively high being, for the most part, areas of decreasing population and high rates of juvenile delinquents.

Economic Segregation.—These areas in which the population is decreasing and being dehoused, and in which as a result of the invasion of industry and commerce the physical deterioration is most evident, are also the areas in which the groups of lowest economic status are concentrated. An indication of this process of economic segregation in Philadelphia is the distribution of equivalent monthly rentals[6] calculated from the federal census of 1930 for the 44 ward areas. These median rentals are presented in Map 32.

It will be noted that the areas of lowest rentals comprise much of the industrial area along the Delaware River which was included in the early settlement of Philadelphia, as well as the areas occupied by or zoned for industry and commerce near the central business district. The areas of highest rentals, on the other hand, include most of the newer outlying areas, where, for the most part, the buildings are new and the population increasing. Areas 7–8 and 9–10, which were included in the original city of Philadelphia and might be expected to have low median rentals, fall into the higher classes. Actually, the economic status of the population in large sections of these areas is no different from that of the population in adjoining areas. The median rental is raised far above that of the adjoining areas, however, by the fact that the population living in the apartments, apartment hotels, and hotels of the Rittenhouse Square district, included within these areas, represents a group of the highest economic status. It is evident, therefore, that the median rental for these two areas is an intermediate value which does not describe the economic status of either of these two widely separated economic groups living within their limits. The same observation might be made for Ward 27, which includes the University of Pennsylvania. The limitation of the median rental as an index of economic status of segments of the population likewise is seen in some of the outlying wards, where small areas of low rental are concealed by the relatively high median for the area as a whole.

A comparison of the rates of delinquents and median monthly rentals for the 44 ward areas reveals that, with the exception of the areas in central Philadelphia just discussed, the areas of low rentals are, for the most part, also those with high rates of de-

[6] As in Chicago, this rental was estimated for owned homes at 1 per cent of the value, so that the median rental might represent all homes in the area.

MAP 32

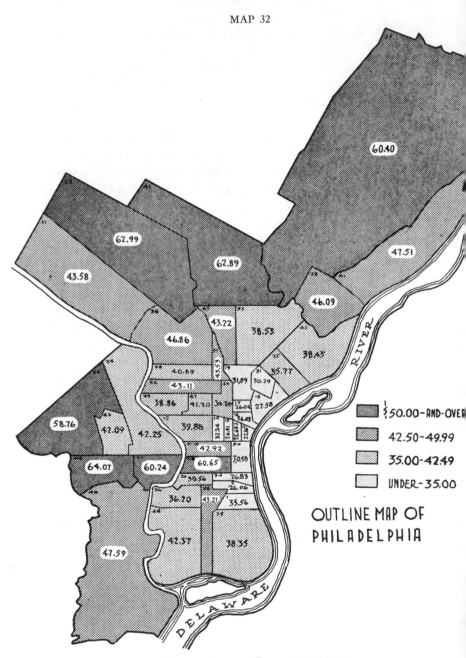

60.40

62.99

47.51

43.58

62.89

46.09

43.22

38.53

46.86

38.45

40.69

43.53

35.77

31.89

30.29

43.11

38.86

41.70

36.26

26.04

27.58

26.03

39.88

31.24

26.61

58.76

42.09

42.25

42.92

30.48

64.07

60.24

60.65

26.83

26.06

38.56

36.20

43.21

33.56

47.59

42.37

38.35

RIVER

DELAWARE

▓	½ 50.00 – AND – OVER
▒	42.50 – 49.99
▒	35.00 – 42.49
░	UNDER – 35.00

OUTLINE MAP OF
PHILADELPHIA

MEDIAN RENTALS, PHILADELPHIA, 1930

linquents, and vice versa. The coefficient of linear correlation between rates of delinquents and median rentals in the 44 areas is
$-.53 \pm .072$. The true relationship probably is curvilinear and
would therefore be represented by a somewhat higher correlation
ratio or coefficient of curvilinear correlation. The small number of
areas precludes the use of these measures here.

The general correspondence between high rates of delinquents
and low rentals is made strikingly apparent when rates of delinquents are calculated for the four groups of areas indicated on
Map 32. These rates are presented in Table 57. The same trends
of association are found whether areas are classed on the basis of
rates of delinquents or combined into zones.

TABLE 57

RATES OF DELINQUENTS FOR AREAS GROUPED
BY MEDIAN RENTAL

Median Rentals	Rate of Delinquents
$50.00 and over	3.5
42.50–$49.99	4.8
35.00–42.49	6.4
Under $35.00	10.4

Home Ownership.—Another index of the differentiating processes in the growth of the city is the percentage of families who
own their own homes. When the percentages of families owning
homes are compared with the rates of delinquents on Map 28, a
high negative correlation is evident. The coefficient of correlation
describing this relationship is $-.86 \pm .02$. When the same rates
of delinquents are correlated with the percentages of families owning homes in 1920, the coefficient is likewise $-.86 \pm .02$.

Segregation of the Foreign-born and Negro Population.—In
Philadelphia, as in Chicago, it is in the areas of physical deterioration and low rentals near the central business district and the
major industrial developments that the group of lowest economic
status is segregated. The fact that this group in Philadelphia
comprises a large proportion of the foreign-born and Negro population is indicated in Table 58. These zones are drawn with a
radius of 2 miles instead of $1\frac{1}{2}$ miles, the radius used in Map 29.
This change was made because it was felt that with the large and

irregular wards fewer problems would be presented in the calculation of rates for large zones, and also to illustrate the fact that the
size of the zone is not important in the presentation of these data.

It is evident from Table 58 that the proportion of foreign born
in the white population is nearly twice as great in Zone I as in
Zone IV and that the proportions changed but little from zone
to zone between 1920 and 1930, except in Zone I, where there was
a distinct decrease. It is evident that the Negro population is
much more highly concentrated than the foreign born in the first

TABLE 58

PERCENTAGE OF FOREIGN BORN IN WHITE POPULATION
AND PERCENTAGE OF NEGROES IN TOTAL POPU-
LATION, BY 2-MILE ZONES: 1920 AND 1930

ZONE	PERCENTAGE OF FOREIGN BORN IN WHITE POPULATION		PERCENTAGE OF NEGROES IN TOTAL POPULATION	
	1920	1930	1920	1930
I........	32.3	26.9	15.6	24.5
II........	22.1	22.2	4.3	9.4
III........	18.6	18.8	3.0	5.9
IV........	16.8	16.3	4.1	3.9

zone, and also that the percentage of Negroes increased markedly,
especially in the first and second zones, in this 10-year period.

These two population groups do not, as a rule, occupy the same
areas. Instead, they are complementary groups, either one or the
other being found in low-rent areas. For this reason it is necessary
to consider them together in making comparisons with other
community characteristics. Since, as already pointed out, "foreign" and "Negro" are not comparable classifications and therefore cannot be combined, we will use, as in Chicago, a population
index representing the percentage of foreign-born heads and Negro
heads of families in the total number of families in each area.

Map 33 shows the percentage of foreign-born and Negro heads
of families in each of the 44 ward areas in Philadelphia in 1930.
The areas with the highest percentages are concentrated north
and south of the central business district. It will be noted that

MAP 33

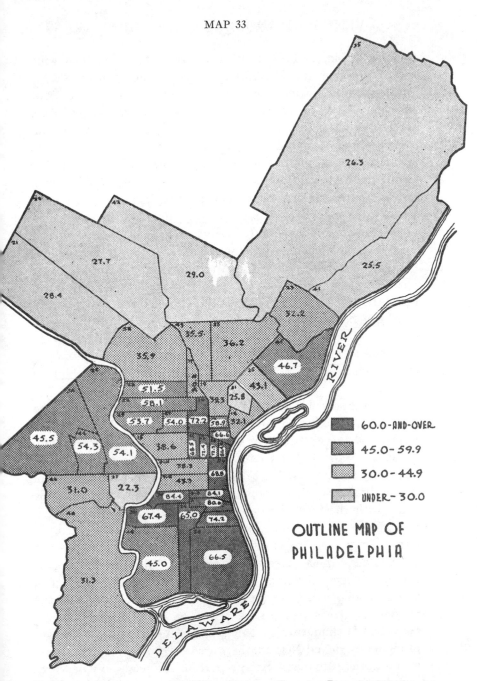

60.0 - AND-OVER

45.0 - 59.9

30.0 - 44.9

UNDER - 30.0

OUTLINE MAP OF
PHILADELPHIA

PERCENTAGE FOREIGN-BORN AND NEGRO HEADS OF FAMILIES, PHILADELPHIA, 1930

this map is similar to, but not identical with, the map showing rates of delinquents. Many of the areas of high rates are areas with a high proportion of foreign-born or Negro population, but some are not. Of the 12 areas with rates of delinquents above 10.0, the family heads in 8 are predominantly foreign born or Negro.

Aside from Areas 7–8 and 9–10, where the rates of delinquents are high and the proportions of foreign-born and Negro heads of families relatively low because of the large adult population in hotels, apartment hotels, and apartments, there are some areas where rates of delinquents are relatively high and the indigenous population is predominantly native white. In Wards 18 and 31, for example, in the Kensington Mill District, the rates of delinquents are high, while the percentages of foreign-born and Negro heads of families are only 32.1 and 25.8, respectively. The population of these areas is made up primarily of second- and third-generation Irish-Americans, who evidently did not move out as did the people of similar areas. At the other extreme, Ward 39 is characterized by a relatively low rate of delinquents (4.9) and a high proportion of heads of families either foreign born or Negro.

From the school census of 1927 it was possible to calculate the proportion of school children with foreign-born or Negro fathers for each of the 134 areas for which rates of delinquents are presented on Map 28. These data, from an entirely separate source, bear out the fact that the areas with the highest proportions of foreign-born and Negro population are, for the most part, the areas with the highest rates of delinquents. With these small areas, however, the exceptions are even more readily noted. In Areas 7–7, 7–8, and 7–9 in Kensington and Areas 5–12 and 7–1 in North Philadelphia, rates of delinquents are high, but the proportions of foreign and Negro fathers of school children are 29.9, 36.0, and 29.4, 36.9, and 38.7, respectively—all of which are below the median. In Areas 3–6, 3–11, and x–2, on the other hand, where the rates of delinquents are only 4.2, 2.5, and 4.1, the percentages of foreign-born and Negro fathers are 90.8, 89.0, and 84.7. These examples indicate that a high proportion of foreign-born or Negro population is not a condition necessarily linked with high delinquency rates.

In spite of such local variations, rates of delinquents and percentage of foreign-born and Negro heads of families are positively correlated, the coefficient being .52 ± .08. Similarly, when the rates of delinquents in the 134 school district areas are correlated with the percentage of foreign-born and Negro fathers of school children, r equals .58 ± .04. The general positive relation between these two variables is likewise seen when rates of delinquents are calculated for the four classes of areas on Map 33. These rates are presented in Table 59.

The distribution of the Negro population in Philadelphia furnishes an opportunity to compare the rates of delinquents in Negro and white areas. While the rates in the Negro areas are high, they are not noticeably higher than in some other areas in

TABLE 59

RATES OF DELINQUENTS FOR AREAS GROUPED BY
PERCENTAGE OF FOREIGN-BORN AND NEGRO
HEADS OF FAMILIES

Percentage of Foreign-born and Negro Heads of Families	Rate of Delinquents
Over 60.0	9.2
45.0–59.9	6.1
30.0–44.9	5.0
Under 30.0	3.2

the same relative geographic position. For example, in South Philadelphia the rates of delinquents in certain areas are almost identical, in spite of differences in the racial composition of the population. From Map 28 it will be seen that Areas 2–3 and 6–8 are contiguous areas about the same distance from the central business district. In Area 2–3, where the population is 81.0 per cent Negro, the rate of delinquents is 9.9; while in Area 6–8, where 81.4 per cent of the fathers of school children are foreign-born whites, the corresponding rate is 10.7.

Older-Boy Commitments.—It has been shown that, with few exceptions, areas of high rates of delinquents are differentiated from low-rate areas by variations in physical, economic, and demographic characteristics. The question arises: Do rates of adult crime exhibit patterns of distribution comparable to those of rates of delinquents?

Obviously, the distribution of juvenile delinquents may be expected to parallel that of young adult criminals, both because delinquents tend to become adult criminals as soon as they pass beyond the juvenile court age and because the presence of young adult offenders probably affects directly the behavior of the younger boys.

Such is the situation in Philadelphia. Map 34 shows rates of older boys committed, based on the geographic distribution of 3,232 boys 16–21 years of age committed to the Eastern Penitentiary, Philadelphia County Prison, and Huntingdon Reformatory in the years 1920–29, inclusive.[7] From these data, rates were calculated for the 44 areas on the basis of the aged 16–21 male population in Philadelphia in 1925. This population was estimated from the aged 16–21 population in 1930, by applying the rate of in-

TABLE 60

RATES OF DELINQUENTS FOR AREAS GROUPED BY
RATE OF OLDER-BOY COMMITMENTS

Rates of Older-Boy Commitments	Rate of Delinquents
9.0 and over	13.7
6.0–8.9	9.9
3.0–5.9	7.5
0.0–2.9	4.4

crease or decrease in population in the different wards between 1920 and 1930.

The rates of older boys thus secured range from 0.6 to 19.7. The median is 3.2, and the rate for the city as a whole 3.4. From Map 34 it will be seen that all the areas with the highest rates (9.0 and over) are clustered around the central business district, while the areas of low rates are in the outlying districts.

Obviously, the distribution of older boys committed and that of juvenile delinquents in Philadelphia are closely related. The coefficient secured when the rates of delinquents in the 44 areas are correlated with the older-boy rates is .79 ± .037. The same general relationship is indicated by the rates of delinquents calculated for the four classes of areas represented on Map 34. Table 60 shows that the rate of delinquents for the areas with the highest

[7] The data on the distribution of these offenders by wards were gathered by the Criminal Justice Association of Philadelphia and published in a bulletin entitled *Older Boys and Crime in Philadelphia* (1932).

MAP 34

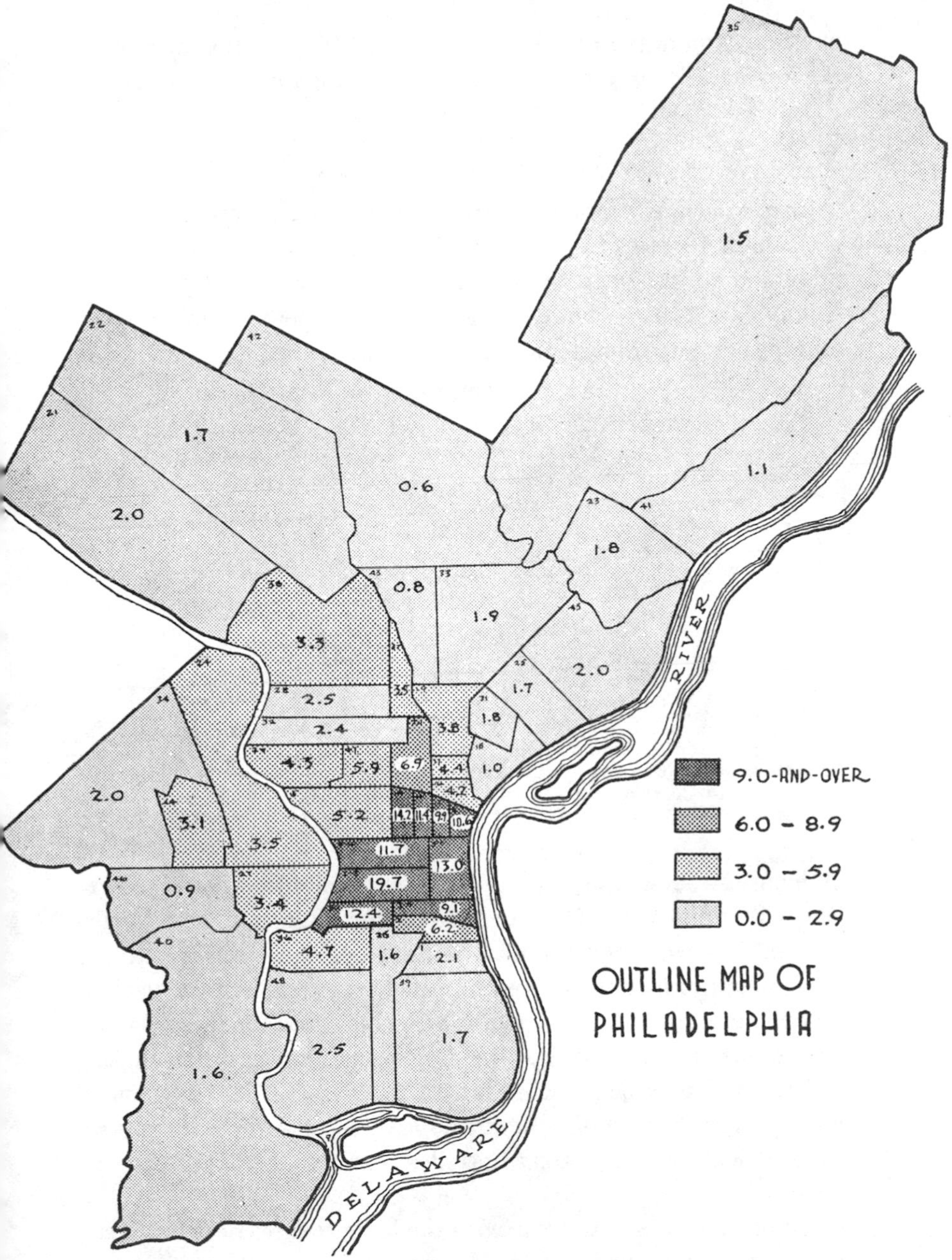

9.0-AND-OVER

6.0 – 8.9

3.0 – 5.9

0.0 – 2.9

OUTLINE MAP OF
PHILADELPHIA

RATES OF OLDER-BOY COMMITMENTS, PHILADELPHIA, 1920–29

older-boy commitment rates is 13.7, while that for the areas with the lowest older-boy rate is only one-third as high, or 4.4.

VARIATION IN COMMUNITY CHARACTERISTICS
WITH RATES OF DELINQUENTS

Comparison by Classes of Areas.—In the discussion of community characteristics for the city of Philadelphia, data have been presented to illustrate the relationship by areas among rates of delinquents and (1) increase or decrease of population, (2) percentage of population dehoused, (3) median rental, (4) percentage

TABLE 61

COMMUNITY CHARACTERISTICS FOR AREAS GROUPED BY
RATE OF DELINQUENTS

COMMUNITY CHARACTERISTICS	AREA RATES OF DELINQUENTS 1926–28			
	Under 4.0	4.0–6.9	7.0–9.9	10.0 and Over
Percentage increase or decrease of population, 1920–30	41.8	3.1	−5.6	−22.1
Percentage population dehoused, 1923–27	0.3	0.5	1.3	6.4
Average median rental, 1930	$53.00	$46.25	$40.00	$35.70
Percentage of families owning homes, 1930	61.8	53.9	39.1	24.9
Percentage foreign-born and Negro heads of families, 1930	30.5	43.7	60.6	61.6
Rate of older-boy commitments, 1920–29	1.3	2.4	4.0	9.6

of home ownership, (5) percentage of foreign-born and Negro heads of families, and (6) rate of older-boy offenders. In addition to computing coefficients of correlation for these series of data, areas were grouped into classes on the basis of each of the various indexes, and rates of delinquents were computed for these classes. To summarize the findings, the data pertaining to other characteristics will now be presented, first, for classes of areas grouped on the basis of rates of delinquents and, second, for zones drawn concentrically at intervals of 2 miles from the center of the city outward.

Table 61 shows that areas with the highest rates of delinquents have, as a class, the most rapidly decreasing population. It is in areas with the highest rates of delinquents that the highest proportion of the population is dehoused by demolition of residences, a consistent decrease being noted in the percentage dehoused in any class of area with a decrease in the rate of delinquents. Again, areas with the highest rates of delinquents have the lowest median rentals, indicating that these are, for the most part, the areas of lowest economic status. Relatively few people own homes in the areas with the greatest concentration of delinquents; but, as the class rate of delinquents decreases, home ownership consistently increases. The concentration of foreign-born and Negro heads of families in the areas with the highest rates of delinquents reflects

TABLE 62

COMMUNITY CHARACTERISTICS BY 2-MILE ZONES

COMMUNITY CHARACTERISTICS	ZONE			
	I	II	III	V
Rate of delinquents....................	10.5	5.5	4.0	2.8
Percentage increase or decrease of population, 1920–30.........................	−13.9	−1.8	22.0	68.8
Percentage of population dehoused, 1923–27	3.8	0.6	0.5	0.4
Median rental, 1930.....................	$37.69	$42.82	$52.23	$56.85
Percentage of families owning homes, 1930..	31.7	50.4	60.1	64.1
Percentage of families with radio sets, 1930.	33.7	54.9	67.4	74.3
Percentage of foreign-born and Negro heads of families, 1930.....................	63.1	45.5	36.2	28.1
Rate of older-boy commitments, 1920–29..	7.1	2.4	1.8	1.4

the existing economic segregation, so that, while there is probably no causal relationship, rates of delinquents and the percentage of foreign-born and Negro heads of families are seen to vary together. Also, the distribution of older offenders parallels that of juvenile delinquents.

Comparison by Zones.—When the several series of data are presented by zones (see Table 62), the patterns of variation are again found to be regular and consistent. There may be numerous small areas within zones which differ significantly, and the dividing-lines between zones may not correspond to any actual social differences; but, by and large, there is a tendency for characteristics to vary continuously from the center of the city outward. Presented in this conceptual scheme, the data illustrate certain concomitants of the process of growth and expansion in Philadelphia: the movement of population from the central areas, where demolitions are highest and physical deterioration most acute; the segregation of the groups of lowest economic status in these central areas where rentals are, on the whole, lowest and where a relatively small proportion of the residents own their homes; the concentration of a large proportion of the foreign-born and Negro population in areas of lowest economic status, resulting in a segregation both economic and racial or nationalistic; and, finally, the differential distribution of delinquency and crime.

SUMMARY

These data reveal that the relationships between rate of delinquents and other community characteristics in Philadelphia parallel closely the relationships which obtain in Chicago. The correlations are intermediate or high when computed between sets of variables in small areas; they are much higher when the analysis is made by zones or classes of areas. This suggests that the relationship is generalized and that, as in Chicago, it results from general processes of city growth which underlie the differences between types of areas.

The fact that the delinquency data for Philadelphia are more than a decade old is unimportant in an analysis of the relationship between the distribution of delinquents and other community characteristics, and probably not very important from a practical or utilitarian point of view. Studies in Chicago and several other cities have revealed that in the absence of significant disturbing influences the configuration of delinquency in a city changes very slowly, if at all. On this basis it may be assumed that in Philadelphia, where the study of successive sets of census data reveals little change in the ranking of areas, the configuration probably would have been much the same a decade earlier or later.

CHAPTER IX

GREATER BOSTON

THE study of the distribution of juvenile delinquents in the Boston metropolitan district may be considered as a study of many cities or of one urban community. For, unlike the other studies in this series, limited for the most part to one municipality, this study of the Boston district includes, in addition to the city of Boston, 15 contiguous cities and towns organically a part of the conurbation but politically distinct and independent. Two of these cities have a population of more than 100,000 each, 3 have a population between 50,000 and 100,000, 7 are between 30,000 and 50,000, and the remaining 3 between 15,000 and 30,000 each. In 1930 the population of Boston was 781,188, and the total population of these 15 cities and towns 750,011, indicating that, of the 1,531,199 persons in this area, about one-half lived within the corporate limits of Boston.

The inclusion of the cities and towns outside of Boston does not unduly complicate the problems inherent in such a study within the city of Boston itself. In other cities the data for the distribution studies have been secured from one court, to which cases were brought from the entire city. This has made possible seemingly valid comparisons between the rates of delinquents in one area of the city and those in another. In Boston, however, cases of juvenile delinquents are heard in 8 municipal courts located in different sections of the city, and the cases from the other cities and towns considered are heard in 7 additional district and municipal courts distributed throughout the area.

When data covering the same period were gathered from each of these 15 courts, it was found that they were similar in character, and there appeared to be no reason to assume that the cases secured from one court in Boston corresponded more closely to cases secured from the other Boston courts than to those from the courts outside. An effort was made to render the different series comparable through the elimination of certain types of cases not common to all. It is probable, however, that the cases are less comparable than they would have been had it proved possible to secure all from a single source. In this study, therefore, relatively more emphasis will be placed on variations in the rates of delinquents within judicial districts and less emphasis on variations in different parts of the cities or in different cities not in the same district. In this way it is hoped that the influence of any possible selective factors will be minimized.

GROWTH OF THE BOSTON AREA

History.—Boston differs from all other cities in this series in its geographic location, in its history, in its population composition, and in the configuration assumed during its development. The area designated as Boston, at the time of settlement in 1630, was a hilly peninsula of about 700 acres, connected with the mainland only by a narrow neck of land. This area of original settlement is now included in the central business district and, together with some additional acreage gained by cutting down the hills and filling in the harbor front and arms of the sea, is still known as "Boston," or "old Boston," as differentiated from the area added to the city through annexation.

By the time of the first federal census in 1790 the population of Boston had increased to 18,320; and in 1825, just 3 years after incorporation as a city, it was 56,003. Although East and South Boston had been annexed at this time, more than 96 per cent of the population was still in the area of original settlement.

However, within the area now included in the city of Boston a number of towns, some settled as early as old Boston, had been developing. It was through the annexation of these towns that the area of the city was extended. Roxbury, with a population of about 30,000, was annexed in 1867. This was followed by Dorchester, with a population of about 12,000, in 1869; by West Roxbury, Brighton, and Charlestown, with a combined population of nearly 50,000, in 1873; and by Hyde Park, with a population of approximately 16,000, in 1911. These towns have retained their identity to a great extent, and their names are used to distinguish them from old Boston, or Boston proper.

Geographically, the city has undergone many changes. The area of Boston proper has been increased from 783 to 1,829 acres by the filling-in of the Back Bay, an arm of the Charles River which spreads south between the Common and the hills of Brookline, and by smoothing the irregularities of the harbor front by cutting down the hills. Through successive annexations the total area was extended to about 50 square miles.

Since most of the large annexations to old Boston were toward the south and west, some of the independent cities on the north, notably Cambridge, Somerville, Everett, and Chelsea, extend almost to the central business district of Boston. Brookline, another independent town, is almost wholly encircled by the city. While these cities and towns are politically independent, they are functionally as much a part of Boston as many of the areas within the city limits and will be so considered for the purpose of this study.

The population growth, since 1870, of the city of Boston and of the other cities and towns included in this study is presented in Table 63. The population in each of these towns and cities increased between 1920 and 1930. The highest rate of increase (44.7 per cent) was in Arlington; and the lowest (4.3 per cent), in Cambridge.

Composition of the Population.—The population of the city of Boston is predominantly white, 97.2 per cent being so classified in the 1930 federal census, while 2.6 per cent were classified as Negro. Of the total white population, 29.4 per cent were foreign born, 25.6 per cent native white of native parentage, 31.9 per cent native white of foreign parentage, and 10.3 per cent native white of mixed parentage. The predominant groups among the foreign-born whites were, in order of their number, those born in Ireland, Canada, Italy, and Russia; while the largest groups of native white of foreign or mixed parentage, classified on the basis of parents' birthplace, were practically the same—Irish, Italians, Canadians, and Russians. One difference between the composition of the foreign-born white population in Boston and in other cities has been the high percentage of English-speaking foreign born. For at least half a century the Irish have been the dominant national group, while the non-French Canadians have been second in rank, at least since 1900.

The composition of the population in some of the other cities and towns in the Boston area was quite different in 1930 from that of Boston. In only one city—Chelsea—was the proportion of foreign-born white population higher (37.2 per cent) or the

TABLE 63

POPULATION GROWTH, 1870–1930, BOSTON
METROPOLITAN AREA

AREA	POPULATION			
	1930	1910	1890	1870
Greater Boston.........	1,531,199	1,155,252	718,646	368,433
City of Boston.........	781,188	670,585	448,477	250,526
Towns and cities outside Boston city limits:				
Arlington............	36,094	11,187	5,629	....
Belmont.............	21,748	5,542	2,098	....
Brookline...........	47,490	27,792	12,103	6,650
Cambridge..........	113,643	104,839	70,028	39,634
Chelsea.............	45,816	32,452	27,909	18,547
Everett.............	48,424	33,484	11,068	2,220
Malden...., ...	58,036	44,404	23,031	7,367
Medford............	59,714	23,150	11,079	5,717
Melrose............	23,170	15,715	8,519	....
Newton.............	65,276	39,806	24,379	12,825
Revere.............	35,680	18,219	5,668	1,197
Somerville..........	103,908	77,236	40,152	14,685
Waltham............	39,247	27,834	18,707	9,065
Watertown..........	34,913	12,875	7,073	....
Winthrop...........	16,852	10,132	2,726	....

percentage native born of native parents lower (15.7 per cent). In Everett, Cambridge, and Somerville the population composition approximated that of Boston with respect to these two groups, while among the communities of over 40,000 the percentage of foreign-born white was conspicuously smaller in Newton (20.8) and in Medford (22.9), and the percentage of native white of native parentage correspondingly higher. Among the smaller places, those with the lowest percentage of foreign-born whites were Melrose (16.8), Winthrop (20.8), Belmont (21.7), and Arlington (22.3).

Outside of Boston the largest number of Negroes were found in Cambridge, where 4.8 per cent of the total population were so classified. In Everett the percentage was 2.1, in Malden 1.1, in Medford 1.0, and in Newton 1.0. In none of the other cities was the proportion of Negroes in the population equal to 1 per cent of the total.

Industrial Configuration.—Large sections of old Boston, Charlestown, East Boston, and South Boston have been zoned for either industry or business. In Boston proper the only areas not zoned for these uses were the residential section known as Beacon Hill, located just north of the Boston Common, and the Back Bay district, located west of the Common along the Charles River. Likewise, there are smaller areas zoned for business and industry in Roxbury; and industrial areas are to be noted along the Dorchester shore line, in the extreme southern part of the city, in the area known as Hyde Park, and in the northern part of Brighton. On the whole, however, the more outlying sections of Boston are residential.

In the cities adjacent to Boston the largest industrial areas are also in the sections of the city closest to central Boston and the harbor. This is noted in Cambridge, Somerville, Everett, and Chelsea, each of which contributes to this industrial hub. In the extreme western part of the metropolitan area the large industrial district of Waltham is located—a separate industrial center representing a development evidently almost completely independent of the major industrial areas of the harbor. A smaller but similar center is found in the northern section of Newton and the southern section of Watertown. The outlying cities and towns, however, are almost completely residential. This is especially true of Belmont, Arlington, Melrose, and Winthrop.

MALE JUVENILE DELINQUENTS IN BOSTON

Series Studied and Types of Offenses.—The data for this study of the distribution of male juvenile delinquents in the Boston metropolitan district were secured, as has been said, from the records of the 15 district and municipal courts in which cases of juvenile delinquency are heard. Eight of these are within the

limits of political Boston, and 7 outside. The cases in old Boston
are heard in the Boston Juvenile Court; those in East Boston in
the East Boston District Court, which includes Winthrop; and
the cases in Charlestown, South Boston, Roxbury, Brighton,
Dorchester, and West Roxbury in the municipal courts which
bear these names.[1]

Data were gathered on all of the boys who appeared in these
courts on delinquency petition between June 1, 1927, and May 31,
1930. In order to make the types of cases in the 15 judicial districts more nearly comparable, however, the series was restricted
to the comparatively serious types of delinquency. This was
necessary because of the variations in policy of the police and
other agencies in regard to disposition of offenders charged with
less serious offenses. In some courts there were no cases where
violation of the motor vehicle laws, trespassing, stealing rides on
street cars, gaming on the Lord's Day, truancy, stubbornness,
obstructing foot traffic, and similar offenses were charged; while
in other courts, where the cases came from areas of about the
same type, such charges were very common. In an effort, therefore, to eliminate these variations due to differences in policy, this
series was limited to the basic types of offenses found in every
court. All cases of stealing or attempted stealing, destruction of
property, sex offenses, and certain other serious types of delinquencies, such as carrying concealed weapons or bootlegging,
were retained, and all others excluded. This was done before any
of the cases in the series were plotted. In some courts very few
cases were eliminated by this method, in others, large numbers.
It is important in this connection that by far the largest number
of cases were eliminated in East Boston, where some of the heaviest concentrations and highest rates of delinquents are to be

---

[1] Four of the district courts outside of the city hear cases from more than one
town or city. The cases from Waltham and Watertown are heard in the Second
District Court of Eastern Middlesex; the cases from Belmont, Arlington, and Cambridge in the Third District Court of Eastern Middlesex; the cases from Medford,
Malden, Melrose, and Everett in the First District Court of Eastern Middlesex;
and the cases from Chelsea and Revere in the Chelsea District Court. Two other
cities have separate district courts, Somerville and Newton; while the cases from
Brookline are heard in the Brookline Municipal Court.

found. These rates would have been still higher if cases had not
been eliminated in the interest of uniformity.

It should be remembered that this selection of cases was made
only to secure some basis for comparison among the judicial districts in the Boston area. Since comparisons within judicial districts will be more often employed than comparisons of one district with another, the validity of the series for its major purpose
is not in question.

Thus defined, this series of cases in the Boston area includes
4,917 alleged male delinquents. Of this number, 77.4 per cent
were charged with stealing or attempted stealing, including petty
larceny, larceny of automobiles, breaking and entering, and holdup. Of the total number of individuals, 13.3 per cent were charged
with destruction of property, 1.3 per cent with sex offenses, and
8.0 per cent with other types of offenses. Only in the classification
"destruction of property" was there considerable variation among
the courts. The noticeably higher percentage of these cases in the
Second District Court of Eastern Middlesex, which includes
Waltham and Watertown, probably explains why the rates of delinquents are higher in these areas than in other communities of
the same general type.

The age distribution of the alleged delinquents included in this
series ranged from 7 to 17 years, although 92.5 per cent were within the aged 10–16-year grouping. The largest percentages were in
the 14-, 15-, and 16-year age groups.

Distribution.—Map 35 shows the distribution by place of residence of the 4,917 alleged male juvenile delinquents. Each dot
represents the home address of one boy, regardless of the number
of courts in which he appeared or the number of appearances in
any one court.[2]

This distribution map indicates great differences between the
number of delinquents in the different sections of the Boston
area, the different sections of the city of Boston, and the different
sections of the other cities and towns. Considering the area as a
whole, heavy concentrations are noted in old Boston, especially
in the areas north and northeast of the Common, known locally

[2] These dots were placed by street and number, at or very near the exact address.

MAP 35

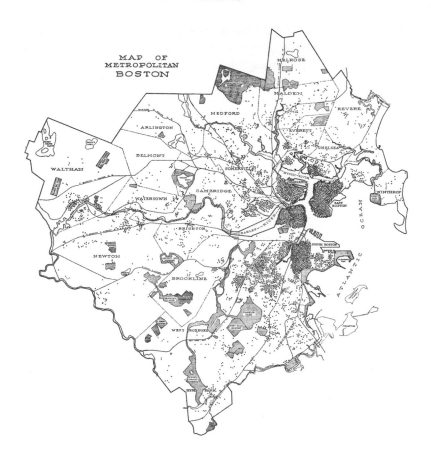

DISTRIBUTION OF 4,917 MALE JUVENILE DELINQUENTS, GREATER BOSTON, 1927-30

as the West End and the North End; and in Charlestown, East Boston, and South Boston. Only slightly less concentrated are the clusters in Roxbury, Cambridge, and Chelsea; while smaller but important concentrations will be observed in Waltham, Newton, Somerville, and Everett. In contrast with these areas of concentration, there are some neighborhoods where the delinquents are widely dispersed, and others from which almost no boys were brought into court.

Variations in concentration are obvious, too, when different sections of the separate cities and towns are compared. This is especially clear in Brookline, Newton, Waltham, Cambridge, Somerville, Everett, and Chelsea, where large proportions of the delinquents are in one section of the city, with relatively few in the remaining sections.

In general, the areas of concentration of delinquents either are zoned for industry or commerce or adjoin industrial or commercial areas. The heaviest concentrations in the city of Boston are clustered around the central business and industrial district; while in Cambridge, Somerville, Everett, and Chelsea the main concentrations, like the industrial areas, appear in those parts closest to the central business and industrial section of Boston.

In the outlying districts, also, correspondence will be observed between the location of industrial and commercial areas and location of delinquents. In Waltham, Newton, Brookline, and Hyde Park this tendency is especially noticeable. Conversely, the areas zoned for residential purposes farthest from industry tend to be the areas of fewest delinquents.

Rates of Delinquents.—For the presentation of rates the Boston metropolitan district has been divided into 120 local areas, 49 within the city of Boston and 71 outside. The 49 areas in the city are subdivisions of the 22 wards into which the city is divided. In making these divisions, all ward lines have been preserved, and, in so far as possible, the boundaries of the areas have been made to conform to the boundaries of the judicial districts. The areas in Cambridge, Chelsea, Everett, Malden, Medford, Newton, Revere, Somerville, and Waltham are wards; the areas in Brookline are arbitrary divisions of the federal census enumeration districts; while Arlington, Belmont, Melrose, Watertown, and Winthrop are presented without divisions. In each of the 120 areas the aged 10–16 male population as estimated[3] was more than 200; and in all but 7 areas, more than 300. The total aged 10–16 male population for the combined areas was 89,666.

The rates of delinquents as presented represent the number of delinquents for the 3-year period per 100 male population aged 10–16, as of 1930. The rate for the metropolitan district as a whole is 5.5, and the median of the 120 area rates is 3.5. For the city of Boston as a whole the rate is 7.0, and for the area outside of Boston it is 4.0.

The rates of delinquents for the 120 areas in the Boston district are presented on Map 36. These may be considered from the point of view of variation within the entire area, within the 15 judicial districts, or within the different towns and cities. When the metropolitan area is considered as a whole, the range of rates is from 0.4 to 18.5. It will be observed that most of the areas of high rates of delinquents are in or near the central business and industrial district of Boston. Rates of 16.0 and 13.0 will be noted in Areas 77 and 78, located north and northeast of the Common; rates of 14.4 and 11.2 in Areas 75 and 76, respectively, in Charles-

---

[3] From the age and sex distribution of the population for Boston as a whole and from the age distribution by wards it was possible to calculate quite accurately the aged 10–16 male population as of 1930 for each ward. On this basis the ward rates of delinquents were calculated. However, since these wards were very large and many included several different types of areas, it was felt that, by dividing them, interesting variations in rates would be revealed. The aged 10–16 male population in each was secured by computing from the federal census enumeration districts the proportion of the total population in each division of the ward and dividing the aged 10–16 male population for the ward as a whole on the basis of this proportion. Such a procedure assumes that the ratio of the aged 10–16 male population to the total population is constant throughout the ward.

In Cambridge, Malden, Medford, Newton, and Somerville the aged 10–16 male population was calculated through the same procedure. For cities under 50,000 the population by age groups for wards was not available. In Chelsea, Everett, Revere, and Waltham, therefore, it was necessary to distribute the aged 10–16 population for the city as a whole on the basis of the proportion of the total population in each ward. In Brookline the same method was employed. As in the other cities, the aged 10–16 male population for Arlington, Belmont, Melrose, Watertown, and Winthrop was secured from the population by age and sex in the federal census publications.

MAP 36

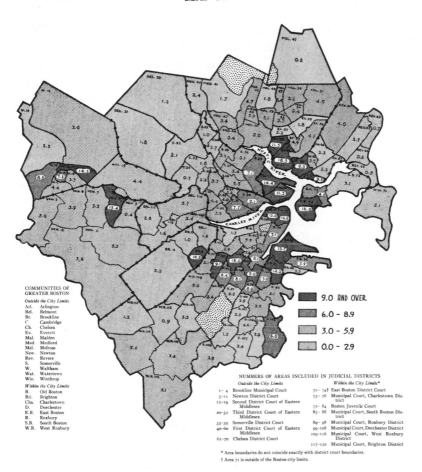

COMMUNITIES OF
GREATER BOSTON

Outside the City Limits

Arl.	Arlington
Bel.	Belmont
Br.	Brookline
C	Cambridge
Ch.	Chelsea
Ev.	Everett
Mal.	Malden
Med.	Medford
Mel.	Melrose
New.	Newton
Rev.	Revere
S.	Somerville
W.	Waltham
Wat.	Watertown
Win.	Winthrop

Within the City Limits

B.	Old Boston
Bri.	Brighton
Cha.	Charlestown
D.	Dorchester
E.B.	East Boston
R.	Roxbury
S.B.	South Boston
W.R.	West Roxbury

9.0 AND OVER

6.0 - 8.9

3.0 - 5.9

0.0 - 2.9

NUMBERS OF AREAS INCLUDED IN JUDICIAL DISTRICTS

Outside the City Limits

1– 4	Brookline Municipal Court
5–11	Newton District Court
12–19	Second District Court of Eastern Middlesex
20–32	Third District Court of Eastern Middlesex
33–39	Somerville District Court
40–60	First District Court of Eastern Middlesex
61–70	Chelsea District Court

*Within the City Limits**

71– 74†	East Boston District Court
75– 76	Municipal Court, Charlestown District
77– 84	Boston Juvenile Court
85– 88	Municipal Court, South Boston District
89– 98	Municipal Court, Roxbury District
99–108	Municipal Court, Dorchester District
109–116	Municipal Court, West Roxbury District
117–120	Municipal Court, Brighton District

* Area boundaries do not coincide exactly with district court boundaries.

† Area 71 is outside of the Boston city limits.

RATES OF MALE JUVENILE DELINQUENTS, GREATER BOSTON, 1927–30, BY AREAS

town; and a rate of 16.0 in Area 74 in East Boston. Only slightly removed from this center are the high rates of 15.7 and 14.2 in Areas 85 and 87 in South Boston, and a rate of 18.0 in Area 90 in Roxbury. Lower than these, but still well above the average, are the rates 7.6 and 8.1 in Areas 80 and 84 in Old Boston; 8.8 in Area 73 in East Boston; 7.9 in Area 86 in South Boston; and 7.0, 8.1, 8.4, 8.9, and 9.0 in Areas 92, 96, 95, 98, and 94, respectively.

Likewise, outside of the city of Boston, areas of high rates of delinquents are to be found near this central business and industrial district. A rate of 18.5 will be observed in Everett in the area closest to Boston, and rates of 9.5 and 9.3 in the same relative position in Chelsea; while in the sections of Somerville and Cambridge that extend closest to Boston proper the rates are 7.1 and 8.1. In each case these rates are the highest in their respective cities.

In outlying districts noticeably high rates are to be observed in Newton (15.4 in Area 8) and in Waltham (14.5 in Area 14). In general, however, the areas in the outlying parts of Boston and the surrounding cities and towns have much lower delinquency rates than those near the central business and industrial district in Boston. As indicated previously, the variations in rates of delinquents among areas within judicial districts are especially significant, since these could not be affected by variations in the policy of the different courts (see Table 64).

It will be observed from this table that with the exception of the Charlestown district, where there are only 2 areas, both with high rates of delinquents, the range in each district is wide, both within and outside the city of Boston. For the Boston Juvenile Court, for example, the rates vary from 1.3 in the fashionable Back Bay district to 16.0 in the North End, an area of immigrant first settlement. Similarly, the variation in South Boston is from 2.7 to 15.7, in Roxbury from 2.2 to 18.0, and in the First District Court of Eastern Middlesex from 0.8 to 18.5. Likewise, the courts which include only one city or town reveal wide variations in rates. This is evident in Brookline, where the range is from 1.0 to 10.3; in Newton, where it is from 0.4 to 15.4; and in Somerville, where it is from 1.0 to 7.1. In almost every instance these variations represent the difference between the rates of delinquents in the high-income residential areas and those in the areas adjacent to either industrial or commercial properties.

From these facts it will be seen that it makes little difference whether variation is considered from the standpoint of the total metropolitan area, of the judicial districts, or of the individual

TABLE 64

RANGE OF RATES AND RATE FOR EACH JUDICIAL
DISTRICT, GREATER BOSTON

Judicial District	Areas	Range of Rates	Rate for District
Brookline Municipal Court......	1– 4	1.0–10.3	3.3
Newton District Court.........	5– 11	0.4–15.4	5.1
Second District Court of Eastern Middlesex.................	12– 19	2.5–14.5	5.2
Third District Court of Eastern Middlesex.................	20– 32	0.7– 8.1	3.5
Somerville District Court.......	33– 39	1.0– 7.1	4.1
First District Court of Eastern Middlesex.................	40– 60	0.8–18.5	3.7
Chelsea District Court.........	61– 70	0.5– 9.5	4.0
East Boston District Court......	71– 74	3.1–16.0	9.9
Municipal Court, Charlestown District..................	75– 76	11.2–14.4	12.7
Boston Juvenile Court.........	77– 84	1.3–16.0	9.8
Municipal Court, South Boston District..................	85– 88	2.7–15.7	10.5
Municipal Court, Roxbury District..................	89– 98	2.2–18.0	8.2
Municipal Court, Dorchester District..................	99–108	1.3– 6.0	2.9
Municipal Court, West Roxbury District..................	109–116	0.9– 5.1	3.0
Municipal Court, Brighton District..................	117–120	1.6– 5.7	3.7

cities. In each case there are wide differences in the rates of delinquents among local areas.

Rates by Zones.—The rates of delinquents by zones for the Boston metropolitan area are presented on Map 37. These zones are constructed by taking a focal point in the central business district of Boston and drawing concentric circles at intervals of $1\frac{1}{2}$ miles. In calculating these rates the metropolitan district was considered, first, as a unit without regard for judicial districts and, second, by segments, taking certain judicial districts for special consideration.

On Map 37 it will be noted that the rates decrease regularly from 11.7 in the first zone to 2.7 in Zone IV, then rise to 4.3 in Zone VI. It is probable that the increase in Zones V and VI is due in part to the fact that Newton, Waltham, and Hyde Park repre-

MAP 37

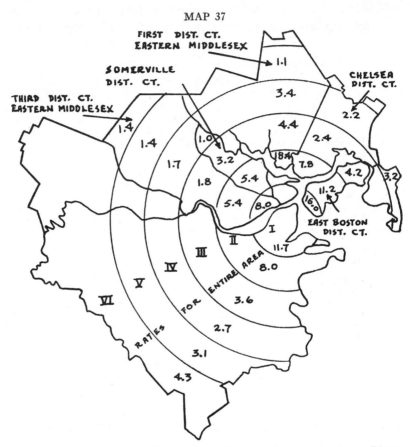

RATES OF MALE JUVENILE DELINQUENTS, GREATER BOSTON, 1927–30, BY ZONES

sent independent outlying centers and in part to differences between courts, since the rates of delinquents in Waltham, Watertown, and Newton are disproportionately high. The cases secured from the courts in these cities contain a somewhat higher percentage of boys charged with minor offenses.

It should be remembered that these zone rates are considered valid only as schematic presentations of general tendencies. Here, perhaps more than in any other city, interesting and significant local variations are eliminated in the calculation of zone rates. For example, in Zone I the rates of delinquents vary from 5.4 to 16.0, while in Zone VI a variation of from 0.7 to 14.5 is to be noted. However, it is significant that, notwithstanding these differences within the zones and the fact that each zone represents parts of separate municipalities and courts, the rate in Zone I is more than four times the rate in Zone IV and nearly three times that in Zone III.

When variations in rates are considered by the segments of zones which fall within certain judicial districts, the decrease out from the center of the metropolitan district is even more marked. The Third District Court of Eastern Middlesex, which includes Cambridge, Belmont, and Arlington, is, for example, represented in each of the 6 zones. The rates for the segments of the larger zones falling within this judicial district are: 8.0, 5.4, 1.8, 1.7, 1.4, and 1.4. The Somerville District Court extends over 3 zones (II–IV) with rates of 5.4, 3.2, and 1.0; while the Chelsea District Court, extending over the same zones, has rates of 7.8, 2.4, and 2.2. Similarly, rates calculated by zones for the East Boston District Court area, which extends over Zones I–IV, are 16.0, 11.2, 4.2, and 3.2. Thus, it will be noted that in these 4 judicial districts, each of which extends from the center of the Boston metropolitan district toward the periphery, the decrease in zone rates from the center of the city outward is sharp and regular.

It appears from the zone map of the Boston area, as well as from the distribution map, that the business district of Waltham might well be taken as a focal point for another set of smaller zones and that these, too, would show a variation from the center outward. The same might be said to be true to a lesser extent for Newton, Watertown, and Hyde Park. With regard to Cambridge and Somerville, the two largest cities in the area outside of Boston, and perhaps some of the others close to the center, it is interesting that the zonal variations are not from the center of these cities outward but *from the center of Boston outward*, as indicated by the rate maps for judicial districts.

Extent of Concentration.—The distribution of male juvenile delinquents in the Boston district was considered finally in relation to the distribution of population and in relation to the total geographic area. The extent of concentration for the metropolitan area was analyzed by ranking the 120 areas of the Boston district according to rate of delinquents, then dividing the male population aged 10–16 into four equal parts. For each of these quartiles the total number of delinquents and the percentage of the city area included were then computed. The results of this division are presented in Table 65.

It will be noted that the quarter of the aged 10–16 male population living in areas with the highest rates of delinquents con-

TABLE 65

PERCENTAGE OF DELINQUENTS AND OF CITY AREA
FOR QUARTILES OF MALE POPULATION AGED
10–16, WHEN AREAS ARE RANKED BY RATE OF
DELINQUENTS

Quartiles of Population	Percentage of Delinquents	Percentage of City Area
Upper one-fourth, in high-rate areas.............	53.9	9.9
Second one-fourth.......	24.6	23.8
Third one-fourth........	14.3	34.0
Lower one-fourth, in low-rate areas.............	7.2	32.3

tributed over half of the total delinquents from the Boston district, although the areas included made up less than one-tenth of the total city area. On the other hand, the 50 per cent of the boys who lived in areas with the lowest rates of delinquents contributed only one-fifth of the total delinquents, drawn from two-thirds of the total area.

When the population of boys aged 10–16 living within any judicial district is divided into four equal groups on the same basis, variations similar to those for the Boston district as a whole are revealed. In the First District Court of Eastern Middlesex, which includes Malden, Medford, Melrose, and Everett, the one-fourth of the aged 10–16 male population in areas with the highest rates contributed 47.2 per cent of the delinquents but was drawn from only 15.5 per cent of the total area of the judicial district. In the Second District Court of Eastern Middlesex, which includes

Waltham and Watertown, the one-fourth of the aged 10–16 male population in areas of highest rates contributed 44.7 per cent of the delinquents but was drawn from 12.1 per cent of the total area of the judicial district. Similarly, in the Roxbury Municipal Court 38.8 per cent of the delinquents came from the one-fourth of the boys aged 10–16 who lived in areas of highest rates, .although the areas themselves comprised only 21.3 per cent of the total area served by this court. On the other hand, the one-fourth of the boys aged 10–16 living in the areas of lowest rates of delinquents contributed only 9.6 per cent of the total delinquents

TABLE 66

PERCENTAGE OF MALE POPULATION AGED 10–16
AND OF CITY AREA FOR QUARTILES OF DELIN-
QUENTS WHEN AREAS ARE RANKED BY RATE OF
DELINQUENTS

Quartiles of Delinquents	Percentage of Population	Percentage of City Area
Upper one-fourth, from high-rate areas........	8.6	3.8
Second one-fourth.......	13.8	5.3
Third one-fourth........	22.8	18.4
Lower one-fourth, from low-rate areas.........	54.8	72.5

dealt with by the Roxbury court, while these areas made up 34.7 per cent of the total area served by the court.

When the 4,917 delinquents in the Boston area are divided, in turn, into quartiles on the basis of the magnitude of rate of delinquents, significant variations in corresponding population distribution and area are again revealed, as seen in Table 66.

It will be noted from Table 66 that half of the delinquents in the areas of highest rates represented 22.4 per cent of the population and only 9.1 per cent of the area. The one-fourth of the delinquents in the areas of lowest rates, on the other hand, came from 54.8 per cent of the population and 72.5 per cent of the area.

Similar variations are found within judicial districts. In the First District Court of Eastern Middlesex the one-fourth of the delinquents from the areas of highest rates came from 8.3 per cent of the population and 5.4 per cent of the area; in the Second District Court of Eastern Middlesex the upper quarter represented 10.0 per cent of the population and 6.1 per cent of the area; and in the Roxbury District Court one-fourth of the delinquents came from 12.6 per cent of the population and 13.7 per cent of the area.

These data indicate a high degree of concentration of delinquents, whether viewed from the standpoint of the area as a whole or from that of the different judicial districts. Only those districts containing the largest number of areas have been treated separately, but the distribution map and the variation in the rates of delinquents indicate that the extent of concentration in each of the others would not differ widely from those presented.

DELINQUENCY IN THE CITY OF BOSTON: LATER DATA

Since the foregoing data were collected, the Boston Council of Social Agencies has published statistics on delinquency in the city of Boston for the years 1931 through 1934.[4] These statistics are given for the 14 "health and welfare areas" established by the Council. A rate of delinquents was computed for each of these areas from a count of the court appearances of juvenile delinquents aged 7–16 residing in the area, both male and female, and from the juvenile population of the same age group in the area.

The rates of delinquents for the 4-year period 1931–34 are shown in Map 38.[5] The rate for the city as a whole is 7.7; the median rate is 6.5; and the range is from 2.8 in West Roxbury to 21.4 in West End. It will again be noted that the highest rates are found in or near the central business and industrial district of Boston. Rates of 21.4 and 16.5 in West End and North End, respectively, are more than double the city rate, and the rate of 15.1 in East Boston is but little lower. Charlestown, South End, and South Boston, all areas zoned for business and industry, are

---

[4] *Social Statistics by Census Tracts in Boston* (Boston: Boston Council of Social Agencies, 1935), II, 14–18.

[5] In order to make these rates roughly comparable in size with the rates already given, the Boston Council of Social Agencies rates are here expressed as the number of delinquents per 100 juveniles aged 7–16 for the entire 4-year period. In the volume from which they are taken, the rates are expressed as the average number of delinquents per year per 1,000 juveniles aged 7–16 (*ibid.*, Table II).

MAP 38

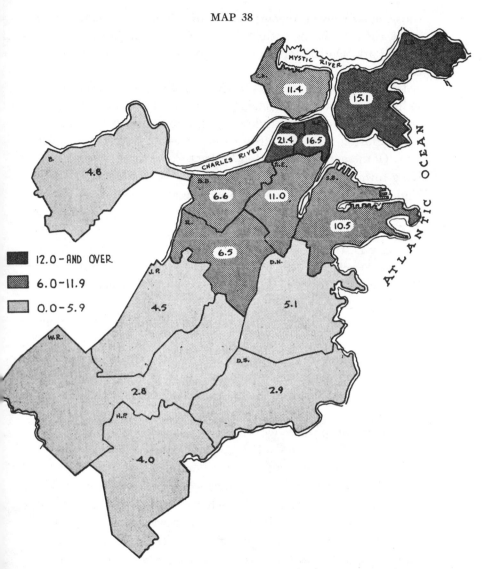

RATES OF JUVENILE DELINQUENTS (MALE AND FEMALE), BOSTON PROPER, 1931-34

conspicuously above average in rates of delinquents. On the other hand, the rates in the outlying areas of Brighton, Jamaica Plain, Hyde Park, Dorchester South, and West Roxbury are considerably below the city rate.

In general, within the city of Boston, the boundaries of the 8 judicial districts do not coincide with those of the health and welfare areas; although in Brighton, Charlestown, East Boston, and South Boston there is a fairly close correspondence between the two. Of these, the East Boston District Court serves also the outlying town of Winthrop. The areas Back Bay, West End, North End, and South End comprise approximately the district served by the Boston Juvenile Court. The areas Hyde Park, Jamaica Plain, and West Roxbury comprise, for the most part, the West Roxbury District of the Municipal Court. Dorchester South and part of Dorchester North are served by the Municipal Court, Dorchester District; while Roxbury and the balance of North Dorchester are served by the Municipal Court, Roxbury District.

It will be apparent, then, that part of the variation among areas may be due to differing practices in different judicial districts, but again there are significant differences among areas in the same judicial district. Moreover, the magnitude of the differences is such as to indicate actual variation in the relative number of delinquents.

Comparison of Two Series of Delinquents.—The general distribution of delinquents in the Boston Council of Social Agencies series for 1931–34 shows a close similarity to that of delinquents from the city of Boston in the 1927–30 series given above.[6] The health and welfare areas by which rates are presented for the 1931–34 series are much larger units, however, than the sections of wards used for the 1927–30 series. It seemed desirable, therefore, to combine and reapportion the samples of delinquents and the juvenile population for the 1927–30 series in order to distribute

[6] Hereafter the series for 1931–34 reported by the Boston Council of Social Agencies will be referred to simply as the "1931–34 series," whereas those cases from the city of Boston in the 1927–30 series of male delinquents will be referred to as the "1927–30 series."

these data by health and welfare areas.[7] The rates thus computed are directly comparable with those for the 1931–34 series.

Table 67 indicates that, in relative size and in rank order, the rates of delinquents for the two series, by health and welfare areas, exhibit an almost perfect correspondence. The coefficient

TABLE 67

RATES OF MALE AND FEMALE DELINQUENTS (1931–34), RATES OF MALE DELINQUENTS (1927–30), AND RANK ORDER OF HEALTH AND WELFARE AREAS

HEALTH AND WELFARE AREAS	1931–34		1927–30	
	Rates of Delinquents	Rank Order of Areas	Rates of Delinquents	Rank Order of Areas
West End.........	21.4	1	16.1	1
North End.........	16.5	2	14.7	2
East Boston........	15.1	3	12.1	4
Charlestown.......	11.4	4	12.6	3
South End.........	11.0	5	9.6	6
South Boston......	10.5	6	10.1	5
Back Bay..........	6.6	7	5.0	8
Roxbury...........	6.5	8	7.9	7
Dorchester North...	5.1	9	4.3	9
Brighton...........	4.8	10	4.1	10
Jamaica Plain......	4.5	11	4.0	11
Hyde Park.........	4.0	12	3.5	12
Dorchester South...	2.9	13	2.5	13
West Roxbury.....	2.8	14	1.3	14

of correlation between the two sets of 14 values[8] is .96 ± .02. This degree of covariance is remarkable when it is remembered that one series includes all male and female delinquents and the other only males who committed serious offenses, that the two series are

[7] It was possible to place delinquents exactly in the proper health and welfare areas, but the male population aged 10–16 could only be estimated in cases where welfare area lines cut across ward lines. For this reason the distribution of the total juvenile population aged 7–16, by health and welfare areas, as given by the Boston Council of Social Agencies report, was used as the best estimate of the proportionate distribution of aged 10–16 males; and these proportions were applied to the total 10–16 male population found previously for the 1927–30 series.

[8] Using Fisher's z-transformation, it is found that the probability is .95 that ρ, the true correlation, lies between .87 and .99. See R. A. Fisher, *Statistical Methods for Research Workers* (London: Oliver & Boyd, 1930), pp. 163 ff.

MAP 39

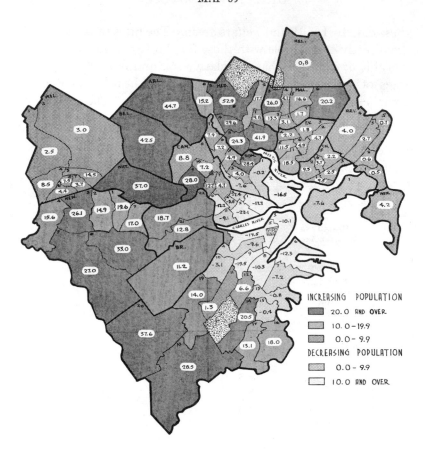

PERCENTAGE INCREASE OR DECREASE OF POPULATION, GREATER BOSTON, 1925–30

for different periods, and that the studies were made by different persons in different organizations without interchange of information.

COMMUNITY CHARACTERISTICS IN RELATION
TO RATES OF DELINQUENTS

A. GREATER BOSTON

As in the discussion of other cities, data will be presented for Boston to show how areas with high rates of delinquents are differentiated from low-rate areas, and to illustrate again the nature of the processes of selection and distribution of the population which seem to be basic to the distribution of delinquents in a metropolitan region.

The industrial configuration of the Boston region and the composition of the population were discussed briefly at the beginning of the chapter. As in other cities, the areas immediately surrounding heavy industrial and commercial concentrations are those of greatest physical deterioration and highest rates of juvenile delinquents.

Increase or Decrease of Population.—In the 5-year period 1925–30, the population of most of the congested areas of Boston decreased, while that of the less densely settled outer areas and the surrounding towns and cities grew. Map 39 shows the rates of increase or decrease of population during this period by wards or cities, or by towns for the Boston area. It will be noted that, generally speaking, the areas of greatest decrease are the areas of highest rates of delinquents, while the areas of increasing population have considerably lower rates of delinquents. When the rates of delinquents (1927–30 series) are correlated with the increase or decrease of population in these 90 areas, the coefficient of correlation, assuming a linear relation, is found to be $-.47 \pm .05$. Since, however, the relationship between rates of increase or decrease of population and rates of delinquents is clearly not linear, the correlation ratio, η, is probably a better measure of their covariance. For these series, $\eta = .60$. There are 2 or 3 areas of increasing population in Newton and Waltham which have much higher rates of delinquents than would be expected from the general trend, but these are industrial districts, which, on the whole, present characteristics much more like the characteristics of central Boston than like those of other outlying areas.

When rates of delinquents are calculated for the five classes of areas represented on Map 39, the relationship between rates of delinquents and percentage increase or decrease of population is strikingly apparent (see Table 68).

TABLE 68

RATES OF DELINQUENTS (1927–30) FOR 90 AREAS
OF GREATER BOSTON GROUPED BY PERCENT-
AGE INCREASE OR DECREASE OF POPULATION,
1925–30

Percentage of Population Change	Rate of Delinquents
Decreasing:	
10.0 and over	10.4
0.0–9.9	7.3
Increasing:	
0.0– 9.9	4.0
10.0–19.9	3.5
20.0 and over	2.8

Unemployed Males.—It has been pointed out that the segregation which takes place in the city proceeds on an economic basis. For the Boston metropolitan district as a whole, there are available few satisfactory indexes of the economic level of constituent areas. Perhaps the most satisfactory is the percentage unemployed among employable males, as determined by the 1934 census of unemployment in Massachusetts.[9] It may be assumed that, on the whole, those individuals who are unemployed and who have not been able to save any appreciable amount from past wages will be forced to gravitate to areas where rents and other living costs are lowest. This being the case, it should be expected that the highest percentage of unemployed would be found in areas with the lowest economic status.

Map 40 shows, for the 22 wards of Boston and for each of the 15 cities and towns in the Boston district, the percentage unem-

[9] *Report of the Census of Unemployment in Massachusetts as of January 2, 1934* (Massachusetts Department of Labor and Industries, November, 1934).

MAP 40

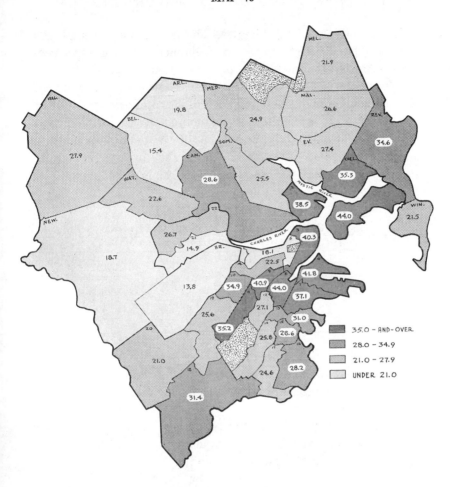

PERCENTAGE UNEMPLOYED AMONG EMPLOYABLE MALES, GREATER BOSTON, 1934

ployed among employable males. The percentages unemployed
were correlated with the rates of delinquents for the same geographic units. The coefficient of correlation based on these 37
pairs of values is .85 ± .03. In the interpretation of this coefficient
it must be pointed out that the percentages of unemployed are as
of January, 1934, while the rates of delinquents are for the period
1927–30. In 1928–29, the mid-point of the delinquency series,
unemployment was, of course, much less than in 1934. It is probable, however, that the areas with the highest percentages of

TABLE 69

RATES OF DELINQUENTS (1927–30) FOR 37 AREAS
OF GREATER BOSTON GROUPED BY PERCENT-
AGE UNEMPLOYED AMONG EMPLOYABLE MALES,
1934

Percentage Unemployed	Rate of Delinquents
35.0 and over	10.1
28.0–34.9	4.3
21.0–27.9	4.0
Under 21.0	2.9

unemployed in 1934 were the areas of lowest economic status
even before 1927. The covariance shown is another indication
that delinquency rates are, on the whole, highest where economic
status is relatively low.

The relationship between the percentage unemployed among
employable males and rate of delinquents is further illustrated in
Table 69, showing the rates of delinquents for classes of areas
grouped according to the percentage of unemployed.

B. BOSTON CITY

In addition to the percentage increase or decrease of population
and the percentage unemployed among employable males, there
are available for the 14 health and welfare areas delimited by the
Boston Council of Social Agencies statistics on such community
characteristics as the percentage of families on relief, rates of older
delinquents, infant mortality, and tuberculosis. Unfortunately,
the health and welfare districts are large areas within which considerable local variation occurs; moreover, coefficients of correlation based on only 14 sets of values are extremely unstable, so

that an accurate estimation of the covariance of the social characteristics of these areas is difficult to attain. Where such coefficients are given, they serve merely to indicate a general association of variables and are not to be interpreted as the correlation to be expected for a much larger number of smaller areas.

Percentage of Families Receiving Public Relief.—This is probably the best simple index of the economic level of an urban community. For the most part, those areas of Boston with the highest percentage of families on relief during 1932–33 have also the highest rates of delinquents. The coefficient of correlation for the two series of 14 values each is .74 ± .07.[10] This coefficient is reduced

TABLE 70

RATES OF DELINQUENTS (1927–30) FOR 14 HEALTH
AND WELFARE AREAS OF BOSTON GROUPED BY
PERCENTAGE OF FAMILIES ON RELIEF, 1932–33

Percentage of Families on Relief	Rate of Delinquents
20.0 and over	11.9
10.0–19.9	5.6
0.0– 9.9	3.0

greatly by the extremely high percentage of families on relief in South End, where the large number of rooming-houses gives this index a different meaning from that which it has in other areas.[11]

When the health and welfare areas are grouped into classes according to percentage of families on relief, the rates of delinquents for these classes vary directly with rates of families on relief (see Table 70 and Map 41).

Older Delinquents.—Statistics on rates of adult criminals are not available by areas for Boston, but rates of older delinquents (17–20 years) for 1930–31 are available for the 14 health and welfare areas. In general, the areas with the highest rates of older delinquents are those with the highest rates of juvenile delinquents, but the range is much narrower for the former. For the 1927–30 series of male delinquents aged 10–16 the rates by health and

[10] Using Fisher's z-transformation, the probability is .95 that the true correlation will be between .34 and .91.

[11] *Social Statistics in Boston* (Boston: Boston Council of Social Agencies, 1933), p. 23.

MAP 41

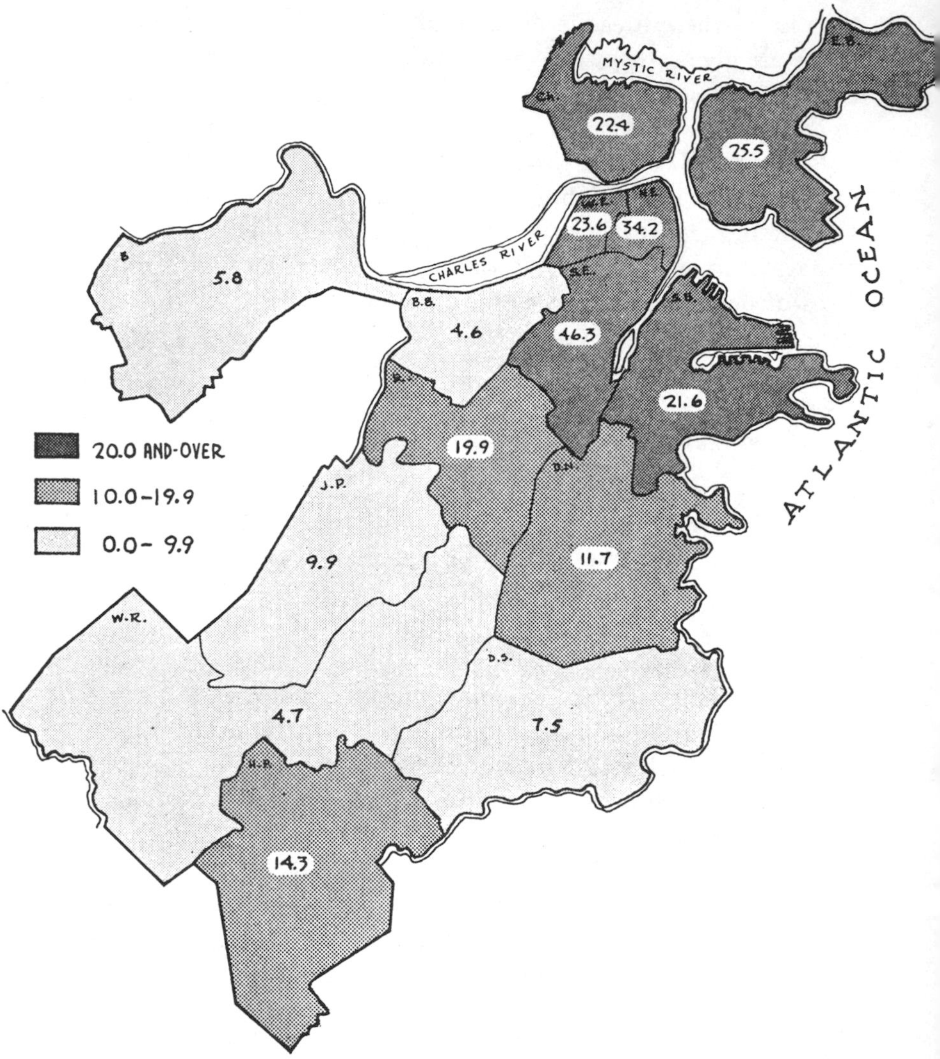

MYSTIC RIVER

E.B.

Ch.

22.4

25.5

ATLANTIC OCEAN

W.L. N.E.

23.6 34.2

CHARLES RIVER

S.E.

B

5.8

B.B.

S.B.

4.6

46.3

21.6

R.

19.9

20.0 AND-OVER

J.P.

D.N.

10.0-19.9

11.7

0.0- 9.9

9.9

W.R.

D.S.

4.7

7.5

H.P.

14.3

Percentage of Families on Relief, Boston Proper, 1932-33

welfare areas range from 1.3 in West Roxbury to 16.1 in West End; for the 1930–34 series the rates of all young delinquents range from 2.8 in West Roxbury to 21.4 in West End; but for the 1930–31 series of older delinquents the range is only from 12.3 in West Roxbury to 26.0 in South Boston and in West End. Particularly among the low-rate areas, the rates of older delinquents show much less variation. Nevertheless, the general covariance of rates of older and younger delinquents is indicated by a coefficient of correlation of .84 ± .05 for the 14 pairs of values, using the 1927–30 male series of juvenile delinquents.

TABLE 71

RATES OF DELINQUENTS (1927–30) FOR 14 HEALTH
AND WELFARE AREAS OF BOSTON GROUPED BY
RATES OF OLDER DELINQUENTS, 1930–31

Rates of Older Delinquents	Rate of Delinquents
22.0–27.9	11.3
16.0–21.9	10.3
10.0–15.9	5.3

When the health and welfare areas are grouped into three classes according to rates of older delinquents, the rates of juvenile delinquents for the classes vary directly with rates of older delinquents (see Table 71 and Map 42).

Infant Mortality.—Rates of infant mortality for 1930–33 show fairly high positive correlation with rates of juvenile delinquents; but the coefficient for 14 pairs of values, .52 ± .12, is too unstable to serve as a satisfactory index of covariance. Two areas, West End and North End, have rates of infant mortality considerably below what one would expect on the basis of other social data, the rate for West End being, in fact, among the lowest, although this area ranks first in rate of juvenile delinquency.

C. VARIATION IN COMMUNITY CHARACTERISTICS
WITH RATES OF DELINQUENTS

In the foregoing discussion of community differentiation in Boston, data have been presented for several series of areas differing in size and in territory covered. For the metropolitan district, which includes Boston and 15 contiguous cities and towns,

MAP 42

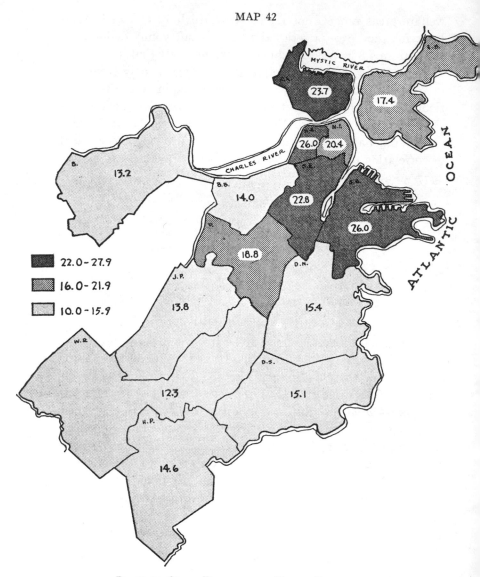

22.0 – 27.9
16.0 – 21.9
10.0 – 15.9

RATES OF OLDER DELINQUENTS, BOSTON PROPER, 1930–31

the percentage of increase or decrease in population has been given for 90 areas, and the percentage unemployed among employable males for 37 areas. It has been pointed out that, when areas are grouped according either to rate of population change or

TABLE 72

PERCENTAGE OF POPULATION CHANGE (1925–30) AND PERCENTAGE OF UNEMPLOYED AMONG EMPLOYABLE MALES (1934) FOR AREAS OF GREATER BOSTON GROUPED BY RATE OF DELINQUENTS

Area Rates of Delinquents	Percentage Increase or Decrease of Population (90 Areas)	Percentage of Unemployed Males (37 Areas)
9.0 and over............	−10.9	41.3
6.0–8.9................	− 8.6	38.7
3.0–5.9................	7.9	26.1
0.0–2.9................	19.6	23.0

TABLE 73

COMMUNITY CHARACTERISTICS FOR 14 HEALTH AND WELFARE AREAS OF BOSTON GROUPED BY RATE OF DELINQUENTS

Area Rates of Delinquents	Percentage Increase or Decrease of Population 1920–30	Rate of Families on Relief 1932–33	Rate of Infant Mortality 1930–33	Rate of Older Delinquents 1930–31
10.0 and over......	−11.3	24.5	6.9	22.3
5.0–9.9..........	− 6.1	21.9	6.8	19.0
0.0–4.9..........	25.0	8.9	5.3	14.4

so percentage unemployed, rates of delinquents for these classes thow a consistent pattern of covariation. The association of these community characteristics with rates of delinquents may also be illustrated by grouping areas according to rates of delinquents and computing the percentage increase or decrease in population and the percentage of unemployed for each class of areas. The results of such a grouping are found in Table 72.

The 14 health and welfare areas, too, have been grouped into classes, by rates of delinquents; and the percentage increase or decrease of population, rates of families on relief, rates of older delinquents, and rates of infant mortality have been computed. These indexes show the same consistent patterns of variation that were found for the larger number of small areas in the district as a whole.

SUMMARY

In general, rates of delinquents by areas in the Boston area vary widely both for the city as a whole and within judicial districts. A series of all delinquents appearing before Boston juvenile courts from 1931–34, presented for the 14 health and welfare areas of the city by the Boston Council of Social Agencies, was compared with the Boston portion of the 1927–30 series of male delinquents. Areas for the two series had almost the same rank order as to rates of delinquents and a high coefficient of correlation obtained between them.

For the Boston area as a whole, areas with high rates of delinquents were found to be characterized by decreasing population, and vice versa. A high positive correlation was found also between rates of delinquents and the percentage unemployed among employable males. For the 14 health and welfare areas within the city, general positive associations were observed between rates of delinquents and rates of families on relief, infant mortality, and older delinquents.

CHAPTER X

CINCINNATI

THE city of Cincinnati, located on the Ohio River in the extreme southwestern corner of the state of Ohio, offers an opportunity to study rates of delinquents and community characteristics as they are related to land elevation. In contrast with the cities discussed previously, all of which have been comparatively level, part of the city of Cincinnati is located on the flats along the river and part is located on the bluffs and the elevated land behind them. This difference in elevation has figured significantly in the growth and development of the city.

GROWTH OF CINCINNATI

History.—Cincinnati originated as a military outpost in 1788. The original settlement was at a point near what is now the foot of Sycamore Street. By the year 1800 it had expanded into a village of 700 inhabitants, and in 1819 the city was incorporated with a population of 9,873 and a geographic area of 3 square miles. Impetus to its early development came with the opening of steam navigation on the Ohio River in 1816, with the completion of the Miami Canal in 1820, and with the later development of railroad transportation. In the course of this development the city expanded outward, increasing from its original area of 3 square miles in 1819 to 71 square miles in 1930.

In 1930 the population of Cincinnati was 451,160, an increase of 12.4 per cent over 1920. The previous decade had seen an increase of 10.4 per cent, and the decade 1900–1910 an increase of 11.6 per cent. Population growth within recent years has thus been somewhat less than that of many urban centers of the United States, but it has proceeded at a fairly even rate.

In Cincinnati, as in other cities studied, the central business district has developed around the point of first settlement. This area, situated on lowlands on the inner side of a curve in the Ohio River, is known as the "Basin." Along the river front, both in the Basin and in the adjoining areas, particularly to the east, are found heavy industrial properties, including railroad yards. Other heavy industries are located on the western and northwestern edges of the Basin, in Mill Creek Valley. Much of the city is extremely hilly, and large sections are as yet unsettled. On the whole, the better residential areas are found at points of considerable elevation, and the industrial property at the lowest points.

Racial and Nationality Distribution.—The classification of Cincinnati's population in 1930 was: native white, 81.6 per cent; foreign-born white, 7.7 per cent; and Negro, 10.6 per cent. The percentage of foreign-born whites is thus considerably smaller than in most northern industrial cities, and the percentage of Negroes somewhat greater. A large part of the present foreign-born population migrated to Cincinnati prior to 1900. The most numerous of the early immigrants were the Germans, who in 1850 comprised nearly one-third of Cincinnati's inhabitants. By 1930 the German born made up only slightly more than 3 per cent of the population but were still far more numerous than any other foreign group. This German population has been largely assimilated and is spread quite evenly throughout the city. More recent immigration brought large numbers of Russians and Italians to Cincinnati. The Russian population, largely Jewish, shows greater concentration in a few areas than either the German or the Italian. A large part of this group is found in the Avondale section in the east central part of the city, which has the largest foreign-born population of any of the subcommunities within Cincinnati. What nucleus there is to the Italian settlement is found on the northern edge of the central business district.

The Negro population has been increasing much more rapidly than the general rate of increase for Cincinnati. The percentage of Negroes in the population rose from 5.4 in 1910 to 7.5 in 1920 and to 10.6 in 1930. The residential segregation of the Negro population is much more marked than that of any European nationality. The heaviest concentration is found in the Basin area, immediately west of the central business district. The second largest area is in Walnut Hills, northeast of the Basin.

For Cincinnati, data on both male and female delinquents have been obtained. The two series will be discussed separately. Both comprise, however, young people who appeared in the Cincinnati Juvenile Court on petitions alleging delinquency during the period between January 1, 1927, and September 1, 1929.[1]

A. MALE DELINQUENTS

Series Studied and Types of Offenses.—The series of male delinquents includes 2,332 boys ranging in age from 7 to 18 years. Only a few were under 10 years or over 17, and a large majority fell in the age group 12–17, inclusive. The modal point of this distribution is between 16 and 17 years of age. The average age of boys in the Cincinnati series is thus somewhat higher than that for other cities studied.

The Cincinnati series of male delinquents probably includes more minor offenders than most of the other series studied, but nearly half were charged with some form of stealing—larceny of auto, burglary, robbery, or other theft. The next most frequent charge was incorrigibility, followed, in the order named, by traffic offenses, loitering or suspicious actions, watching autos, and malicious mischief.

Distribution.—The distribution of male delinquents by place of residence is shown on Map 43. Each dot on the map represents an individual offender and is plotted approximately at his home address. The heaviest concentration of dots is found in the Basin area. The central business district (centered at the intersection of Sixth and Vine streets) has few delinquents, for there are not many residences and the juvenile population is small; but to the north and to the west, in the area between the business district and the Mill Creek Valley industrial areas, the concentration of delinquents is marked. Along the river to the east of the Basin and at several points to the east of Mill Creek are clusters of delinquents living in proximity to industrial properties. Smaller

---

[1] Data on these delinquents were secured through the co-operation of the Hon. Charles M. Hoffman, judge, and Mr. Galen F. Aschauer, referee, of the Cincinnati Juvenile Court.

MAP 43

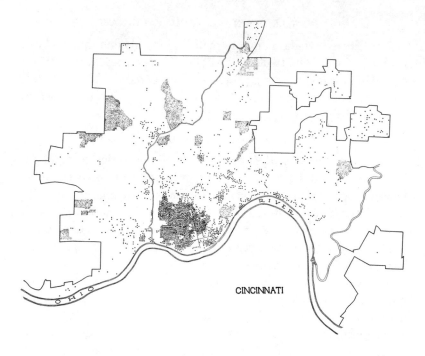

DISTRIBUTION OF 2,332 MALE JUVENILE DELINQUENTS, CINCINNATI, 1927–29

concentrations may be noted in the central part of the city, northeast of the Basin area, and at the northernmost and the northeastern extremities. The first of these areas includes Avondale, Cincinnati's nearest approach to an immigrant community, and the section just to the south, which has a large colored population. The northern extremity contains considerable industrial property and is, in fact, a minor business and industrial center. Large areas of this map of Cincinnati indicate few or no delinquents. These comprise the high-income residential areas of the city and certain sections of the steeper, hilly areas within the city which have little population.

Rates of Delinquents.—Rates of delinquents have been computed for 28 of the 29 statistical areas of Cincinnati used in the 1930 census[2] on the basis of the 1930 male population aged 10–17 years. While the 1930 census was 2 years removed from the mid-year of this series of delinquents, in most areas the population change during this period was slight. Only in those outlying parts of the city where the increase from 1920 to 1930 was exceedingly large would the rates of delinquents, as here computed, differ to any considerable degree from those based on the actual 1928 population. The smallest number of males aged 10–17 years in any area was 276 (Area 21). In all but 5 areas the sample of boys in this age group exceeded 500.

Rates of male delinquents per 100 boys aged 10–17, for the 28 areas, are indicated on Map 44. The range of rates is from 0.3 in Area 15 to 34.5 in Area 1.[3] The rate for the city as a whole is 9.0, and the median 5.3. Areas with the highest rates are those which showed also the greatest concentration of individual delinquents. These are the areas which comprise the Basin and Area 13 with its large river frontage.

[2] The twenty-ninth area, which extends far to the west along the Ohio River, has not been used because of inadequate data on the number of delinquents in this area.

[3] The two lowest rates shown, 0.3 in Area 15 and 1.9 in Area 28, are almost certainly spuriously low. Both of these areas extend some distance out from the city along the river. It is probable that some delinquents in these areas either were dealt with locally or for some reason escaped tabulation in the period under consideration.

Area 1, with a rate of 34.5, is primarily a railroad and industrial area. Area 3, which has a rate only slightly lower, includes the central business district in its northeastern portion and considerable industrial property to the south. Median rentals are low in all of the Basin areas, and the percentage of home ownership is very small.

MAP 44

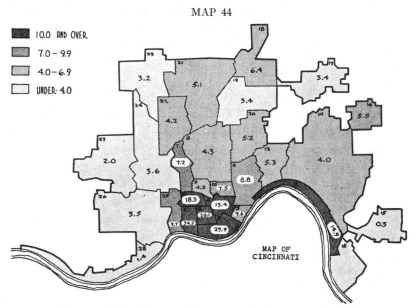

RATES OF MALE JUVENILE DELINQUENTS, CINCINNATI, 1927–29

Areas with the lowest rates of delinquents are, for the most part, those on the periphery of the city. These peripheral areas comprise the "better" residential sections, characterized by relatively high rentals and a high percentage of home ownership. Areas 16 and 18, with higher rates than might be expected, already have been mentioned as containing clusters of delinquents in proximity to industrial properties.

Extent of Concentration.—When the 28 areas of Cincinnati are ranked in order of rates of delinquents and the male population aged 10–17 is divided into quartiles, the corresponding percentages of male delinquents and of total city area indicate clearly the extreme concentration of delinquents (see Table 74). The one-

fourth of the aged 10–17 male population living in areas of highest
rates of delinquents contributed 56.9 per cent of Cincinnati's delinquents but was drawn from only 9.6 per cent of the city's area,
for the period 1927–29. On the other hand, the one-fourth living

TABLE 74

PERCENTAGE OF DELINQUENTS AND OF CITY AREA
FOR QUARTILES OF MALE POPULATION AGED
10–17, WHEN AREAS ARE RANKED BY RATE OF
DELINQUENTS

Quartiles of Population	Percentage of Delinquents	Percentage of City Area
Upper one-fourth, in high-rate areas............	56.9	9.6
Second one-fourth........	22.5	27.3
Third one-fourth.........	12.2	32.6
Lower one-fourth, in low-rate areas............	8.4	36.5

TABLE 75

PERCENTAGE OF MALE POPULATION AGED 10–17
AND OF CITY AREA FOR QUARTILES OF DELIN-
QUENTS WHEN AREAS ARE RANKED BY RATE
OF DELINQUENTS

Quartiles of Delinquents	Percentage of Population	Percentage of City Area
Upper one-fourth, from high-rate areas........	7.8	4.1
Second one-fourth.......	12.5	4.4
Third one-fourth........	22.5	13.2
Lower one-fourth, from low-rate areas........	57.2	78.3

in areas with the lowest rates accounted for only 8.4 per cent of
the delinquents, although their areas of residence comprised 36.5
per cent of the total city area.

When, in turn, delinquents are grouped by quartiles and the
corresponding percentages of population and of city area are
computed, the concentration is again strikingly apparent, as
shown in Table 75.

B. FEMALE DELINQUENTS

The series of female delinquents includes 1,497 girls brought to the Juvenile Court of Cuyahoga County on petition alleging delinquency. A spot map of female delinquents would show concentrations very similar to those noted for the males. Rates of female delinquents based on the same 28 areas previously dis-

MAP 45

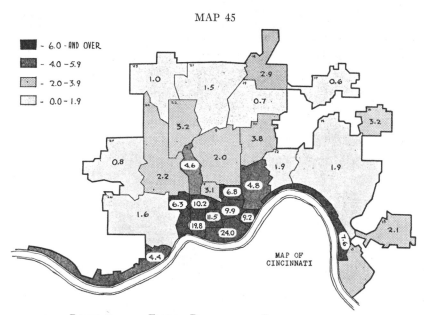

RATES OF 1,497 FEMALE DELINQUENTS, CINCINNATI, 1927–29

cussed are presented on Map 45. The range of rates is from 0.6 in Area 17 to 24.0 in Area 3, the highest rate thus being forty times as great as the lowest. In general, the same areas have high rates of male and female delinquents. Areas 15 and 28, however, which had the lowest rates of male delinquents, have intermediate rates for the girls.

The degree of association between rates of male and female delinquents is evidenced by a coefficient of correlation between the two series of .95 ± .01. On the scatter diagram, however, Areas 15 and 28 fall so far below the regression line that they are isolated from all other points. This would seem to support the hypothesis that the rates of male delinquents in these areas are spuriously low.

Rates by Zones.—Rates by concentric zones have been computed for Cincinnati, taking as a focal point the intersection of Sixth and Vine streets in the central business district, and using an interval of $1\frac{1}{2}$ miles. These zone rates for male and female delinquents are shown in Table 76.

TABLE 76

RATES OF DELINQUENTS BY $1\frac{1}{2}$-MILE ZONES*

Zone	Rate of Male Delinquents	Rate of Female Delinquents
I.................	18.3	12.7
II................	9.4	5.5
III...............	4.8	2.6
IV................	4.4	2.4
V.................	3.9	2.1

*Centered on intersection of Sixth and Vine streets.

The range of rates of male delinquents is from 18.3 in the first zone, which includes most of the Basin area, to 3.9 in the fifth zone, indicating the greater prevalence of influences making for delinquent behavior in the central area. The spread between the central zone and the peripheral zone (12.7 to 2.1) is even greater for female delinquents.

COMMUNITY CHARACTERISTICS IN RELATION TO RATES OF DELINQUENTS

The familiar concentration of delinquents near areas of business and industrial development has been noted also for Cincinnati. The relationship between juvenile delinquency and such characteristics of local areas as percentage increase or decrease in population, median rental, and rate of adult criminals will now be considered.

Increase or Decrease in Population.—During the decade from 1920 to 1930 the population of Cincinnati increased 12.4 per cent. In this same interval, however, six areas lost in population. These were the Basin areas 1, 2, 3, 4, and 5, and Area 13 along the river

to the east. Map 46 shows for each of the 28 city areas the percentage increase or decrease. The greatest drop took place in
Area 3, which includes the central business district. As the business district expanded, it encroached upon the homes in this area.
Likewise, in Area 1, the industrial section of Mill Creek Valley—
railroads, warehouses, and factories—crowded out residences.

MAP 46

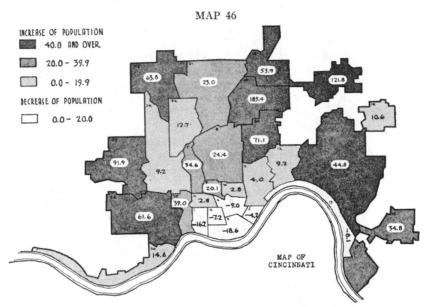

INCREASE OF POPULATION
40.0 AND OVER
20.0 - 39.9
0.0 - 19.9
DECREASE OF POPULATION
0.0 - 20.0

MAP OF
CINCINNATI

PERCENTAGE INCREASE OR DECREASE OF POPULATION, CINCINNATI, 1920–30

Lesser industrial development and business expansion took place
in other areas with decreasing population.

A comparison between the map showing percentage increase
or decrease in population and Map 44, showing rates of delinquents, reveals that those areas with decreasing population had,
in general, the highest rates of delinquents, while areas with increasing population had rates inversely related to the percentage
of population increase. When rates of male delinquents are correlated with the percentage increase or decrease of population,
the coefficient is $-.51 \pm .09$. The relationship between these two
variables is clearly curvilinear, however; so the actual degree of
association is certainly higher than the linear coefficient would

indicate. The small number of areas makes impractical the use of a more exact technique.

When rates of delinquents are computed for each of the four classes of areas indicated on Map 46, the relationship between increase or decrease in population and rates of both male and female delinquents again is apparent (see Table 77).

Median Rentals.—Median monthly rental may be used as an index of economic status. Map 47 shows for each area the median rental as of 1930. The lowest was $17.14 in Area 1; the highest,

TABLE 77

RATES OF MALE AND FEMALE DELINQUENTS FOR
AREAS GROUPED BY PERCENTAGE INCREASE OR
DECREASE OF POPULATION, 1920–30

Percentage Increase or Decrease in Population 1920–30	Rate of Male Delinquents	Rate of Female Delinquents
Decreasing:		
0.0–19.9 (*10.8*)*..	19.0	12.9
Increasing:		
0.0–19.9 (*7.7*)*..	7.2	4.5
20.0–39.9 (*26.6*)*..	5.0	3.1
40.0 and over (*63.9*)*..	3.9	1.8

* Rate for class as a whole.

$96.95 in Area 20. It will be noted that the lowest rentals were found in the Basin area and along the river. For the most part, these areas had the highest rate of male and female delinquents. On the other hand, those more outlying residential areas with highest median rentals were the areas with lowest rates of delinquents. The coefficient of correlation between the two series of 28 values is $-.50 \pm .09$. Here again, however, the apparent relationship between the variables is not linear, and the degree of association is, no doubt, higher than the linear coefficient would indicate. Moreover, Areas 15 and 28 have much lower rates of delinquents relative to the median rentals in these areas than any of the other 28 areas. If these areas are omitted from the correlation, the coefficient becomes $-.65 \pm .08$.

When rates of delinquents are calculated for the four classes of areas indicated on Map 47, a regular pattern of inverse variation may be noted between the median rental for each class and the rates of male and female delinquents for the class (see Table 78).

MAP 47

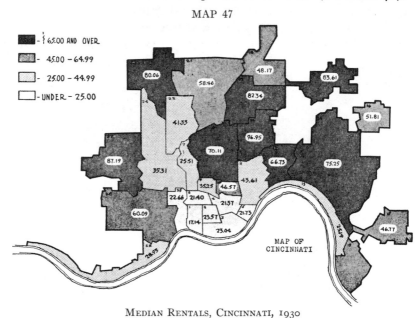

MEDIAN RENTALS, CINCINNATI, 1930

TABLE 78

RATES OF MALE AND FEMALE DELINQUENTS FOR
AREAS GROUPED BY MEDIAN MONTHLY
RENTAL, 1930

Median Monthly Rentals	Rate of Male Delinquents	Rate of Female Delinquents
Under $25.00............	18.6	12.5
$25.00– 44.99...........	6.0	4.0
45.00– 64.99..........	4.5	2.6
65.00 and over........	4.1	1.9

Rates of Adult Males Arrested.—Area rates of adult males arrested have been calculated on the basis of the home addresses of 1,206 individuals. These rates, as shown on Map 48, are expressed in terms of the numbers of arrested male adults per 100 males aged 18–45. It will be noted that the range of rates is rela-

tively much greater than in the case of either male or female delinquents, being from 0.1 in Areas 21 and 17 to 5.1 in Area 3.
Rates of 1.0 and over are found in all areas of the Basin district,
and rates of 0.5 or less in most of the outlying areas. The similar-

MAP 48

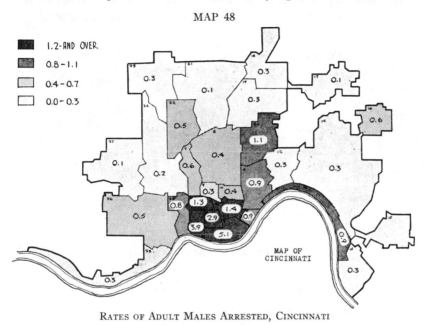

RATES OF ADULT MALES ARRESTED, CINCINNATI

TABLE 79

RATES OF MALE AND FEMALE DELINQUENTS
FOR AREAS GROUPED BY RATE OF
ADULT MALES ARRESTED

Rates of Adult Males Arrested	Rate of Male Delinquents	Rate of Female Delinquents
1.2 and over............	20.2	13.3
0.8–1.1................	8.7	5.0
0.4–0.7................	5.2	3.3
0.0–0.3................	4.0	2.3

ity of the distribution of adult male criminals and male delinquents is indicated by the coefficient of correlation, .93 ± .02.

The covariance of rates of adult criminals and of delinquents is
indicated also in Table 79, which shows rates of male and female
delinquents for the four classes of areas indicated on Map 48.

VARIATION IN COMMUNITY CHARACTERISTICS
WITH RATES OF DELINQUENTS

Comparison by Classes of Areas.—In the preceding section correlations were presented to indicate the degree of association between rates of delinquents and various community characteristics.

TABLE 80

COMMUNITY CHARACTERISTICS FOR AREAS GROUPED
BY RATE OF MALE DELINQUENTS

Rates of Male Delinquents	Rate of Female Delinquents	Percentage Increase or Decrease in Population 1920–30	Median Rental 1930	Rate of Adult Males Arrested
10.0 and over......	12.9	− 9.8	$21.95·	2.8
7.0–9.9...........	6.1	9.3	32.02	0.7
4.0–6.9...........	2.5	28.8	60.47	0.4
Under 4.0.........	1.7	51.9	63.04	0.3

TABLE 81

COMMUNITY CHARACTERISTICS BY 1½-MILE ZONES

Zone	Rate of Male Delinquents	Rate of Female Delinquents	Percentage Increase or Decrease in Population 1920–30	Median Rental 1930	Rate of Adult Males Arrested
I	18.3	12.7	− 9.6	$13.87	2.77
II.........	9.5	5.5	14.6	16.58	0.78
III.........	4.8	2.6	28.8	22.94	0.50
IV.........	4.4	2.4	37.6	28.28	0.41
V	3.9	2.1	46.0	33.52	0.29

Rates of delinquents were presented for classes of areas based on variation in each of these indexes. As a summary of the associations noted, and as an indication of their consistency, in Table 80 measures of various community characteristics are presented for classes of areas based on rates of male delinquents. Again the co-variation of these series indicates that areas with high rates of delinquents differ significantly in a number of characteristics from areas with low rates and that the trend of variation is found to be consistent for each of the characteristics.

Comparison by Zones.—Rates of male and female delinquents by $1\frac{1}{2}$-mile zones have already been presented. Comparable zone figures have been computed for percentage increase or decrease in population, median rental, and rate of adult criminals. These are presented in Table 81.

It will be noted that all the consistent variations in indexes which might be expected on the basis of the correlations and of previous findings are again revealed. As one passes from the central to the outermost zone, rates of male and female delinquents and of adult criminals progressively decrease, the population change becomes one of greater increase, and the mean median rental consistently increases.[4]

SUMMARY

Rates of both male and female delinquents vary widely among areas in Cincinnati. Most of the areas with the highest rates are in the Basin along the Ohio River. These areas are also those where the trend of the population indicates change in the use of land; where the economic status, as indicated by median rentals, is lowest; and where adult crime, as reflected in rates of arrested individuals, is highest. These variables are associated closely with one another in all of the areas of the city.

[4] For additional information on the differential characteristics of areas in Cincinnati see James A. Quinn, Earle Eubank, and Lois E. Elliott, *Population Characteristics by Census Tracts, Cincinnati, Ohio—1930 and 1935* (Columbus: Ohio State University, 1940).

CHAPTER XI

GREATER CLEVELAND

CLEVELAND, like Chicago, is a large northern, east-central Great Lakes city with a relatively recent origin and a history of very rapid growth. It is, like both Chicago and Philadelphia, an industrial center with a large proportion of foreign born and a comparatively small but rapidly increasing Negro population. Like these two cities, also, Cleveland is surrounded by high-class residential suburbs; but, in contrast with the studies confined to the corporate limits of Chicago and Philadelphia, it has been possible to include four cities contiguous to Cleveland. These four suburbs—Lakewood, East Cleveland, Cleveland Heights, and Shaker Heights—each a separate municipality, will be considered a part of greater Cleveland, for the purposes of this study.

THE GROWTH OF CLEVELAND

History.—The city of Cleveland is situated on the southern shore of Lake Erie at the mouth of the Cuyahoga River. The first settlement was made on the east bank of the river in 1786; but it was not until 1814, when the population of the settlement was approximately 100, that it was incorporated as the "Village of Cleveland." "The original village plot was confined to a mile square bounded virtually by the lake, the river, Huron, and Erie streets."[1] The present Public Square was included in the original survey and constituted the approximate geographic center of the village.

In the meantime a rival settlement had sprung up on the west bank of the Cuyahoga River. This settlement was founded in 1807 as Ohio City and received a charter as such in 1836. In the same year Cleveland, having expanded, though still confined to the east side of the river, was incorporated as a city, with a population of about 5,000. These two cities were united in 1853.

[1] S. P. Orth, *A History of Cleveland* (Cleveland: S. J. Clark Pub. Co., 1910), p. 45.

The federal census of 1860, the first after the consolidation, gave the population of Cleveland as 43,417. By 1900 the population had reached 381,768; in 1910 it was 560,663; in 1920, 796,841; and in 1930, 900,429. The rate of increase between 1910 and 1920 was 42.1 per cent; between 1920 and 1930, 13.0 per cent. The growth of the cities of Lakewood, East Cleveland, Cleveland Heights, and Shaker Heights has been relatively recent. In 1910 the combined population was 27,602. This population grew to 85,510 in 1920, an increase of 213.4 per cent; and to 178,904 in 1930, an increase of 106.8 per cent over 1920.

In 1930 the population of the five-city area was 93.1 per cent white, 6.8 per cent Negro, and 0.1 per cent of other races. The population classified as foreign-born white was 23.6 per cent of the total, while 31.4 per cent was native white of native parentage.

The topography of Cleveland has played an important part in determining the directions of expansion. The Cuyahoga River valley, with its meandering course, its considerable depth, and its width, has constituted an effective natural barrier to free transportation in a southerly direction. The result has been that the directions of greatest expansion have been eastward and westward from the central business district rather than toward the south.

The Cuyahoga River valley has also rather effectively divided the east and west sides. Since the business center is east of the river, access to it is much easier from the east than from the west. The result has been that, although the city has annexed large areas west of the river, the greatest population concentration is on the east side. More than two-thirds of the population in the five cities under consideration live east of the Cuyahoga River and the Public Square.

The configuration of Cleveland proper has been influenced not only by the natural barriers just discussed but also by political barriers. The expansion of its boundaries has been blocked since 1900 by Lakewood on the west and East Cleveland and Cleveland Heights on the east. The result is that the city proper has extended toward the northeast, the southeast, and the southwest until its extremities are farther from the Public Square than any of the four suburban cities under consideration.

The area of Cleveland in 1920 was 56.7 square miles; and the combined area of Lakewood, East Cleveland, Cleveland Heights, and Shaker Heights, 22.9 square miles. The area of these four suburban cities changed little between 1920 and 1930, but Cleveland proper annexed West Park and some other smaller sections, raising its total area to 70.9 square miles and the area of the five cities to 94.1 square miles.

The Industrial Configuration of Cleveland.—The processes through which areas are differentiated in Cleveland become much more intelligible when considered with reference to the configuration taken by the city's business and industry. Map 49 shows the industrial areas, railroad property, and economic level of families.

The two outstanding districts of industrial development in Cleveland paralleled the lake shore and Cuyahoga River, respectively. The first of these extends to a point about 2 miles east, being terminated by large properties included in Cleveland's public park system. Excellent transportation facilities, provided by the water front and the New York Central Railroad, which traverses this entire stretch, resulted in the early acquisition of this property for commercial and industrial purposes.

The second of these outstanding industrial districts follows the meandering course of the Cuyahoga River south to the city limits. The river and paralleling railroads here also afford excellent transportation facilities for commerce and industry. This district may be observed to fork at a point approximately 3 miles from the river's mouth, one branch following the river to the southwest and another following railroad right-of-ways to the southeast.

Other industrial districts are to be noted adjacent to railroad properties extending through the western portion of the city, and especially to the extreme northeast, in the area known locally as Collingwood, where the New York Central railroad yards and other industrial properties constitute a district of considerable proportions.

MALE JUVENILE DELINQUENTS IN CLEVELAND

Series Studied and Types of Offenses.—The distribution of delinquents will be discussed, first, for the 4-year period 1928–31

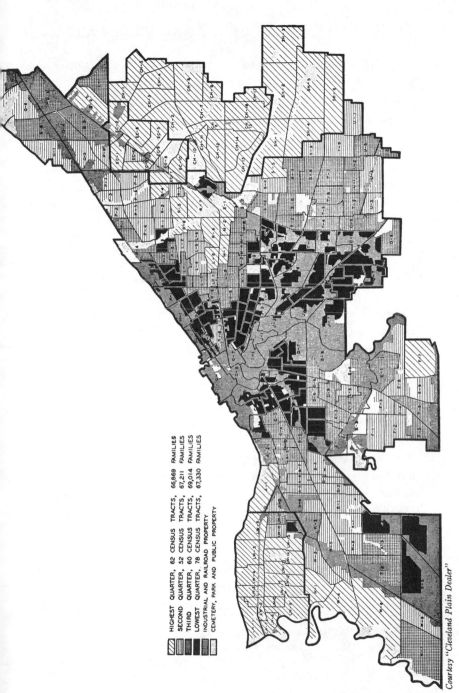

INDUSTRIAL CONFIGURATION AND ECONOMIC CLASSIFICATION OF CENSUS TRACTS, CLEVELAND, 1930

HIGHEST QUARTER, 62 CENSUS TRACTS, 66,869 FAMILIES
SECOND QUARTER, 52 CENSUS TRACTS, 67,211 FAMILIES
THIRD QUARTER, 60 CENSUS TRACTS, 69,014 FAMILIES
LOWEST QUARTER, 78 CENSUS TRACTS, 67,330 FAMILIES
INDUSTRIAL AND RAILROAD PROPERTY
CEMETERY, PARK AND PUBLIC PROPERTY

and, second, for the 3-year period 1919–21. Both series of cases comprise boys brought into the Cuyahoga County Juvenile Court from Greater Cleveland. The two series thus afford a basis for comparisons over a 10-year interval.

A. THE 1928–31 JUVENILE COURT SERIES

The 1928–31 juvenile court series includes 6,876 male delinquents brought into the Cuyahoga County Juvenile Court from Cleveland, Lakewood, East Cleveland, Cleveland Heights, and Shaker Heights during the years 1928–31, inclusive. These were all official cases; that is, the offenses charged were serious enough to warrant official action by the court. Unofficial cases, where the complaint was settled without formal court action, were not included.

These boys were brought to court for a wide variety of offenses, the most common involving the theft of property. Auto larceny was the most common form of stealing, with burglary and larceny second. The next largest general group was made up of such offenses as incorrigibility, truancy, carrying concealed weapons, disorderly conduct, and similar offenses. A smaller number were charged with acts of violence or sex offenses.

Ages of boys taken to the Cuyahoga County Juvenile Court extended through the seventeenth year. The number of boys in each age group increased up to the age of 16, with a somewhat smaller number 17 years of age.

Distribution.—Map 50[2] shows the geographic distribution by tracts of the 6,876 juvenile delinquents included in this series. In contrast with all of the other distribution maps in this volume the delinquents are plotted within the limits of the census tract in which they live rather than by exact street and number. Since there are 252 tracts (see Map 49) in the five cities, the distribution

---

[2] The tabulation by tracts of the delinquents in this series was secured through the courtesy of Dr. C. E. Gehlke, of Western Reserve University. The same data were used by H. D. Shelden, Jr., in the study "Problems in the Statistical Study of Juvenile Delinquency," *Metron*, XII, 1934.

MAP 50

CLEVELAND

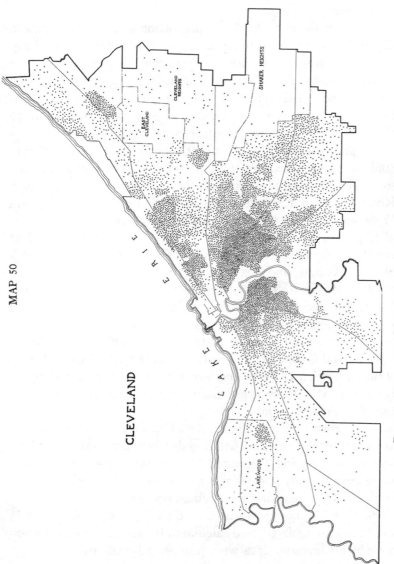

DISTRIBUTION OF 6,876 MALE JUVENILE DELINQUENTS, CLEVELAND, 1928–31

by tracts approximates the actual distribution by home address rather closely.[3]

This map shows that a large proportion of the delinquents in Cleveland are concentrated in a few areas, with the others widely scattered. Most of these areas of great concentration are near the central business district or heavy industrial properties, while the areas of fewest delinquents are in the outlying residential communities or in the suburbs. This, as already noted, appears to be the typical configuration for American cities.

The largest area of heavy concentration of delinquents in Cleveland is found southeast of the central business district, extending from the industrial properties on the east bank of the Cuyahoga River eastward for several miles along Central, Scowle, and Woodlawn avenues. Another area of concentration, almost completely surrounded by heavy industry, is located directly south of the Public Square on the west side of the Cuyahoga River, north of Clark Avenue, and east of Scranton Road.

Other areas with many delinquents will be noted west of the Cuyahoga River and the Public Square, along the industrial properties on the shores of Lake Erie, and along Broadway southeast of the central business district out toward the city limits.

Two notable concentrations are seen in the outlying areas. One is in the portion of Cleveland which adjoins Cleveland Heights. Here in a little valley is a densely populated district with all of the physical and social characteristics of an area of immigrant first settlement. Similar characteristics were found in an area in the southeast corner of Lakewood, where concentration of delinquents is especially marked. Aside from these small areas, there are relatively few delinquents in any of the four suburbs or in the outlying sections of Cleveland proper.

Rates of Delinquents.—Rates of male juvenile delinquents in Cleveland for 1928–31 were calculated for the 40 statistical areas for which Cleveland data were published by the federal census,

---

[3] A map showing the actual distribution of the male delinquents, together with that of the female delinquents brought into the Juvenile Court during the same period, is published in the 1930 annual report of the Juvenile Court of Cuyahoga County.

for Lakewood divided into two parts, and for East Cleveland, Cleveland Heights, and Shaker Heights as individual units. Since these 45 areas represent combinations of the 252 census tracts, the aged 10–17 male population for each area was secured by totaling the number of boys in this age group in all the tracts in each area.[4] The number of delinquents likewise represents the sum of those in all tracts within each statistical area. The total number of boys was 77,207, an average of about 1,700 boys per area. The smallest number in any area was 721 (Area 29), the largest, 3,103 (Cleveland Heights).

The rate of delinquents in each area represents the number of delinquents brought to court on official petition during this 4-year period per 100 boys of the same age group as of 1930, not including those who may have moved into the area subsequent to a court appearance in some other part of the city.

The range of rates is from 0.6 to 37.7 (see Map 51). The median is 7.1, and the rate for the metropolitan area as a whole 8.9. It will be noted that in Cleveland, as in the other cities, the distribution of rates is skewed positively, with the median value relatively close to the lower end of the range. This means that a large number of areas are characterized by low rates of delinquents, and relatively few by very high rates.

The areas of high rates of delinquents in Cleveland are those characterized also by concentrations of delinquents. The highest rates, it will be noted, are in Areas 23 (37.7) and 20 (29.7). These areas include part of the central business district, the deteriorated areas which adjoin the central business district on the south and east, the industrial area along the east bank of the Cuyahoga River, and the railroads which extend outward from the center of the city toward the southeast.

The areas with lowest rates of delinquents are in the outlying sections of Cleveland and in the suburbs, where there is little in-

[4] These data are included in Table 1 of *Population Characteristics by Census Tracts, Cleveland, Ohio, 1930*, ed. Howard W. Green (published by the Cleveland Plain Dealer). Included in this volume is an exhaustive analysis by census tracts of the socioeconomic characteristics of Cleveland areas.

MAP 51

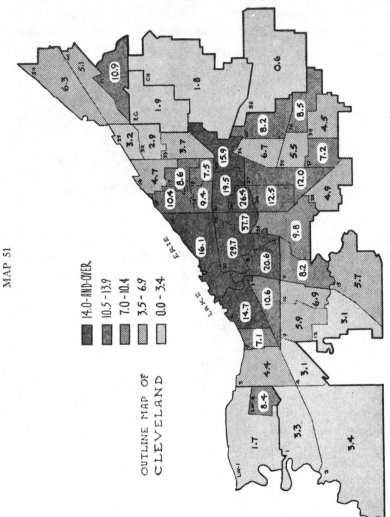

OUTLINE MAP OF
CLEVELAND

■ 14.0 - AND - OVER
▓ 10.5 - 13.9
▒ 7.0 - 10.4
░ 3.5 - 6.9
□ 0.0 - 3.4

RATES OF MALE JUVENILE DELINQUENTS, CLEVELAND, 1928–31

dustry, where incomes are high, and where conditions of life are most favorable. In Shaker Heights the rate is only 9.6; in Lakewood it is 1.7; in Cleveland Heights, 1.8; and in East Cleveland, 1.9. Other rates less than 3.5 may be noted for Areas 32, 12, 4, 29, 1, and 2 within the city of Cleveland.

B. THE 1919–21 JUVENILE COURT SERIES

This series includes the 5,155 boys dealt with as official delinquents by the Cuyahoga County Juvenile Court during the period 1919–21. The series, centered around 1920, furnishes a basis for a study of changes in the different areas between 1920 and 1930. It should be noted that this 3-year series, like the later 4-year series, is based upon individuals rather than upon cases. In other words, a boy is counted only once, even though he may have appeared in court many times.

Distribution.—Map 52 shows the distribution by home address of the 5,155 boys in this series, plotted by street and number. This is the actual distribution of these alleged delinquents, therefore, in contrast with the approximate distribution of the series presented in Map 50.

The general distribution of delinquents is similar to that in the 1928–31 series. Map 52 again shows a heavy concentration in the section south of Euclid Avenue from the Cuyahoga River eastward, although the concentration east of Fifty-fifth Street is not so dense as for the later period. Another area of heavy concentration will be noted directly south of the Public Square, on the west side of the river. A smaller but extremely dense cluster of dots is found in the community just west of Cleveland Heights.

The most marked difference between the distributions of delinquents in the two periods is seen just east of Fifty-fifth Street in the southern part of the city. This industrial area shows a heavy concentration for the 1919–21 period, as compared with 1928–31. On the other hand, the southeastern corner of Lakewood shows a lesser concentration of delinquents in the earlier period.

Rates of Delinquents.—Rates of delinquents for the 1919–21

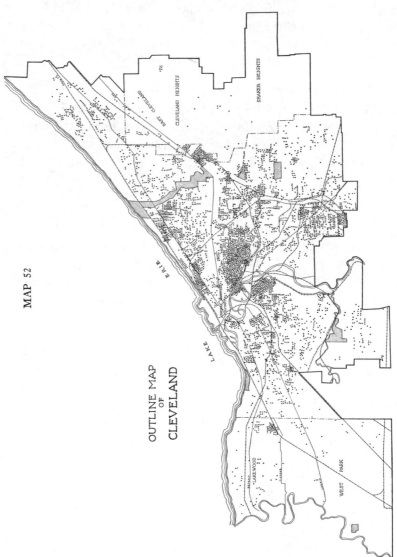

MAP 52

OUTLINE MAP
OF
CLEVELAND

DISTRIBUTION OF 5,155 MALE JUVENILE DELINQUENTS, CLEVELAND, 1919–21

series were calculated for the same 45 areas used for the 1928–31 series.[5] All the areas had populations of 400 or more boys in the 10–17 age group, except Area 1 and Shaker Heights, with 215 and 144 boys, respectively.

The range of rates is from 3.0 in Cleveland Heights and in Lakewood to 22.1 in Area 20 (see Map 53). The median rate is 6.6, and the rate for Greater Cleveland as a whole 9.2. The rates represent the number of boys brought to the Juvenile Court during the 3-year period, per 100 boys in the 10–17 age group as of 1920.

It will be noted that the areas with the highest rates are, for the most part, those that showed the greatest concentration of dots on Map 52. The highest rate is 22.1 in Area 20, which includes much of the central business district. Area 8, just south of the central business section, has a rate of 18.6; while Area 14, including that section of the central business district north of Area 20 and along the lake front, has a rate of 13.6. The next highest rates are found not in areas contiguous to these three but in the narrow strip running almost north and south from the area of immigrant first settlement just west of Cleveland Heights (Area 22) through Area 27 to the large immigrant settlement in Area 28.

Surrounding the central areas of high rates on all sides, there are intermediate-rate areas; and beyond these, with the exception of the narrow strip of high rates mentioned above, a gradual tapering-off in magnitude. In general, the outlying sections of the city had low rates of delinquents in 1920, although those in the extreme northeastern portion were higher than average. Sizable industrial developments and immigrant settlements were found in these areas.

The eastern suburbs—East Cleveland, Cleveland Heights, and Shaker Heights—all had rates of delinquents less than 4.0, as had Area 1 of Lakewood. Six areas within Cleveland itself (Areas 1, 3, 12, 13, 29, and 32), all of them located on the periphery of the city, had rates less than 5.0.

[5] Data for 1920 on the aged 10–17 male population by census tracts were furnished by Howard W. Green.

MAP 53

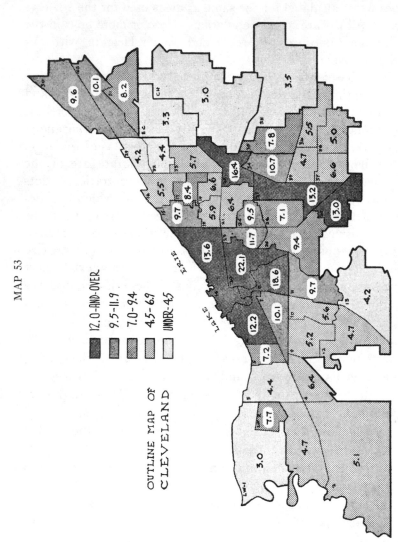

OUTLINE MAP OF
CLEVELAND

12.0-AND-OVER
9.5-11.9
7.0-9.4
4.5-6.9
UNDER-4.5

RATES OF MALE JUVENILE DELINQUENTS, CLEVELAND, 1919–21

A comparison of Map 53 with Map 51 reveals a few changes in
the distribution of high rates of delinquents from 1920 to 1930.
Most apparent is the shift eastward of the highest rates, so that in
the 10-year period Area 23 rose in rank from eighth to first, Area
24 moved from fifteenth to third, and Area 21 from twenty-fifth to
fifth. During this period a great change in population composition
and in social and economic characteristics took place in these
areas.

Another change in rate will be observed in Area 28, which in
1920 ranked sixth, with a rate of 13.0, but in 1930 stood thirty-
first, with a rate of only 4.9. There are no readily apparent reasons for this extreme change, since the population composition remained about the same, as did the economic status of the area.
Whether the practices of law enforcement in Area 28 underwent
a complete change between 1920 and 1930 or whether the community achieved a degree of organization which led to a drop in
the actual number of delinquents is not known, but certainly the
proportionate number of boys brought to court diminished greatly
during 10 years.

Apart from these and a few minor changes, the general distribution of delinquents and of high and low rates of delinquency
is closely similar for the two periods. There was greater concentration of delinquents in 1930, and a much greater range of area
rates—from 0.6 to 37.7, as against 3.0 to 22.1 in 1920—but the
ranking of most of the areas was not greatly changed. The coefficient of linear correlation, .72 ± .05, between the two sets of
rates in the 45 areas indicates that the general similarity of the distributions is sufficient to offset the two differences discussed
above.

Extent of Concentration.—A further comparison of the two
series is afforded by the extent of concentration of delinquents
with regard to population and area for each period. The 45 areas
were ranked in descending order of rates of delinquents and
grouped by quartiles of male population aged 10–17. The corre-

sponding percentage of delinquents and of city area was then computed. The results are given in Table 82.

It will be noted that in 1919–21 the one-fourth of the male population aged 10–17 living in areas with highest rates of delinquents contributed 42.2 per cent of all delinquents taken to the Cuyahoga County Juvenile Court from Greater Cleveland, drawn from only 14.4 per cent of the total area, while in 1928–31 the corresponding quarter of the population contributed 52.4 per

TABLE 82

PERCENTAGE OF DELINQUENTS AND OF CITY AREA FOR QUARTILES OF MALE POPULATION AGED 10–17, WHEN AREAS ARE RANKED BY RATE OF DELINQUENTS: 1928–31 AND 1919–21

QUARTILES OF POPULATION	1928–31		1919–21	
	Percentage of Delinquents	Percentage of City Area	Percentage of Delinquents	Percentage of City Area
Upper one-fourth, in high-rate areas.......	52.4	19.0	42.2	14.4
Second one-fourth......	25.3	14.7	27.4	15.2
Third one-fourth	15.1	20.6	18.6	16.1
Lower one-fourth, in low-rate areas...........	7.2	45.7	11.8	54.3

cent of the total delinquents and occupied 19.0 per cent of the total area. This represents increased concentration of delinquents with respect to population if not with respect to area.

Table 83 shows the percentage of male population aged 10–17 and the percentage of city area when delinquents in turn are divided into four equal groups, according to area rates. The greater concentration of delinquents in areas of highest rates for 1928–31, as compared with 1919–21, is again indicated; but for both periods it is clear that a majority of the delinquents were drawn from a relatively small proportion of the male population aged 10–17, occupying an even smaller proportion of the city area. In 1928–31, for example, one-half of all the delinquents were drawn from 23.6 per cent of the aged 10–17 male population, as of 1930, representing only 17.3 per cent of the total area of greater Cleveland.

Rates by Zones.—Rates of delinquents by zones for Cleveland have been calculated for both time series (see Table 84). Zones

TABLE 83

PERCENTAGE OF MALE POPULATION AGED 10–17 AND OF CITY AREA FOR QUARTILES OF DELINQUENTS WHEN AREAS ARE RANKED BY RATE OF DELINQUENTS: 1928–31 AND 1919–21

QUARTILES OF DELINQUENTS	1928–31		1919–21	
	Percentage of Population	Percentage of City Area	Percentage of Population	Percentage of City Area
Upper one-fourth, from high-rate areas.......	8.4	5.5	12.8	7.8
Second one-fourth.......	15.2	11.8	18.6	9.1
Third one-fourth........	23.7	14.4	24.7	17.7
Lower one-fourth, from low-rate areas........	52.7	68.3	43.9	65.4

TABLE 84

RATES OF DELINQUENTS BY 2-MILE ZONES*
1928–31 AND 1919–21

Zone	Rate 1928–31	Rate 1919–21
I...............	19.5	15.4
II...............	11.0	8.3
III...............	5.7	7.7
IV...............	4.5	6.0

* Drawn concentrically with Public Square as focal point.

were drawn concentrically at 2-mile intervals, taking the focal point at the Public Square. Where an area lay in two zones, the aged 10–17 male population and the number of delinquents were split proportionally.

The zone rates for the two series of cases indicate not only the general concentration of delinquents near the center of the city but also the greater incidence of high-rate areas near the center for the later series.

COMMUNITY CHARACTERISTICS IN RELATION TO
RATES OF DELINQUENTS

Data now will be presented to give an objective picture of the association between the distribution of juvenile delinquents and other community characteristics, such as the percentage increase and decrease in population, the percentage of families on relief in recent years, and the percentage of foreign-born and Negro heads of families in any area. For purposes of this description the 1928–31 delinquency series will be used, since more complete data are available for this period than for the earlier one.

TABLE 85

RATES OF DELINQUENTS, 1928–31, FOR AREAS
GROUPED BY PERCENTAGE INCREASE OR
DECREASE OF POPULATION, 1920–30

Percentage of Population Change 1920–30	Rate of Delinquents 1928–31
Decreasing:	
15.0 and over (− 29.0)*	22.6
0.0–14.9 (− 9.8)*	12.6
Increasing:	
0.0–29.9 (8.8)*	6.0
30.0–59.9 (49.3)*	5.5
60 and over (132.7)*	4.5

* Percentage for class as a whole.

Increase and Decrease of Population.—Between 1920 and 1930 the population of Greater Cleveland increased 22.2 per cent. There were, however, 14 areas within the city in which the population decreased over the 10-year span. Map 54 shows the percentage of population change for each of the 45 areas of Greater Cleveland from 1920 to 1930. It will be noted that the areas which dropped in population were concentrated in the central portion of the city and that the greatest decrease took place in the areas comprising, or immediately adjacent to, the central business district. These were the areas with highest rates of delinquents in 1928–31, as may readily be seen by comparing Map 54 with Map 51, showing rates of delinquents. The degree of association between the rate of delinquents and the percentage increase or de-

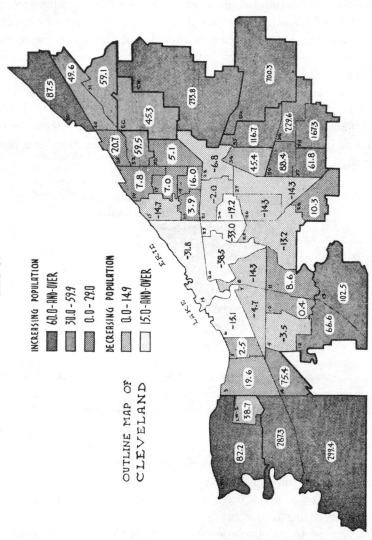

MAP 54

INCREASING POPULATION

■ 60.0-AND-OVER
▨ 30.0-59.9
▨ 0.0-29.0

DECREASING POPULATION

□ 0.0-14.9
□ 15.0-AND-OVER

OUTLINE MAP OF
CLEVELAND

PERCENTAGE INCREASE OR DECREASE OF POPULATION, CLEVELAND, 1920–30

crease in population is indicated by the coefficient of linear correlation between the two series of 45 values, which is −.65 ± .06. Since the relationship is clearly curvilinear, the actual degree of association is somewhat higher than the linear coefficient would indicate.

Rates of delinquents have been computed for each of the five classes of areas indicated on Map 54. These are shown in Table 85. These again indicate clearly that high rates of delinquents tend to be found in areas with a decreasing population, and vice versa.

TABLE 86

RATES OF DELINQUENTS, 1928–31, FOR AREAS
GROUPED BY PERCENTAGE OF FAMILIES
ON RELIEF, 1937

Percentage of Families on Relief 1937	Rate of Delinquents 1928–31
20 and over (28.0)*....................	16.9
15.0–19.9 (17.9)*....................	14.2
10.0–14.9 (11.8)*....................	8.0
5.0– 9.9 (7.6)*....................	6.2
0.0– 4.9 (2.0)*....................	3.2

* Percentage for class as a whole.

Families on Relief.—The percentage of families on relief is perhaps the most satisfactory index available of the relative economic levels of areas. Map 55 shows for each of the 45 areas of Greater Cleveland the percentage of families on relief in 1937.[6] The same general pattern of distribution that obtained for rates of delinquents may be noted. The coefficient of correlation for the two series (of 45 values each) is .93 ± .02.

When rates of delinquents are calculated for the five classes of areas (according to percentage of families on relief) indicated on Map 55, the trend of relationship between these two variables is again clearly evident (see Table 86). It may be added that, although the percentage of families on relief relates to 1937, the

[6] Data on the total number of families as of October, 1937, and the number of families who received relief during the year 1937 are given by census tracts in Howard W. Green, *Two Hundred Million for Relief in Cleveland, 1928–1938* (see esp. Table 13).

MAP 55

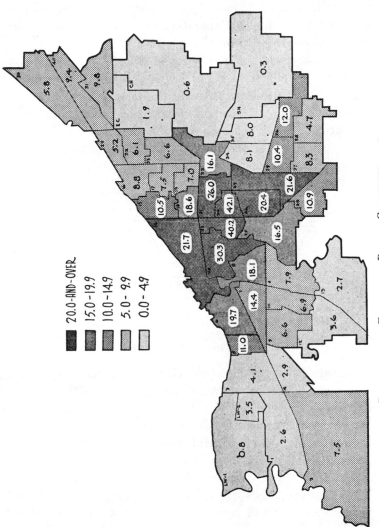

20.0-AND-OVER
15.0-19.9
10.0-14.9
5.0- 9.9
0.0- 4.9

PERCENTAGE OF FAMILIES ON RELIEF, CLEVELAND, 1937

ranking of the areas in terms of economic status probably changed very little between 1930 and 1937; and, if so, no serious error is introduced by using available data for the latter year as an index of conditions in the former.

Foreign-born and Negro Heads of Families.—It has been pointed out that the foreign-born and Negro population is usually compelled by circumstances to settle in the deteriorated areas surrounding the central business district and heavy industrial concentrations. As a single index of the distribution of racial and nativity groups, the percentage of foreign-born and Negro heads of families has been selected. This is shown on Map 56. It will be

TABLE 87

RATES OF DELINQUENTS, 1928–31, FOR AREAS GROUPED
BY PERCENTAGE OF FOREIGN-BORN AND
NEGRO HEADS OF FAMILIES, 1930

Percentage of Foreign-born and Negro Heads of Families, 1930	Rate of Delinquents 1928–31
70.0 and over (79.6)*	20.1
58.0–69.9 (63.7)*	10.5
46.0–57.9 (55.1)*	7.0
34.0–45.9 (39.9)*	6.0
Under 34.0 (23.1)*	3.1

* Percentage for class as a whole.

seen that, in general, the areas with a high percentage of foreign-born and Negro heads of families are the areas with highest rates of delinquents. The coefficient of linear correlation between the two series of 45 values each is .92 ± .02. This does not mean that areas have high rates of delinquents *because* they have a high percentage of foreign-born and Negro heads of families but, rather, that these variables characterize the same areas. It is likely that the forces which lead to a segregation of the groups with lowest economic status in deteriorated areas are related to the forces which make for social disorganization and a breakdown of community controls within these areas.

When rates of delinquents are calculated for the five classes of areas indicated on Map 56, the consistent covariance of the rates with the percentage of foreign-born and Negro heads of families may be noted (see Table 87).

MAP 56

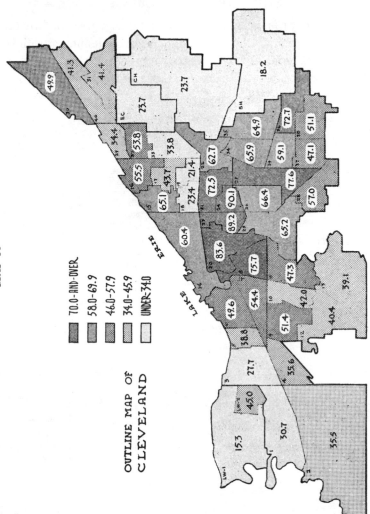

OUTLINE MAP OF
CLEVELAND

70.0-AND-OVER
58.0-69.9
46.0-57.9
34.0-45.9
UNDER-34.0

PERCENTAGE FOREIGN-BORN AND NEGRO HEADS OF FAMILIES, CLEVELAND, 1930

VARIATION IN COMMUNITY CHARACTERISTICS
WITH RATES OF DELINQUENTS

Comparison by Classes of Areas.—When the 45 areas of Greater
Cleveland are grouped, according to rates of delinquents, into
the five classes indicated on Map 51, other social characteristics
for these classes show consistent trends of variation (see Table 88).

TABLE 88

SOCIAL CHARACTERISTICS OF GREATER CLEVELAND FOR
AREAS GROUPED BY RATE OF DELINQUENTS
1928–31

Area Rates of Delinquents 1928–31	Percentage Increase or Decrease of Population 1920–30	Percentage Foreign-born and Negro Heads of Families 1930	Percentage Families on Relief 1937
14.0 and over (21.2)*....	− 22.2	71.0	25.6
10.5–13.9 (11.5)*....	− 1.9	59.6	16.3
7.0–10.4 (8.8)*....	19.7	49.9	10.5
3.5– 6.9 (5.3)*....	31.6	46.7	6.8
0.0– 3.4 (2.3)*....	106.8	28.1	2.2

* Rate for class as a whole.

TABLE 89

SOCIAL CHARACTERISTICS OF GREATER
CLEVELAND BY ZONES

Zone	Rates of Delinquents 1928–31	Percentage Increase or Decrease of Population 1920–30	Percentage Foreign-born and Negro Heads of Families 1930	Percentage Families Owning Homes 1930	Percentage Families on Relief 1937
I........	19.5	− 25.1	66.7	21.4	21.9
II.......	11.0	4.0	50.8	31.4	14.5
III.......	5.7	46.6	47.3	43.2	6.6
IV.......	4.5	123.4	34.0	50.4	3.9

Areas with the highest rates of delinquents for 1928–31 showed,
as a class, the greatest decrease in population from 1920 to 1930,
the highest percentage of foreign-born and Negro heads of families
in 1930, and the highest percentage of families on relief in 1937.
The reverse was true of areas with relatively few delinquents.

Comparison by Zones.—The indexes presented above have been
computed also for the concentric zones at 2-mile intervals for

which rates of delinquents were reported. These data are presented in Table 89 and constitute further evidence of the concentration of certain social conditions and social problems in areas nearest to the center of the city.

SUMMARY

Cleveland is an industrial center with a relatively recent origin and a history of very rapid growth. Four contiguous suburban cities—Lakewood, East Cleveland, Cleveland Heights, and Shaker Heights—were included with Cleveland proper for purposes of this study.

Two series of juvenile delinquents were presented, comprising boys taken to the Cuyahoga County Juvenile Court from Greater Cleveland during the periods 1919–21 and 1928–31. The ages of the boys ranged from 10 years through 17, with the 16-year-olds most numerous.

For both series the greatest concentration of delinquents was found near the central business district and in the areas surrounding heavy industrial properties, with the widest scattering in the residential suburbs. Rates of delinquents for the 45 areas showed interesting changes in rank and in range over the 10-year period that separated the two series of cases. The cluster of highest-rate areas, which in 1919–21 had its focus approximately in the central business district, moved slightly eastward and southward by 1928–31, accompanying a change in other characteristics of these areas. Several outlying areas which had rather high rates of delinquents in 1919–21 showed more moderate rates a decade later.

A high degree of association was found between rate of delinquents and the percentage increase or decrease in population over a 10-year period, areas with decreasing population having, in general, the highest rates of delinquents. Areas with a high percentage of foreign-born and Negro heads of families tended to have high rates of delinquents, and a high positive correlation obtained also between rates of delinquents and the percentage of families on relief.[7]

[7] See chap. vi for a discussion of race and nationality as compared with economic factors.

CHAPTER XII

RICHMOND

RICHMOND, Virginia, differs in several respects from the northern cities thus far discussed. First, it is an old southern city. This fact in itself implies racial and national differences, as well as the presence of somewhat divergent traditions and culture. Second, Richmond is probably more completely a political and governmental center than the other cities. Boston is a state capital, and Philadelphia has been capital of both state and nation; but probably in neither of these larger industrial centers was the effect so great as in Richmond, which has been the state capital since 1779 and was also capital of the Confederate States during the Civil War. Finally, Richmond is a city whose rate of growth has been slow, compared with that of many northern industrial communities. Although one of the oldest cities in this series, its population in 1930 was only about one-eighteenth as great as that of Chicago and one-eleventh that of Philadelphia.

With the stability of age and in the absence of the disorganization which presumably accompanies rapid change, Richmond should represent, as a whole, a relatively organized, integrated, and stable community—a somewhat different setting for consideration of the distribution of delinquents.

THE GROWTH OF RICHMOND

History.—The first settlement within the present limits of the city of Richmond was made in 1737 at the head of tidewater on the James River. There the town of Richmond, with an area of $\frac{1}{5}$ square mile, was incorporated in 1742 with a population of about 250. The most striking fact about the city's growth was that the business center did not remain at the place of original settlement but moved westward and northward to the higher land, where it is today. Most of the major early annexations were in that direction, where, because of the elevation, the land was considered much more desirable for residential purposes.

In 1782, when the population had increased to about 800 and the area to a little over a square mile, the city of Richmond was incorporated. By 1810 the population had reached 9,785, and the total area 2.4 square miles. At this time the geographic center of the city was near the point which is today the heart of the central business district.

In 1910, when the area had increased to about 10 square miles, the old city of Manchester on the south side of the James River was annexed. This was followed by further annexations on both sides of the river in 1914, at which time the corporation line was extended in practically all directions, increasing the total area of the city to 24 square miles. The political boundary has not been extended since that time. Today there are several built-up areas contiguous to the city but outside of the corporate limits, and therefore not included in our study.

The population of Richmond as given in the federal census was 27,570 in 1850, 85,050 in 1900, and 182,929 in 1930. The increase in population between 1920 and 1930 was 6.6 per cent.

Composition of the Population.—The population of Richmond differs as regards both nativity and race from that of the northern cities previously considered. In 1930, 71.0 per cent of the population were white, and 29.0 per cent Negro. Of the white population, 96.9 per cent were native white and 91.8 per cent native white of native parentage. The foreign born constituted 3.1 per cent of the white population and 2.2 per cent of the total. The most noticeable trends in population composition during the last 30 years are the decreases in the proportion of the foreign born and of Negroes. The percentage of the foreign born decreased from 3.3 in 1900 to 2.2 in 1930, and the percentage of Negroes in the total population dropped from 37.9 to 29.0 in the same period.

Industrial Configuration.—The pattern of industrial configuration of the city of Richmond is indicated on Map 57, adapted from the zoning map which shows the areas zoned for heavy and light industry. The streets either occupied by or subject to occupancy by business also are indicated.

It will be noted that the distribution of heavy industry follows the lowlands very closely. The two sides of the river and the islands are industrial; the areas in black in the southeastern part

MAP 57

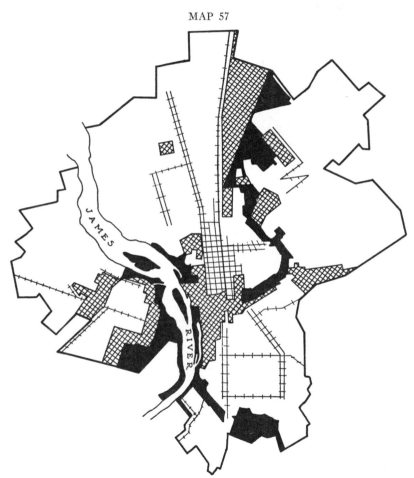

INDUSTRIAL CONFIGURATION OF RICHMOND, VIRGINIA

of the city are on the flats along the river; and the line of industrial areas which circles to the north and then toward the northwest is in a sharp geographic depression over which viaducts have been constructed at the important streets. The light industrial areas, it will be noted, are located, in most instances, adjacent to the heavy industrial areas or the central business district. It is interesting that the area included in the old town of Richmond and the area through which the business district has passed in its movement to the present location are both zoned entirely for either light or heavy industry.

MALE JUVENILE DELINQUENTS IN RICHMOND

Series Studied and Types of Offenses.—The cases included in this study were secured from the records of the Juvenile and Domestic Relations courts. Practically all boys arrested in Richmond are brought to the Juvenile Court, where a large proportion are dismissed with a warning. Because of the large number of boys brought to this court charged with very minor offenses, it was necessary to limit our series to those cases where the court order indicated that the offense was of a more serious nature. This selection was made in order that the cases in this series would be in some degree comparable to those in other cities where minor offenses are disposed of without court action. The present series, which comprises cases brought to court between May 1, 1927, and April 30, 1930, thus includes 1,238 boys.

Of these boys, 60.4 per cent were charged with some form of stealing (10.1 per cent larceny of automobiles, 14.0 per cent burglary or robbery, and 36.3 per cent other types of theft); 6.5 per cent were charged with sex offenses; and 33.1 per cent with other offenses, such as truancy, violation of probation, destruction of property, disorderly conduct, incorrigibility, and drunkenness.

The age distribution of the delinquents in the Richmond series is somewhat different from the distribution in Chicago and Philadelphia. In Richmond the upper age limit is the eighteenth birthday, whereas the upper limit in Chicago is the seventeenth, and in Philadelphia the sixteenth birthday. Three and four-tenths per cent of the boys were 9 years of age or younger, 4.6 per cent were 10, 4.7 per cent were 11, 7.7 per cent 12, 10.9 per cent 13, 14.5 per cent 14, 17.1 per cent 15, 17.7 per cent 16, and 17.7 per cent 17 years of age. The remaining 1.4 per cent of the boys were over 17 years of age.

Distribution.—Map 58 shows the distribution by home address of the 1,238 male juvenile delinquents. It will be observed that there are marked variations in the extent of concentration of cases in the different areas in Richmond. Very heavy concentrations are seen north of the central business district and in the section north of Riverview and Hollywood cemeteries, with lesser concentrations east of the business center in the Church Hill districts, in Fulton, and in South Richmond. On the other hand, there are relatively few cases in the West End, Ginter Park, Barton Heights, and Highland Park districts.

A comparison of Map 58 with Map 57, showing the industrial configuration of the city, reveals that the distribution of delinquents is related to this configuration. Most of the major concentrations of delinquents are in the oldest sections of Richmond and adjacent either to heavy or light industrial property or to the central business district. On the other hand, the areas where there are relatively few delinquents are the newer sections of the city, in general farther removed from industry and commerce.

It may be observed also that the areas of heaviest concentration of delinquents are largely, although not exclusively, the areas of Negro population. It should be noted also that most of the Negroes live in areas adjacent to industry and commerce, and that non-Negro areas of the same type are also characterized by concentrations of delinquents.

Rates of Delinquents.—The 19 areas for which rates of delinquents are presented in this study represent combinations of the 1930 federal census enumeration districts. The irregularities in the shape of these areas reflect the irregularities of these districts. The male juvenile population in each area was computed from the total population.[1]

Map 59 shows the rates of delinquents in each area. These 3-year rates represent, as in other cities, the number of delinquents per 100 of the aged 10–17 male population as of 1930.

---

[1] It was necessary to use this total population, secured for enumeration districts directly from the Federal Census Bureau, as a basis for the computation of the aged 10–17 male population, since population data by age groupings were not available for Richmond either for enumeration districts or for other small areas. Each of the 19 areas had a computed population of not fewer than 250 boys aged 10–17 years.

MAP 58

DISTRIBUTION OF 1,238 MALE JUVENILE DELINQUENTS, RICHMOND, VIRGINIA, 1927–30.

The rates of delinquents in the 19 areas range from 1.6 to 25.1, with a median of 10.7 and a rate for the city as a whole of 12.3.[2]

MAP 59

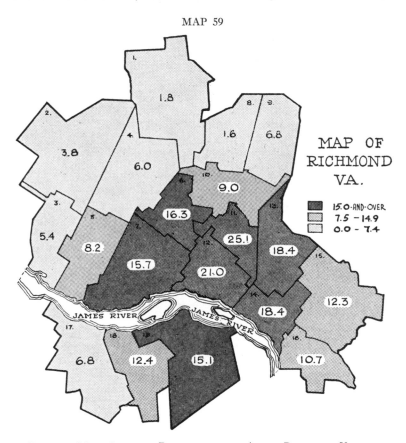

RATES OF MALE JUVENILE DELINQUENTS, BY AREAS, RICHMOND, VIRGINIA

The area (11) with the highest rate of delinquents (25.1) extends from the central business district to the industrial districts on the north. Area 12, with the next highest rate (21.0), includes

[2] The fact that the rates of delinquents in Richmond are somewhat higher than in some of the other cities should not be interpreted to mean that there is more delinquency in Richmond. These materials furnish no basis for any conclusion on this question. In this study, as stated previously, we are interested in the variation in rates of delinquents among areas in the same city and have made no effort to study the comparative number of delinquents or the amount of delinquency in the different cities.

most of the central business district and some of the residential areas adjacent. Surrounding these two central areas are others with relatively high rates of delinquents. Area 6, which is largely

MAP 60

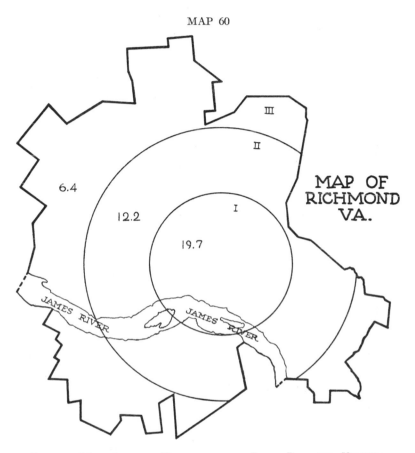

RATES OF MALE JUVENILE DELINQUENTS, BY ZONES, RICHMOND, VIRGINIA

Negro in population, has a rate of 16.3; Area 7, both Negro and white, a rate of 15.7; Area 13, predominantly white, a rate of 18.4; and Area 14, which is almost exclusively white, a rate of 18.4. These figures indicate that the areas close to industrial and commercial areas in Richmond have high rates of delinquents whether occupied by Negro or by white population. Likewise, Area 19, closest to the central business district and to industrial areas on the south side of the river, has a high rate of delinquents (15.1), while the rates in the other two areas on the south side (18 and 17) are decidedly lower, 12.4 and 6.8, respectively. In contrast with the areas with high rates of delinquents, those with low rates are, without exception, on the periphery of the city.

Zone Rates.—The tendency of the rates of delinquents to decrease outward from the center of Richmond to the periphery is presented schematically on Map 60. The zones were drawn at

TABLE 90

PERCENTAGE OF DELINQUENTS AND OF CITY AREA FOR QUARTILES OF MALE POPULATION AGED 10–15, WHEN AREAS ARE RANKED BY RATE OF DELINQUENTS

Quartiles of Population	Percentage of Delinquents	Percentage of City Area
Upper one-fourth, in high-rate areas	41.7	16.2
Second one-fourth	31.5	25.4
Third one-fourth	18.9	23.8
Lower one-fourth, in low-rate areas	7.9	34.6

intervals of 1 mile, with the focal point at the center of the business district.

The variation in rates of delinquents, it will be noted, is from 19.7 in Zone I to 6.4 in Zone III. In other words, more than three times as many boys, per 100 of the population, appeared in the Juvenile Court on serious charges from Zone I as from Zone III.

Extent of Concentration.—In Richmond, as in other cities, the concentration of delinquents has been studied in relation to the distribution of the population and the total city area. The extent of this concentration, when the areas of the city are ranked by rate of delinquents and divided into four groups with equal aged 10–15 male population, is indicated in Table 90. While the percentage of delinquents in the four population groups varies widely, the corresponding percentages of the city area show relatively little fluctuation.

Likewise, when the 1,238 delinquents are divided into four equal groups on the basis of the magnitude of the rates in the areas of residence, significant variations in the population and city area again appear. These are presented in Table 91. Half of the city's delinquents, it is revealed, come from 31 per cent of the population, occupying less than one-fifth of the total city area.

TABLE 91

PERCENTAGE OF MALE POPULATION AGED 10–15 AND OF CITY AREA FOR QUARTILES OF DELIN-QUENTS WHEN AREAS ARE RANKED BY RATE OF DELINQUENTS

Quartiles of Delinquents	Percentage of Population	Percentage of City Area
Upper one-fourth, from high-rate areas........	13.7	9.3
Second one-fourth.......	17.3	9.5
Third one-fourth........	21.0	19.5
Lower one-fourth, from low-rate areas.........	48.0	61.7

COMMUNITY CHARACTERISTICS IN RELATION
TO RATES OF DELINQUENTS

That there are wide and patterned variations in the rates of delinquents among areas in Richmond has been demonstrated. In the present section an effort will be made to analyze some of the factors underlying these differences and to distinguish the areas with high rates of delinquents from those with low rates by means of certain physical and social indexes.

Physical Status.—The correspondence between the pattern of distribution of delinquents and the industrial and commercial configuration of Richmond has been pointed out. As in the larger industrial cities already discussed, the areas adjacent to industry and to the central business district have characteristics in common which differentiate them from areas farther removed. In Richmond the growth of the city has been less rapid than that of the northern industrial cities studied, and the encroachment of industry on residential areas has not been such as to produce the sudden deterioration of these areas. Yet, in time, deterioration has taken place; and the older, central areas have become, for the most part, less attractive places of residence than the newer outlying developments. Homes grow old even when their existence is not threatened by the invasion of industry. The general proximity of business and industry, coupled with the relative undesirability of the lowlands in which they are located, has tended to prevent new residential construction in these areas and has led in time to deterioration. The differentiation of areas in Richmond is thus a product of the natural process of city growth, particularly as related to aging and to the shifting of residential areas from the lowlands to higher ground.

Average Rentals.—An index of economic level among the areas differentiated in this process, giving a clue to the physical attractiveness of the several areas of Richmond for residential purposes, is presented in Map 61, which shows the average monthly home rentals for 13 different areas. These are the so-called "market areas" within the city limits of Richmond, used by the Chesapeake and Potomac Telephone Company of Virginia in their commercial survey of rentals and telephone-users. The average rentals here presented were computed from the summary of the number of families in each rental class as established by this survey.

It will be noted that these average rentals vary from $10.37 in Area I to nearly six times this amount, or $58.08, in Area E. With the exception of Area A, the central business district, where the average rental is increased by the presence of some large homes and rooming-houses and a few high-class apartments, the areas close to the center of the city are areas of low rents. On the other hand, the more outlying areas, C, E, and F, have average rentals of $50.37, $58.08, and $43.09, respectively. The only exception to this general variation is in Fulton, or Area J, a semi-industrial, geographically low section along the river front and the railroad yards, cut off from the rest of the city by several large hills. The average rental here, $11.88, indicates that the characteristics of the area are much more like those of the central congested areas than those of other peripheral residential neighborhoods.

Although these 13 market districts and the 19 areas for which rates of delinquents were presented do not coincide, a comparison of the map showing the distribution of delinquents with that showing average rentals indicates that the areas of low rents are, in general, the areas of high rates of delinquents, and vice versa.

MAP 61

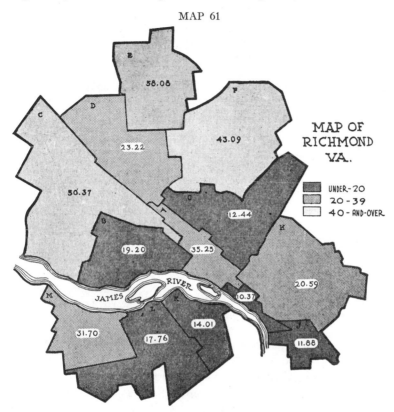

MAP OF
RICHMOND
VA.

UNDER- 20
20 - 39
40 - AND-OVER

AVERAGE RENTALS, RICHMOND, VIRGINIA, 1928

In South Richmond a striking comparison is afforded among 3 comparable areas, where, as the rates of delinquents decrease from 15.1 to 6.8, average rentals increase from $14.01 to $31.70. The only apparent exception to this general correspondence is in Fulton, where, on the basis of the average rents, a somewhat higher rate of delinquents would be expected.

The average rental in any of these areas cannot be said to "explain" the amount of delinquency in the area. It does, however, indicate the approximate economic level of the families and, to some extent, the physical attractiveness of the area. In Area G, which had in 1928 an average rental among the lowest in Richmond ($12.44), the physical conditions are described in a report of the Negro Welfare Survey Committee of Richmond:

At least two-thirds of the rented houses visited needed essential repairs or alterations. Almost everything seemed to be wrong with the houses; leaking roofs were mentioned again and again; plastering was down; paper, painting or kalsomining was needed everywhere; many porches, fences, gutters were broken; plumbing defects of every kind were noted. A large number of the very old houses in Jackson Ward could only be described as generally dilapidated and hardly fit for human habitation.[3]

Conditions are similar in Area J, known as the Fulton district, where unpleasant home conditions go hand in hand with extreme deterioration and low rents. In these areas at the time of the survey the houses were dilapidated and without sanitary facilities, and many streets were unpaved and poorly lighted.

In Fulton . . . . the summary of the condition of streets compiled from block sheets made by the Survey Field workers, reads: "The streets of one-half of the blocks had never been paved. Over one-third of the blocks surveyed are without sidewalks. In wet weather it was noted by the surveyors that mud makes some of the streets and sidewalks almost impassable. In some of the blocks, dirt paths run along paved or partially paved or oiled roads. A large portion of the district is without curbs or gutters."[4]

The physical and economic differences among areas, important as they may be, probably reflect even more significant differences in the social life of these contrasting areas.

It is evident that the areas with the lowest rentals and the highest rates of delinquents were, at the time of the writing, predominantly Negro areas. It is important to note, however, that low-rent areas almost as deteriorated were occupied by white population and that the rates of delinquents in these areas were also high. Almost without exception, it is the group with the lowest economic status which is forced into the old sections of the city near its center, the areas close to industrial property, or areas geographically low and undesirable. In Chicago, areas of this

[3] *The Negro in Richmond* (Richmond Council of Social Agencies, 1929), p. 72.
[4] *Ibid.*, p. 74.

type have remained areas of high rates of delinquents over a long period, notwithstanding almost complete change in the population makeup. Probably the same would be found to be true in Richmond if the trends could be studied.

MAP 62

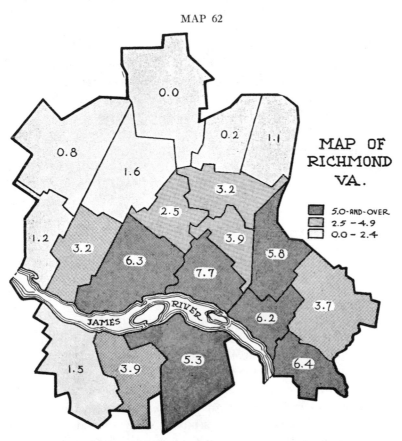

RATES OF DEPENDENCY IN RICHMOND, VIRGINIA, 1929

Rates of Dependency.—Another index of the economic level of areas and of the difference between areas of high and low delinquency rates is the distribution of the 1,467 families who received aid from the Family Service Society of Richmond during the year 1929. The home addresses of these families were plotted on a map, and rates of dependents were calculated for the same 19 areas used to determine rates of delinquents. These rates represent the number of families receiving aid per 100 families in each area as of 1930.

These rates of dependents are presented in Map 62. The range is from 0.0 in Area 1 to 7.7 in Area 12. It will be observed that most of the areas with low rates of dependency are near the periphery of the city, where the rates of delinquents are also low, and that in general the areas with high rates of dependents are those with high rates of delinquents, near the city's center. Two areas with high rates of delinquents, however, do not have high dependency rates as measured by this index. These areas were occupied by Negroes, many of whom would have been dependent if funds had been made available for their care.

TABLE 92

RATES OF DELINQUENTS FOR AREAS GROUPED BY
RATE OF DEPENDENT FAMILIES, 1929

Rates of Dependent Families	Rate of Delinquents
5.0 and over...........................	16.9
2.5–4.9...............................	14.0
0.0–2.4...............................	6.8

The extent to which rates of dependents vary with rates of delinquents is indicated by the coefficient of correlation, .78 ± .06.[5] This correspondence is further shown when rates of delinquents are calculated for the three groups of areas outlined on Map 62 (see Table 92).

Rates of Adult Criminals.—A further index of variation in the influences to which children are subjected is the distribution of adult criminals. For such a study a series of male offenders brought into the Bureau of Identification in Richmond on charges of stealing or attempted stealing between 1927 and 1930 was secured.

The 819 individuals included were plotted on a map by home address, and rates of adult criminals calculated for the same areas were used for the rates of delinquents. The rate in each area represents the number of adult criminals in this series per 100 of the

[5] Using Fisher's z-transformation, the 2σ limits are .50 and .91.

aged 20–35 male population as calculated from the federal census of 1930.

The rates of adult criminals are presented in Map 63. The range is from 0.3 to 14.3, the median rate is 2.5, and the rate for

MAP 63

RATES OF ADULT CRIMINALS, RICHMOND, VIRGINIA, 1927–30

the city as a whole 3.6. It will be observed that 2 areas in the central part of Richmond have rates of adult criminals distinctly higher than those in the other areas. Area 12, which includes the central business district, has a rate of 14.3, and Area 11, just north of the central business district, a rate of 9.0. Toward the north and west the rates decrease successively to the periphery of the city, where the 7 areas with the lowest rates are to be found.

As in the other series, the rates decrease regularly in the 3 areas in South Richmond, and also designate Fulton (Area 16) as an area with distinctly different characteristics from those in the northern and western parts of the city.

When rates of delinquents in the 19 areas are correlated with rates of adult criminals, the resulting coefficient is .81 $\pm$ .05.[6] The close association is also evident when rates of delinquents are calculated for the four groups of areas shown on Map 63 (see Table 93). This very evident correspondence establishes the fact that, without question, adult offenders and juvenile delinquents have the same general distribution in the city of Richmond.

TABLE 93

RATES OF DELINQUENTS FOR AREAS GROUPED BY
RATE OF ADULT CRIMINALS, 1927–30

Rates of Adult Criminals	Rate of Delinquents
6.0 and over	23.2
3.0–5.9	15.8
1.0–2.9	9.2
0.0–0.9	4.0

The variation in the rates of adult criminals among areas in Richmond signifies more than just a high or low proportion of criminal population: it signifies very real differences in effectiveness of the communities in preventing delinquency or criminality, on the one hand, and in the presence of positive influences toward delinquency or criminality, on the other.

VARIATION IN COMMUNITY CHARACTERISTICS
WITH RATES OF DELINQUENTS

Comparison by Areas.—The extent to which the variations in delinquency rates throughout the city parallel similar variations in the rates of family dependency and adult criminals is further indicated when the latter rates are calculated for the three groups of areas shown on Map 59 (see Table 94). These data indicate that, quite apart from location in the city, areas of low rates of delinquents are characterized also by low rates of dependent families and adult criminals, while the high-rate areas also correspond.

[6] Using Fisher's z-transformation, the 2σ limits are .57 and .92.

Comparison by Zones.—In considering the distribution of delinquents, rates were presented for three 1-mile zones. In Table 95
the data on community characteristics are presented, together
with rates of delinquents, for these zones.[7]

The indexes here presented indicate even more strongly than
those previously given not only that areas of high rates of de-

TABLE 94

RATES OF DEPENDENTS AND OF ADULT CRIMINALS
FOR AREAS GROUPED BY RATE
OF DELINQUENTS

Rates of Delinquents	Rate of Dependents	Rate of Adult Criminals
15.0 and over..........	5.3	5.7
7.5–14.9..............	3.9	2.6
0.0– 7.4.............	0.7	0.9

TABLE 95

COMMUNITY CHARACTERISTICS BY 1-MILE ZONES

Community Characteristics	Zone I	Zone II	Zone III
Rate of delinquents......	19.7	12.2	6.4
Average rental..........	$16.81	$22.43	$33.84
Rate of dependents......	5.2	3.8	1.7
Rate of adult criminals...	7.7	2.9	1.3

linquency may be differentiated from areas of low rates, but also
that high rates of delinquents are in themselves indications of the
basic differentiation of areas that takes place in the process of city
growth. As a result of this process the types of areas which are
physically deteriorated, in which rents are low, and in which delinquents, dependents, and adult criminals are found tend to be
concentrated near the central business and industrial districts.

[7] As with rates of delinquents, the rentals, rates of dependents, etc., are presented
for the zones as drawn. In the calculation, when an area was divided by one of the
concentric circles, the division of the total rental, population, and number of dependents, etc., was made on the basis of the percentage of the area in each zone.

SUMMARY

Richmond, an old southern city, differs in many respects from the northern industrial cities under consideration in this study, the population being relatively small, the rate of growth slow, and the predominant population groups the native white of native parentage and the Negroes.

In spite of these differences, the distribution of delinquents in Richmond differs little from the pattern found in the other cities studied. Both the actual geographic distribution of the boys included in the study and the rates based on the 1930 population of similar age reveal concentrations of delinquents near the central business district and the industrial areas, in contrast with a wide dispersion of cases in the newer outlying residential areas. The areas of high rates of delinquents in Richmond were found to be characterized by relatively low average rentals, with high rates of family dependency and of adult crime. These indexes indicate variations in the facilities offered by the community and family for the satisfaction of the normal desires of children, variations in the amount of control exercised by the community, and variations in extent of possible contact with criminals or criminal traditions.

PART IV

CHAPTER XIII

CONCLUSION

SUMMARY AND INTERPRETATION

I T IS clear from the data included in this volume that there is a direct relationship between conditions existing in local communities of American cities and differential rates of delinquents and criminals. Communities with high rates have social and economic characteristics which differentiate them from communities with low rates. Delinquency—particularly group delinquency, which constitutes a preponderance of all officially recorded offenses committed by boys and young men—has its roots in the dynamic life of the community.

It is recognized that the data included in this volume may be interpreted from many different points of view. However, the high degree of consistency in the association between delinquency and other characteristics of the community not only sustains the conclusion that delinquent behavior is related dynamically to the community but also appears to establish that all community characteristics, including delinquency, are products of the operation of general processes more or less common to American cities. Moreover, the fact that in Chicago the rates of delinquents for many years have remained relatively constant in the areas adjacent to centers of commerce and heavy industry, despite successive changes in the nativity and nationality composition of the population, supports emphatically the conclusion that the delinquency-producing factors are inherent in the community.

From the data available it appears that local variations in the conduct of children, as revealed in differential rates of delinquents, reflect the differences in social values, norms, and attitudes to which the children are exposed. In some parts of the city attitudes which support and sanction delinquency are, it seems, sufficiently extensive and dynamic to become the controlling forces in the development of delinquent careers among a relatively large number of boys and young men. These are the low-income areas, where delinquency has developed in the form of a social tradition, inseparable from the life of the local community.

This tradition is manifested in many different ways. It becomes meaningful to the child through the conduct, speech, gestures, and attitudes of persons with whom he has contact. Of particular importance is the child's intimate association with predatory gangs or other forms of delinquent and criminal organization. Through his contacts with these groups and by virtue of his participation in their activities he learns the techniques of stealing, becomes involved in binding relationships with his companions in delinquency, and acquires the attitudes appropriate to his position as a member of such groups. To use the words of Frank Tannenbaum: "It is the group that sets the pattern, provides the stimulus, gives the rewards in glory and companionship, offers the protection and loyalty, and, most of all, gives the criminal life its ethical content without which it cannot persist."[1]

In these communities many children encounter competing systems of values. Their community, which provides most of the social forms in terms of which their life will be organized, presents conflicting possibilities. A career in delinquency and crime is one alternative, which often becomes real and enticing to the boy because it offers the promise of economic gain, prestige, and companionship and because he becomes acquainted with it through relationships with persons whose esteem and approbation are vital to his security and to the achievement of satisfactory status. In this situation the delinquent group may become both the incentive and the mechanism for initiating the boy into a career of delinquency and crime and for sustaining him in such a career, once he has embarked upon it.

In cases of group delinquency it may be said, therefore, that from the point of view of the delinquent's immediate social world, he is not necessarily disorganized, maladjusted, or antisocial. Within the limits of his social world and in terms of its norms and expectations, he may be a highly organized and well-adjusted person.

[1] *Crime and the Community* (New York: Ginn & Co., 1938), p. 475.

The residential communities of higher economic status, where the proportion of persons dealt with as delinquents and criminals is relatively low, stand in sharp contrast to the situation described above. Here the norms and values of the child's social world are more or less uniformly and consistently conventional. Generally speaking, the boy who grows up in this situation is not faced with the problem of making a choice between conflicting systems of moral values. Throughout the range of his contacts in the community he encounters similar attitudes of approval or disapproval. Cases of delinquency are relatively few and sporadic. The system of conventional values in the community is sufficiently pervasive and powerful to control and organize effectively, with few exceptions, the lives of most children and young people.

In both these types of communities the dominant system of values is conventional. In the first, however, a powerful competing system of delinquency values exists; whereas in the second, such a system, if it exists at all, is not sufficiently extensive and powerful to exercise a strong influence in the lives of many children. Most of the communities of the city fall between these two extremes and represent gradations in the extent to which delinquency has become an established way of life.

It is important to ask what the forces are which give rise to these significant differences in the organized values in different communities. Under what conditions do the conventional forces in the community become so weakened as to tolerate the development of a conflicting system of criminal values? Under what conditions is the conventional community capable of maintaining its integrity and exercising such control over the lives of its members as to check the development of the competing system? Obviously, any discussion of this question at present must be tentative. The data presented in this volume, however, afford a basis for consideration of certain points which may be significant.

It may be observed, in the first instance, that the variations in rates of officially recorded delinquents in communities of the city correspond very closely with variations in economic status. The communities with the highest rates of delinquents are occupied by those segments of the population whose position is most disadvantageous in relation to the distribution of economic, social, and cultural values. Of all the communities in the city, these have the fewest facilities for acquiring the economic goods indicative of status and success in our conventional culture. Residence in the community is in itself an indication of inferior status, from the standpoint of persons residing in the more prosperous areas. It is a handicap in securing employment and in making satisfactory advancement in industry and the professions. Fewer opportunities are provided for securing the training, education, and contacts which facilitate advancement in the fields of business, industry, and the professions.

The communities with the lowest rates of delinquents, on the other hand, occupy a relatively high position in relation to the economic and social hierarchy of the city. Here the residents are relatively much more secure; and adequate provision is offered to young people for securing the material possessions symbolic of success and the education, training, and personal contacts which facilitate their advancement in the conventional careers they may pursue.

Despite these marked differences in the relative position of people in different communities, children and young people in all areas, both rich and poor, are exposed to the luxury values and success patterns of our culture. In school and elsewhere they are also exposed to ideas of equality, freedom, and individual enterprise. Among children and young people residing in low-income areas, interests in acquiring material goods and enhancing personal status are developed which are often difficult to realize by legitimate means because of limited access to the necessary facilities and opportunities.

This disparity in the facilities available to people in different communities for achieving a satisfactory position of social security and prestige is particularly important in relation to delinquency and crime in the urban world. In the city, relationships are largely impersonal. Because of the anonymity in urban life, the individual is freed from much of the scrutiny and control which characterize life in primary-group situations in small towns and rural communities. Personal status and the status of one's community are, to a very great extent, determined by economic achievement. Superior status depends not so much on character as on the possession of those goods and values which symbolize success. Hence, the kind of clothes one wears, the automobile one drives, the type of building in which one lives, and the physical character of one's community become of great importance to the person. To a large degree these are the symbols of his position— the external evidences of the extent to which he has succeeded in the struggle for a living. The urban world, with its anonymity, its greater freedom, the more impersonal character of its relationships, and the varied assortment of economic, social, and cultural backgrounds in its communities, provides a general setting particularly conducive to the development of deviations in moral norms and behavior practices.

In the low-income areas, where there is the greatest deprivation and frustration, where, in the history of the city, immigrant and migrant groups have brought together the widest variety of divergent cultural traditions and institutions, and where there exists the greatest disparity between the social values to which the people aspire and the availability of facilities for acquiring these values in conventional ways, the development of crime as an organized way of life is most marked. Crime, in this situation, may be regarded as one of the means employed by people to acquire, or to attempt to acquire, the economic and social values generally idealized in our culture, which persons in other circumstances acquire by conventional means. While the origin of this tradition of crime is obscure, it can be said that its development in the history of the community has been facilitated by the fact that many persons have, as a result of their criminal activities, greatly improved their economic and social status. Their clothes, cars, and other possessions are unmistakable evidence of this fact. That many of these persons also acquire influence and power in politics and elsewhere is so well known that it does not need elaboration at this point. The power and affluence achieved, at least temporarily, by many persons involved in crime and illegal rackets are well known to the children and youth of the community and are important in determining the character of their ideals.

It may be said, therefore, that the existence of a powerful system of criminal values and relationships in low-income urban areas is the product of a cumulative process extending back into the history of the community and of the city. It is related both to the general character of the urban world and to the fact that the population in these communities has long occupied a disadvantageous position. It has developed in somewhat the same way as have all social traditions, that is, as a means of satisfying certain felt needs within the limits of a particular social and economic framework.

It should be observed that, while the tradition of delinquency and crime is thus a powerful force in certain communities, it is only a part of the community's system of values. As was pointed out previously, the dominant tradition in every community is conventional, even in those having the highest rates of delinquents. The traditionally conventional values are embodied in the family, the church, the school, and many other such institutions and organizations. Since the dominant tradition in the community is conventional, more persons pursue law-abiding careers than careers of delinquency and crime, as might be expected.

In communities occupied by Orientals, even those communities located in the most deteriorated sections of our large cities, the solidarity of Old World cultures and institutions has been preserved to such a marked extent that control of the child is still sufficiently effective to keep at a minimum delinquency and other forms of deviant behavior. As Professor Hayner has pointed out . . . , the close integration of the Oriental family, the feeling of group responsibility for the behavior of the child, and the desire of these groups to maintain a good reputation in American communities have all been important elements in preserving this cultural solidarity.[2]

It is the assumption of this volume that many factors are important in determining whether a particular child will become involved in delinquency, even in those communities in which a system of delinquent and criminal values exists. Individual and personality differences, as well as differences in family relationships and in contacts with other institutions and groups, no doubt

[2] See Norman S. Hayner, "Five Cities of the Pacific Northwest," Chapter XVI in the original edition of this volume.

influence greatly his acceptance or rejection of opportunities to engage in delinquent activities. It may be said, however, that if the delinquency tradition were not present and the boys were not thus exposed to it, a preponderance of those who become delinquent in low-income areas would find their satisfactions in activities other than delinquency.

In conclusion, it is not assumed that this theoretical proposition applies to all cases of officially proscribed behavior. It applies primarily to those delinquent activities which become embodied in groups and social organizations. For the most part, these are offenses against property, which comprise a very large proportion of all the cases of boys coming to the attention of the courts.

IMPLICATIONS FOR PREVENTION AND TREATMENT

The theoretical formulation set forth in the preceding pages has certain definite implications with regard to the task of dealing with the problem of delinquency in large American cities. Some of the more important may be stated as follows:

1. Any great reduction in the volume of delinquency in large cities probably will not occur except as general changes take place which effect improvements in the economic and social conditions surrounding children in those areas in which the delinquency rates are relatively high.

2. Individualized methods of treatment probably will not be successful in a sufficiently large number of cases to result in any substantial diminution of the volume of delinquency and crime.

3. Treatment and preventive efforts, if they are to achieve general success, should increasingly take the form of broad programs which seek to utilize more effectively the constructive institutional and human resources available in every local community in the city. Tannenbaum states this point vividly: "The criminal is a product of the community, and his own criminal gang is part of the whole community, natural and logical to it; but it is only part of it. In that lies the hope that the rest of the community can do something with the gang as such."[3]

---

[3] *Op. cit.*, p. 474.

It is suggested that one way in which current methods of dealing with the problem of delinquency in high-rate areas may be strengthened is through programs of community action, initiated and carried on by the concerted efforts of citizens and local residents interested in improvement of the community life in all its aspects. Such programs provide an opportunity to all residents to use their talents, energies, interests, and understanding in a common effort to strengthen, unify, and extend the constructive forces of the community. Through the leadership of local residents it is possible to effect a closer co-ordination of local institutions, groups, and agencies into a unified program for the area as a whole. By this means those private organizations maintained by persons residing outside of the community may take on more of the nature of instrumentalities through which the local residents seek to deal with their own problems.

It was for the purpose of assisting in the development of such programs of community action in low-income areas that in 1932 the Institute for Juvenile Research and the Behavior Research Fund initiated the work of what is now known as the Chicago Area Project, a private corporation with a board of directors made up of prominent citizens interested in delinquency prevention. Aid in the form of funds and personnel has been provided by foundations and a variety of city-wide public and private agencies, as well as by local residents, institutions, and agencies. The major features of the project are here set forth briefly, in order to indicate one way in which constructive forces in a neighborhood may be more effectively utilized.

The Neighborhood as the Unit of Operation.—The local community area or neighborhood is the unit of operation in the Chicago Area Project. Thus far, activities have been developed in six small geographic areas, varying in size from approximately $\frac{1}{2}$ square mile to $2\frac{1}{2}$ square miles, with populations ranging from 10,000 to 50,000. The work is developed upon a neighborhood basis because it is assumed that delinquency is a product chiefly of community forces and conditions and must be dealt with, therefore, as a community problem, even though it is recognized that the delinquency-producing communities themselves may be products of more general processes.

Planning and Management by Local Residents.—In each area the activities are planned and carried on by a committee composed of representative local citizens. These committees include members of churches, societies, labor unions, trades and professions, business groups, athletic clubs, and a miscellany of other groups and organizations. These committees function as boards of directors and assume full responsibility for sponsoring and managing all aspects of the community program.

This procedure of placing responsibility for the planning and managing of the program in the hands of local residents stands in sharp contrast to traditional procedures whereby many institutions and programs operating in low-income areas have been controlled and managed by boards of directors whose members live, for the most part, in outlying residential areas. Although the local residents may be partly dependent upon sources of financial support outside the community, they assume full leadership in the management of their welfare activities. They are participants in a creative enterprise in which their talents, capacities, and energies find opportunities for expression in socially significant affairs of the neighborhood. Instead of suffering the humiliations often entailed in receiving the services of philanthropy, they achieve a sense of self-reliance, preserve their self-respect, and enhance their status among their neighbors by contributing time and energy to the creation of better opportunities for children. The Area Project program is, therefore, a development by the people within a local community rather than a ready-made program or institution imposed from the outside. It seeks to build solidarity and unity of sentiments among the people by encouraging and aiding them to work together toward common objectives.

Employment of Local Workers.—In so far as practicable, the staff in each neighborhood is recruited locally. Indigenous workers have intimate and significant relationships with local organizations, institutions, groups, and persons which are of great value in promoting programs of social action. Through institutes and

training courses the local leaders are familiarized with the special-
ized knowledge and techniques necessary to their program work.

The emphasis placed upon local residents does not in any way
minimize the value of the services of skilled, specially trained
workers. By operating in conjunction with or through the committees of local residents, the professional worker in these communities has a chance to translate his special knowledge more
effectively into the thinking, planning, and practices of the neighborhood people. While there is much that the lay resident can
learn from the professional, it is equally true that the professional
can learn from the lay resident.

Utilizing and Co-ordinating Community Resources.—In developing the work in each area, the committee of local residents
seeks the co-operation of churches, schools, recreation centers,
labor unions, industries, societies, clubs, and other social groupings in a program of concerted action for the improvement of the
neighborhood. The mothers and fathers participating in the
citizens' committees, who understand the problems of their communities and have a vital interest in all local matters that bear
upon the lives of their children and young people, thereby become
instrumentalities through which the services of welfare agencies in
the community are co-ordinated.

Activity Programs.—Through the sponsorship of the committees of residents a great variety of activities is carried on.
These include recreation, summer camping, scouting, handicraft,
forums, and interest trips. Efforts have been made to improve
housing, the physical appearance of the area, and sanitary conditions. Parent-teacher groups have been organized to effect a
more satisfactory working relationship between school and community. To a limited extent, employment opportunities for
young persons have been augmented. Especial attention has been
directed to the task of providing for the needs of problem children
and delinquents. In so far as possible, the committees concern
themselves with all phases of community life, with special emphasis on those which bear upon the well-being of children.

Credit Given to Local Residents.—It has been an established
policy of the Chicago Area Project that all publicity concerning

the program activities in the neighborhood shall be controlled by the local committees and that all credit for accomplishments in connection with the program shall be given to the local residents and the organizations and agencies co-operating with them. Actually the work of the project has been publicized primarily by reports released by the local committees. The board of directors and staff of the Chicago Area Project function as aids to these committees.

In this description of the Chicago Area Project no attempt has been made to give a detailed picture of the many activities and accomplishments of the program. Complete reports are being prepared by certain of the local neighborhood committees. At least two such reports will be ready for publication within the next year.

It may be said, however, that the achievements of the committees have been sufficiently outstanding to demonstrate the feasibility and desirability of programs of neighborhood action as a means of making more effective the welfare activities carried on in low-income areas of large cities. In each community where such programs have been undertaken, the residents have responded enthusiastically. They have demonstrated that they possess, contrary to widespread opinion, the talents and capabilities essential to effective participation in the planning and management of welfare institutions, agencies, and programs. As already suggested, they have planned, developed, and operated summer camps and community centers, planned and promoted health and sanitation programs, functioned effectively in relation to the improvement of their schools, contributed in a significant manner to the adjustment of juvenile and adult offenders, and in many other ways initiated activities designed to further the welfare of children and young people.

Altogether apart from what the achievements of the Area Project may be, the data in this volume provide a basis for the conclusion that programs for the prevention of delinquency in low-income areas of American cities are not likely to succeed unless they can effect certain basic changes in the conditions of life surrounding children. As long as the present condition exists, little change in the volume of delinquency should be expected.

Year after year, decade after decade, large cities—and especially certain areas in large cities—send to the courts an undiminished line of juvenile offenders. Year after year, decade after decade, likewise, society continues to organize or construct new agencies or institutions designed to reduce the number of these offenders and to rehabilitate those who have already offended against the law. Perhaps the unsatisfactory results of these treatment and prevention efforts have been due, in part at least, to the fact that our attention has been focused too much upon the individual delinquent and not enough upon the setting in which delinquency arises.

James S. Plant, on the basis of many years' experience in a psychiatric clinic, arrives at somewhat the same conclusion. He states:

Society is, and has been, aroused over its misfits and the mass of human breakdown that is in the wake of its progress. It has erected every conceivable type of agency to study, salvage, or merely sweep up this debris. As the wreckage mounts, new agencies are demanded or "better standards of service" asked of those existing. The folly of believing that happiness and goodness can be fabricated by machinery (agencies) will be exposed only when we understand that the ills, corruptions, and hypocrisies of a cultural pattern flow into the child and man and "become a part of him for the day, for the year, or for stretching cycles of years." If it is true that the triumphs and tragedies of the street flow into and become a part of the child, then all programs of personality change must manage somehow to change the street.[4]

Whether or not we care to admit it, most delinquent boys reflect all too accurately what they have learned in the process of living in their own communities. If we wish to have fewer delinquents, or if we wish to modify the mode of life of those who already are delinquent, a way must be found to modify those aspects of the community life which provide the appropriate setting for delinquency careers and which give to these careers the sanction and approbation on which all social behavior depends.

[4] *Personality and the Cultural Pattern* (New York: Commonwealth Fund, 1937), p. 18.

PART V

CHAPTER XIV

RECENT RATES OF DELINQUENTS AND COMMITMENTS IN CHICAGO: DISTRI-BUTION AND TRENDS

INTRODUCTION

R ATES of delinquents and rates of commitments included in the original edition of *Juvenile Delinquency and Urban Areas* were based on data representing the first three and one-half decades of this century. A spot map (Map 9) showing the geographic distribution of delinquents in Chicago for the period 1934–40 was included in that edition, but rate maps for the same period were not. In the present addition to this volume rate maps for Chicago and Chicago suburbs for the period 1934 intermittently through 1966 are included. This means that the revised volume includes rates of delinquents by areas in Chicago for a period of 65 years, which is something more than one-half of the life of the city.

During this period great changes have taken place in the numbers and distribution of population both in Chicago and in the suburbs of Chicago. If the total period covered in the study is divided into two parts, the first including the period 1900–1930, and the second period 1930–66, some contrasts are evident. For example, the population of Chicago doubled between 1900 and 1930 with the addition of about one and two-thirds million persons, while between 1930 and 1960 the increase was only about 5 per cent.

In contrast, the population in Cook County outside of Chicago increased by less than half a million persons between 1900 and 1930 but increased by about a million between 1930 and 1960. In other words, Chicago was the area of rapid population growth in one period; the suburbs represented the area of rapid growth in the other. This is reflected in the increase in the number of cities. In 1930 there were 17 cities with a population of

10,000 or over in Cook County outside of Chicago. Three decades later this number had almost tripled, since in 1960 there were 47 cities with a population of 10,000 or over in Cook County, outside of Chicago. In addition, in 1960, there were 46 other cities in Cook County with a population of between 2,500 and 10,000. This means that in 1960, using the census definition, there were 95 cities in Cook County in addition to Chicago.

All of Cook County is served by the Cook County Juvenile Courts. During the early decades of this century, few children were brought to the court on petition alleging delinquency from the area outside of Chicago. With the outward movement of population this number has increased steadily. Therefore, in this revision, rates of delinquents for the series computed after 1945 have been computed for all Cook County cities with a population of 10,000 or over. It is not assumed that the rates for the suburbs furnish a basis for comparison with rates for Chicago communities, but they do furnish a basis for interesting and valid comparisons with other suburbs.

Changes in Chicago and Cook County, other than population changes, which are somewhat related to variations in rates of delinquents by areas, have been numerous during the past 30 years, both in Chicago and suburbs. Several of these will be enumerated.

In the first place the arrangement of types of areas within the city is not so orderly as it was a few decades ago. Then the suburbs were stretched out like fingers along the suburban railroad lines and were rather uniformly of high economic status. Within the city the configuration of the population followed the street car lines, and the economic level of the population tended to increase rather uniformly with distance from the center of the city.

Several factors were important in changing this situation. One was the arrival of the automobile economy, which made it possible for people to live farther away from their work or in areas where there was no public transportation. When the vacant living space within the city was gone, the movement continued into the suburbs. Bus lines, not restricted by rails, followed the population. The result of this flow of population into the suburbs was that suburban towns, instead of being uniformly of high economic status, showed a wide variation in income, type of dwelling, and life style. Some of these differences are related also to the very wide variation in rates of delinquents among suburban cities.

Another factor was the Supreme Court decision which held that restrictive covenants were not enforceable in the courts. This decision permitted many families to move from the sections of the city to which they had been restricted, to whatever areas were available. When coupled with a large Negro, Mexican, and Puerto Rican migration, this movement meant that many areas which had been middle class or declining middle class took on the characteristics of immigrant areas. The result has been that although the variations in rates of delinquents among areas are as great as in earlier series the gradients are not so regular as they were in the first decades of this century.

Partly for this reason and partly because the concept of zone has limited utility, the data in the revised section will not be presented by zones. Zone rates were included in the early edition because they revealed the rather regular decreases of rates as one moved out from the center of the city, and not because it was assumed that zones really existed. Furthermore, if zone rates were to be presented for the materials in this section they would involve a combination of rates for Chicago areas and rates for suburban communities. For reasons which will be elaborated when the data are presented, these data are not comparable.

All of the Chicago data in this chapter will be presented by communities. Originally, rates of delinquents and other indexes of community life were presented by square-mile areas, communities, subcommunities, or other areas created by combining census tracts in different ways. Since the time of first publication of this volume, however, the U.S. census has adopted the 75 communities as the geographical units for which detailed census data are made available. As a result of this decision, the use of almost all other kinds of divisions of the city for study purposes has disappeared.

For statistical work the Chicago communities leave much to be desired, both because of the great disparity in numbers of population and because some of the areas lack homogeneity. On the positive side, however, they are stable, they are widely used for the presentation of great varieties of economic and social data, and they furnish a permanent basis for the study of trends. Some of the data presented by square-mile areas in the earlier chapters of this volume have since been translated into rates by communities for the purpose of trend analysis.

First to be presented are five sets of rates of male delinquents for Chicago communities covering, collectively, the years 1934–65. These series vary somewhat in terms of the manner in which the data were collected, the number of years included in each series, and the age group included in the population base. For this reason the absolute rates are valuable only in the study of variation in rates of delinquents among areas at a given period. In the original form they cannot be used to indicate either increases or decreases in rates of delinquents in a particular community, or from one series to the next; nor can the mean rate or the grand mean be used to determine whether rates of delinquents are upward or downward in particular areas since many other elements would have to be taken into consideration before such a conclusion could be drawn.

To meet these difficulties the findings in this study will be presented by means of rates and indexes. The number of offenders, the age grouping, and the size of the population base will be presented in the introduction to each series, together with the range of rates, the median, the mean, and the grand mean. To focus attention on the relative magnitude of rates in any one series and to facilitate comparison among series, all the rates in all of the series have been translated into indexes by dividing each community rate by the grand mean (the mean of the community rates) of that series. Thus 1.00 automatically becomes the mean, 0.50 is half as great as the mean, and an index of 2.00 indicates that the rate in an area is twice as high as the mean.

The shading used on the maps has been based on the indexes
of relative magnitude of the type of deviant behavior under consideration.

RATES OF MALE DELINQUENTS

The 1934–40 Juvenile Court Series.—The indexes of rates of
male delinquents presented on Map 64 are based on the 9,849
male delinquents against whom petitions were filed in the Cook
County Juvenile Court during the years 1934–40. All of these
delinquents are separate individuals because subsequent appearances in the same or subsequent years were eliminated as
duplications.

The numbers of delinquents were counted by census tracts
and then combined into communities or the other statistical
areas into which Chicago is divided. In the presentation of
these data and the data in the series which follow, community 32, the Central Business District of Chicago, and the
home of very few adolescent males, has been combined with
community 33 which adjoins it on the south. As a result the
data are presented for 74 rather than 75 areas.

Because the communities vary widely in size and in population, the actual count of delinquents by areas is not easy to
interpret. It is of some interest, however, to note that in the
years 1934–40 eight areas produced fewer than 10 delinquents
each while at the other extreme 13 areas produced more than
200 each and four areas produced more than 450 delinquents
each in the 7-year period.

Rates of Delinquents.—Using these data, rates of delinquents
representing the ratio of delinquents to a population base were
computed for each of the 74 city communities in Chicago. The
population used in the computations was the number of male
youths 10–16 years of age in each community computed for the
midyear (1937.5) on the assumption that the trend followed a
straight line between the number in this population group in

1940 and the number in 1950. The population thus computed was 181,786.

The rates are stated as the number per hundred, that is, the number of official delinquents per 100 males 10–16 years of age at the midpoint of the series. The range of rates of male delinquents for the 1934–40 series is from 0.4 to 22.3. The median rate is 3.5; the mean rate is 5.4; and the grand mean is 5.01. The fact that this distribution is not just a chance distribution around the mean is seen in the fact that 24 areas have rates less than 3.0 and seven areas have rates of more than 11.0. Since the mean of each series is 1.00, the index reveals immediately the relation of the rate in each area to the mean, and to the rate in each of the other areas.

While these indexes facilitate comparisons of the magnitude of rates of delinquents among areas, their most important advantage is the fact that they furnish a basis for study of the relative magnitude of the rate in any area with the rate in the same area at another time. Thus if indexes of rates are higher in successive series of rates of delinquents, rates of delinquents in that area have been increasing relative to the other areas and vice versa.

Rates of delinquents for this series, reduced to indexes, are presented on Map 64. The range of the indexes is from .08 in community 72 to 4.44 in community 35, or from 8 per cent of the grand mean to nearly $4\frac{1}{2}$ times the grand mean. This wide difference in rates of delinquents among areas in this period is not unlike the findings presented for the earlier years in this century, or from those which are to follow. As compared with earlier studies it appears that rates of delinquents decreased somewhat in areas 24 and 28, as the assimilative process progressed, and increased in other areas, such as 7 and 42, where rapid and significant changes were taking place.

This stability in the city is quite understandable, since neither the city of Chicago nor its suburbs grew very much during the thirties. The flow of new immigrants from Europe had been slowed both by the absence of demand for cheap labor and by restrictive legislation, and the depression tended to reverse the

MAP 64

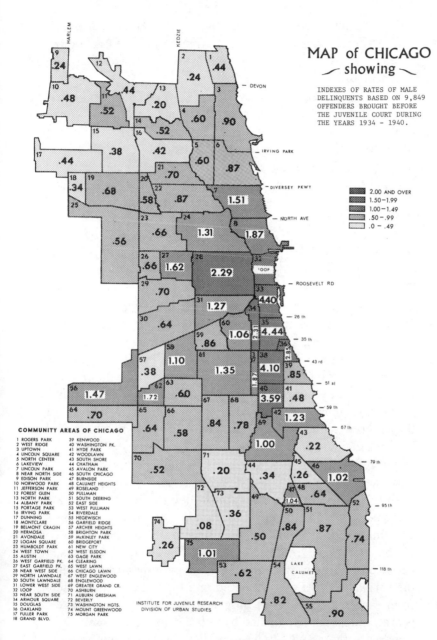

INDEXES OF RATES OF MALE DELINQUENTS BASED ON 9,849 OFFENDERS BROUGHT BEFORE THE JUVENILE COURT DURING THE YEARS 1934–40.

flow of young people from the country to the city. Movement within the city also was slowed. Immigrant groups stayed in areas of first settlement, and the movement toward the suburbs was negligible.

The 1945–51 Juvenile Court Series.—The second set of rates and indexes is based on the 8,041 male juvenile offenders brought before the Cook County Juvenile Court on official petition for the first time during the calendar years 1945–51. As in earlier series a large proportion of the delinquent boys were brought to court from a few communities. Three areas produced more than one-quarter, and ten areas more than one-half, of all the official delinquents.

The population base for these calculations consisted of the male population 10–16 years of age as computed for the midpoint of this series from the 1940 and 1950 Federal Census of Population. The smaller number of adolescent males (140,842) in the same age group represents the sharp decrease in the adolescent population between 1930 and 1950, a fact which reduced the amount, but not necessarily the rate, of delinquents.

In this series of rates of delinquents, as in some of the series presented in the first edition, the rates of delinquents have two meanings. They show, first, the variation in the relative number of official offenders among different communities, and, second, they represent the actual proportion of the juvenile population brought to court on official petitions. In all rates of delinquents which follow this series, the rates of delinquents will indicate only the relative amount of delinquent behavior.

In this series the range of rates of delinquents in the 74 areas is from 0.3 to 16.9. The median rate is 3.8; the city rate is 5.7; and the grand mean of the community rates is 4.84. The range of the indexes is from .06 to 3.49. Expressed as indexes, the variations in rates of delinquents among areas in Chicago for the period 1945–51 are presented on Map 65. Not much change from earlier maps is to be observed, but some trends have appeared which will be clarified by subsequent data. Some of these trends are the result of the fact that the last large immigrant groups from Europe did not move out of the inner-city areas to

MAP 65

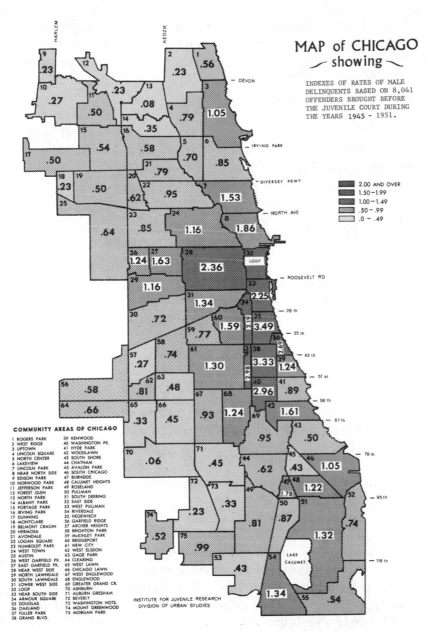

MAP of CHICAGO
~ showing ~

INDEXES OF RATES OF MALE
DELINQUENTS BASED ON 8,041
OFFENDERS BROUGHT BEFORE
THE JUVENILE COURT DURING
THE YEARS 1945 - 1951.

2.00 AND OVER
1.50 – 1.99
1.00 – 1.49
.50 – .99
.0 – .49

HARLEM
KEDZIE
— DEVON
— IRVING PARK
— DIVERSEY PKWY
— NORTH AVE
LOOP
— ROOSEVELT RD
— 26 th
— 35 th
— 43 rd
— 51 st
— 59 th
— 67 th
— 79 th
— 95 th
— 118 th

LAKE
CALUMET

COMMUNITY AREAS OF CHICAGO

1 ROGERS PARK	39 KENWOOD
2 WEST RIDGE	40 WASHINGTON PK.
3 UPTOWN	41 HYDE PARK
4 LINCOLN SQUARE	42 WOODLAWN
5 NORTH CENTER	43 SOUTH SHORE
6 LAKEVIEW	44 CHATHAM
7 LINCOLN PARK	45 AVALON PARK
8 NEAR NORTH SIDE	46 SOUTH CHICAGO
9 EDISON PARK	47 BURNSIDE
10 NORWOOD PARK	48 CALUMET HEIGHTS
11 JEFFERSON PARK	49 ROSELAND
12 FOREST GLEN	50 PULLMAN
13 NORTH PARK	51 SOUTH DEERING
14 ALBANY PARK	52 EAST SIDE
15 PORTAGE PARK	53 WEST PULLMAN
16 IRVING PARK	54 RIVERDALE
17 DUNNING	55 HEGEWISCH
18 MONTCLARE	56 GARFIELD RIDGE
19 BELMONT CRAGIN	57 ARCHER HEIGHTS
20 HERMOSA	58 BRIGHTON PARK
21 AVONDALE	59 McKINLEY PARK
22 LOGAN SQUARE	60 BRIDGEPORT
23 HUMBOLDT PARK	61 NEW CITY
24 WEST TOWN	62 WEST ELSDON
25 AUSTIN	63 GAGE PARK
26 WEST GARFIELD PK.	64 CLEARING
27 EAST GARFIELD PK.	65 WEST LAWN
28 NEAR WEST SIDE	66 CHICAGO LAWN
29 NORTH LAWNDALE	67 WEST ENGLEWOOD
30 SOUTH LAWNDALE	68 ENGLEWOOD
31 LOWER WEST SIDE	69 GREATER GRAND CR.
32 LOOP	70 ASHBURN
33 NEAR SOUTH SIDE	71 AUBURN GRESHAM
34 ARMOUR SQUARE	72 BEVERLY
35 DOUGLAS	73 WASHINGTON HGTS.
36 OAKLAND	74 MOUNT GREENWOOD
37 FULLER PARK	75 MORGAN PARK
38 GRAND BLVD.	

INSTITUTE FOR JUVENILE RESEARCH
DIVISION OF URBAN STUDIES

INDEXES OF RATES OF MALE DELINQUENTS BASED ON 8,041 OFFENDERS BROUGHT
BEFORE THE JUVENILE COURT DURING THE YEARS 1945–51.

make room for the new immigrant. As a result of earlier observations, it is to be expected that rates of delinquents will have
decreased in some inner areas where immigrant groups have
been located, while the rates in areas into which immigrant
groups have moved will tend to increase significantly.

Examination of the index map for this series of data reveals
that in about two-thirds of the communities the indexes are less
than 1.00, and that in about one-third of the areas the indexes
are above 1.00. Translated into more personal terms, this means
that nearly two-thirds of the children live in areas with rates of

TABLE 96

PERCENTAGE OF DELINQUENTS COMMITTED
TO INSTITUTIONS, BY RATE OF DELIN-
QUENTS INDEXES, CHICAGO COMMUNI-
TIES, COOK COUNTY JUVENILE COURT,
1945–51

Indexes of Rates of Delinquents	Percentage of Delinquents Committed to Institutions
2.00 and over.......	36.7
1.50–1.99...........	28.8
1.00–1.49...........	24.8
0.50–0.99...........	19.3
0–0.49...........	15.2

delinquents below the mean, and slightly more than one-third
live in areas with rates above the mean. In the eight areas with
indexes of 2.00 or more the probability of children becoming
delinquent is at least twice as great as it is in the 48 areas with
rates below the mean, and more than four times as great as it
is in the 17 areas with indexes below 0.50.

The data for this series included not only the number of
offenders for each community in Chicago but also the number
of these offenders who were committed to institutions. From
these data the percentage of offenders committed from each area
of the city during this period has been computed. The results,
by class of area based on indexes, are presented in Table 96.

This table reveals that the rate of commitment varies directly
with the rate of delinquents. In other words, the higher the rate
of delinquents the higher the proportion of delinquents who are

committed. This is entirely consistent with the findings presented in Chapter V of this volume.

The 1954–57 Juvenile Court Series.—This set of rates of delinquents by communities in Chicago is based on 9,830 male individuals brought before the Juvenile Court of Cook County during the 4-year period 1954–57. This series and all which follow represent a change in the procedure of collecting data from the juvenile court. Earlier series were based on the number of individuals who came into court on delinquency petition for the first time in a specified period. The present data, in original form, includes *all male individuals who came into court during a specific period on petitions alleging delinquency*. This means that data on the same individual were collected as many times as that individual came to court during the period. These duplications were eliminated for present purposes so that the rates would represent persons and not appearances.

At the same time the age group used in the computations of rates was changed from 10–16 to 12–16 years primarily because most of the delinquents are included in the 12–16 age range. This does not create a problem, because the focus of interest is on the *relative* magnitude of the rates, and because cross-section data cannot be used to represent statistical probabilities of delinquent behavior.

The population base for each area was computed as a straight-line trend between the aged 12–16 male population in each area from the 1950 and 1960 federal censuses. By this method the estimated population was found to be 113,827, or an average of 1,538 males 12–16 years of age for each area. The range in number of delinquents per area was from 12 to 872.

Rates of delinquents computed for the 74 areas were found to range from 2.1 to 25.9. The mean rate is 8.6; the grand mean is 8.04; and the median rate is 6.5. When these rates are translated into indexes of rates of delinquents the range is from 0.26 to 3.22, or from one-quarter of the mean to 3¼ times the mean. Again more than two-thirds of the areas were found to have rates of delinquents lower than the grand mean, as indicated by an index of less than 1.0. These indexes are presented on Map 66.

MAP 66

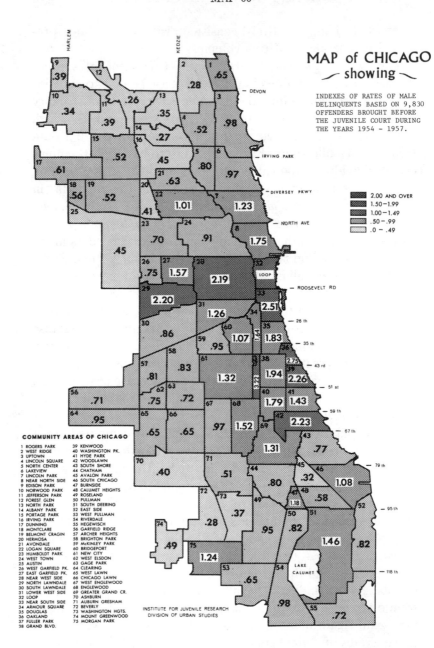

MAP of CHICAGO
~ showing ~

INDEXES OF RATES OF MALE
DELINQUENTS BASED ON 9,830
OFFENDERS BROUGHT BEFORE
THE JUVENILE COURT DURING
THE YEARS 1954 - 1957.

▓	2.00 AND OVER
▓	1.50 – 1.99
▒	1.00 – 1.49
░	.50 – .99
	.0 – .49

HARLEM

KEDZIE

— DEVON

— IRVING PARK

— DIVERSEY PKWY

— NORTH AVE

— ROOSEVELT RD

— 26 th

— 35 th

— 43 rd

— 51 st

— 59 th

— 67 th

— 79 th

— 95 th

— 118 th

9 .39
12
10 .34
11 .26
13 .35
2 .28
1 .65
3 .98
.52
14 .27
15 .52
16 .45
5 .80
6 .97
17 .61
.39
18 .56
19 .52
20 .63
21 .63
.41
22 1.01
7 1.23
25
23 .70
24 .91
8 1.75
.45
26 .75
27 1.57
28 2.19
32 LOOP
29 2.20
31 1.26
33 2.51
30 .86
34
59 .95
60 1.07
35 1.83
36
57 .81
58 .83
61 1.32
38 2.75
39 1.94
40 2.26
56 .71
62 .75
63 .72
37 1.79 1.43
64 .95
65 .65
66 .65
67 .97
68 1.52
69 2.23
43 .77
1.31
70 .40
71 .51
44
45 .32
46
47 1.08
72 .80
48 .58
49 1.18
50
51
52 .82
73 .37
.28
95 .82
1.46
74 .49
75 1.24
53
54
LAKE CALUMET
.65
.98
55 .72

COMMUNITY AREAS OF CHICAGO

1	ROGERS PARK	39	KENWOOD
2	WEST RIDGE	40	WASHINGTON PK.
3	UPTOWN	41	HYDE PARK
4	LINCOLN SQUARE	42	WOODLAWN
5	NORTH CENTER	43	SOUTH SHORE
6	LAKEVIEW	44	CHATHAM
7	LINCOLN PARK	45	AVALON PARK
8	NEAR NORTH SIDE	46	SOUTH CHICAGO
9	EDISON PARK	47	BURNSIDE
10	NORWOOD PARK	48	CALUMET HEIGHTS
11	JEFFERSON PARK	49	ROSELAND
12	FOREST GLEN	50	PULLMAN
13	NORTH PARK	51	SOUTH DEERING
14	ALBANY PARK	52	EAST SIDE
15	PORTAGE PARK	53	WEST PULLMAN
16	IRVING PARK	54	RIVERDALE
17	DUNNING	55	HEGEWISCH
18	MONTCLARE	56	GARFIELD RIDGE
19	BELMONT CRAGIN	57	ARCHER HEIGHTS
20	HERMOSA	58	BRIGHTON PARK
21	AVONDALE	59	McKINLEY PARK
22	LOGAN SQUARE	60	BRIDGEPORT
23	HUMBOLDT PARK	61	NEW CITY
24	WEST TOWN	62	WEST ELSDON
25	AUSTIN	63	GAGE PARK
26	WEST GARFIELD PK.	64	CLEARING
27	EAST GARFIELD PK.	65	WEST LAWN
28	NEAR WEST SIDE	66	CHICAGO LAWN
29	NORTH LAWNDALE	67	WEST ENGLEWOOD
30	SOUTH LAWNDALE	68	ENGLEWOOD
31	LOWER WEST SIDE	69	GREATER GRAND CR.
32	LOOP	70	ASHBURN
33	NEAR SOUTH SIDE	71	AUBURN GRESHAM
34	ARMOUR SQUARE	72	BEVERLY
35	DOUGLAS	73	WASHINGTON HGTS.
36	OAKLAND	74	MOUNT GREENWOOD
37	FULLER PARK	75	MORGAN PARK
38	GRAND BLVD.		

INSTITUTE FOR JUVENILE RESEARCH
DIVISION OF URBAN STUDIES

INDEXES OF RATES OF MALE DELINQUENTS BASED ON 9,830 OFFENDERS BROUGHT
BEFORE THE JUVENILE COURT DURING THE YEARS 1954–57.

The 1958–61 Juvenile Court Series.—Since this series of delinquents is centered on a census year it may properly be assumed that these rates of delinquents reveal the differences among areas somewhat more accurately than do the other series. It will be noted, however, that the findings in all of the series are very much the same. As indicated earlier, the absolute rate of delinquents does not establish the proportion of the boys in an area who become delinquent, but rather the relative magnitude of the rates among areas.

The delinquents in this series are the 14,167 boys who were brought into the Cook County Juvenile Court on petitions alleging delinquency during the 4-year period 1958–61. The number of boys in the 12–16 age group in 1960 was 123,537. The number of delinquents in the different areas ranges from 10 to 140; the rates from 1.8 to 34.5. The rate of delinquents for the city is 11.5; the grand mean is 10.21; and the median rate is 6.8.

When these rates are translated into indexes the range in the variation among areas is from 0.18 to 3.38. These rates are presented on Map 67. The rates in this series exhibit a slightly greater range than the rates in most of the other series, but the differences are not great. Series centered on census years and series for which the population has been computed on a straight line between census years have built into them a degree of stability. Projections of population beyond census years involve higher probability of error.

From the data in this series, also, it was possible to compute rates of recidivism for each of the 74 communities. Using the same class groupings as were employed for the 1945–51 juvenile court series, similar results were obtained (see Table 97).

The total percentage of delinquents committed to institutions in this series probably would exceed the percentage for the 1945–51 series, because the delinquent careers of some of the delinquents had not been completed when the data for this series were collected. In all probability the differences in rates of commitments for the different classes of areas would not be changed significantly by the addition of a few more commit-

MAP 67

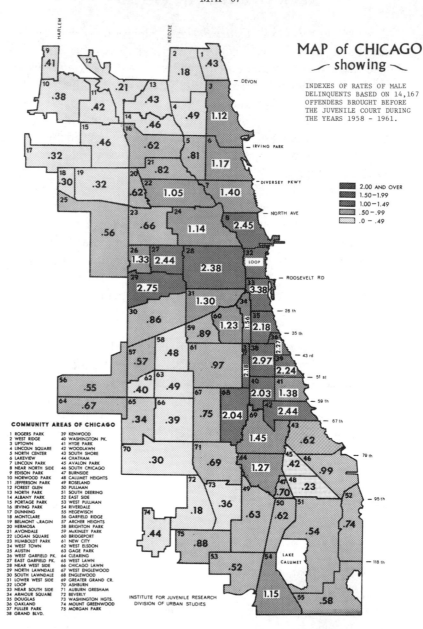

MAP of CHICAGO
~ showing ~

INDEXES OF RATES OF MALE
DELINQUENTS BASED ON 14,167
OFFENDERS BROUGHT BEFORE
THE JUVENILE COURT DURING
THE YEARS 1958 - 1961.

2.00 AND OVER
1.50 – 1.99
1.00 – 1.49
.50 – .99
.0 – .49

COMMUNITY AREAS OF CHICAGO

1 ROGERS PARK	39 KENWOOD
2 WEST RIDGE	40 WASHINGTON PK.
3 UPTOWN	41 HYDE PARK
4 LINCOLN SQUARE	42 WOODLAWN
5 NORTH CENTER	43 SOUTH SHORE
6 LAKEVIEW	44 CHATHAM
7 LINCOLN PARK	45 AVALON PARK
8 NEAR NORTH SIDE	46 SOUTH CHICAGO
9 EDISON PARK	47 BURNSIDE
10 NORWOOD PARK	48 CALUMET HEIGHTS
11 JEFFERSON PARK	49 ROSELAND
12 FOREST GLEN	50 PULLMAN
13 NORTH PARK	51 SOUTH DEERING
14 ALBANY PARK	52 EAST SIDE
15 PORTAGE PARK	53 WEST PULLMAN
16 IRVING PARK	54 RIVERDALE
17 DUNNING	55 HEGEWISCH
18 MONTCLARE	56 GARFIELD RIDGE
19 BELMONT ..RAGIN	57 ARCHER HEIGHTS
20 HERMOSA	58 BRIGHTON PARK
21 AVONDALE	59 McKINLEY PARK
22 LOGAN SQUARE	60 BRIDGEPORT
23 HUMBOLDT PARK	61 NEW CITY
24 WEST TOWN	62 WEST ELSDON
25 AUSTIN	63 GAGE PARK
26 WEST GARFIELD PK.	64 CLEARING
27 EAST GARFIELD PK.	65 WEST LAWN
28 NEAR WEST SIDE	66 CHICAGO LAWN
29 NORTH LAWNDALE	67 WEST ENGLEWOOD
30 SOUTH LAWNDALE	68 ENGLEWOOD
31 LOWER WEST SIDE	69 GREATER GRAND CR.
32 LOOP	70 ASHBURN
33 NEAR SOUTH SIDE	71 AUBURN GRESHAM
34 ARMOUR SQUARE	72 BEVERLY
35 DOUGLAS	73 WASHINGTON HGTS.
36 OAKLAND	74 MOUNT GREENWOOD
37 FULLER PARK	75 MORGAN PARK
38 GRAND BLVD.	

INSTITUTE FOR JUVENILE RESEARCH
DIVISION OF URBAN STUDIES

INDEXES OF RATES OF MALE DELINQUENTS BASED ON 14,167 OFFENDERS BROUGHT
BEFORE THE JUVENILE COURT DURING THE YEARS 1958–61.

ments. These data support once more the findings presented in Chapter V, namely, that before the completion of their careers a higher proportion of boys are committed to institutions from areas of high rates than from areas of low rates.

The 1962–65 Juvenile Court Series.—These rates of delinquents for Chicago communities are based on the 12,844 male offenders taken to the juvenile court on delinquency petitions during the 4-year period 1962–65. Again, duplications have been eliminated. The population base is the aged 12–16 male population estimated for each community on the basis of a straight-line

TABLE 97

PERCENTAGE OF DELINQUENTS COMMITTED TO INSTITUTIONS, BY RATE OF DELINQUENTS INDEXES, CHICAGO COMMUNITIES, COOK COUNTY JUVENILE COURT, 1958–61

Indexes of Rates of Delinquents	Percentage of Delinquents Committed to Institutions
2.00 and over........	34.1
1.50–1.99............	34.5
1.00–1.49............	29.0
0.50–0.99............	27.3
0–0.49............	16.6

trend for this age group between 1950 and 1960, extended to 1964. By this method of computation the estimated total aged 12–16 male population in Chicago as of January 1, 1964, was 132,678.

The rates of delinquents for Chicago communities computed on the basis of these data range from 1.7 to 30.0. The rate for the city is 9.7; the median rate is 6.5; and the grand mean is 8.97. Indexes of these rates, computed by dividing each rate by the grand mean of the area rates, are presented on Map 68. The range of these indexes is from 0.19 to 3.34. Since, by definition, the mean rate is 1.0, the 11 areas in this series in which the index is more than 3.00 all have rates more than 3 times the mean.

This is the last of the five series of rates of male delinquents for the 75 communities in Chicago. Inspection reveals that in

MAP 68

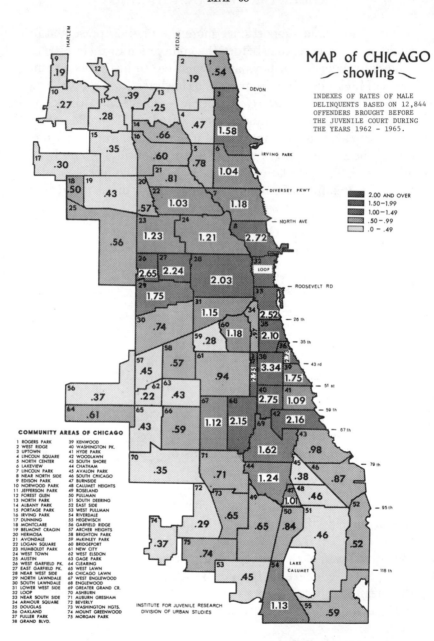

MAP of CHICAGO
~ showing ~

INDEXES OF RATES OF MALE
DELINQUENTS BASED ON 12,844
OFFENDERS BROUGHT BEFORE
THE JUVENILE COURT DURING
THE YEARS 1962 - 1965.

2.00 AND OVER
1.50–1.99
1.00–1.49
.50–.99
.0 – .49

COMMUNITY AREAS OF CHICAGO

1 ROGERS PARK
2 WEST RIDGE
3 UPTOWN
4 LINCOLN SQUARE
5 NORTH CENTER
6 LAKEVIEW
7 LINCOLN PARK
8 NEAR NORTH SIDE
9 EDISON PARK
10 NORWOOD PARK
11 JEFFERSON PARK
12 FOREST GLEN
13 NORTH PARK
14 ALBANY PARK
15 PORTAGE PARK
16 IRVING PARK
17 DUNNING
18 MONTCLARE
19 BELMONT CRAGIN
20 HERMOSA
21 AVONDALE
22 LOGAN SQUARE
23 HUMBOLDT PARK
24 WEST TOWN
25 AUSTIN
26 WEST GARFIELD PK.
27 EAST GARFIELD PK.
28 NEAR WEST SIDE
29 NORTH LAWNDALE
30 SOUTH LAWNDALE
31 LOWER WEST SIDE
32 LOOP
33 NEAR SOUTH SIDE
34 ARMOUR SQUARE
35 DOUGLAS
36 OAKLAND
37 FULLER PARK
38 GRAND BLVD.

39 KENWOOD
40 WASHINGTON PK.
41 HYDE PARK
42 WOODLAWN
43 SOUTH SHORE
44 CHATHAM
45 AVALON PARK
46 SOUTH CHICAGO
47 BURNSIDE
48 CALUMET HEIGHTS
49 ROSELAND
50 PULLMAN
51 SOUTH DEERING
52 EAST SIDE
53 WEST PULLMAN
54 RIVERDALE
55 HEGEWISCH
56 GARFIELD RIDGE
57 ARCHER HEIGHTS
58 BRIGHTON PARK
59 McKINLEY PARK
60 BRIDGEPORT
61 NEW CITY
62 WEST ELSDON
63 GAGE PARK
64 CLEARING
65 WEST LAWN
66 CHICAGO LAWN
67 WEST ENGLEWOOD
68 ENGLEWOOD
69 GREATER GRAND CR.
70 ASHBURN
71 AUBURN GRESHAM
72 BEVERLY
73 WASHINGTON HGTS.
74 MOUNT GREENWOOD
75 MORGAN PARK

INSTITUTE FOR JUVENILE RESEARCH
DIVISION OF URBAN STUDIES

INDEXES OF RATES OF MALE DELINQUENTS BASED ON 12,844 OFFENDERS BROUGHT
BEFORE THE JUVENILE COURT DURING THE YEARS 1962–65.

most communities there was little change in the relative magnitude of the rates. In a few there has been a steady upward
trend in rates of delinquents, and in a few the trend has been
steadily downward. These trends appear to be associated with
significant changes in the social life of the areas. The areas
showing the greatest increase have experienced disruptive
changes brought about by new migration, while areas of greatest
decrease are previously high-rate areas in which institutions

TABLE 98

DISTRIBUTION BY MAGNITUDES OF INDEXES OF RATES OF MALE
DELINQUENTS FOR CHICAGO COMMUNITIES IN EACH OF
FIVE JUVENILE COURT SERIES

INDEXES OF RATES OF DELINQUENTS	SERIES					TOTAL	
	1934–40	1945–51	1954–57	1958–61	1962–65	Mean	Percentage
3.00 and over...	4	2	1	1	1	1.8	2.4
2.50–2.99......	1	3	2	2	5	2.6	3.5
2.00–2.49......	2	3	4	10	6	5.0	6.8
1.50–1.99......	5	6	7	1	4	4.6	6.2
1.00–1.49......	11	12	11	12	12	11.6	15.7
Above mean....	23	26	25	26	28	25.6	34.6
Below mean.....	51	48	49	48	46	48.4	65.4
0.50–0.99......	32	31	34	24	23	28.8	38.9
0–0.49......	19	17	15	24	23	19.6	26.5

have stabilized during the period under study. Changes in the
distribution around the mean of rates of delinquents, stated as
indexes, also have been small, as is indicated in the following
data.

*Summary of Comparative Distribution of Five Sets of Rates
of Delinquents.*—Table 98 summarizes the distribution of each
of the five sets of rates of delinquents around its own mean. The
distributions are surprisingly similar. The great suburban development, significant changes in the composition of the population, and the expansion of industry, *together,* seem not to have
changed very significantly the number of different types of delinquency-producing areas in Chicago. There has been a slight

increase both in the number of areas above the mean—these are areas into which new groups have expanded—and in the number of areas with rates which are less than one-half the mean, perhaps indicating a slight tendency toward polarization of communities in the production of officially recorded delinquency.

RATES OF FEMALE DELINQUENTS AND SCHOOL TRUANTS

The 1945–51 Female Delinquent Series.—Of the young offenders who appeared in Cook County Juvenile Court from Chicago for the first time during the years 1945–51, about one-fourth were girls. These offenders have been taken as a basis for analysis of the distribution of female delinquents, and the calculation of rates of female delinquents for Chicago communities. The total number of female juvenile offenders involved in these calculations is 2,792.

Female juvenile offenders appear to be somewhat more concentrated in a few areas than are male offenders. For example, there were ten or fewer offenders in each of 33 communities, and more than 300 in each of three. The variations are reflected in the rates of female delinquents calculated for each community on the basis of the number of female offenders for each area and the aged 11–17 female population as of 1948.5, estimated on the basis of a straight-line trend between the 1940 and the 1950 censuses. The number of females in this age group was computed to be 139,631. The rate of female offenders computed for the 74 Chicago communities ranges from 0.0 to 10.3. The rate for the city as a whole is 2.0; the grand mean is 1.62; and the median rate is 1.1.

The extreme variation of rates of female offenders among areas in Chicago is reflected in the indexes which have been computed and presented on Map 69. It will be observed that in 54 areas the rates are below the mean and that in six areas the rates are more than 3 times the mean. The *pattern* of distribution, however, differs little from the pattern of distribution of male offenders.

The 1945–51 Male School Truants Series.—During the years 1945–51, 2,662 male individuals were brought before the Cook

MAP 69

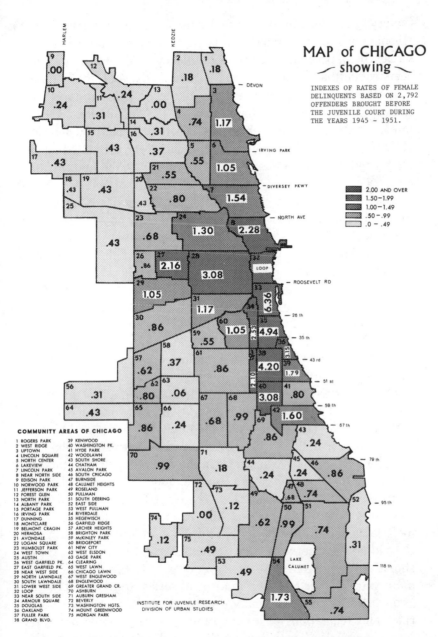

MAP of CHICAGO
~ showing ~

INDEXES OF RATES OF FEMALE
DELINQUENTS BASED ON 2,792
OFFENDERS BROUGHT BEFORE
THE JUVENILE COURT DURING
THE YEARS 1945 - 1951.

▓	2.00 AND OVER
▓	1.50 – 1.99
▓	1.00 – 1.49
▒	.50 – .99
░	.0 – .49

COMMUNITY AREAS OF CHICAGO

1 ROGERS PARK	39 KENWOOD
2 WEST RIDGE	40 WASHINGTON PK.
3 UPTOWN	41 HYDE PARK
4 LINCOLN SQUARE	42 WOODLAWN
5 NORTH CENTER	43 SOUTH SHORE
6 LAKEVIEW	44 CHATHAM
7 LINCOLN PARK	45 AVALON PARK
8 NEAR NORTH SIDE	46 SOUTH CHICAGO
9 EDISON PARK	47 BURNSIDE
10 NORWOOD PARK	48 CALUMET HEIGHTS
11 JEFFERSON PARK	49 ROSELAND
12 FOREST GLEN	50 PULLMAN
13 NORTH PARK	51 SOUTH DEERING
14 ALBANY PARK	52 EAST SIDE
15 PORTAGE PARK	53 WEST PULLMAN
16 IRVING PARK	54 RIVERDALE
17 DUNNING	55 HEGEWISCH
18 MONTCLARE	56 GARFIELD RIDGE
19 BELMONT CRAGIN	57 ARCHER HEIGHTS
20 HERMOSA	58 BRIGHTON PARK
21 AVONDALE	59 McKINLEY PARK
22 LOGAN SQUARE	60 BRIDGEPORT
23 HUMBOLDT PARK	61 NEW CITY
24 WEST TOWN	62 WEST ELSDON
25 AUSTIN	63 GAGE PARK
26 WEST GARFIELD PK.	64 CLEARING
27 EAST GARFIELD PK.	65 WEST LAWN
28 NEAR WEST SIDE	66 CHICAGO LAWN
29 NORTH LAWNDALE	67 WEST ENGLEWOOD
30 SOUTH LAWNDALE	68 ENGLEWOOD
31 LOWER WEST SIDE	69 GREATER GRAND CR.
32 LOOP	70 ASHBURN
33 NEAR SOUTH SIDE	71 AUBURN GRESHAM
34 ARMOUR SQUARE	72 BEVERLY
35 DOUGLAS	73 WASHINGTON HGTS.
36 OAKLAND	74 MOUNT GREENWOOD
37 FULLER PARK	75 MORGAN PARK
38 GRAND BLVD.	

INSTITUTE FOR JUVENILE RESEARCH
DIVISION OF URBAN STUDIES

INDEXES OF RATES OF FEMALE DELINQUENTS BASED ON 2,792 OFFENDERS
BROUGHT BEFORE THE JUVENILE COURT DURING THE YEARS 1945–51.

County Juvenile Court on petitions alleging truancy from school. Some of these truants may have appeared in court subsequently on petitions alleging delinquency, and some may have been committed to institutions subsequently, but these data show the distribution at the time of the first appearance for truancy. The population base used in the calculation of the rates was the same as the base used in the calculation of rates of delinquents for the same period, namely, the estimated aged 10–16 male population as of 1948.5 (140,842), the midyear of the series.

The range of rates, by communities, in this series is from 0.0 to 6.9. The median rate is 0.9; the rate for the city is 1.9; and the mean of the rates is 1.50. These rates, translated into indexes, are presented on Map 70. The range of the indexes of the rates of school truants is from 0.0 to 4.6. Clearly the variation among city areas is very great. In 12 of the areas the rates are more than twice the magnitude of the grand mean. In the delinquency series for the same period the indexes of only 8 areas were greater than twice the grand mean. This suggests that the concentration of truants into a few areas is even greater than the concentration of delinquents.

Discussion.—The rates of delinquents presented in this volume are based on a complete enumeration of the offenders dealt with under the law from each community in given periods of time. In addition, these rates can be used as indexes of the relative amount of violative behavior in the different communities of the city. All offenders have not been included in the calculation of these rates. Those who have challenged the values of the community vigorously, and at the wrong time and place, are included as official court cases, and those who have challenged the values so vigorously that it has been adjudged that they should be removed from participation in the life of the community are included in the commitment series. But beyond these two categories there are many degrees of nonconformity to the rules and regulations of a community. Some juvenile nonconformists are dealt with by police, school principals, park directors, and others in positions of authority, and other young

MAP 70

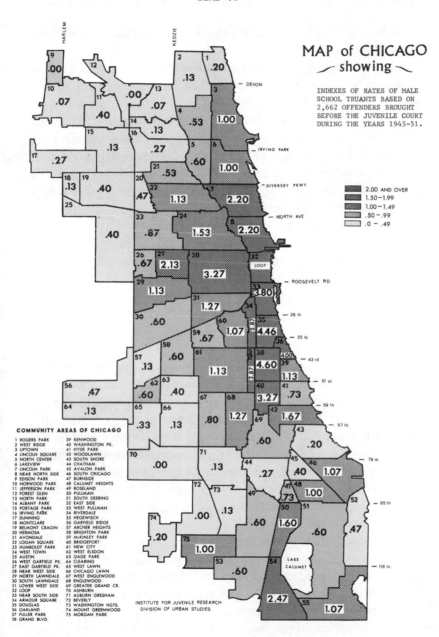

INDEXES OF RATES OF MALE SCHOOL TRUANTS BASED ON 2,662 OFFENDERS BROUGHT BEFORE THE JUVENILE COURT DURING THE YEARS 1945–51.

people engaging in violative behavior are not apprehended or even identified.

From this perspective a rate of delinquents of 4.0 in an area suggests not only that the rate is twice as great as the rate in an area where the rate is 2.0 but also that there is approximately twice as much violative behavior ranging from the telling of falsehoods to assault with a deadly weapon. This emphasizes the fact that the magnitude of the rate of delinquents is important only in relation to the rate of delinquents in other areas. It should be evident that rates based on different types of data serve essentially the same purpose if the sample is adequate to establish their validity.

As a practical question, however, it may be important to know just what segment of the population is involved in what kinds of institutions. Some of the data which follow help to answer this question as well as to furnish answers about the stability of these data.

RATES OF COMMITMENTS FOR CHICAGO COMMUNITIES

The 1945–51 Male Commitment Series.—Another index of variation in rates of delinquents among areas in Chicago is based on commitments to correctional institutions. These rates are based very largely on that proportion of the juvenile court population which recidivated, perhaps several times, and finally was committed. In this instance commitments represent about 28 per cent of the 8,041 offenders who appeared in court for the first time during the 7-year period 1945–51. These committed cases are the young offenders who continued to challenge the values of the community until the judge decided that they should be removed from the community and given custodial care.

The series is based on 2,239 committed male offenders. The extreme concentration of committed juveniles is indicated by the fact that 37 per cent of the total number of commitments from the 74 areas in Chicago came from only three areas. By way of contrast, there were no commitments from five communities.

The rates of commitments in communities are based on the

aged 10-16 male population as of 1948.5, computed for the 1945–51 series of juvenile delinquents. The rate of commitment for the city is 1.59,[1] the median rate is 0.73, and the mean of the area rates is 1.23. The range of the rate index is from 0.0 to 6.70. The extreme variation in the rates of commitment by communities is suggested by the fact that in six areas the rates are more than 3 times the mean rate, and at the other extreme the rates in 32 areas are less than 0.50. These rates are presented on Map 71.

The 1958–62 Male Commitment Series.—The second set of rates of male commitments by communities is based on the count of committed individuals by areas as released by the Illinois Youth Commission. Included are the 5,294 males committed to correctional institutions from the 74 areas in Chicago during the 5-year period 1958-62. The population base is the same as that used in calculating rates of delinquents in the aged 12–16 male population as of 1960. The rates, as in all the other calculations, represent the number of committed individuals per one hundred population in the aged 12–16 male population.

The range of rates of commitments in the 74 areas in Chicago is from 0.19 to 13.79. The median rate is 2.60; the rate for the city is 4.28; and the mean of the rates is 3.80. When these rates are translated into indexes the range is from 0.05 to 3.63. The distribution in the city is presented on Map 72. It should be remembered that in the indexes for all the different kinds of data the mean for the series is 1.0. In this series the rates in 48 of the areas fall below the mean, and in 26 areas the rates are above the mean. In six of these 26 areas the index reveals that the rates are more than 3 times the mean of all the rates.

The 1963–66 Male Commitment Series.—Rates of male commitments were calculated from the reports of the number of male offenders sent to the State Training Schools by the Youth Commission during the 4-year period 1963–66 and the esti-

---

[1] Rates of commitments are presented as percentages, or number per hundred, just as are the rates of delinquents. However, because in many instances the number of commitments from an area is small, the opportunity for comparison among areas has been increased by extending the computation two places to the right of the decimal point.

MAP 71

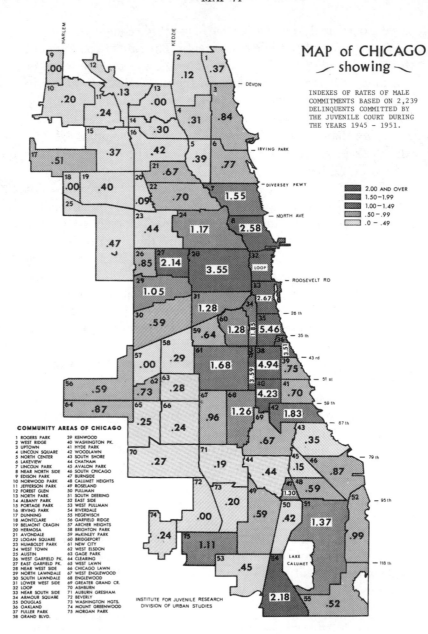

MAP of CHICAGO
~ showing ~

INDEXES OF RATES OF MALE
COMMITMENTS BASED ON 2,239
DELINQUENTS COMMITTED BY
THE JUVENILE COURT DURING
THE YEARS 1945 – 1951.

2.00 AND OVER
1.50–1.99
1.00–1.49
.50–.99
.0 – .49

COMMUNITY AREAS OF CHICAGO

1 ROGERS PARK	39 KENWOOD
2 WEST RIDGE	40 WASHINGTON PK.
3 UPTOWN	41 HYDE PARK
4 LINCOLN SQUARE	42 WOODLAWN
5 NORTH CENTER	43 SOUTH SHORE
6 LAKEVIEW	44 CHATHAM
7 LINCOLN PARK	45 AVALON PARK
8 NEAR NORTH SIDE	46 SOUTH CHICAGO
9 EDISON PARK	47 BURNSIDE
10 NORWOOD PARK	48 CALUMET HEIGHTS
11 JEFFERSON PARK	49 ROSELAND
12 FOREST GLEN	50 PULLMAN
13 NORTH PARK	51 SOUTH DEERING
14 ALBANY PARK	52 EAST SIDE
15 PORTAGE PARK	53 WEST PULLMAN
16 IRVING PARK	54 RIVERDALE
17 DUNNING	55 HEGEWISCH
18 MONTCLARE	56 GARFIELD RIDGE
19 BELMONT CRAGIN	57 ARCHER HEIGHTS
20 HERMOSA	58 BRIGHTON PARK
21 AVONDALE	59 McKINLEY PARK
22 LOGAN SQUARE	60 BRIDGEPORT
23 HUMBOLDT PARK	61 NEW CITY
24 WEST TOWN	62 WEST ELSDON
25 AUSTIN	63 GAGE PARK
26 WEST GARFIELD PK.	64 CLEARING
27 EAST GARFIELD PK.	65 WEST LAWN
28 NEAR WEST SIDE	66 CHICAGO LAWN
29 NORTH LAWNDALE	67 WEST ENGLEWOOD
30 SOUTH LAWNDALE	68 ENGLEWOOD
31 LOWER WEST SIDE	69 GREATER GRAND CR.
32 LOOP	70 ASHBURN
33 NEAR SOUTH SIDE	71 AUBURN GRESHAM
34 ARMOUR SQUARE	72 BEVERLY
35 DOUGLAS	73 WASHINGTON HGTS.
36 OAKLAND	74 MOUNT GREENWOOD
37 FULLER PARK	75 MORGAN PARK
38 GRAND BLVD.	

INSTITUTE FOR JUVENILE RESEARCH
DIVISION OF URBAN STUDIES

INDEXES OF RATES OF MALE COMMITMENTS BASED ON 2,239 DELINQUENTS
COMMITTED BY THE JUVENILE COURT DURING THE YEARS 1945–51.

MAP 72

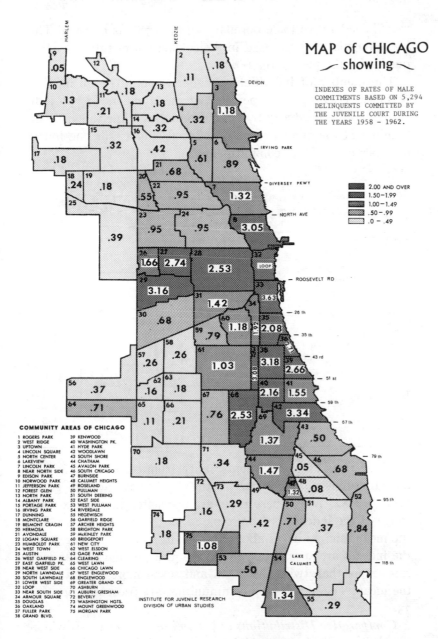

MAP of CHICAGO
~ showing ~

INDEXES OF RATES OF MALE
COMMITMENTS BASED ON 5,294
DELINQUENTS COMMITTED BY
THE JUVENILE COURT DURING
THE YEARS 1958 – 1962.

2.00 AND OVER
1.50–1.99
1.00–1.49
.50–.99
.0 – .49

COMMUNITY AREAS OF CHICAGO

1 ROGERS PARK
2 WEST RIDGE
3 UPTOWN
4 LINCOLN SQUARE
5 NORTH CENTER
6 LAKEVIEW
7 LINCOLN PARK
8 NEAR NORTH SIDE
9 EDISON PARK
10 NORWOOD PARK
11 JEFFERSON PARK
12 FOREST GLEN
13 NORTH PARK
14 ALBANY PARK
15 PORTAGE PARK
16 IRVING PARK
17 DUNNING
18 MONTCLARE
19 BELMONT CRAGIN
20 HERMOSA
21 AVONDALE
22 LOGAN SQUARE
23 HUMBOLDT PARK
24 WEST TOWN
25 AUSTIN
26 WEST GARFIELD PK.
27 EAST GARFIELD PK.
28 NEAR WEST SIDE
29 NORTH LAWNDALE
30 SOUTH LAWNDALE
31 LOWER WEST SIDE
32 LOOP
33 NEAR SOUTH SIDE
34 ARMOUR SQUARE
35 DOUGLAS
36 OAKLAND
37 FULLER PARK
38 GRAND BLVD.

39 KENWOOD
40 WASHINGTON PK.
41 HYDE PARK
42 WOODLAWN
43 SOUTH SHORE
44 CHATHAM
45 AVALON PARK
46 SOUTH CHICAGO
47 BURNSIDE
48 CALUMET HEIGHTS
49 ROSELAND
50 PULLMAN
51 SOUTH DEERING
52 EAST SIDE
53 WEST PULLMAN
54 RIVERDALE
55 HEGEWISCH
56 GARFIELD RIDGE
57 ARCHER HEIGHTS
58 BRIGHTON PARK
59 McKINLEY PARK
60 BRIDGEPORT
61 NEW CITY
62 WEST ELSDON
63 GAGE PARK
64 CLEARING
65 WEST LAWN
66 CHICAGO LAWN
67 WEST ENGLEWOOD
68 ENGLEWOOD
69 GREATER GRAND CR.
70 ASHBURN
71 AUBURN GRESHAM
72 BEVERLY
73 WASHINGTON HGTS.
74 MOUNT GREENWOOD
75 MORGAN PARK

INSTITUTE FOR JUVENILE RESEARCH
DIVISION OF URBAN STUDIES

INDEXES OF RATES OF MALE COMMITMENTS BASED ON 5,294 DELINQUENTS COM-
MITTED BY THE JUVENILE COURT DURING THE YEARS 1958–62.

mated aged 12–16 male population (132,678) as of 1964. This is the population base used in the calculation of rates of delinquents for the period 1962–65.

The number of individual offenders committed during this period was 4,256. Forty per cent of the offenders (1,720 individuals) were produced by six communities while the six communities at the other extreme produced only 11, or one-fourth of 1 per cent of the commitments.

TABLE 99

DISTRIBUTION BY MAGNITUDES OF INDEXES OF RATES OF MALE
COMMITMENTS FOR CHICAGO COMMUNITIES IN EACH
OF THREE COMMITMENT SERIES

INDEXES OF RATES OF COMMITMENT	SERIES			TOTAL	
	1945–51	1958–62	1963–66	Mean	Percentage
3.00 and over.............	6	6	7	6.3	8.6
2.50–2.99.................	2	5	1	2.7	3.6
2.00–2.49.................	2	2	4	2.7	3.6
1.50–1.99.................	4	3	3	3.3	4.5
1.00–1.49.................	8	10	8	8.7	11.7
Above mean...............	22	26	23	23.7	32.0
Below mean...............	52	48	51	40.3	68.0
0.50–0.99.................	20	16	18	18.0	24.3
0–0.49.................	32	32	33	32.3	43.7

These rates of commitments range from 0.09 to 14.18. The median rate is 1.75; the rate for the city is 3.21; and the grand mean is 2.82. When these rates are translated into indexes the range of the indexes is from 0.03 to 5.03, with 51 areas below the mean, and 23 areas above the mean. As in the other series the indexes are spread out above the mean with 12 areas with rates more than twice the mean and seven more than 3 times the mean. The indexes, by communities, are presented on Map 73.

Comparative Distributions of Commitment Series.—It will be noted from Table 99, which summarizes the distribution of indexes by class of areas in these three series of commitments

MAP 73

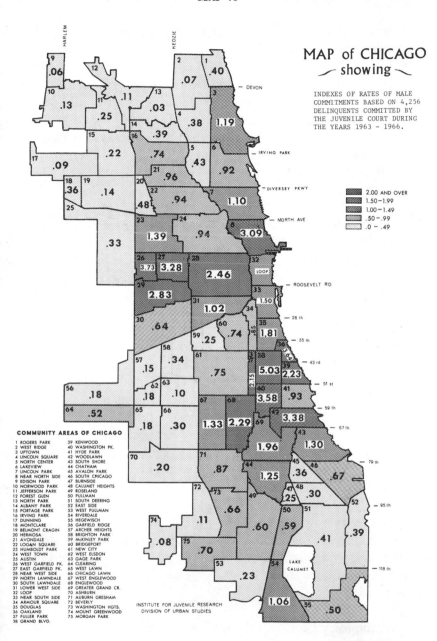

MAP of CHICAGO
~ showing ~

INDEXES OF RATES OF MALE
COMMITMENTS BASED ON 4,256
DELINQUENTS COMMITTED BY
THE JUVENILE COURT DURING
THE YEARS 1963 - 1966.

2.00 AND OVER
1.50 – 1.99
1.00 – 1.49
.50 – .99
.0 – .49

COMMUNITY AREAS OF CHICAGO

1 ROGERS PARK
2 WEST RIDGE
3 UPTOWN
4 LINCOLN SQUARE
5 NORTH CENTER
6 LAKEVIEW
7 LINCOLN PARK
8 NEAR NORTH SIDE
9 EDISON PARK
10 NORWOOD PARK
11 JEFFERSON PARK
12 FOREST GLEN
13 NORTH PARK
14 ALBANY PARK
15 PORTAGE PARK
16 IRVING PARK
17 DUNNING
18 MONTCLARE
19 BELMONT CRAGIN
20 HERMOSA
21 AVONDALE
22 LOGAN SQUARE
23 HUMBOLDT PARK
24 WEST TOWN
25 AUSTIN
26 WEST GARFIELD PK.
27 EAST GARFIELD PK.
28 NEAR WEST SIDE
29 NORTH LAWNDALE
30 SOUTH LAWNDALE
31 LOWER WEST SIDE
32 LOOP
33 NEAR SOUTH SIDE
34 ARMOUR SQUARE
35 DOUGLAS
36 OAKLAND
37 FULLER PARK
38 GRAND BLVD.

39 KENWOOD
40 WASHINGTON PK.
41 HYDE PARK
42 WOODLAWN
43 SOUTH SHORE
44 CHATHAM
45 AVALON PARK
46 SOUTH CHICAGO
47 BURNSIDE
48 CALUMET HEIGHTS
49 ROSELAND
50 PULLMAN
51 SOUTH DEERING
52 EAST SIDE
53 WEST PULLMAN
54 RIVERDALE
55 HEGEWISCH
56 GARFIELD RIDGE
57 ARCHER HEIGHTS
58 BRIGHTON PARK
59 McKINLEY PARK
60 BRIDGEPORT
61 NEW CITY
62 WEST ELSDON
63 GAGE PARK
64 CLEARING
65 WEST LAWN
66 CHICAGO LAWN
67 WEST ENGLEWOOD
68 ENGLEWOOD
69 GREATER GRAND CR.
70 ASHBURN
71 AUBURN GRESHAM
72 BEVERLY
73 WASHINGTON HGTS.
74 MOUNT GREENWOOD
75 MORGAN PARK

INSTITUTE FOR JUVENILE RESEARCH
DIVISION OF URBAN STUDIES

INDEXES OF RATES OF MALE COMMITMENTS BASED ON 4,256 DELINQUENTS
COMMITTED BY THE JUVENILE COURT DURING THE YEARS 1963–66.

from Chicago communities, that these distributions closely re-semble one another and differ in some ways from the indexes of rates of delinquents. These differences are most distinct at the extreme. On the average, 8.6 per cent of the areas are character-ized by rates more than 3 times the mean, and at the other extreme an average of 43.7 per cent of the areas have rates less than one-half the mean. This concentration of areas at the lower end of the range is partly the result of the fact that there is less recidivism in these low-rate areas, and it is usually recidivists who are committed.

The 1958–66 Female Commitment Series.—Rates of female commitments by communities, based on the records of 2,118 individual offenders, as published by the Illinois Youth Com-mission for the years 1958–66, also were computed for the 74 Chicago communities. The population used was the estimated aged 13–17 female population in each area as of 1962, the mid-point of the series. These rates are stated as the number of juve-nile female offenders committed to correctional institutions from each 100 females in this age group in the population. The population was estimated to be 125,318.

For the city as a whole the rate of female commitments is 1.69, the mean of the rates is 1.55, and the median rate is 0.59. The range of the rates in the 74 communities is from 0.0 to 6.56. These rates, translated into indexes ranging from 0.0 to 4.23, are presented on Map 74. It is readily observable from this map that the variations in rates of female commitments are greater than the variations computed from other data. Of the 74 areas, 53 (72 per cent) of the indexes are below the mean, and in 42 areas the indexes are less than one-half of the mean. At the other extreme, 18, or nearly one-quarter of the areas, are characterized by indexes of more than twice the magnitude of the mean.

CONCLUSION

Delinquency among girls in large cities is quite different from delinquency among boys. The offenses for which girls are brought to court are largely sex offenses, although the official

MAP 74

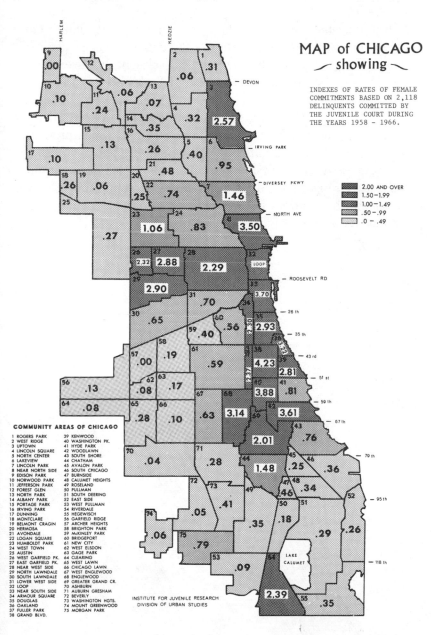

MAP of CHICAGO
~ showing ~

INDEXES OF RATES OF FEMALE
COMMITMENTS BASED ON 2,118
DELINQUENTS COMMITTED BY
THE JUVENILE COURT DURING
THE YEARS 1958 - 1966.

2.00 AND OVER
1.50—1.99
1.00—1.49
.50 —.99
.0 —.49

COMMUNITY AREAS OF CHICAGO

1 ROGERS PARK	39 KENWOOD
2 WEST RIDGE	40 WASHINGTON PK.
3 UPTOWN	41 HYDE PARK
4 LINCOLN SQUARE	42 WOODLAWN
5 NORTH CENTER	43 SOUTH SHORE
6 LAKEVIEW	44 CHATHAM
7 LINCOLN PARK	45 AVALON PARK
8 NEAR NORTH SIDE	46 SOUTH CHICAGO
9 EDISON PARK	47 BURNSIDE
10 NORWOOD PARK	48 CALUMET HEIGHTS
11 JEFFERSON PARK	49 ROSELAND
12 FOREST GLEN	50 PULLMAN
13 NORTH PARK	51 SOUTH DEERING
14 ALBANY PARK	52 EAST SIDE
15 PORTAGE PARK	53 WEST PULLMAN
16 IRVING PARK	54 RIVERDALE
17 DUNNING	55 HEGEWISCH
18 MONTCLARE	56 GARFIELD RIDGE
19 BELMONT CRAGIN	57 ARCHER HEIGHTS
20 HERMOSA	58 BRIGHTON PARK
21 AVONDALE	59 McKINLEY PARK
22 LOGAN SQUARE	60 BRIDGEPORT
23 HUMBOLDT PARK	61 NEW CITY
24 WEST TOWN	62 WEST ELSDON
25 AUSTIN	63 GAGE PARK
26 WEST GARFIELD PK.	64 CLEARING
27 EAST GARFIELD PK.	65 WEST LAWN
28 NEAR WEST SIDE	66 CHICAGO LAWN
29 NORTH LAWNDALE	67 WEST ENGLEWOOD
30 SOUTH LAWNDALE	68 ENGLEWOOD
31 LOWER WEST SIDE	69 GREATER GRAND CR.
32 LOOP	70 ASHBURN
33 NEAR SOUTH SIDE	71 AUBURN GRESHAM
34 ARMOUR SQUARE	72 BEVERLY
35 DOUGLAS	73 WASHINGTON HGTS.
36 OAKLAND	74 MOUNT GREENWOOD
37 FULLER PARK	75 MORGAN PARK
38 GRAND BLVD.	

INSTITUTE FOR JUVENILE RESEARCH
DIVISION OF URBAN STUDIES

INDEXES OF RATES OF FEMALE COMMITMENTS BASED ON 2,118 DELINQUENTS
COMMITTED BY THE JUVENILE COURT DURING THE YEARS 1958–66.

charge may be "away from home" or "out late at night." On the other hand larceny is the most common charge against males. Comparison of the maps reveals clearly, however, that the communities where the rates for females are highest also are the areas where the rates of male offenders are concentrated.

These commitment data suggest that the more restricted the index the more sharply it differentiates the areas which produce or are most likely to produce serious offenders. This is in keeping with early chapters in this volume in which the point is made that rates of recidivism and rates of commitment vary directly with variations in the magnitude of rates of delinquents among city areas.

CHAPTER XV

RATES OF DELINQUENTS AND COMMITMENTS FOR CHICAGO SUBURBS: DISTRIBUTION AND TRENDS

THE foregoing 11 sets of rates of offenders for Chicago communities, added to the findings set forth in the original publication, provide a basis for the study of change in Chicago over a period of about 65 years. No similar study of change can be made for the suburbs, but 7 sets of rates of delinquents for Chicago suburbs do furnish a basis for the comparison of rates of delinquents among these suburbs, and to a lesser extent of changes over time. Analyses of rates of delinquents for Chicago communities and for the suburbs have been dealt with separately. For a variety of reasons, these data do not furnish a basis for valid comparisons between rates in city communities and those in the suburbs.

RATES OF DELINQUENTS FOR TWENTY-ONE CHICAGO SUBURBS

Rates of delinquents for suburbs of Chicago were not included in this volume when it was first published. Since that time, most of the increase in population in Cook County has taken place in the suburbs. In 1940 the population outside of Chicago was about two-thirds of a million; by 1960 this number had increased to about 1.58 million, or 2.25 times the 1940 population. By 1960 Cook County included, in addition to Chicago, 15 cities with a population of 25,000 or over, and 32 additional cities with a population of 10,000 or over.

Since all of these cities share the Cook County Juvenile Court it was decided to use court data to compute relative magnitudes of rates of delinquents for each of these suburban cities. In this comparison, therefore, differences within cities are ignored, although wide differences are recognized here just as in the City of Chicago. In each community the rate is quite likely an average of wide variations in rates among the neighborhoods which make up the community.

Furthermore, it is quite possible that rates of delinquents based on official appearances in court bear a somewhat different relationship to the total amount of violative behavior among juveniles in the suburbs than is the case in Chicago. In Chicago, working arrangements between the Youth Division and other units of the Chicago Police Department have been worked out and stabilized over a long period of time. Since it is quite unlikely that these arrangements have been duplicated in the suburbs, it is probable that Chicago and suburban rates are not comparable. For this reason rates of delinquents for cities outside of Chicago are compared only with other cities outside of Chicago. Even this should be done cautiously because of possible differences in policy among suburban cities, and changes in policy within each city over time.

The 1945–51 Juvenile Court Male Delinquent Series.—Rates of male delinquents for 21 suburban cities in Cook County with a total population of 10,000 or more in 1950 were computed on the basis of the 362 young offenders from these areas brought before the Juvenile Court of Cook County on petitions alleging delinquency during the 7-year period 1945–51. The population base, the male population 10–16 years of age, was estimated for 1948.5 (the midyear of the series) on the basis of a straight-line trend between the population in this age group in 1940 and the number in the comparable age group in 1950. This number was estimated to be 22,118. The rates represent the number dealt with as official delinquents per hundred males 10–16 years of age.

The rates of male delinquents in these suburban cities range from 0.4 to 3.3. The mean of the rates, or grand mean, is 1.34. When these rates are translated into indexes by dividing each rate by the grand mean the range is from 0.30 to 2.47. These indexes showing the relative magnitude of rates of delinquents are presented for the 21 cities on Map 75.

MAP 75

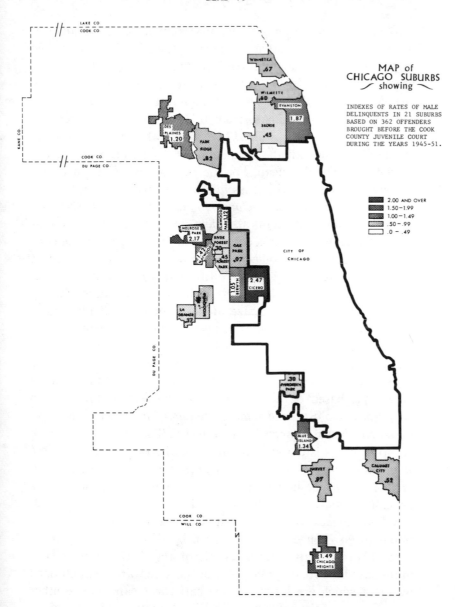

INDEXES OF RATES OF MALE DELINQUENTS IN 21 SUBURBS BASED ON 362 OF-
FENDERS BROUGHT BEFORE THE COOK COUNTY JUVENILE COURT DURING THE YEARS
1945-51.

While the proportion of young males involved in delinquency which resulted in official appearance in the juvenile court is low in the suburban communities, the variation in rates among areas, as revealed by the indexes, is similar to that within the city. Missing are the areas of very high rates which characterize the central city, but apart from this difference the spread in rates is roughly comparable. For example, the rates in six areas are less than one-half the mean, and the rates in three areas are more than twice the mean. For the 21 cities the rates in 12 are below the mean, and the rates in nine are above the mean.

The 1945–51 Juvenile Court Female-Delinquent Series.— Rates of female delinquents also have been computed for these 21 cities. The sample is small, consisting of only 124 female offenders. Presumably this tabulation is complete, because until recent years the Cook County Juvenile Court was not widely used by suburban communities in dealing with female offenders. For the purpose of this study the size of the sample is not important, since it is the relative magnitude and not the absolute magnitude of the rates which is emphasized.

Rates of female delinquents were computed for these 21 cities on the basis of an estimated female population aged 11–17 years of 21,871, based on a trend line for this age group between 1940 and 1950. Rates of female offenders for the 21 cities computed on this basis range from 0.0 to 1.6. The rate for the entire group of cities is 0.6 and the mean of the rates is 0.47. There were no official offenders from five of these 21 cities, and 67, or more than one-half of the total number of offenders, were brought to court from only three cities.

When indexes were computed for these rates the range was found to be from 0.0 to 3.39, when by definition the mean is 1.00. The distinctive characteristic of the distribution is seen in the fact that 10, or 43 per cent of the areas, are characterized by rates which are less than one-half the mean. At the other extreme two of the areas with the highest indexes also are areas with the highest rates of male offenders. The indexes, representing these rates, are presented on Map 76.

MAP 76

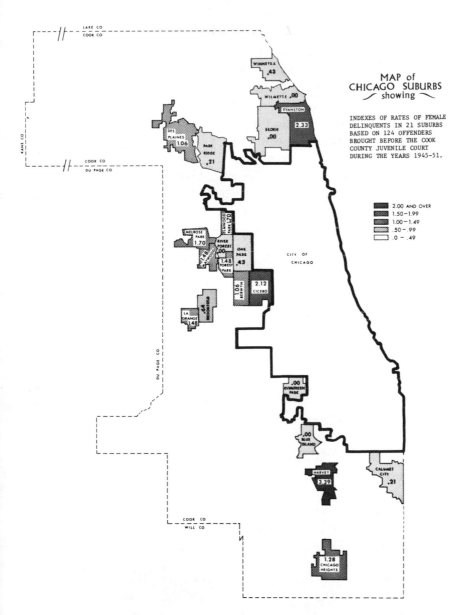

INDEXES OF RATES OF FEMALE DELINQUENTS IN 21 SUBURBS BASED ON 124
OFFENDERS BROUGHT BEFORE THE COOK COUNTY JUVENILE COURT DURING THE
YEARS 1945–51.

The 1954–57 Juvenile Court Series.—Federal census reports indicate that in 1960 there were 47 cities in Cook County, Illinois, each with a population of more than 10,000 persons. Rates of male delinquents based on data from the Cook County Juvenile Court will be presented for three 4-year periods, covering the years 1954–65. The first series covers the years 1954–57.

According to the records at our disposal 964 different male offenders from these 47 cities were brought to the Cook County Juvenile Court for official action during the years 1954–57. During this 4-year period more than 60 male offenders were taken to court from three different suburban cities, 40 to 59 from three others, and between 20 and 39 from 10 other areas.

Data were translated into rates of delinquents using the estimated number of males 12–16 years of age (35,030) as of the year 1947.5. The rates range from 0.0, in one of the 47 cities, to 6.4. The rate for the cities as a group is 2.8, the grand mean is 2.41, and the median is 2.3. When these rates are translated into indexes so that they can be compared with other series, the range is from 0.0 to 2.66 with 22 areas above the mean and 25 areas below. Of the 47 areas the indexes reveal that the rates in five areas are more than twice the mean. These indexes are presented on Map 77.

The view that suburbs differ less among themselves than do communities within Chicago is supported by the clustering of the areas around the mean, and by the fact that in these three delinquency series no index is more than 3 times the mean. Part of the reason for this lies in the fact that the suburbs, by definition, are part of a metropolitan complex which has only one inner-city area around which areas of very high rates are concentrated.

The 1958–61 Juvenile Court Series.—In the years 1958–61, 1,414 male delinquents were brought before the Cook County Juvenile Court on petitions alleging delinquency from these 47 suburban cities. The number of official delinquents sent to court from the different suburbs ranged from 1 to 121, with an av-

MAP 77

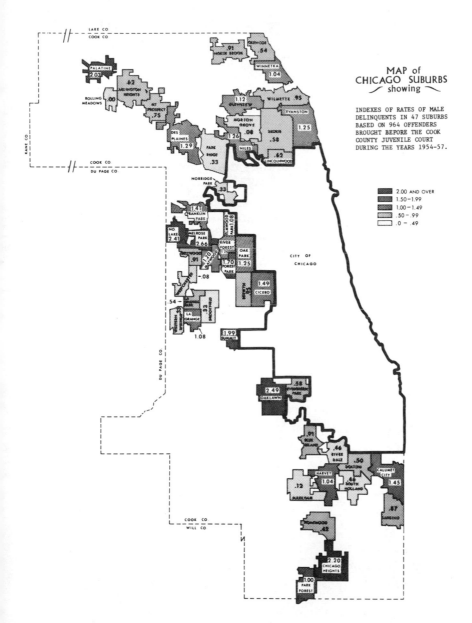

MAP of
CHICAGO SUBURBS
~ showing ~

INDEXES OF RATES OF MALE
DELINQUENTS IN 47 SUBURBS
BASED ON 964 OFFENDERS
BROUGHT BEFORE THE COOK
COUNTY JUVENILE COURT
DURING THE YEARS 1954-57.

2.00 AND OVER
1.50-1.99
1.00-1.49
.50 - .99
.0 - .49

Indexes of Rates of Male Delinquents in 47 Suburbs Based on 964 Offenders Brought before the Cook County Juvenile Court during the Years 1954–57.

erage of 30 per city over the 4-year period. The actual distribution, however, showed great concentration in a few areas.
More than 70 official delinquents came from each of eight cities,
while nine produced fewer than 10 each.

Rates of male delinquents for these cities were calculated
using the aged 12–16 male population as set forth in the 1960
U.S. census. This population was computed to be 45,811. The
rates were found to range from 0.2 to 7.4. The median rate is
2.41, the grand mean of the rates is 2.86, and the mean for the
suburbs as a whole is 3.1. When these rates are translated into
indexes the range is from .07 to 7.4. These indexes are presented
on Map 78. The distribution of areas by classes of indexes reveals little change from the previous series. In both of these
series the rates in five areas are more than 2 times the mean,
and in three instances the same areas are involved.

The 1962–65 Juvenile Court Series.—During the years 1962–
65 a total of 1,457 juvenile male offenders were brought before
the court from these 47 suburban cities. The estimated base
population for the midyear of the period was 54,023. The range
of rates computed from these data is from 0.6 to 6.1. The median
rate is 2.5; the rates for the suburbs as a whole and the grand
mean are the same, 2.70. When these rates are translated into
indexes the pattern is quite similar to the pattern in previous
series, with somewhat less deviation from the mean. The range
in the indexes is from 0.22 to 2.26. Thirty-three areas fall between 0.50 and 1.50, with rates in four areas more than twice
the mean rate. These indexes are presented on Map 79.

The findings in these three suburban series can be summarized in two propositions: first, for the most part, the indexes
reveal that the relative position of most of the suburbs changed
little over this 12-year period, and, second, when there was a
sharp trend in the indexes of rates of delinquents in certain
suburbs it appeared to be associated with large population
movements as revealed by the census, or with major industrial
developments.

The distribution, by class of area, for these three sets of rates
of delinquents for 47 suburbs is presented in Table 100. Two

MAP 78

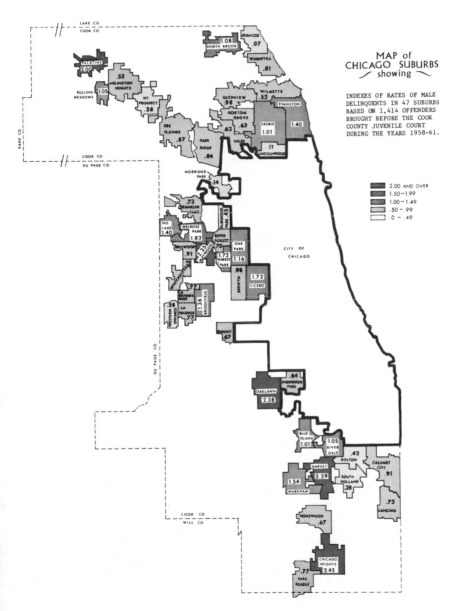

MAP of
CHICAGO SUBURBS
showing

INDEXES OF RATES OF MALE
DELINQUENTS IN 47 SUBURBS
BASED ON 1,414 OFFENDERS
BROUGHT BEFORE THE COOK
COUNTY JUVENILE COURT
DURING THE YEARS 1958-61.

2.00 AND OVER
1.50 - 1.99
1.00 - 1.49
.50 - .99
.0 - .49

INDEXES OF RATES OF MALE DELINQUENTS IN 47 SUBURBS BASED ON 1,414 OF-
FENDERS BROUGHT BEFORE THE COOK COUNTY JUVENILE COURT DURING THE
YEARS 1958-61.

MAP 79

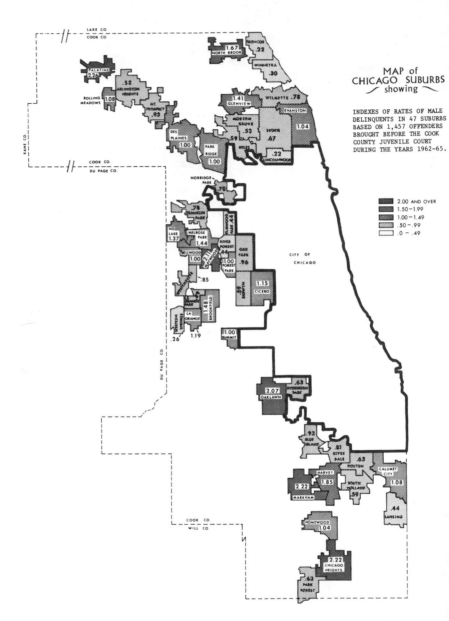

INDEXES OF RATES OF MALE DELINQUENTS IN 47 SUBURBS BASED ON 1,457 OF-
FENDERS BROUGHT BEFORE THE COOK COUNTY JUVENILE COURT DURING THE
YEARS 1962–65.

points are noteworthy. The first is that the distributions for the three are quite similar; the other is that the rates in proportionately fewer areas deviate widely from the mean than do the rates for Chicago communities. It will be noted that two-thirds of the rates fall within the range 0.50 and 1.50.

TABLE 100

DISTRIBUTION BY MAGNITUDE OF INDEXES OF RATES OF MALE
DELINQUENTS FOR 47 SUBURBS IN EACH OF THREE
JUVENILE COURT SERIES

INDEXES OF RATES OF COMMITMENTS	SERIES			TOTAL	
	1954–57	1958–61	1962–65	Mean	Percentage
2.50 and over.............	1	1	0	0.67	1.4
2.00–2.49...............	4	4	5	4.33	9.2
1.50–1.99...............	2	4	2	2.67	5.7
1.00–1.49...............	15	9	15	13.00	27.7
Above mean..............	22	18	22	20.67	44.0
Below mean..............	25	29	25	26.33	56.0
0.50–0.99...............	15	21	18	18.00	38.3
0–0.49...............	10	8	7	8.33	17.7

RATES OF COMMITMENTS FOR FORTY-SEVEN SUBURBAN CITIES

The 1958–66 Juvenile Court Male-Commitment Series.— Rates of male and female commitments to the State Training Schools for the years 1958–66 have been computed for these same 47 cities on the basis of data made available by the Illinois Youth Commission. The population base for the male series was computed from the male population in 1960 which would be expected to constitute the 12–16 age grouping in 1962. Projection of a straight-line trend between 1950 and 1960 proved not to be applicable to the suburbs, where the rate of growth over time is quite uneven. Instead, 80 per cent of the difference between the aged 12–16 population in the census and the population which would be in the age group 12–16 in 1960, added to the 1960 population, was taken as the base. The estimated population, as of 1962, is 49,915.

The number of male individuals committed to the Illinois Youth Commission from these 47 suburbs from 1958 to 1966 was 651. These committed individuals are even less evenly distributed over the suburbs than are commitments among Chicago communities. There were two or fewer cases in seven communities, and more than 40 cases in four communities. When these data are translated into rates of commitments the range is from 0.0 to 4.60. The rate for all 47 cities is 1.30, with a median of 0.88, and a mean of 1.26. When the rates are translated into indexes the range is from 0.0 to 3.67. The concentration of delinquents in a few areas is indicated by the fact that the rate in 32 communities is below the mean while in three areas the rates are more than 3 times the mean. These indexes are presented on Map 80.

The 1958–66 Juvenile Court Female-Commitment Series.— Rates of commitments for females have been calculated for the 15 cities outside of Chicago with a total population of more than 25,000 population in 1960. The estimated female population 13–17 years of age in these cities in 1962 was 24,269. There were no commitments to the Illinois Training School for Girls from two of these areas, and in the 9-year period 1958–66 the total number of commitments from the 15 cities was 87. Of this number 55, or 63 per cent, were committed from three cities.

Rates of female commitments, computed on the basis of the estimated aged 13–17 female population in each community in 1962, ranged from 0.0, in two areas, to 1.37. The median rate is 0.18, the rate for these 15 cities taken as a unit is 0.36, and the mean of the rates (the grand mean) is 0.38. Only about seven out of each 2,000 girls in these cities were committed to the training school during this 9-year period. When these rates are translated into indexes the range is from 0.0 to 3.62. These indexes are presented on Map 81. This map reveals that the rates in ten of these 15 suburbs are below the grand mean, while at the other extreme the rates in three areas are more than twice the grand mean.

MAP 80

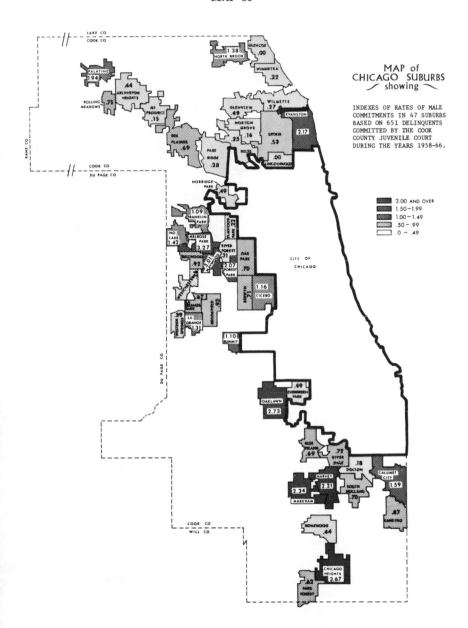

MAP of
CHICAGO SUBURBS
showing

INDEXES OF RATES OF MALE
COMMITMENTS IN 47 SUBURBS
BASED ON 651 DELINQUENTS
COMMITTED BY THE COOK
COUNTY JUVENILE COURT
DURING THE YEARS 1958-66.

2.00 AND OVER
1.50—1.99
1.00—1.49
.50—.99
.0 — .49

INDEXES OF RATES OF MALE COMMITMENTS IN 47 SUBURBS BASED ON 651 DE-
LINQUENTS COMMITTED BY THE COOK COUNTY JUVENILE COURT DURING THE
YEARS 1958–66.

MAP 81

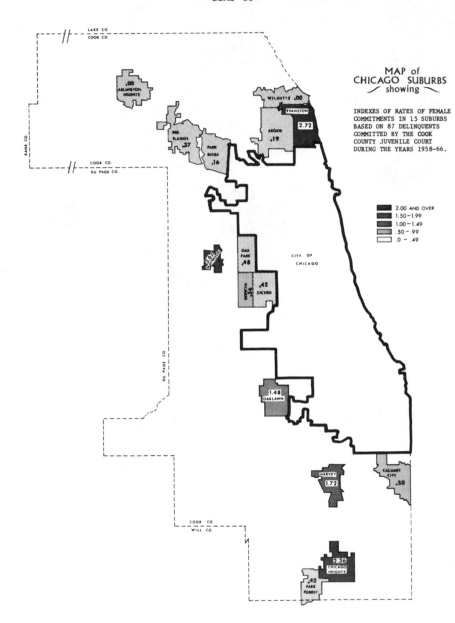

INDEXES OF RATES OF FEMALE COMMITMENTS IN 15 SUBURBS BASED ON 87 DE-
LINQUENTS COMMITTED BY THE COOK COUNTY JUVENILE COURT DURING THE
YEARS 1958–66.

CONCLUSION

It should be remembered that these indexes are not measures of the amount of violative behavior in these communities. It can be said, however, on the basis of past experience, that variation among areas represents real differences which, in the absence of great changes, are likely to be duplicated in the future. It should be reiterated, also, that indexes based on the mean of the rates in these 15 areas do not furnish a basis for any conclusions about the amount of delinquency in our society. They do, however, furnish a basis for comparison with rates in other areas over a given period of time, and with the relative magnitude of rates of delinquents in the same area at different times.

CHAPTER XVI

RATES OF DELINQUENTS AND COMMITMENTS

DISCUSSION AND CONCLUSIONS

T HE most persistent finding in this examination of rates of delinquents among areas in Chicago has been the absence of significant changes in the production of delinquents in most city areas relative to other city areas. In most communities there has been no striking upward or downward movement. A far more interesting finding, however, is derived from the fact that in a few areas rates have been increasing rapidly, while in some areas decreases have been similarly rapid.

In earlier chapters of this volume it was pointed out that one European ethnic group after another moved into the areas of first settlement, which were for the most part inner-city areas, where their children became delinquent in large numbers. As these groups became assimilated and moved out of the inner-city areas their descendants disappeared from the Juvenile Court and their place was taken by offenders from the groups which took over the areas which had been vacated.

From these data it was possible to make several generalizations relevant to delinquent behavior. The first is that most of the delinquents in Chicago have been produced, in turn, by the newest large immigrant or migrant groups in the city. During the first decades of this century a large proportion of the delinquents were the children of German or Irish immigrants. Thirty years later a large proportion of the offenders were the children of the Polish and Italian immigrants who replaced the German and the Irish in the inner-city areas.

Because of World War I and the Great Depression there was little pressure from incoming groups to move resident groups out of the inner-city areas. As a result resident groups became well established in the inner-city areas and resisted rather successfully the pressure for space from new migrant groups which later came to the city in large numbers. Consequently these migrants spread out over the city into other areas where decay and age had reduced values and resistance. Thus, it has followed that many areas outside of the inner-city have taken on some of the characteristics of inner-city areas. This has resulted in some increase in the number and proportion of areas with high rates of delinquents. More recently large segments of the second- and third-generation Polish and Italian population have been moving out from the inner-city areas and are being replaced by Spanish-speaking peoples and some of the new Negro and white migrants from the South.

In any evaluation of the meaning of these data it should be remembered that just as there is wide variation in rates of delinquency among areas in a city, so there are wide variations in rates among the subgroups of any population group in different parts of the city. As was indicated in Chapter VI, variation within nativity, nationality, or racial groups is as great as variation among areas. Thus, as earlier immigrant groups moved out, rates of delinquents in these groups decreased as the proportion of each group in the different types of areas was changed. It follows that the role of each group in the delinquency-producing process at any moment has tended to be a function of its distribution in the city.

TRENDS IN RATES IN CERTAIN CHICAGO COMMUNITIES

Probably the most interesting and no doubt the most important fact about rates of delinquents among areas in Chicago is that while the change in rates of delinquents among areas, either upward or downward, has been slight, there has been a sharp increase, relative to other areas, in a small number of communities, and a sharp decrease in about the same number of areas. Here we refer to trends in relation to other city areas, quite apart from the question of whether there is more or less delinquency in the city as a whole.

In Chicago it is widely recognized that during the past two decades rates of delinquents have been increasing rapidly in communities 29 (Lawndale), 42 (Woodlawn), and 68 (Englewood). In order to establish rates of change, trend lines based on indexes for these areas have been computed using the 1934–40, and 1945–51, and the 1958–61 Juvenile Court Series. These series represent approximately 11-year intervals at their midpoints, with the 1958–61 series representing the three Juvenile Court Series centered around the 1960 census.

TRENDS IN RATES OF DELINQUENTS

To describe the trends more clearly, trend lines have been fitted to the original values and an equation describing the trend has been computed for each of these three areas. The values represent the midpoints of the series, but for the purpose of showing the entire range the value for the intercept, that is, for January 1, 1934, is presented also.

The equation for the trend line for community 29 is $Y = 0.20 + .0914X$; the equation for community 42 is: $Y = 0.97 + .0538X$; and the equation for community 68 is: $Y = .053 + .0560X$. The actual and the computed values for these three areas are presented in Table 101.[1]

The area of greatest increase, it will be noted, is in area 29, where the variation in original values is from 0.70 of the grand mean at the midpoint of the 1934–40 series to 2.75 times the grand mean at the midpoint of the 1958–61 series. This is an increase of more than 2 times the grand mean. The range is even greater when stated in terms of the computed values.

These three areas are the areas into which large Negro populations have moved during the past two decades. The charge is made that Negro youth are much more delinquent than white youth, which at this stage of urbanization is undoubtedly true. But this is only half the story. The other half is seen in the fact that the areas of greatest *decrease* in rates of delinquents also are areas where the population is predominantly Negro. Following are the trend lines computed for communities 35, 38, and 40,

---

[1] Trend data for some Chicago communities, translated into standard scores, were published in the Task Force Report *Juvenile Delinquency* and *Youth Crime* published by the President's Commission on Law Enforcement and the Administration of Justice. The observed trends are very much the same as those presented here notwithstanding the fact that the periods of time were not identical.

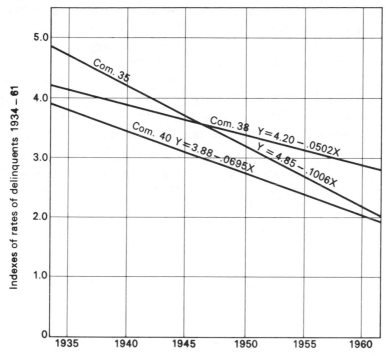

FIG. 26.—Trends in rates of delinquents in communities 29, 42, and 68, 1934–61.

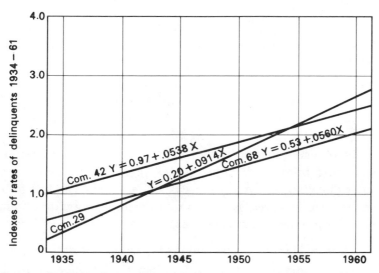

FIG. 27.—Trends in rates of delinquents in communities 35, 38, and 40, 1934–61.

the communities which include most of the area between the Loop and Washington Park. *These are areas in which Negro population has been concentrated for several decades.*

The equation for the trend line for community 35 is: $Y = 4.85 - .1006X$. This downward trend is slightly greater than the upward trend in community 29. The population in both, it should be remembered, is predominantly Negro. Similarly, the downward trend in rates in communities 38 and 40 is about the

TABLE 101

ACTUAL AND COMPUTED TREND VALUES FOR INDEXES OF RATES OF
DELINQUENTS IN THREE CHICAGO COMMUNITIES (29, 42, 68),
1934–40, 1945–51, 1958–61

COMMUNITY	VALUES	PERIOD				
		Intercept January 1, 1934	1934–40	1945–51	1958–61	Intercept December 31, 1961
29..............	Actual		0.70	1.16	2.75	
(Lawndale)......	Computed	0.20	0.52	1.52	2.57	2.76
42..............	Actual		1.23	1.61	2.44	
(Woodlawn).....	Computed	0.97	1.16	1.75	2.37	2.48
68..............	Actual		0.78	1.24	2.04	
(Englewood).....	Computed	0.53	0.73	1.34	1.99	2.10

same as the upward trend in communities 42 and 68. The equation for the *downward* trend line in community 38 is $Y = 4.20 - .0502X$, and the equation for the downward trend in community 40 is $Y = 3.88 - .0695X$.

The observed and computed values for these three areas of decreasing rates of delinquents are presented in Table 102. Rates of delinquents in these areas still are high. The fact to be emphasized, however, is their rapid decrease, notwithstanding increases in rates in adjacent areas.

TRENDS IN RATES OF COMMITMENTS IN CHICAGO COMMUNITIES

Because rates of commitments are not available for the 1934–40 series, parallel trend data cannot be presented. However, trend lines based on commitment data for two series, extending over an 18-year period at the extremes, are available for the same areas. Since there are only two points on the trend line the actual and computed values are identical. The equations for the increase in rates of commitments, and the original and computed values for each of the two series, plus the values at the extremes, will be presented for the same areas used in the presentation of trends for rates of delinquents (see Table 103).

TABLE 102

ACTUAL AND COMPUTED TREND VALUES FOR INDEXES OF RATES OF
DELINQUENTS IN THREE CHICAGO COMMUNITIES (35, 38, 40),
1934–40, 1954–57, 1958–61

COMMUNITY	VALUES	PERIOD				
		Intercept January 1, 1934	1934–40	1945–51	1958–61	Intercept December 31, 1961
35.............	Actual		4.44	3.49	2.18	
(Douglas)........	Computed	4.85	4.49	3.39	2.23	2.03
38............. (Grand Boulevard).........	Actual		4.10	3.33	2.97	
	Computed	4.20	4.03	3.48	2.90	2.80
40............. (Washington Park).........	Actual		3.59	2.96	2.03	
	Computed	3.88	3.64	2.87	2.07	1.93

TABLE 103

TREND LINE EQUATIONS AND VALUES FOR INDEXES OF RATES OF
COMMITMENTS IN THREE CHICAGO COMMUNITIES (29, 42, 68),
1945–51 AND 1958–62

COMMUNITY	EQUATION	Intercept January 1, 1945	PERIOD		Intercept December 31, 1962
			1945–51	1958–62	
29............. (Lawndale)	$Y = .44 + .1758X$	.44	1.05	3.16	3.60
42............. (Woodlawn)	$Y = 1.39 + .1258X$	1.39	1.83	3.34	3.65
68............. (Englewood)	$Y = 0.89 + .1058X$	0.89	1.26	2.53	2.79

The communities in which the rates of commitments decreased most rapidly also are the areas of greatest decrease in rates of delinquents. The equation for the trend in rates of commitments in these areas and the observed and computed values are presented in Table 104.

It will be noted that increases in rates of commitments in communities 29, 42, and 68 are greater than those based on rates of delinquents. Similarly, the decreases in rates of commitments in communities 35, 38, and 40 are greater than those for rates of delinquents in the same areas. When trend lines for

TABLE 104

TREND LINE EQUATIONS AND VALUES FOR INDEXES OF RATES OF
COMMITMENTS IN THREE CHICAGO COMMUNITIES (35, 38, 40),
1945-51 AND 1958–62

COMMUNITY	EQUATION	Intercept January 1, 1945	PERIOD		Intercept December 31, 1962
			1945–51	1958–62	
35 .... (Douglas)	$Y = 6.45 - .2817X$	6.45	5.46	2.08	1.38
38 .... (Grand Boulevard)	$Y = 5.45 - .1467X$	5.45	4.94	3.18	2.81
40 .... (Washington Park)	$Y = 4.83 - .1725X$	4.83	4.23	2.16	1.73

rates of delinquents were computed for the two series used in computing trends in rates of commitments (1945–51 and 1958–62), it was found that the trends were sharper than the trends based on three series, but not so sharp as the trends for rates of commitments. These findings suggest strongly that rates of commitments differentiate very sharply the areas which produce the most serious delinquents. The years included in the 1945–51 and 1958–62 series were the years of great population movement and change in some Chicago communities.[2]

[2] Commitment rates calculated for the 1963–66 series after these trend lines had been computed do not support the existence of a continuous downward trend in the rates of commitment in communities 38 and 40. It is possible that these findings represent a counter trend, but it is far more likely that for these areas, the rates for the years since 1960 are spurious because of the absence of information

The term "delinquency areas," used originally to indicate the areas or communities in a city where the rates of delinquents are highest, has been used often to suggest that delinquent behavior is common to only a few areas and that the other areas do not have to face conduct problems among young people. This is probably never true, and surely it is not the situation either in Chicago or its suburbs. Examination of the maps reveals that rates are spread rather evenly between areas with the lowest and those with the highest rates. Although it is true that many of the cases are concentrated in a few areas, there are no non-delinquency areas.

Neither are rates of delinquents measures of all violative behavior. Rates of commitments, based on smaller numbers of more serious offenders, are equally good indexes of the relative incidence of violative behavior; and rates of police arrests, more inclusive in nature, presented in Chapter III, present the same general picture. These data, plus extensive interviews with all the male children in certain small areas, indicate that rates of delinquents based on official records suggest the relative amount, but never the absolute amount, of violative behavior among areas. In some areas the proportion of youthful males who engage in conduct which would be defined as delinquent may approximate 100 per cent.

It was pointed out in the earlier edition of this volume that indexes of community life can be used to describe the communities in which delinquents are found, but that these characteristics do not furnish an explanatory system. It was suggested also that delinquent behavior seemed to be closely related to the struggle for a more favorable position in the social order. As Professor Short has pointed out in the new introduction to this

---

about the size of the juvenile population. This unusual situation arises from the fact that parts of these areas have been depopulated by extensive demolition, and after some time they have been repopulated following the completion of large housing projects. When such extensive changes are taking place any estimate of the size of the adolescent population, at a particular moment in time, is subject to wide error.

volume, this point of view has been developed much further by Robert K. Merton, Albert Cohen, Cloward and Ohlin, and many others. Surely their formulations apply well to the delinquency data for Chicago and suburbs which are being added in these chapters. Analyses of the community rates presented here in sequence furnish new materials which may be relevant to an understanding of the young offender. It was noted earlier that rates of delinquents decrease in population groups as they move out from the inner city. The data presented here establish the fact that over time, rates of delinquents decrease in population groups even if these groups are not able to move to other areas. This is seen in the old Negro areas and in some immigrant areas where the assimilative process has been almost completed.

Analyses of the data also reveal that the areas of high rates of delinquents, over the more than 60 years included in this study, have been those most disrupted by incoming population. This occurred because institutional roles of the area into which migrants came were not readily accessible to new settlers, and because institutions and institutional roles which the new settlers brought with them did not prepare them for important roles in the new situation. This has been especially true with reference to economic, political, and educational institutions. Because most of the European immigrants brought with them institutions not too different from the ones they found here, the disruption of their social life, although serious, tended to disappear as they made their way into the political and economic life of the American city. This was accompanied by outward movement from areas of first settlement to more stable communities where the rates of delinquents among their children decreased rather rapidly. Thus was brought about the situation in which, at a given time, widely different rates of delinquents could be computed for different segments of the same ethnic population group.

More recent migrant groups to the city have met with more serious problems. Although some members of these groups did not have the language barrier of earlier groups, they were less familiar with the institutions of a highly industrialized society, and some of their basic institutions differed more widely from the institutions of a large American city than did those of the European immigrants. In addition, some of these more recent migrants have been denied participation in many of the basic activities through which assimilation into urban life takes place.

The data on trends also demonstrate with equal sharpness the rapid rise in rates of delinquents in certain areas when a population with a different history and different institutions and values takes over areas in a very short period of time. These are almost classic cases of the process of organization and disorganization described by Thomas and Znaniecki in *The Polish Peasant*. What is unusual is the documentation of the "reorganization" process without outward movement of population.

Clearly all social orders fall at some point on the continuum. Slowly changing social orders tend to be both orderly and restrictive. Rapidly changing social orders, such as our own, maintain a precarious balance between change and order. But when the change involves the introduction of a new population with different institutions and practices, institutional disruption and role discontinuity are to be expected. It was pointed out in Part II of this volume that, as groups made their adjustment and moved out, the rates of delinquents in these groups decreased. It has been suggested here that some stabilization of community life and institutions takes place without outward movement.

Disorganization accompanying rapid change may be virtually complete. If the institutions and social roles of the newcomers do not meet the needs of the new situation, and if the population is not able or is not given opportunities to perform the roles in their traditional institutions, the disruption in the incoming group is serious. The evidence, however, is that these problems tend to get solved except in a few areas where rapid change is a permanent characteristic. Given time, some groups make adjustment and move out, and others make their adjustments without moving out. Projection of the downward trends, discussed above, suggests that a new equilibrium of social control has been achieved, or is in the process of being achieved, in these communities.

In the transition from simpler forms of social life to the complex life of the city, role problems of the adolescent male probably are more serious than are the problems of other age groups. With the exception of the school, for which he may not be adequately prepared, no meaningful conventional institutional setting is available to him in urban communities. If the adolescent male fails in school or drops out, or for other reasons finds school roles unsatisfactory or unplayable, he finds himself in an institutional void. He is not wanted in industry or commerce, he is too young for military service, and odd jobs traditionally available to his age group are decreasing in numbers. The problem is complicated enormously by the fact that, where racial or ethnic barriers to employment are encountered, non-participation in economic roles may be extended into young adulthood. The result is that youth gangs in the city may include both boys and young men.

SUMMARY OF CONCLUSIONS

1. Rates of delinquents and rates of commitments vary widely and consistently among Chicago communities, and almost as widely and consistently among suburbs of Chicago. This means that the probability of an adolescent's becoming involved in violative conduct, to the extent that he or she is dealt with officially by legal agencies, varies widely among areas. The evidence indicates that these probabilities are stable and persistent.

Delinquency-producing characteristics of communities with high rates of delinquencies are cumulative. This means that the higher the rate of delinquents, the greater the probability that the offender will become a recidivist and the greater the probability that eventually the same offender will be committed to a training school.

2. It is not assumed that geographic areas produce delinquent children. Rather, rates of delinquents reflect the effectiveness of the operation of processes through which socialization takes place and the problems of life are encountered and dealt with.

Low rates of delinquents reflect the existence of a stable institutional structure. Although this does not require the absence of change, it suggests that if population change takes place, newcomers are able and willing to play existing roles in the institutions. This is the situation which can be found in many outlying areas of the city.

3. A high incidence of delinquent behavior indicates a breakdown of the machinery through which the needs of different segments of the population are met through conventional institutions. Usually in cities this breakdown is the result of rapid change in the population. If the new population is not prepared to play significant roles in the traditional political and economic institutions, or if these are denied them, the disruption may be very great.

Evidence presented in this chapter, however, suggests that although the disruption in a population group may be very great, after a period of time movement toward stability occurs. At varying rates of speed such changes tend to occur in all areas and in all groups. Historically this process has been greatly accelerated, in many groups, by outward movement into better communities.

4. High or low rates of delinquents are not permanent characteristics of any ethnic or racial group. Each population group experienced high rates of delinquents when it occupied the areas of first settlement, and these rates went down as the groups either moved out to better areas or moved toward stability in the same areas.

Probably there is thus no such thing as a valid rate of delinquents for a population group, because there are as many rates for every group as there are types of areas in which segments of the groups are located. It follows that the rate of delinquents in any particular group at any moment is a function of the distribution of that group in different types of areas.

5. Rates of delinquents by communities correlate closely with many economic and social characteristics of Chicago communities. Details of these correlations have not been presented, be-

cause these relationships were investigated so fully in the original edition of this volume, and their updating would require research beyond the scope of this revision.

There is good reason to believe that the value of these correlations has diminished. Once it has been established that certain kinds of problems are concentrated in certain types of city areas through the natural processes of city growth, high correlations are "built in," and low correlations become more interesting than high correlations. In addition, it has been quite well established that correlations do not furnish a satisfactory explanatory system for human conduct. Attention has shifted more to influences affecting the vertical ordering of the population and to the question of opportunity for upward mobility.

6. Rates of delinquents and commitments among suburban cities in Cook County vary in much the same manner as rates among communities in the city of Chicago. As in Chicago, suburbs with the highest rates tend to be the more industrialized centers which have attracted the newest immigrant or migrant populations. All of these suburbs, like Chicago, are served by the Cook County Juvenile Court. It is quite probable that the referral system may differ among the suburbs, and the suburban referral systems may differ from the system in Chicago. Therefore, these rates should be interpreted cautiously. It is probable that for the suburbs commitment rates furnish the best basis for comparison.

If population data were available it is quite probable that the variation in rates in areas within some of the suburban cities would be as great as the variation among these cities.

7. There are a few surprises in community trends in rates of delinquents and commitments. The position of most areas, relative to other areas, has changed very little. Areas where rates have increased most rapidly have been areas of great population change; while areas of greater decrease are those in which rates have been high, but have decreased as the foreign born became assimilated, or other migrant groups moved toward new or more stable institutional forms.

8. Probably the most interesting finding in this study is the evidence that rates of delinquents went sharply up in certain areas which were newly occupied by Negro populations, while at the same time the rates went sharply down in communities also occupied very largely by Negroes. The latter were the areas of highest rates of delinquents in the city in the twenties and thirties.

In a sense the whole story of change in urban communities is bound up in these findings. Areas disrupted by change have high rates of delinquents, but after a while movement toward stability can be observed as new institutional forms are developed or old institutions are modified to meet new problems. This is followed by a downward trend in the rates of delinquents. There is comfort in the fact that communities do move toward stability even though it is recognized that change is a permanent characteristic of many city areas.

This cycle, so clearly revealed by these data, no doubt resembles very closely the experiences of social groups whenever or wherever change has been so rapid that controls have broken down. In Chicago the process can be seen clearly in immigrant areas which have not been pressed by any new incoming group. In these situations rates have gone steadily down.

9. The emphasis on disruption of institutional roles presented in this report is not inconsistent with prevailing opportunity theories of delinquent behavior. Opportunity is created through chances to participate in meaningful roles, and these roles were not available to migrant youth. Youth gangs, often delinquent, have been one answer to this dilemma.

One of the clearest facts about many male youths in the modern city is the absence of any meaningful role outside of the school. For those who are not able to play the school role satisfactorily there are few opportunities. Boys out of school are not wanted in industry or commerce, and they cannot get into the army either because they are too young or cannot qualify because of lack of training. Neither can they run away to sea or go West because there is no market here for their talents or lack of talents; and odd jobs, even if available, do not help many to find a place in the urban community. Illegitimate activities furnish one possible answer to this quest.

This absence of opportunity was very real to immigrant youth, but it is much more serious for youth in the migrant populations which have moved to the city more recently. Among the reasons for the complications are deficiencies in early schooling, discrimination, and the ever increasing level of education required for good jobs.

10. The consistency with which certain communities produce large numbers of delinquents, over a long period of time, focuses attention on the community as the basic unit for programs aimed at an understanding of the offender, treatment, or the prevention of violative behavior. Surely the processes of the community must be understood before programs, based on this understanding, can be brought into operation. Full recognition of the implications of the fact that a large proportion of young offenders come from a few areas should lead to further concentration on the neighborhood or the community as the appropriate units for social action.

In the original edition of this volume details of one such program, the *Chicago Area Project,* were sketched. In his Introduction Professor Short discusses this program as a social movement and evaluates its impact on public policy in both public and private agencies. It is his view that the impact has been substantial.

It is not inappropriate to reiterate that the strength of the Chicago Area Project as a social movement lies in the fact that its program is oriented toward the encouragement of participation in neighborhood and community life by the persons who live in the problem areas; by its efforts to help these persons increase the educational, recreational, and occupational opportunities of children and young people; and by its efforts to encourage and help local residents to reach the offender through the efforts of those who know his problems and his world.

During recent years some of the basic ideas of the Chicago

Area Project have been incorporated into the field-services program of the Illinois Youth Commisison. More recently the board of directors of the Chicago Area Project has completed an arrangement whereby it becomes an agency through which Chicago Community Fund allocations are distributed to small neighborhood organizations and committees. This means that the Chicago Area Project, as a social movement, has been incorporated into stable institutional forms both at the governmental level and as a private agency.

INDEX

Abbott, Edith, 11
Adler, Herman, 12
Adult offenders: distribution and rates of, 93–98, 217–20, 249–52, 266–67, 308–10; juvenile delinquents and, xxxi, xxxvi, 133–34, 182–83
Allison, Archibald, 8, 9
Anderson, Robert T., xxxvi
Anomie, xxxvii–xl
Aschaffenburg, Gustav, 7, 8
Aschauer, Galen F., 257

Baittle, Brahm, xlvi
Baltimore, community characteristics associated with delinquency rates in, xxvii
Becker, Howard S., xxvi
Bell, Daniel, xxxvii
Berger, Bennett M., xli
Biehl, K., 142
Blackmar, F. W., 11, 12
Bloch, H., xl
Bogue, Donald J., xlvi
Booth, Charles, 10
Bordura, David J., xxvii
Boston: community characteristics in, 245–54; distribution and rates of delinquents in, 227–45; history and growth of, 224–27. See also "Cornerville"
Botein, Bernard, 12
Boy's own story, 176–82
Breckinridge, S. P., 11
Bunce, J. Thackray, 6
Burgess, E. W., xxv–xxvi, xliv, xlvi, 11, 12, 18

Burt, Cyril, 9

Cahr, Frances, 12
Capone, Al, xxxviii
Cartwright, Desmond S., xxvii
Cayton, Horace, xxx, xxxi
Chicago: community characteristics in, 24–42, 90–107, 170–89; delinquency and community characteristics in, 140–55, 164–69; distribution and rates of juvenile court delinquents in, 50–67, 329–50, 376–84; history and growth of, 22–27; rates of commitments in, 72–77, 350–58; rates of police arrests in, 81–85; series comparisons and correlations, 67–72, 75–81, 85–87. See also Indexes, of rates of; Suburbs, Chicago
Chicago Area Project, xxv, xxxiii, xlv, 322–25; as a social movement, xlvi–liv, 388–89; detached workers and, liii–liv
Chilton, Roland J., xxvii, xl
Cincinnati: community characteristics in, 263–69; distribution and rates of delinquents in, 257–63; history and growth, 255–57
Cleveland: community characteristics in, 285–93; distribution and rates of delinquents in, 272–85; history and growth of, 270–72
Cloward, Richard, xxxi, xxxv, xxxvii, xxxviii, xxxix, xli, xliii
Cohen, Albert, xxxv, xli, xliii
Commitment and rates of delinquents, 123–26, 129–32, 136–38, 338–39, 343, 376–84

The index to the introduction was prepared by Stuart Hadden, with support from the Social Research Center, Washington State University, Pullman, Washington.

390